USS *Monitor*

ED RACHAL FOUNDATION NAUTICAL ARCHAEOLOGY SERIES

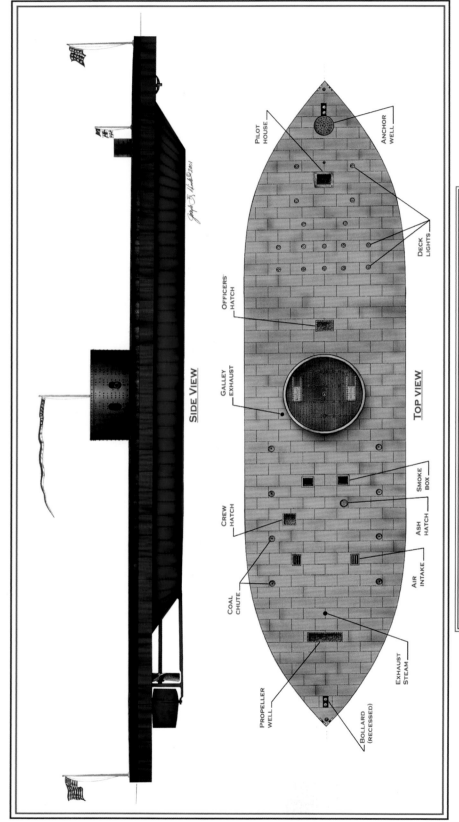

SIDE VIEW

TOP VIEW

PILOT HOUSE

ANCHOR WELL

DECK LIGHTS

OFFICERS' HATCH

GALLEY EXHAUST

CREW HATCH

SMOKE BOX

ASH HATCH

COAL CHUTE

AIR INTAKE

PROPELLER WELL

BOLLARD (RECESSED)

EXHAUST STEAM

U.S.S. MONITOR

THE U.S.S. MONITOR WAS THE PROTOTYPE, TURRETED, ARMORED WARSHIP THAT CHANGED THE COURSE OF NAVAL HISTORY FOREVER. MADE FAMOUS BY ITS DUEL WITH THE CSS VIRGINIA ON MARCH 9, 1862, THIS VALIANT AND INNOVATIVE SHIP MET DISASTER IN A GALE OFF CAPE HATTERAS AND SANK WITH A GREAT LOSS OF LIFE IN LATE 1862.

HULL LENGTH: 172'-0" BEAM: 41'-0" DRAFT: 10'-5" SPEED: 8 KNOTS CREW: 59 ARMOR: 11" TURRET, 5" SIDES, 1" DECK, 9" PILOTHOUSE. ARMAMENT: TWO 11" DAHLGREN SMOOTHBORES

USS *Monitor*

A Historic Ship Completes Its
Final Voyage

John D. Broadwater

Foreword by James P. Delgado

TEXAS A&M UNIVERSITY PRESS
COLLEGE STATION

This paper meets the requirements of ANSI/NISO z39.48-1992 (Permanence of Paper).
Binding materials have been chosen for durability.

Publication of this volume is supported by generous funding from the National Marine Sanctuary Foundation.

The story of the USS *Monitor*, as told in the pages of this book, lives on. It lives on, however, only through public-private partnerships such as this publication facilitated through the National Marine Sanctuary Foundation. The Foundation is committed to ongoing efforts to preserve *Monitor*, protect its resting place in the ocean, and promote its unique story in US history. You can support these efforts with a donation, and can learn how and get more information about the Foundation by visiting www.NMSFocean.org.

LIBRARY OF CONGRESS CATALOGING-IN-PUBLICATION DATA

Broadwater, John D.
  USS *Monitor* : A historic ship completes its final voyage / John D. Broadwater.—1st ed.
      p.   cm. — (Ed Rachal Foundation nautical archaeology series)
  Includes bibliographical references and index.
  ISBN-13: 978-1-60344-473-6 (cloth : alk. paper)
  ISBN-10: 1-60344-473-4 (cloth : alk. paper)
  ISBN-13: 978-1-60344-474-3 (pbk. : alk. paper)
  ISBN-10: 1-60344-474-2 (pbk. : alk. paper)
  1. Monitor (Ironclad) 2. Shipwrecks—North Carolina—Hatteras, Cape. 3. Underwater archaeology—North Carolina—Hatteras, Cape. 4. Excavations (Archaeology)—North Carolina—Hatteras, Cape. 5. Hatteras, Cape (N.C.)—Antiquities. 6. *Monitor* National Marine Sanctuary (N.C.) 7. United States—History—Civil War, 1861–1865—Naval operations. I. Title.
II. Series: Ed Rachal Foundation nautical archaeology series.
  E595.M7B76 2012
  973.7'58—dc23
                                                                    2011036725

Frontispiece: Plan and profile views of USS *Monitor,* based in part on archaeological evidence from NOAA. © Joseph Hinds

———◆———

*This book is dedicated to United States Navy personnel,
current and former, who unselfishly volunteered to defend our nation,
and especially to the hundreds of dedicated Navy men and women
who raised significant parts of USS Monitor from its watery grave
along with two of its missing sailors,
who can now be honored and laid to rest.*

———◆———

CONTENTS

Foreword ix
Preface xi
Acknowledgments xiii

PROLOGUE
First Encounter 1

CHAPTER ONE
"The *Monitor* Is No More" 5

CHAPTER TWO
Discovery 14

CHAPTER THREE
Story of an Ironclad 28

CHAPTER FOUR
A Sanctuary for America 62

CHAPTER FIVE
Charting a New Course for *Monitor* 98

CHAPTER SIX
Implementing the Recovery Plan 117

CHAPTER SEVEN
Engineering the Recovery of *Monitor*'s Machinery 139

CHAPTER EIGHT
***Monitor* Completes Its Final Voyage** 166

CHAPTER NINE
In *Monitor*'s Turret 183

EPILOGUE
The Story Continues 207

Notes 217
Bibliography 225
Index 235

FOREWORD

———————

The *Monitor* became and remains a part of the American mind, its bare mention conjuring up images of what we are as a people, of our experiences as a people, and of some of the major events and motifs in our history.

—LARRY E. TISE, 1978

This book reaches the American people on the 150th anniversary of the key events in the yearlong career of USS *Monitor*, beginning with its launch on January 30, its commissioning on February 25, its battle with CSS *Virginia* on March 9, its refit at Washington Navy Yard in October, and its loss, with sixteen officers and crew, on December 31, 1862.

Born out of necessity in the first "modern" conflict, the American Civil War, *Monitor* was a product of the ingenious mind of John Ericsson, the industrial prowess and economic might of the Union, and a harbinger of a new type of war, where increasingly deadlier arms—the product of the laboratory and the factory—merged to wreak havoc. Herman Melville, in response to the arrival of *Monitor* and its famous battle at Hampton Roads, wrote

> *Hail to Victory, without the gaud*
> *Of Glory; zeal that needs no fans*
> *Or banners; plain mechanic power*
> *Plied cogently in War now placed—*
> *Where War belongs—*
> *Among the trades and artisans.*

Monitor's technology, with its low freeboard, iron hull, and rotating turret, demonstrated the efficiency of a turreted warship, just as *Virginia*'s armored casemate and the havoc its guns wrought on the non-armored ships of the Union fleet demonstrated the end of wooden warships. In response to these two ships and the Battle of Hampton Roads, both the Union and the Confederacy turned to armored craft and monitors (fifty-nine monitors were ordered by the US Navy after *Monitor*'s perceived success) and foreign navies also adapted to the new technology, culminating in the development of iron and steel-hulled turreted capital ships, the progenitors of the battleship.

While the engineering, architecture and the art of the iron maker defined in part the mundane aspects of *Monitor*, the circumstances of *Monitor*'s birth and the battle with CSS *Virginia* quickly became fixed into American mythology, representing as all myths do real and fictional stories, recurring themes or character types that appeal to the consciousness of a people, by embodying cultural ideas or giving expression to deep, commonly felt emotions. *Monitor*, like another famous Civil War craft, the Confederate submarine *H. L. Hunley*, inspired a national mania that continues 150 years later, an impact reflected in popular culture that resounds even now with phrases like an "ironclad" guarantee. In the aftermath of the Battle of Hampton Roads, a hero-cult arose around *Monitor*'s designer, builders, officers, and crew, reflected in the breathless prose of Oliver Wendell Holmes, who opined in response to the news of *Monitor*'s intervention against *Virginia*'s rampage at Hampton Roads, "is it not the age of fable, and of heroes, and of demi-gods over again?"

The mythic qualities of *Monitor*, and its role as a symbol of the American people, a physical embodiment of the national myth, compelled both memorialization and a quest to locate a ship lost in the dark seas off Cape Hatteras at depths then beyond reach in 1862, inspiring *Monitor*'s paymaster William Keeler, who survived the sinking, to write to his wife that "the *Monitor* is no more. What the fire of the enemy failed to do, the elements have accomplished." That quest resulted in the discovery of the wreck nearly four decades ago. Since then, as John Broadwater chronicles in these pages, generations removed by space and time from the events of the Civil War, but mindful of the passions of that conflict, have responded to the discovery of *Monitor*. The find led to the designation of America's first National Marine Sanctuary, the creation of the *Monitor* Center at The Mariners' Museum in Newport News, Virginia, and finally, the decision to raise, conserve, and display portions of the sunken warship.

The decision to raise portions of the ship was not made lightly. For many archaeologists, the preferred option is to leave sunken ships and other sites untouched. That this was ultimately not done with *Monitor* was the result of long discussion, and hard decisions over what was best for a publicly owned resource, the consequences of environmental changes and human impacts, the exigencies of funding, and the simple fact that the recovery of key features of *Monitor*'s technology provided the means for a larger public audience to see and again interact with the famous ship. The process of recovery, as recounted by

Broadwater, and the work done inside *Monitor*'s turret, also reminded all of us that this is a human story, the saga of people, especially that of the two as yet unidentified sailors who, like many in history, have either been "ordinary" folk rendered heroic by the circumstances into which they were thrust, as well as all who have been caught up in something larger than life and paid a price—in this case the ultimate price—as a result.

The pages that follow are a unique, compelling, and personal account by the archaeologist who has spent more time than any other interacting with USS *Monitor*. John Broadwater was there at the beginning of the modern saga, was one of the first to again touch *Monitor* after its loss, and to enter the "tomb" of the ironclad's turret. He was a key player in the planning and management of *Monitor*, and his voice and perceptions are an important part of *Monitor*'s ongoing saga. This book is an appropriate and powerful human account for the 150th anniversary. It is not the final archaeological report, which NOAA's Office of National Marine Sanctuaries is now working to complete. Archaeology continues long after the excavation ends, both in the laboratory and in the archives. Work to identify *Monitor*'s lost sailors continues, as does the ongoing conservation of the turret, machinery, and artifacts. A comprehensive and extensive report is forthcoming. For now, in 2012, however, we pause to be reminded again, in John Broadwater's prose, that this ship, and its saga, are first and foremost a human story.

JAMES P. DELGADO
Director, Maritime Heritage Program
Office of National Marine Sanctuaries
National Oceanic and Atmospheric Administration

PREFACE

The story of the ironclad warship USS *Monitor* and its famous Civil War battle with the Confederacy's CSS *Virginia* (ex-*Merrimack*) is learned by every American school child. The story is compelling: the "little ironclad that could" proved itself worthy against a larger, heavily-armored foe, helping preserve the Union that we Americans hold so dear. *Monitor*'s fame quickly spread throughout the world and is still one of the most recognized historic warships. *Monitor* sank during a storm on the last day of the year in which it was launched, but that loss proved to be merely the end of the first chapter of *Monitor*'s legend. Discovered in 1973 off Cape Hatteras, North Carolina, *Monitor* once again became front-page news. Subsequent expeditions by numerous organizations maintained the public's interest in the wreck until the late 1990s, when significant parts of *Monitor*'s hull and machinery were recovered to prevent their disintegration due to the corrosive saltwater environment.

In this book I have attempted to document the second chapter in *Monitor*'s story, which spans three decades and includes *Monitor*'s discovery, protection, management, and partial recovery. I am very fortunate to be the only person who has been directly involved with *Monitor* nearly from discovery through recovery. I was not with the team that discovered *Monitor*'s remains in 1973 (I was searching for it elsewhere), but I was a member of the expedition that verified the discovery the following spring. In 1979 I was one of three archaeologists who conducted the first excavation within *Monitor*'s hull. Over the years I participated in additional *Monitor* expeditions and served on advisory panels. Then in April 1992 I was selected as manager of the *Monitor* National Marine Sanctuary, the federal marine preserve that protects and manages the wreck. For the next decade I was actively involved in all aspects of *Monitor* research and was the onsite chief scientist for the National Oceanic and Atmospheric Administration (NOAA) during all research and recovery expeditions.

Last year, at the urging of Daniel J. Basta, director of the Office of National Marine Sanctuaries, I put aside my work on a *Monitor* archaeological and engineering report long enough to write this account of the *Monitor* story for a general audience. I have drawn heavily on my personal knowledge and experience to describe this unique period in *Monitor*'s history in considerable detail in the hope that I can impart to readers a sense of the concerns, deliberations, decision making, excitement, and elation that I and others experienced while helping save *Monitor* for future generations. For accuracy and completeness, I relied extensively upon our expansive archive of *Monitor*-related historical material, our volumes of expedition data and technical reports, and on input from other managers and researchers who were involved over the years.

This book is, in a sense, also the history of NOAA's National Marine Sanctuary Program, which was created by federal law in 1972, the same year that several groups were making plans to search for *Monitor* off Cape Hatteras. In January 1975, *Monitor* became America's first National Marine Sanctuary, and the management decisions made at that time formed the basis for management of all the sanctuaries to come.

This book will be followed by a very detailed archaeological and engineering report that will present and analyze the data recovered from the site since *Monitor*'s discovery. Even that lengthy report will not be the end of *Monitor*'s story. Chapter three began when *Monitor*'s gun turret, the last major component to be recovered, arrived at The Mariners' Museum for conservation and eventual exhibition. This new chapter will continue indefinitely, as the slow and painstaking process of stabilizing and conserving more than 150 tons of iron and other materials proceeds at the museum. With each object, another small part of *Monitor*'s history emerges, like adding a new piece to a puzzle, contributing its bit of knowledge to our overall picture of *Monitor*, its officers and crew, and the events that led to its loss.

I have made every effort to present *Monitor*'s history, discovery, management, research, and recovery as accurately as possible. However, the story spans a century and a half, so I am undoubtedly guilty of occasional mistakes and omissions. I alone am responsible for any errors in this book, and my comments and conclusions do not necessarily represent the opinion of the National Oceanic and Atmospheric Administration or the US Government.

Please join me now as we travel through 150 years of *Monitor*'s history.

JOHN D. BROADWATER
Williamsburg, Virginia

ACKNOWLEDGMENTS

—➤◆◄—

As I was writing this book I began keeping a detailed list of those who deserved acknowledgment, but when the draft reached nearly a dozen pages, I realized that in a work of this scope—spanning nearly four decades of research and stewardship—it would be nearly impossible to adequately recognize and thank the scores of organizations and hundreds of individuals who have contributed to the USS *Monitor*'s preservation and remarkable ongoing story. Therefore, I have mentioned as many key participants as possible within the manuscript, so that this book itself became essentially one long acknowledgment, but with the same caveat that such an attempt can never be fully complete after so many participants over so lengthy a passage of time. To any whose names do not appear, I hope you will forgive the omission and take pride in what we, collectively, have accomplished over the years to ensure that *Monitor*'s story will continue to expand and be told and retold for many generations to come.

This book would not have happened without the encouragement and support of Daniel J. Basta, the Director of NOAA's Office of National Marine Sanctuaries (ONMS), as well as that of Margo Jackson, Acting ONMS Deputy Director, Jason Patlis, President and CEO of the National Marine Sanctuary Foundation, and James P. Delgado, Director of ONMS' Maritime Heritage Program. Jim Delgado was committed to this publication even before he

joined NOAA, and he served as an essential go-between in this process, and on his own time completed an outstanding edit of the first draft of this manuscript. I gratefully acknowledge his key role in seeing this publication through completion. I am also grateful to David W. Alberg, Superintendent of the *Monitor* National Marine Sanctuary, and William B. Cogar, Director of The Mariners' Museum in Newport News, Virginia, for their assistance and that of their staffs in the research and image selection during the preparation of this book.

The National Marine Sanctuary Foundation also provided generous funding that made possible the publication of this book at such high production values. With the Foundation's support, the story of the *Monitor* and its excavation is presented with the color and drama that allow readers to grasp the importance of the project.

I also must thank those who reviewed this manuscript and offered their insights and advice: David Alberg, William Andahazy, Daniel Basta, Philip Beierl, Reed Bohne, Tane Casserley, Thomas Clark, David Conlin, James Delgado, David Dinsmore, Russell Green, Anna Holloway, Joseph Hoyt, Jeffrey Johnston, James Kelly, David Krop, Richard Lawrence, Don Liberatore, Wayne Lusardi, David Mindell, Jay Moore, Craig Mullen, Larry Murphy, Christopher Murray, Cathryn Newton, Barbara Scholley, Robert Schwemmer, Robert Sheridan,

William Still, Bruce Terrell, Joseph Uravitch, Hans Van Tilburg, Ole Varmer, and Gordon Watts. Their contributions added significantly to this book, but any errors and omissions are my responsibility.

Editor-in-Chief Mary Lenn Dixon of Texas A&M University Press and her team have added their skills and enthusiasm to make this book a reality, as have their partners at Graphic Composition. I particularly want to acknowledge Thom Lemmons, Diana Vance, Mary Ann Jacob, Kevin Grossman, and the marketing department at Texas A&M University Press, and Rachel Cabaniss, Ellen Graben, and Deborah McClain at GCI.

I am personally indebted to countless people for the success of our *Monitor* research and recovery efforts, especially Captain Christopher Murray (USN Ret.), who found a way to involve the US Navy in the propeller recovery, then worked tirelessly and innovatively to keep the Navy engaged throughout the entire recovery program. Captain Barbara "Bobbie" Scholley (USN Ret.), was involved from the beginning as well, playing several key roles on and off site. Both are amazing divers and salvage experts as well as exceptional individuals, and I consider myself very fortunate to have had the honor of working with them. I must also thank John Rayfield, veteran staffer in the House of Representatives, whose commitment to saving *Monitor* was essential to our success. Finally, I want to acknowledge Jeff Johnston, who joined the *Monitor* staff just in time for the recovery operations. Jeff became an unequaled expert on *Monitor*'s history and construction, and during our many weeks of 24-7 onsite research Jeff alternated twelve-hour watches with me, sharing responsibility for representing NOAA.

Finally, I want to thank my wife, Sharon, and my daughters, Jennifer and April, for their patience, understanding, and encouragement during all the years that I spent way too much time with *Monitor* instead of at home.

In closing, I offer my sincere thanks, gratitude, and respect to all who have tirelessly worked on or for *Monitor*, from those who saw it designed and built in a hundred days, to those who served in it—some of whom paid a high price, including their lives—and all who have worked for the past four decades to discover, document, recover, conserve, preserve, protect, and share *Monitor* with current and future generations.

USS *Monitor*

Prologue

—————➤●◄—————

FIRST ENCOUNTER

I twist my body to peer through the tiny viewport. The cobalt blue Gulf Stream water darkens to ever-deeper shades as we descend toward the sea floor. Huddled in a cramped aluminum cylinder, I'm struggling to control my fear of close spaces. I have to stay focused, because I am sealed in the dive chamber of the *Johnson-Sea-Link*, an incredible research submersible that can reach depths of 1,000 feet. Even though we aren't going nearly that deep, my claustrophobia leapt out as soon as the hatch closed.

Across the chamber, my dive tender, Don Liberatore, is concentrating on the sub's gauges, digital numbers, and lights, but I know he's also keeping a close eye on me. Don will make sure I don't get into trouble today, since this will be my first deep sub dive. He is an experienced research diver with the Harbor Branch Foundation, the Florida-based oceanographic institution that designed, built, and operates this sub. Don clearly senses my apprehension, gives me a confident grin and quips, "Well, you're finally going to see her, John."

I grin back, because that's the reason I'm willing to stuff myself into this little dive chamber that I described to my friends as "a fifty-five-gallon drum with a hatch." I'm getting ready to dive on the famous Civil War ironclad USS *Monitor*. As a boy, I built a plastic model of it, as an archaeologist I searched for it, and in 1974 I helped produce a mosaic photograph of its remains. Now, five years later, I am one of a

small team of archaeologists and research divers that will explore it in person, 240 feet below, sixteen miles offshore of Cape Hatteras, North Carolina.

"Bottom in sight," reports Roger Cook from the pilot sphere forward of us. Roger is Harbor Branch's mission director and our sub pilot.

"Bottom in sight," Don responds into his headset.

A flash of light catches my eye and I see a large fish just outside the viewport.

"There's the amberjacks," Don says. "The *Monitor* must be pretty close." Apparently, the jacks hear the sub's thruster motors and see its floodlights so they've ventured out from the wreck to see who's come to visit.

"Wreck in sight," Roger calls out, right on cue.

"Roger, wreck in sight," Don acknowledges. "Better get ready, John."

High-pitched whirring sounds from the thrusters signal us that Roger is crabbing the sub into the current that almost always flows over the wreck. Another sound, higher in pitch and longer in duration, reverberates off the chamber walls. From our training dives I know that's the sub communicating with the mother ship on the surface through hydrophones. It's Roger reporting our status to the mission coordinator on the bridge.

As I zip up my wet suit jacket, Don taps me on the shoulder and points out the starboard viewport. At first I can't see anything, but as I lean closer to the

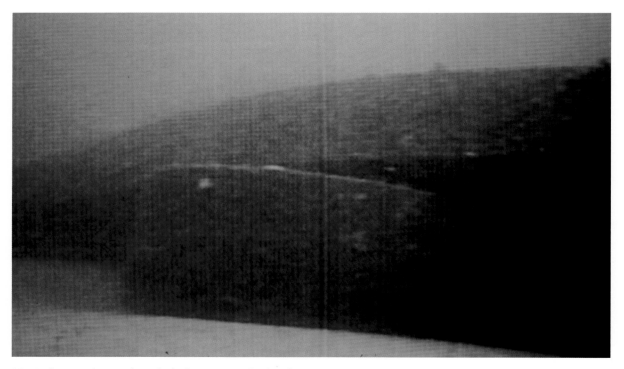

Monitor's stern, showing how the hull rests on its displaced gun turret. Courtesy NOAA
Monitor Collection

port I detect a dark shape. As the sub moves forward the shape materializes into a recognizable image: it's *Monitor*'s bow. The unique circular anchor well is clearly visible, and I can see anchor chain draped over the side of the armor belt and disappearing into the sand.

A slender vertical shape comes into view; it's the plastic pipe that our archaeological director, Gordon Watts, installed yesterday. My job is to complete the installation of two more reference pipes, one near the turret and one at the bow. Our goal is to install a row of four survey pipes, parallel to *Monitor*'s hull, which we will use for mapping the wreck.

Roger expertly settles the sub onto the seabed near *Monitor*'s port side, in the lee of the Gulf Stream's flow. "On bottom."

Don acknowledges, and Roger reports poor visibility, only twenty to thirty feet, adding that the sub is positioned near *Monitor*'s amidships bulkhead, facing the turret. Gordon thoroughly briefed me on my assignment, and I understand exactly what I am to do. I'm just a bit apprehensive—I've been this deep before, just never with all this equipment and all the procedures associated with diving from a submersible.

Don undogs the exit hatch, which is being held tightly in place by the outside water pressure. Next he carefully checks all my equipment and asks if I'm ready. Trying to appear confident, I muster a firm "Roger." With that, Don opens a valve. A hissing roar fills the chamber as a mixture of helium and oxygen gasses rushes in from a storage tank, raising the pressure inside the chamber. I immediately feel the pressure on my eardrums, reminding me that I need to pinch my nose and blow forcefully to balance the pressure on both sides of my eardrums. The medical term is the "Valsalva maneuver" but most divers call it "equalizing."

Don calls out, "Fifty feet," but his voice is two octaves higher. A combination of increasing pressure and the helium in our breathing gas makes him sound like Alvin the chipmunk. He's giving me the "okay" signal, which I return to indicate that he can keep pressurizing the chamber. Pulling on my band mask—which covers my whole face and includes a gas regulator and communications gear—I hear Don call out "Hatch open!"

Sure enough, I look down and I'm staring at the Atlantic Ocean! The pressure inside has reached the same as that outside, letting the hatch drop open. I

The author in the dive chamber of the *Johnson-Sea-Link* submersible, preparing for a research dive on *Monitor*. Courtesy NOAA *Monitor* Collection

dives we didn't breathe helium, so it's the first time I've sounded like one of the chipmunks.

After sliding my feet down through the hatch I get one last checkout from Don. He gives me a shoulder tap and I hear him report, "Diver leaving the sub." I push myself down and onto the seabed. I'm out. I crawl out from beneath the sub and stand up next to the armor belt. I'm seeing everything in deep shades of blue. I turn to face the pilot sphere, a thick acrylic bubble that gives the two people inside a panoramic view of the scene. I give them an "okay" sign, then pull the water hose off the sub and start walking (we don't wear fins on this project). Don feeds my umbilical out through the hatch and asks if I'm okay. I reply, "okay." I am; in fact, I'm very excited to finally be here. Walking aft, following the armor belt and the guide rope that Gordon set in place yesterday, I pass the first plastic pipe. Ahead I can barely see the faint shape of the pipe I am assigned to install.

I reach the pipe, a ten-foot long section of white, thick-walled PVC pipe, lying in the sand next to the reference marker that tells me where to install it. Following my dive plan, I secure a "leveling collar" around the center of the pipe. This device, fitted with two bubble levels set at right angles to one another, will ensure that I keep the pipe vertical as I sink it into the seabed. I then insert the jetting tube that will force high-pressure water through the pipe, thus

know that's how it works, of course, but somehow it seems more dramatic now that we're in such deep water.

I tighten the straps on my band mask and take a breath. The regulator's hiss is followed by a comforting inrush of cool gas. My squeaky "Comms check" comes across as a real surprise. During our training

The author's first *Monitor* dive involved installing a reference pipe near *Monitor*'s famous gun turret. Courtesy NOAA *Monitor* Collection

washing out a hole that will let the pipe slide into the seabed.

Suddenly, my focus leaps from the task at hand to the surrounding scene. I've just become acutely aware that I'm actually standing next to the USS *Monitor*, America's first modern warship. I am only a few feet from *Monitor*'s most iconic feature: its armored gun turret. I look back toward the sub. The water hose and my umbilical trail off along the bottom, but the sub is lost in the blue haze. Yielding to a nearly irresistible urge, I set down the water hose and walk to the turret.

Twenty-two feet in diameter and nine feet high, the turret towers over me, covered with more than a century of corrosion and marine growth. I reach out and gently place the palm of my hand against the turret. I can almost sense the flow of history into my body. This is why I became an archaeologist, why I love investigating shipwrecks. My mind is reeling with images of *Monitor*'s battle with CSS *Virginia* (ex-*Merrimack*) in 1862, of shot and shell crashing against this very iron, of that terrible night when *Monitor* sank out here, taking sixteen men to the bottom.

"Ready for me to turn on the water, John?" It's Roger, trying to keep me on schedule. I only have a few minutes before I must return to the protection of the sub and begin the slow ascent to the surface. Quickly, I return to the pipe, raise it to vertical, and call out, "Ready."

The rest of the dive is fairly routine. I am able to jet the reference pipe the desired five feet into the sediment before moving to the pipe at the bow. The operation begins well, but after sinking only three feet, the pipe strikes a hard surface and won't go deeper. I keep pushing the pipe until my dive time is up and Roger tells me to return to the sub immediately. I barely make it back into the sub before the maximum dive time of sixty minutes. Beyond that limit, Don and I would have been subjected to a much longer decompression time because of the extra gasses our bodies would have absorbed under pressure.

As I stow my band mask I hear Roger call out, "Leaving bottom."

I also hear gas hissing as Richard Roesch, in the forward sphere with Roger, begins methodically reducing the pressure in our dive chamber to begin the decompression process, just as the pressure would have decreased had we been ascending to the surface as swimmers. I watch as the sub is recovered from the sea and "mated" (docked) with a hatch on the ship's deck. When pressures are equalized, our hatch opens again and we slide through a short metal trunk into a large decompression chamber where we eat a hot meal and complete our return to atmospheric pressure.

My first encounter with *Monitor*'s turret will remain a vivid memory that I will cherish for the rest of my life. And, although I didn't know it at the time, I was to have many more visits with *Monitor* in the coming years.

Chapter One

———✦———

"THE *MONITOR* IS NO MORE"

FOLLOWING NEW ORDERS

As dawn broke over the Outer Banks of North Carolina on the morning of Tuesday, December 30, 1862, the sun's dim glow silhouetted a strange procession on the cold Atlantic Ocean. Far offshore, two sidewheel steamships were slowly making their way through gentle swells as they headed south-southeast. Each steamer was towing what a casual observer might assume was an elliptical barge, each "barge" so low in the water that waves lapped over its hull. At the center of each was a large cylinder, behind which vertical projections trailed curls of smoke. The two pairs of vessels were miles apart but unmistakably traveling in company.

A closer look would have left the observer dumbfounded, for the odd "barges" being towed were the first of their kind, harbingers of a new age of fighting ships: the Union Navy's new iron-armored warships USS *Monitor* and USS *Passaic*. A brilliant Swedish-American inventor, John Ericsson, had conceived the "monitor" design for defense of harbors and inland waters. Their hulls were almost completely submerged to protect them from enemy gunfire, while their own guns and crews were shielded within heavily armored, cylindrical turrets.

On March 9, 1862, the USS *Monitor*, prototype of this new design, had fought the Confederate iron-clad CSS *Virginia* at Hampton Roads, Virginia, in a battle that precipitated global changes in naval warfare. Just over nine months since that battle, the now-famous *Monitor* was under tow, heading south to Beaufort, North Carolina, in company with USS *Passaic*, the first of a new class of larger and somewhat more seaworthy monitors. The previous week, on Christmas Eve, Commander John P. Bankhead, *Monitor*'s commanding officer, had received confidential orders instructing him to "proceed in tow of the *Rhode Island*, with the *Monitor* under your command, to Beaufort, N.C., and wait further orders. Avail yourself of the first favorable weather."[1]

Monitor was ready for the voyage. The ship had been refitted at the Washington Navy Yard in October. There, workers overhauled its hull and machinery and armored and extended its smoke pipes and fresh air funnels, raising them higher off the deck to prevent seawater from entering. To commemorate their battle with CSS *Virginia*, the officers had *Monitor*'s two 11-inch Dahlgren guns engraved with "Monitor & Merrimac [*sic*]." Then one gun was engraved "Ericsson" for the builder, the other "Worden" for the commanding officer at the time of the battle.

Improvements continued to be made after *Monitor* returned to Hampton Roads the following month. The crew moved the helm to a temporary steering station atop the turret. Previously, the wheel was mounted in a pilothouse near the bow

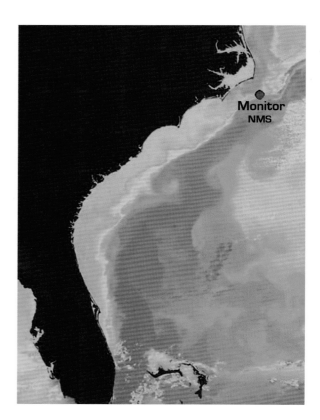

Satellite image of the southeastern coast of the US, showing surface water temperatures and the location of the *Monitor* National Marine Sanctuary; the confrontation off Cape Hatteras between the northerly-flowing Gulf Stream (red) and southerly-flowing Labrador Current (blue) is clearly visible. Courtesy NOAA Office of Exploration and Research

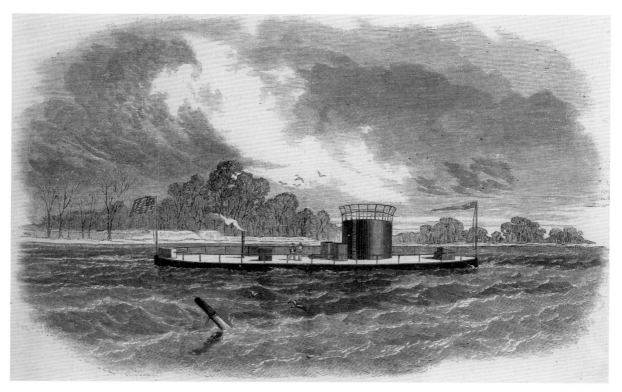

Illustration of USS *Monitor* from *Harper's* Magazine, published March 22, 1862, less than two weeks after its battle with CSS *Virginia*. Most of the details are accurate. Courtesy The Mariners' Museum

U.S.S. RHODE ISLAND. 19 -14 - 14

Photograph of USS *Rhode Island*, the sidewheel steamer that was towing *Monitor* the night the ironclad sank. Courtesy The Mariners' Museum

Photograph of USS *Passaic,* the first of a new class of Union Navy monitors, somewhat larger and more seaworthy than the original *Monitor*. Courtesy The Mariners' Museum

Commander John Bankhead was *Monitor*'s commanding officer at the time the ironclad sank. Courtesy The Mariners' Museum

that projected several feet above the deck and was nearly always awash when underway.[2]

Preparations for the voyage had been extensive. On March 7, during *Monitor*'s transit from New York to Hampton Roads, a storm caused water to enter the ship at the base of the turret and down the two ventilator openings, creating problems with internal ventilation and endangering the ship and crew. *Monitor*'s executive officer later wrote his father and brother,

[T]he sea suddenly . . . came up with tremendous force through our anchor-well, and . . . our hawse-pipe . . . and then the water would rush through in a perfect stream, clear to our berth deck, over the wardroom table. The noise resembled the death-groans of twenty men, and was the most dismal, awful sound I have ever heard. . . . We began to think the 'Monitor' would never see daylight.[3]

As a result of that experience, *Monitor*'s officers undoubtedly paid close attention to identifying and sealing potential sources of leaks in December. As an extra precaution, the crew installed a high-capacity centrifugal water pump to enhance the ship's ability to more quickly empty the bilges if *Monitor* took on water.

Monitor's new surgeon, Greenville Weeks, reported that "the turret and sight holes were caulked, and every possible entrance for water made secure."[4] Engine room fireman George Geer played an active role in those final preparations, spending most of Christmas day caulking and sealing. Geer wrote his brother that he had "secured the hatches with red lead putty and for the port holes [deck lights and, possibly, coal scuttles] I made rubber gaskets, one inch thick and in fact, had everything about the ship in the way of an opening water tight."[5]

The turret was rotated so that the gunports faced directly to starboard, which lined up hatches in the turret deck with openings to the ship below. Then, against the builder's instructions, the crew apparently raised the turret and inserted a tarred hemp gasket or oakum packing between the turret and deck. Once the turret was lowered onto the gasket, the crew may have caulked the seam between the turret and deck as well.[6] The port stoppers, heavy iron pendulums that closed the gun ports, were secured inside with their own ropes and pulleys; wooden bucklers (plugs) were placed in the gun ports and secured with bolts that passed through the small implement holes in the stoppers. The bucklers were caulked in place. Inside, the two guns were secured by tightening up their tackle and clamping the carriage brakes securely.

When the anchor was raised for the voyage, the crew jammed packing into the eight-inch diameter hawse pipe, where the anchor chain passed out of the ship only five inches above the waterline.[7] Surely, the officers must have recalled the stream of water ejected from this opening during the voyage from New York, and seen to it that the hawsehole was well sealed.[8]

FACING THE CAPE

In spite of all these preparations, as the two monitors approached Cape Hatteras on that December morning they faced a threat for which they were not designed—the perils of open sea. To ease their passage, both were under tow by sturdy, reliable sidewheel steamers—*Monitor* by USS *Rhode Island* and *Passaic* by USS *State of Georgia*. Despite the tow, both ironclads were experiencing unsettling motion. As seas began to build, both began to leak despite the extensive efforts at caulking. A light wind from the south-southwest had generated gentle swells, causing water to periodically wash across the monitors' low decks.[9] Worse weather was on its way; cloudbanks on the horizon to the southwest were spreading across the sky.[10]

Both ships were following courses plotted to round Cape Hatteras at a respectful distance.[11] Even in the age of steam, mariners well knew to maintain adequate "sea room" when passing the Cape.[12] Cape Hatteras and the shallow Diamond Shoals that extend seaward comprise the easternmost projection on the mid-Atlantic coast, often snaring ships that venture too near. Danger from the constantly-shifting shoals is compounded by the volatile and violent weather produced by the collision there of the cold, southerly-flowing Labrador Current with the warm, northerly-flowing Gulf Stream.

In spite of the treacherous shoals, Commander Stephen D. Trenchard, commanding *Rhode Island*, and *Monitor*'s commanding officer, Commander John P. Bankhead, agreed to navigate as close to land as they deemed prudent. They took this riskier course to try and slip past Diamond Shoals inside the Gulf Stream, which flows north at an impressive speed of 2 to 4 knots, sufficient to significantly impede their progress. *State of Georgia* and *Passaic*, on the other hand, stood a few miles further offshore, accepting a slower pace in exchange for the relative safety of deeper water.[13] Both steamers took frequent soundings, keeping a close watch on water depth, by which they could estimate their distance from shore.[14]

As they continued south, both monitors began to feel the Cape's power. Colliding warm and cold water from the two opposing sea currents, along with an approaching low-pressure front, were brewing up a major storm. *Rhode Island*'s deck officers initially estimated the wind at Force 2 from southwest by west.[15] Although wind of Force 2 on the Beaufort Scale is only 4 to 6 knots—defined as a "light breeze" producing "small wavelets"—the complex natural forces at Hatteras obviously amplified the wind's effect. The real concern was that the ironclads under tow, heavy and riding low in the water, would become unwieldy and dangerous in any but calm seas.

At 6:40 a.m., *Monitor* signaled *Rhode Island* to heave to so that additional chafing protection could be parceled onto the two towlines.[16] These large hawsers, 3½ and 4¾ inches in diameter and approximately 300 feet long, had begun to wear due to the constant working of the towlines in the chocks. If the towlines could not be adequately padded, they would eventually part, casting *Monitor* adrift. The hard work of the sailors notwithstanding, chafing continued and would become a much more serious problem before the day was done.

Further offshore, *Passaic* had been heading into Force 4 winds (11 to 16 knots) from the southwest since the previous evening. *Passaic*'s logbook stated, "At 12, Cape Hatteras Light House bore West (true) distant ten miles. Moderate swell from South West."[17] An hour later, *Rhode Island* "made Cape Hatteras Light House bearing W.S.W. distant 14 miles. Sounded in 13 fathoms [seventy-eight feet]."[18]

By afternoon, as weather conditions continued to deteriorate, the four vessels drew closer together. Deck officers on *State of Georgia* reported seeing "the 'Monitor' . . . on the starboard bow 5 miles distant. . . . stormy weather, with several vessels in sight." Astern, *Passaic* was struggling with disabled bilge pumps and clogged limbers (openings in the bilge frames that let water flow to the pumps). *Passaic*'s logbook described the crew's struggles: "Latter part [of the noon-to-4:00 p.m. watch] making a quantity of water. One watch constantly bailing water . . . and engineers and firemen employed in trying to settle the turret, but are as yet unsuccessful." *Passaic*'s turret, like *Monitor*'s, was held in place only by its immense weight (more than 150 tons) and a shaft coupling. It is frightening to imagine that massive turret, containing two large guns and other equipment, rising off the deck with the erratic motion of the ship and the buffeting seas, allowing water to pour through the widened gap at the turret base and into the ironclad's interior. Equally frightening is the image of men attempting to "settle" the enormous cylinder.[19]

From 4:00 to 6:00 p.m., *Passaic*'s log noted that the winds were unchanged and that the sea was "comparatively smooth."[20] At 4:15 *State of Georgia* paused briefly to bury one of their crew at sea, Landsman William N. Kearny, who had died at 7:00 a.m. from acute laryngitis. As they paused, the crews of *State of Georgia* and *Passaic* saw *Rhode Island* and *Monitor* in the distance, inshore approximately six miles and bearing west-southwest.[21]

On board *Monitor*, the officers were enjoying themselves in spite of the weather. Paymaster William F. Keeler later wrote to his wife that they gathered atop the turret and,

[A]mused ourselves for an hour or more by watching two or three sharks. . . . We made no water of consequence; a little trickled down about the pilot house & some began to find its way under the turret rendering it wet & cheerless below.

At 5 o'clock we sat down to dinner, every one cheerful & happy & though the sea was rolling & foaming over our heads . . . all rejoicing that at last our monotonous, inactive life had ended.[22]

Keeler's mood changed when he returned to the top of the turret around 6:30, to find the night dark and tempestuous:

We were now off Cape Hatteras, the Cape Horn of our Atlantic Coast. The wind was blowing violently; the heavy seas rolled over our bows dashing against the pilot house &, surging aft, would strike the solid turret with a force to make it tremble, sending off on either side a boiling, foaming torrent of water.[23]

Grenville Weeks, the ship's surgeon, later wrote that "the little vessel plunged through the rising waves instead of riding on them as they increased in violence . . . so that, even when we considered ourselves safe, the appearance was of a vessel sinking." Weeks heard one sailor lament, "Give me an oyster-scow! Anything!—only let it be wood, and something that will float over, instead of under the water!"[24]

Monitor steamed close to *Rhode Island* and Bankhead used a speaking trumpet to shout that if *Monitor* needed assistance during the night they would hoist a single red lantern from the signal mast. Soon they were once again under way, maintaining a speed of 6 knots.[25]

During the night a series of squalls passed over the convoy. *Passaic*'s log noted that "from 6 to 8 p.m., ship laboring in head sea. Leaking badly forward in anchor well. Hands bailing water from under berth deck [beneath the turret] and passing it into fire room, and from there pumped out." Mean-

while, *Monitor*'s crew managed to remain in a good mood—even taking time to cheer at getting ahead of *Passaic* and being "the first iron-clad that ever rounded Cape Hatteras."[26] Below, second assistant engineer Joseph Watters was keeping an eye on the engine and bilge pumps, while readying the auxiliary pumps for instant use.[27]

Francis Butts, a landsman who had volunteered for duty on *Monitor* in November, was assisting at the helm atop the turret. He later recalled:

The vessel was making very heavy weather, riding one huge wave, plunging through the next as if shooting straight for the bottom of the ocean, and splashing down upon another with such force that her hull would tremble, and with a shock that would sometimes take us off our feet, while a fourth would leap upon us and break far above the turret, so that if we had not been protected by a rifle-armor that was securely fastened and rose to the height of a man's chest, we should of been washed away.[28]

IRONCLADS IN DISTRESS

Shortly after 7:30 p.m. *Monitor*'s port towline parted. The hawser had finally chafed until it broke, and *Monitor* began "yawing very much," and began taking in "more water around the base of the tower."[29] Conditions were about to get worse. During the 8:00 p.m.-to-midnight watch, the situation on board each monitor became more and more critical. The wind increased to Force 4 (11 to 16 knots) out of the southwest by west, and squalls were creating periods of much stronger winds and higher seas. Commander Bankhead reported that at 8:00 p.m.,

[T]he sea . . . commenced to rise very rapidly, causing the vessel to plunge heavily, completely submerging the pilot house and washing over and into the turret and at times into the blower pipes. . . . the under surface of the projecting armor would come down with great force . . . loosening still more of the packing around [the turret's] base.[30]

Passaic was experiencing a similar crisis. Her commanding officer, Captain Percival Drayton, later reported, "I found that the forward armor projection thumping into the sea was gradually making a large opening there, through which the water poured in a large stream."[31] *Passaic*'s log recorded the emergency: "frequent squalls, with rain. Ship leaking badly. All hands employed at bailing water, as before, and throwing over shot. Threw overboard 340 32-lb. shot."[32]

On *Monitor*, engineer Watters reported to Bankhead that the bilge pumps were unable to keep up with the inflow of water. He recommended that they start the high-capacity centrifugal pump. Bankhead immediately ordered him to do so, but a short time later Watters reported that even with all pumps operating the water was still gaining, having risen to several inches above the engine room floor where it dampened the coal and splashed into the ash pits.[33]

On *Passaic*, efforts to lighten the ship proved insufficient, especially with water continuing to en-ter and the pumps disabled by bilge debris. Drayton later reported that "at 10 p.m., finding that I could not stand the thumping of the heavy southwest sea, I directed the *State of Georgia* to run north and get a lee north of Hatteras."[34] *Passaic*'s log records that "at 10:30 kept the ship off before the wind to run back."[35] Even that drastic action did not guarantee safety, and during the latter part of the watch, half of the crew was jettisoning more ballast to lighten the ship.[36] Captain Drayton's decisions that night saved *Passaic*, thus avoiding a double tragedy for the Union.

At the same time *Passaic* began retreating to the north, Commander Bankhead received word that even with all *Monitor*'s pumps operating, water was still rising and would soon quench the boiler fires. Once the fires were out, steam pressure would drop rapidly and the pumps would not operate. As Sur-geon Weeks noted, "When [the fires] were reached, the vessel's doom was sealed; for with their extinc-tion the pumps must cease, and all hope of keeping the Monitor above water more than an hour or two expire."[37] Already, boiler pressure was dropping be-cause of wet coal and the demands of all the pumps. Bankhead ordered the engines slowed to divert as much steam as possible to the pumps.

PANORAMA OF HORROR

Shortly after 10:30 p.m., Bankhead consulted his of-ficers. All were in agreement that with power failing and water rising, *Monitor* could not be saved. Bank-head gave the order to hoist a red lantern atop the turret to alert *Rhode Island* to their peril. Some of the crew formed bucket brigades, fruitlessly passing up buckets of water, trying to keep busy and possibly delay the inevitable. In the engine room, water was already above the ash pits, choking airflow to the fires.[38] The Navy's powerful new warship had very little time remaining.

Standing on the turret, Bankhead assessed his ship's desperate situation. The remaining towline, hanging slack over the bow, was making *Monitor* unmanageable. He asked for volunteers to go for-ward and cut the thick hawser. Master Louis Stod-der, Boatswain's Mate John Stocking, and Quarter Gunner James Fenwick jumped to the task, clam-bering down the slippery sides of the turret to make their way forward. As the sea washed over them, the men clung desperately to a lifeline threaded through stanchions positioned along the edge of the deck. The wave took Fenwick and Stocking, sweeping them overboard. Stodder succeeded in cutting the line and alone made his way back to the turret.[39]

Spotting the red lantern, Commander Trenchard responded immediately, turning about and sending out two of *Rhode Island*'s boats—the launch and first cutter—which began pulling for the stricken *Moni-tor*. On the foundering ironclad, the situation was chaotic. Paymaster Keeler recalled,

It was a scene well calculated to appall the boldest heart. Mountains of water were rushing cross our decks & foaming along our sides; . . . the howling of the tempest, the roar & dash of waters; the hoarse orders through the speaking trumpets of the officers; the response of the men; the shouts of encouragement and words of caution; 'the bubbling cry of some strong Swimmer in his agony;' and the whole scene lit up by the ghastly glare of the blue lights burning on our con-sort, formed a panorama of horror which time can never efface from my memory.[40]

Monitor pulled close to *Rhode Island* to aid the boats in reaching them, but the vessels nearly collided, and *Monitor* staved in the launch. At that dangerous moment, with the two ships close together, some of *Rhode Island*'s men threw ropes down to *Monitor*'s deck, but few attempted to reach them through the heavy seas that washed over the hull. Several men had gathered on the turret roof, unsure or unwill-ing to attempt the perilous passage down the turret ladder, across the flooded deck and onto the boat.[41]

Rhode Island pulled forward, and a third boat was launched to carry off more of *Monitor*'s men.[42] Although the launch was badly damaged, its passengers managed to keep it afloat long enough to get back to *Rhode Island*.

To make matters worse, *Monitor*'s drifting hawser tangled one of *Rhode Island*'s paddlewheels, causing the steamer to lose maneuverability and drift away from its overloaded boats. Before the next boat attempted to return to *Monitor*, *Rhode Island* had drifted nearly two miles away.[43]

Bankhead's report of January 1, 1863, states:

At 11:30, my engines working slowly, and all the pumps in full play, but water gaining rapidly, sea very heavy, and breaking entirely over the vessel. . . . While waiting for the boats to return, the engineer reported that the engines had ceased to work, and shortly after all

the pumps stopped also, the water putting out the fires, and leaving no pressure of steam.[44]

The appended report by Joseph Watters, Second Assistant Engineer, corroborated Bankhead's account of the loss of engine and pumps:

[T]he amount of water in the ship increased, until it reached the fires and gradually extinguished them. The pressure of steam in the boilers at that time was five pounds per square inch, and the main engine stopped; the . . . pumps still working slowly, but finally stopped.

I reported the circumstances to Captain Bankhead. A few minutes later I received an order to leave the engine room, and proceed to get in the boats. It was then between the hours of 12 p.m. and 1 a.m., and the fires nearly extinguished.[45]

USS *Monitor* foundered off Cape Hatteras, North Carolina, early in the morning of December 31, 1862, its towship, USS *Rhode Island*, rescuing all but 16 of its officers and crew. From *Harper's Weekly*, January 3, 1863. Courtesy The Mariners' Museum

Bankhead wrote that without power, *Monitor* had "fallen off into the trough [of the wave] and rolling so heavily as to render it impossible for boats to approach." Hoping to bring *Monitor*'s head back into the wind, Bankhead "ordered the anchor to be let go and all the chain given her." He then "ordered all the men left on board to leave the turret and endeavor to get into the two boats which were then approaching us."[46]

Rhode Island's men conducted themselves well that night, the boat crews performing remarkable acts of bravery and heroism. Acting Master's Mate D. Rodney Browne, returning to *Monitor* for a second time, overloaded his boat in hopes of saving as many of the remaining men as possible. As Browne later reported, it was then around 1:00 a.m. and, "We had now got in my boat all of the 'Monitor's' crew that could be persuaded to come down from the turret for they had seen some of their shipmates . . . washed overboard and sink in their sight." Browne began pulling away for *Rhode Island*, vowing to return for the remaining men.[47] Bankhead's report confirmed, "there were several men still left upon and in the turret who, either stupefied by fear or fearful of being washed overboard . . . would not come down."[48]

The men who remained in the turret could see Browne's overloaded boat struggling against huge waves, its crew pulling toward *Rhode Island*, which must have seemed impossibly far away. They may have decided that even if they had managed to reach the boat, the odds of surviving the long pull to *Rhode Island* would be slim. At least on *Monitor*, there was a chance they would somehow weather the storm.

"THE *MONITOR* IS NO MORE"

When the first cutter reached *Rhode Island*, half of the boat's crew allowed themselves to be pulled aboard along with *Monitor*'s survivors. At around 1:30, despite extreme exhaustion and the loss of half his crew, Browne and his remaining men immediately set off again for *Monitor*. Browne reported, "We made but slow progress and before we reached her, her light disappeared." They continued on to where they last saw *Monitor*'s light, but all they found was an eddy, apparently produced by the sinking ironclad.[49]

Later, Weeks reminisced about standing safely at the rail of *Rhode Island*, witnessing the *Monitor*'s final minutes:

For an hour or more we watched from the deck of the Rhode Island the lonely light upon the Monitor's turret — a hundred times we thought it gone forever, a hundred times it reappeared."[50]

At approximately 1:30 on the morning of New Year's Eve, 1862, *Monitor*'s red lantern winked out for the last time. Paymaster Keeler wrote to his wife, "The *Monitor* is no more. What the fire of the enemy failed to do, the elements have accomplished."[51]

Chapter Two

DISCOVERY

Following *Monitor*'s loss, Bankhead submitted an official report, as did the commanding officers of *Rhode Island*, *Passaic*, and *State of Georgia*. Based on those reports, and most probably on their own sea experience, Navy Board officials concluded that the officers and men of *Monitor* and *Rhode Island* had done everything possible to prevent *Monitor* from sinking. We know this because the Navy Board did not commission a board of inquiry to investigate the vessel's loss, and they took no action against any of the officers.

As for the ship, *Monitor* was a total and irretrievable loss. The Navy Department would have concluded that *Monitor* lay beyond the reach of available technology. The ironclad's last position was not precisely known. Even if the officers had been able to record exact bearings, the limits of navigation accuracy at that time would have made it nearly impossible to relocate the wreck. More importantly, the water depth—estimated at that time to be in excess of 300 feet—and the hazardous offshore location, would have prevented any salvage attempt. Given the circumstances and the exigencies of war, the Navy soon forgot about their first ironclad.

Because of this combination of factors, it is not surprising that *Monitor* lay undisturbed on the seafloor for nearly a century. The Navy turned its attention to improved and larger monitor-type warships, but many veterans and citizens sustained memories of the original. Their interest carried over into a new century, as aficionados kept *Monitor*'s story alive and indeed molded the story of the little ironclad into an American legend.

EARLY ATTEMPTS TO LOCATE *MONITOR*

Following World War II, improvements in deep-sea technology inspired thoughts of finding, and even recovering *Monitor*, sparking searches that ultimately discovered the ironclad's resting place and led to years of protection, research, and recovery.

The earliest known planned search for *Monitor* was in May 1950, when the US Navy sought to locate the wreck using a newly-developed sonar device designated the "Underwater Object Locator (UOL) Mark 4."[1] The Navy reported having located a sunken object that was approximately the right size and position to be *Monitor*, but apparently there was no further attempt to identify the site at that time. We have found no other information about this brief but intriguing project and one can only speculate as to what inspired this naval unit to look for *Monitor*.[2]

The most highly publicized *Monitor* search up until the time of the actual discovery in 1973 was conducted in 1955 by Marine Corporal Robert Marx, who later became a well-known treasure hunter. Marx managed to interest the editors at *Life* magazine, who sent reporter Clay Blair to Hatteras to cover the story. Even the federal government was drawn into the drama. In July *Life* arranged a brief visit by the US Coast and Geodetic Survey vessel *Stirni*, which conducted a sonar survey and a wire drag. The wire appeared to briefly contact an object, but subsequent wire drags and sonar searches failed to verify a target.[3]

Marx claimed to have located *Monitor* on July 12 in forty-five feet of water, within two miles of the Cape Hatteras Lighthouse at a location later recorded by *Stirni*. Both Marx and Blair published detailed accounts of the discovery, but their books disagree on details. The wreck was later found many miles from the lighthouse in much deeper water, so the 1955 discovery was simply not *Monitor*.[4]

There are other early reported searches for *Monitor*, most—but not all—of which seem to have taken place near the Marx site. In 1967 and 1968 North Carolina Tidewater Services Inc., with authorization from the State of North Carolina, towed a magnetometer—an instrument capable of detecting ferrous metal—behind a Norfolk tugboat to search "a specific area adjacent to Cape Hatteras."[5]

That same year the Navy's Supervisor of Salvage, Captain William F. Searle Jr., asked the Naval History Division if it were interested in a renewed search for *Monitor* by the US Navy. Apparently, no action was taken.[6] As the 1970s began, several groups independently applied more scientific approaches for finding *Monitor*. One researcher, who ultimately played a major role in *Monitor*'s discovery, was Captain Ernest W. Peterkin, USNR, of the Naval Research Laboratory. In 1970, Captain Peterkin's interest in all things historical led him to plot the track of USS *Rhode Island*, the steamer that was towing *Monitor* on the night it sank. Peterkin made his results known and attempted to generate interest in a search for *Monitor* at his predicted coordinates, a position determined from careful analysis of historical data. It was well offshore and southeast of Diamond Shoals.[7] There was no immediate response, but Peterkin's research was eventually put to very good use.

The "Year of the Monitor"—1973

In 1973, as if attracted by a siren's song, at least seven different groups conducted searches for *Monitor*, a phenomenon that one researcher termed "the Year of the *Monitor*." Another quipped that 1973 was the "Great *Monitor* Sweepstakes."[8] It was during this time that I first became involved with the lost ironclad.

In May of 1973 several midshipmen at the US Naval Academy set out on a recreational dive to relocate *Monitor* where Marx had reported finding it in 1955. Bad weather, a typical situation during Hatteras summers, prevented their dives but sparked an interest that led to the formation of "Project Cheesebox" as an official Naval Academy independent research project. "Cheesebox" eventually involved eight midshipmen, attracted support from Naval Academy faculty and numerous naval units, and resulted in a significant research report edited by Edward M. Miller.[9]

At about the same time, three private not-for-profit groups teamed up to determine once and for all whether *Monitor* lay near the coordinates Marx published in his book.[10] I headed a research team organized by Underwater Archaeological Associates Inc. and Marine Archaeological Research Services Inc., an organization I cofounded. Not long after we began our search near the lighthouse, we learned that we had company—a search team from the USS *Monitor* Foundation. We soon joined forces, eventually searching a nine-square-mile area centered on the Marx coordinates. Four separate searches, utilizing state-of-the-art side-scan sonars and magnetometers, determined that the area contained no metallic object anywhere near the size and iron mass of *Monitor*.[11]

On July 17, our combined survey team was surprised by a low-level fly-by of a Navy "Orion" aircraft, a distinctive "stinger" (magnetic sensor boom) protruding from its tail. Looking up, one of our team members quipped, "That's what we need to find the *Monitor*!" Little did we know that the RP-3D Orion was, indeed, searching for *Monitor*, on behalf of yet another group of researchers![12] The Orion, from squadron VXN-8, was equipped with a powerful airborne magnetometer.[13] William J. Andahazy, a magnetics specialist with the Naval Research and Development Center arranged the search in support of "Project Cheesebox" at the Naval Academy. That data-gathering flight, conducted by the Naval Oceanographic Office's "Project Magnet" included a brief examination of "Search Area A," the so-called Marx site. Out of a total of twelve targets, Andahazy recommended four for further investigation.

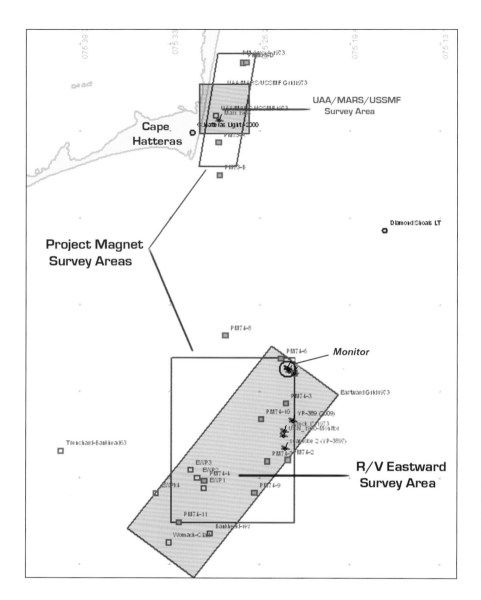

Map of Cape Hatteras area, showing four search rectangles where various groups searched for the wreck of USS *Monitor* in 1973. Courtesy NOAA *Monitor* Collection

Two were well north and two well south of the Marx site.[14]

While all this action was taking place in shallow water near the Cape Hatteras Lighthouse, three separate groups were preparing for surveys much further offshore and southeast of the lighthouse, one based on the 1950 Navy survey and two on charted tracks of *Rhode Island* and *Monitor*.

Roland Wommack, a 1959 graduate of the Naval Academy, believed the Navy had located *Monitor* in 1950 with their Underwater Object Locator, and he was determined to prove it. Wommack's "Monitor Project" team included a diver willing to descend to the 300-foot depth in order to identify *Monitor*. During their August 1973 expedition, however, equip-

ment and weather problems prevented them from completing their survey.[15]

DISCOVERY AND POSITIVE IDENTIFICATION OF *MONITOR*

The R/V Eastward *Cruise, August 1973*

During August 17–31, 1973, a scientific team on board the Duke University Marine Laboratory research vessel *Eastward* conducted an oceanographic cruise off North Carolina. The investigators had two objectives: first, a geological study of a ridge and swale feature on the Continental Shelf off Cape Hatteras, and

The magnetometer sensor probe, or "stinger," of a P-3 *Orion* aircraft is clearly visible in this photo. This aircraft from the US Navy's "Project Magnet" was used to search for *Monitor* in 1973. Courtesy NOAA *Monitor* Collection

second, a search for *Monitor*. The principal investigators were John G. Newton, marine superintendent at Duke's Marine Lab, who headed the expedition; Harold E. Edgerton, from the Massachusetts Institute of Technology; Robert E. Sheridan, a geologist at the University of Delaware; and Gordon P. Watts Jr., underwater archaeologist with the North Carolina Division of Archives and History. Principal funding was from the National Science Foundation and the National Geographic Society.[16]

The stated scientific purpose for the attempt to find *Monitor* was to evaluate the capabilities of a suite of remote-sensing instruments for locating and identifying relatively small, submerged objects. *Monitor* was an ideal subject, since its unique size and shape was not shared by any other vessel known or believed to have sunk near Hatteras.[17]

Following successful completion of the geological survey, the team turned its attention to a 7.5 by 16.5 nautical mile search rectangle. This search area was defined by Gordon Watts, based on a wide range of historical data, including the surviving deck log

WAS *MONITOR* "DISCOVERED" DURING WORLD WAR II?

Some researchers have speculated that *Monitor*'s initial discovery was inadvertent and unrecognized. In 1942, war returned to the coastal waters of North Carolina as the shores of Cape Hatteras became a battlefield in the deadly "Battle of the Atlantic." German U-Boats patrolled the coast, sinking tankers and freighters in incredible numbers. So great was the slaughter that the area became known as "Torpedo Junction." To meet this threat, throughout most of World War II the US Navy conducted coastal patrols along the Atlantic coast in

search of U-Boats. *Monitor*'s wreck lies within one of the most active U-Boat attack zones.

Sonar (sound navigation and ranging) was developed just after World War I, but effective and accurate devices were still under development at the outbreak of World War II, when U-Boats began visiting the North American coast. Early sonar equipment could only display sonar signal returns in very vague patterns, so even skilled operators could not accurately interpret the size and shape of a "target" resting on the seabed. Therefore,

it was common practice for antisubmarine patrols to drop depth charges on every large sonar contact. Captain Ernest Peterkin, USN (ret), posed the theory that since that practice continued throughout the war years, it was possible that *Monitor*'s hull was mistaken for a U-Boat and damaged by Navy depth charges. Based on his theory, Peterkin developed a predictive model of the pattern of debris scatter from a depth charge attack. So far we have no solid evidence to support this scenario.

MONITOR'S CODISCOVERERS

In 1972, John G. Newton and Gordon P. Watts Jr. first discussed the feasibility of using newly developed marine survey equipment to search for shipwrecks off the North Carolina coast.[1] Newton, marine

for, since it was the state's most historic shipwreck and its unique shape would make it easy to identify. Newton was soon able to schedule time for a *Monitor* search as the final leg of a 1973 geology cruise directed by a young

join the cruise, and brought along one of his dual-channel side-scan sonars, with which he obtained acoustic images of *Monitor*.

This team of four men, each an expert in a marine survey specialty, comprised an ideal mix of academic disciplines and skills. They were supported by the crew of Duke University's R/V *Eastward* and by Western Electric Company's Hydrographic Division, which provided an underwater video system and a skilled operator, John Harris. With that system, Harris recorded the video images that Gordon Watts later used to determine that they had actually discovered *Monitor*'s remains. Others who did not participate in the 1973 *Eastward* discovery cruise, but who played major roles in *Monitor* research, included Captain Ernest W. Peterkin, USN (ret), and a group of US Naval Academy midshipmen, led by Edward M. Miller. Through the systematic application of sound research practices, and possibly a measure of luck, the "Duke Team" succeeded where many others had failed.

Monitor's co-discoverers in *Eastward*'s galley. (l-r: Gordon Watts, Robert Sheridan, John Newton and his daughter Cathryn, and Harold Edgerton. Courtesy NOAA *Monitor* Collection

superintendent at the Duke University Marine Laboratory in Beaufort, North Carolina, had a strong interest in history and had just coauthored an oceanographic atlas that included a long list of shipwrecks off the North Carolina coast.[2] Watts had recently been hired as North Carolina's first state underwater archaeologist.

Newton and Watts agreed on USS *Monitor* as the ideal wreck to search

assistant professor at the University of Delaware, Robert E. Sheridan. Sheridan participated in the *Monitor* search and provided useful geological data on the seabed in *Monitor*'s vicinity.

Harold E. "Doc" Edgerton, professor of electrical engineering at the Massachusetts Institute of Technology and inventor of the strobe light, was a pioneer in scanning sonar technology. He accepted Newton's invitation to

Notes:

1. Miller (1974); Newton (1975); Sheridan (2004); Watts (1975).
2. Newton, Pilkey, and Blanton (1971).

of USS *Rhode Island* (*Monitor*'s towship), along with the logs of USS *Passaic* (the second monitor to enter service), and its towship, USS *State of Georgia*, both of which had been traveling in company with *Monitor* and *Rhode Island*.[18]

Initially, twenty-one targets were located, but only one, lying at a depth of 320 feet, correlated well with the expected characteristics of *Monitor*. The team decided to investigate that target, which they designated Site 22643. Deepwater visual examination

was not a simple process with the equipment being used on *Eastward*. As the ship approached the target, still and video cameras suspended from cables were placed in the water and lowered until they were close to the bottom. In order to successfully image a wreck, *Eastward* had to set a course that would tow the cameras directly over the target, and the cable lengths had to be adjusted so that the cameras would be close enough to the bottom to film the wreck, but not close enough that they would be snagged. This

The research vessel *Eastward*, from the Duke University Marine Laboratory, which supported the successful search for USS *Monitor* in August 1973. Courtesy NOAA *Monitor* Collection

procedure required continual compensation for wind and current while, at the same time, estimating where the cameras—trailing beneath the ship and subject to subsurface currents—were located relative to the target. This process was difficult under even the best sea conditions, and required numerous passes over the site.[19]

The team laboriously inspected the site over a period of three days and nights before collecting sufficient imagery to tentatively identify the site as a twentieth-century trawler.[20] (Note that in 2009, the National Oceanic and Atmospheric Administration relocated this wreck during a survey conducted as part of the Office of National Marine Sanctuaries' "Battle of the Atlantic" initiative. The NOAA team positively identified the wreck as the US Navy patrol boat YP-389, a converted trawler sunk by the German submarine U-701 in 1942.[21] I checked data from the Navy's 1950 Underwater Object Locator search and discovered that this site is only about a quarter mile from the reported location of the 1950 Navy target, a discrepancy easily explained by improvements in navigational accuracy since that time. If this is the same target, the 1950 wreck location is approximately four nautical miles further offshore and approximately eighty feet deeper than *Monitor*.)[22]

At that point the *Eastward* team was somewhat discouraged, since only a few days remained on the cruise schedule. They decided to move to the northeast portion of the search area. On the night of August 27, Fred Kelly, Duke's electronics chief, was stowing his fishing gear when he spotted an innocuous black squiggle on the fathometer. Although the target was not very impressive, Kelly suggested that they check it out. *Eastward* reversed course for another look, and this target was designated Site number 22662. The laborious imaging process was repeated, and this time the scientists observed what they believed to be the uniquely shaped hull of the USS *Monitor*, lying approximately sixteen nautical miles south-southeast of Cape Hatteras Lighthouse in 220 feet of water.

After three days and nights of data collection, however, the team became baffled by some of the recorded images, which did not match *Monitor*'s expected appearance. They had to satisfy themselves

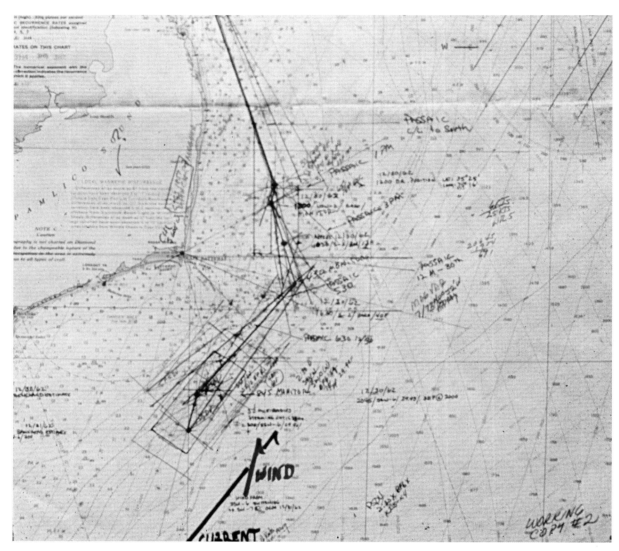

NOAA navigational chart on which Gordon Watts plotted the search area in which *Monitor* was located. Courtesy NOAA *Monitor* Collection

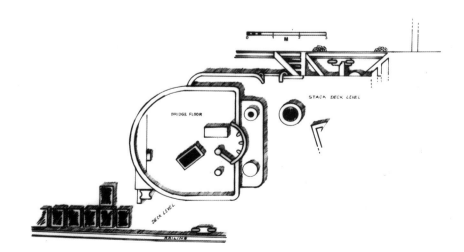

Gordon Watts' drawing of Site 1, the wreck of a trawler that was examined during the 1973 *Eastward* cruise. Courtesy NOAA *Monitor* Collection

The first indication of *Monitor*'s location: a black "squiggle" on *Eastward*'s fathometer chart. Courtesy NOAA *Monitor* Collection

with blurry black-and-white video, since Duke's still camera had become entangled in the wreck and was lost. When they returned to shore, the *Eastward* team cautiously reported that after careful examination of four and a half hours of video footage they believed that *Monitor* "may well" have been located. Archaeologist Watts, cleverly dodging an absolute declaration and yet keeping hopes alive, stated, "Nowhere in these tapes can we find anything that allows us to say this is not the *Monitor*."[23]

The cruise ended, and Watts returned home where he stared for months, off and on, at the videotapes and photos. I was working part-time for Watts at North Carolina's Kure Beach facility, so in late December he invited me to review his findings and offer my opinion. He showed me the video and several black-and-white prints he had made by freezing the video on his home television set and photographing the screen with a still camera. I did not think that the fuzzy images looked much like *Monitor*'s unique hull, pilothouse, or turret. Then Watts said, "Now look at the video again, but this time assume the wreck is upside down and somehow the turret is displaced and partially exposed beneath the hull."

Suddenly, everything made sense. Watts' epiphany had come only after literally scores, if not hundreds of hours of staring at the video, stills, and *Monitor* drawings. He continued refining his theory for a few weeks longer, making sketches and additional photographs to support his conclusion. Fi-

R/V *Eastward* towing still and video cameras over the wreck of USS *Monitor,* as depicted in a *National Geographic* painting. © *National Geographic* magazine

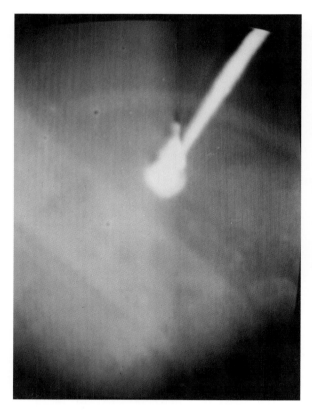

This hazy video frame from the *Eastward* cruise is one of the first glimpses of *Monitor*'s armor belt and turret. Courtesy NOAA *Monitor* Collection

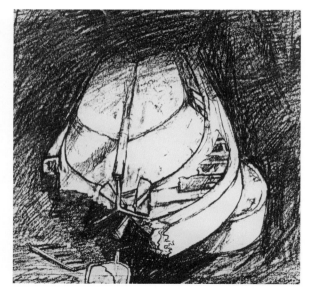

Gordon Watts' first interpretive sketch of *Monitor*'s inverted hull, based on the *Eastward* video. Courtesy NOAA *Monitor* Collection

nally, on January 21, 1974, Watts wrote to *Eastward* cruise leader John Newton, "This is to confirm the identification of site #2 [22662] as that of the Iron-clad U.S.S. MONITOR."[24]

Navy Magnetic Survey of "Area B," January 1974

Even though the Navy's Project Magnet staff was aware that *Monitor* had most likely been located, they conducted a second, previously scheduled Hatteras aerial survey in January 1974. This time they searched "Area B," further offshore where both Watts and Peterkin predicted *Monitor* should lie. Area B was in the vicinity surveyed the previous August by the Duke team. This Navy survey detected eleven uncharted magnetic targets, three of which matched the magnetic signature expected from *Monitor*. One of the three was very near *Eastward*'s Site 2, and another was near Site 1. Target coordinates from these detections were given to the Naval Research Laboratory, which was contemplating a survey of its own.[25]

The Project Magnet airborne shipwreck surveys in 1973 and 1974 proved to be significant beyond the initial goal of looking for *Monitor*'s remains. Andahazy and others from the Navy Ship Research and Development Center demonstrated that magnetic data from properly designed low-altitude flights could be processed by specialized computer software to yield predictions on the locations and characterizations of sunken ships, based upon the magnetic characteristics of the ferrous metals the wrecks contained. Andahazy and his colleagues later applied the same techniques using a high-resolution gradiometer on a small boat to the location of shipwrecks in the York River and elsewhere.[26]

ANNOUNCEMENT AND AFTERMATH

Finally, on March 7, 1974, at a Durham, North Carolina, news conference, John Newton and Gordon Watts announced that the wreck they located during their 1973 cruise had been positively identified as USS *Monitor*.[27] The announcement generated a great deal of excitement—and some skepticism, as was discovered four days later when *Monitor* researchers and interested parties met at the Naval Research Laboratory in Anacostia, Maryland. The purpose of the meeting was to review the Duke data and to discuss a planned mapping expedition by *Alcoa Seaprobe*, an all-aluminum research vessel owned by Alcoa Marine and chartered by the Navy.[28] Watts convincingly presented his interpretation of the *Eastward* data, the midshipmen of "Project Cheesebox" reported on their research, and Andahazy offered corroborating data from the January Project Magnet survey of Area B.[29]

The meeting adjourned, albeit with some doubts remaining, but the *Washington Post* reported that there was "general agreement among all those present" that *Monitor* had probably been located and that this historic ship "deserves to be treated as a nationally valuable archaeological find and not as plunder for the first diver down."[30] The imaging cruise being planned for the following spring would utilize some of the most sophisticated survey equipment in the world with the goal of producing positive and stirring proof that *Monitor* had indeed been located.

THE R/V *ALCOA SEAPROBE* MAPPING CRUISE, APRIL 1974

In late 1973, following the apparently successful Duke survey, codiscoverer Harold Edgerton and several groups, including participants from "Project Cheesebox," encouraged the US Navy to assist in verifying *Monitor*'s discovery. Craig Mullen, Alcoa Marine's Vice President of Operations, attended the meeting and suggested that inspection of the alleged *Monitor* site would be an excellent assignment for the advanced research vessel *Alcoa Seaprobe*, a ship that the Navy already planned to evaluate at sea. This was an important development, since *Seaprobe* was capable of high-resolution deepwater imaging, search, assessment, and, importantly, precisely remaining over a position on the ocean floor.[31] Additionally, Alcoa Marine, the Alcoa subsidiary that operated *Seaprobe*, was already under contract to the Navy for deep ocean search and recovery tasks. To ensure sufficient operating time and publicity, the National Geographic Society offered to cofund the cruise and become a partner in the expedition. Mullen, freshly back from leading a Navy search off Vietnam, would head the Alcoa team.

The Navy approved the project, and the survey took place during the first week of April, 1974. The list of investigators reads like a "Who's Who in Deepwater Oceanography." In fact, although it was

A *National Geographic* painting showing the R/V *Seaprobe* lowering its search pod to the wreck of USS *Monitor*.
© *National Geographic* magazine

not widely known at the time, the *Seaprobe* team included several experts in Cold War submarine operations.[32] Key participants were Commander Colin M. Jones, the Navy's project officer on *Seaprobe*; Chester "Buck" Buchanan, Naval Research Laboratory, who had produced photomosaics on other Navy projects; Andreas Rechnitzer, from the Office of the Oceanographer of the Navy (evaluating *Seaprobe* for a classified Navy project); John Newton, Gordon Watts, and John Harris from the Duke survey; midshipman Edward M. Miller and Ernest W. Peterkin, Project Cheesebox; William J. Andahazy, Project Magnet; Dorothy Nicholson and Nathan Benn, from *National Geographic* magazine; other naval personnel, and support teams from the North Carolina Division of Archives and History and the US Army Reserve.[33]

On April 1, *Seaprobe* deployed its two-ton "search pod," equipped with gyrocompass, several types of sonar, still and video cameras, and strobe and flood lighting. The pod was also fitted with thrusters, small propellers used to adjust the pod's position relative to *Monitor*'s hull. Even with

ALCOA SEAPROBE

The research vessel *Alcoa Seaprobe* was a remarkable ship that in many ways was as unique and innovative as *Monitor*. Designed and built by Alcoa Marine Inc. under the direction of visionary oceanographer Willard Bascom, in length, fitted with an oil-rig-type derrick capable of lowering a string of four-inch diameter steel drill pipes to which could be attached a rugged rectangular steel framework "Pod" fitted with an impressive array of video and still cameras, lights, side scan and a

The remarkable all-aluminum research vessel *Alcoa Seaprobe*, preparing to depart Morehead City, North Carolina, to verify the identity of a wreck believed to be USS *Monitor*. Courtesy NOAA *Monitor* Collection

Seaprobe was designed to search, core, drill, and sample the seabed in water as deep as 18,000 feet and recover 200-ton objects from 6,000 feet depths. In fact, Bascom envisioned *Seaprobe* as a tool for recovering ancient shipwrecks from the deep floor of the Mediterranean Sea.

Seaprobe was all aluminum, 243 feet forward scan sonar as well as a variety of lifting tools powered by seawater pumped through the drill string. The equipment was deployed through a large rectangular well, or "moon pool" opening, in the ship's bottom, which measured roughly twenty by twenty-six feet, placing the drill string near the ship's center of movement for maximum stability and control. The advantage of the drill string deployed sensor package versus a cable towed survey system is its ability to deploy the sensor almost directly underneath the ship and to control its orientation or heading. Free-swimming ROVs (remotely operated vehicles) later replaced this concept.

Precision deepwater work was made possible by the ship's unique advanced positioning system: twin Voith-Schneider cycloidal propellers at bow and stern, controlled through the ship's computer, could vector their thrusts in any direction, giving *Seaprobe* the ability to move in any direction or to maintain a fixed position over a spot on the ocean floor regardless of wind, waves, or other factors. On a Navy project in the Azores islands, *Seaprobe* once demonstrated the ability to thread a cable through a six-inch eye lying 900 feet below the ocean surface, pick up a giant acoustic array tower and, rotating a precise distance, gently return it to the sea floor. Ironically, *Monitor* presented a challenge for *Seaprobe* due to its relatively shallow depth relative to *Seaprobe*'s deep ocean system design.[1]

Notes:

1. Bascom (1976); Miller (1974, 911–12; 1978, 95); Mullen (2010, pers. comm.); Newton (1975, 61).

all the advanced equipment, locating a small object on the seabed was a difficult procedure. Finally, at 4:05 p.m., *Monitor*'s image flashed into view on the control center's video screens. At that point the Alcoa team deployed an underwater acoustic reference beacon to mark the site in case the local surface navigation system failed. The science team looked on with excitement as *Seaprobe* began maneuvering the search pod methodically along the sunken hull in steady transects, recording the site on video and snapping a still photograph every eight seconds. Eventually the expedition produced more than 1,200 black-and-white images and 450 color photographs. In addition, more than four hours of videotape were recorded.[34]

With the first recovery of the search pod, just

Preparing to deploy *Seprobe*'s massive search pod through the "moon pool" to the wreck of *Monitor*. Courtesy NOAA *Monitor* Collection

after 2:00 a.m., Chester "Buck" Buchanan began developing and printing the film. I had been standing by with "Doc" Edgerton and other personnel aboard an Army Reserve landing craft, fighting seasickness, when I was invited aboard *Seaprobe* to assist Buchanan in the darkroom. I quickly accepted. In fact, to get off that bucking and tossing landing craft, I might have accepted an invitation to attempt a breath hold dive on *Monitor*. In *Seaprobe*'s darkroom, we made several copies of images from the search pod still camera.

Before long the entire science party was crowded around tables set up in a large area just outside the Operations Center, referred to as "Times Square" due to its central location in the ship. Everyone was helping assemble jigsaw-puzzle segments of *Monitor*'s hull, using scissors and tape to trim and join the small black-and-white prints. As these simple mosaics began to take shape, it did not take us long to realize that *Monitor*'s identity was no longer in doubt. The unmistakable double-ended hull shape was evident, as was the unique anchor well. In the wee hours following the first night's survey effort, Glen Tillman, *Seaprobe*'s photographer, pieced together the first mosaic of the armor belt resting on the turret that proved without a doubt *Monitor* had indeed been located. For additional proof, our rough measurements taken from the photographs confirmed *Monitor*'s known dimensions.

Everyone was busy day and night, but our eclectic group of scientists and crew found time for in-

formal discussions. *Seaprobe*'s first mate, Norman Cubberly, was very excited about the project, and he spent as much time with us as his job allowed. Norm had an impressive general knowledge of naval history and engineering and was an accomplished sketch artist. He and "Pete" Peterkin generated some amazing hypothetical sketches and "exploded" mechanical views of various *Monitor* components.

Early in the expedition we were given an extensive tour of our all-aluminum research ship. A tour highlight was the "moon pool"—the large rectangular opening in the bottom of the hull through which the search pod and other equipment was lowered. Mounted on the surrounding walls in the moon

Edward Miller (right) takes a turn working with Captain Peterkin on the *Monitor* photomosaic on board *Seaprobe*. Courtesy NOAA *Monitor* Collection

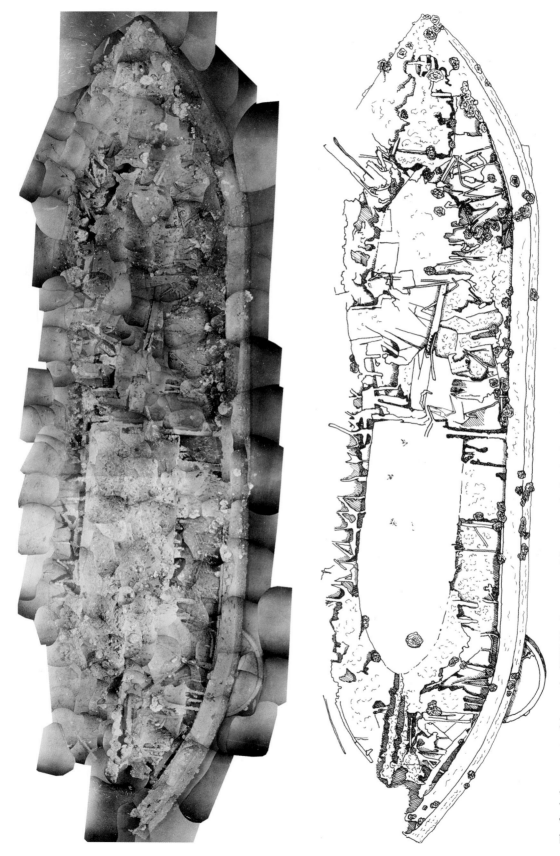

The final photomosaic of the wreck of USS *Monitor* prepared from *Seaprobe* data by the Naval Intelligence Support Center. Courtesy NOAA *Monitor* Collection

This detailed line drawing of the *Monitor* wreck site was based on the *Seaprobe* photomosaic. Courtesy NOAA *Monitor* Collection

pool were devices of all shapes and sizes that could be attached to the end of the drill pipe and lowered to the seafloor. In a prominent location against the forward bulkhead was a huge steel clamshell bucket that our guide reverently referred to as "Kong," an indication of the device's ability to rip out large chunks of whatever came within its grasp. One afternoon as we watched the search pod moving smoothly along *Monitor*'s hull, we were discussing whether we should continue documenting *Monitor*'s hull with still and video photography, or if we should consider recovering hull samples and "Doc" Edgerton's camera. All of a sudden, one of the crewmen who had obviously been listening to our deliberations with growing frustration, blurted out, "Well, I think it's time we let Kong *eat!*" Needless to say, his artifact recovery proposal was rejected, but to this day Gordon and I still find appropriate opportunities to use that colorful phrase.

Actual time spent documenting *Monitor*'s wreck was limited by adverse weather and a requirement to survey additional "Project Magnet" targets. However, by the time we departed, *Monitor*'s entire hull and immediate surrounding area were fully covered by overlapping still photographs and hours of videotape. Following the *Seaprobe* expedition, our *Monitor* documentation was delivered to the Naval Intelligence Support Center, which generated a complete photomosaic of *Monitor*. The Navy released this dramatic image to the public in October 1974, putting to rest any remaining debate concerning the positive identification of *Monitor*'s remains.[35] The photomosaic appeared as a large foldout illustration in John Newton's account of the discovery, which appeared in the January 1975 issue of *National Geographic* magazine.[36]

Announcements of *Monitor*'s discovery, followed by Newton's *National Geographic* article, generated a great deal of interest and excitement around the world, just as news of the ship's remarkable standoff against the Confederate ironclad CSS *Virginia* had done in 1862. The little ironclad's story was remembered and retold. For *Monitor*, one could say that a second life had begun.

Chapter Three

STORY OF AN IRONCLAD

Throughout history there have been events so powerful that they changed the world in significant ways. Similarly, certain technological innovations have been so remarkable that they created fundamental new ways of doing things. Such changes sometimes come about through the actions of a single individual, or may be the work of many. Occasionally, a technological breakthrough makes possible a watershed event, which adds significance to the event itself. Such was the case when USS *Monitor* fought CSS *Virginia* in Hampton Roads in March of 1862. *Monitor* captivated the nation, and then the Western world's attention, as the harbinger of a new type of naval warfare, and a new type of ship and tactics to fight at sea.

Built in one hundred days by an already famous inventor, *Monitor* was well publicized, even before its hasty voyage south to join the Union Navy fleet at Hampton Roads. That fleet, assigned to blockade the Virginia coast, came under attack by the Confederate ironclad CSS *Virginia*, which sank and damaged wooden ships with impunity while suffering little damage from an almost constant bombardment by Union warships. That naval action, on March 9, 1862—early in the American Civil War—gave the world its first glimpse of two new and remarkable types of fighting ships. Both ironclads imaginatively

combined the best state-of-the-art naval technology, and did so in ways uniquely American. The first day of the Battle of Hampton Roads shockingly and cruelly demonstrated the mortal vulnerability of wooden warships to an iron-armored vessel capable of firing its broadsides at close range without suffering significant damage to its own hull or crew. The second day dramatically established the astounding battle endurance of armored vessels—even when pitted against one another—when *Monitor* appeared just in time to fight *Virginia* to a standstill.

Immediately afterward, the battle was touted as a resounding victory of iron and steam over wood and sail, as well as an indisputable exhibition of American ingenuity. While those on both sides of the conflict had ample cause for pride, few were aware that the battle, for all its importance, was just one of many significant milestones on the endless path of naval technology. Indeed, ironclad warships were neither first conceived nor invented in America. Iron-armored warships were in service in France and England years before *Monitor* and *Virginia* were launched. In order to fully appreciate the global significance of the "clash of ironclads" at Hampton Roads, it is necessary to examine the ships and the battle within the context of the nineteenth-century arms race.

THE EVOLUTION OF NAVAL TECHNOLOGY

Warships and Naval Guns

By the middle of the fifteenth century both northern and southern Europe were building three-masted, square-rigged ships that were fully capable of venturing into uncharted, deep-water oceans.[1] Standardized forms emerged, including seagoing carracks, caravels, and galleons, which made possible the "Age of Exploration" and the global expansion of European capitalism through naval power. In the following century, large vessels with overlapping "clinker" planking gave way to smooth plank-on-frame "carvel" planking. This significant improvement simplified and sped the construction of wooden warships. Smooth carvel planking also allowed shipbuilders to cut gunports into ships' sides, ushering in an age of heavily armed warships carrying rows of heavy guns within their hulls along with lighter ones on the open weather deck.

That successful warship design persisted, fundamentally unchanged, for three centuries. By the early nineteenth century, those large, sturdy, and heavily armed ships, built of wood and powered by wind, represented the zenith of wooden warship construction. They had reached the maximum size that the strength of wood would allow, the largest measuring over 200 feet on the main gun deck and mounting 120 guns or more. Spain's *Santísima Trinidad*, the largest warship in the Battle of Trafalgar,

HMS *Victory*, a first-rate warship commanded by Admiral Horatio Nelson at the Battle of Trafalgar in 1805. Carrying 104 Guns, *Victory* represented the pinnacle of sailing wooden warship development and can still be visited in its drydock at the Portsmouth Historic Dockyard, England. Courtesy The Mariners' Museum

1805, was 187 feet long, mounted 136 guns on four decks, weighed nearly 5,000 tons, and carried a crew of more than 1,000 men. Although significant improvements were made between 1810 and 1840, the end of the wooden sailing warship was already close at hand. That is not to say the wooden warship tradition disappeared overnight. The British first-rate ship HMS *Victoria*, the largest wooden battleship that ever entered service, had a hull length of 260 feet and was not launched until November 1859, on the eve of the American Civil War.[2]

North American shipwrights also built large vessels, taking advantage of seemingly unlimited forests of suitable wood. In 1794, the United States Congress passed an act calling for the construction, equipping, and manning of six wooden sailing frigates. These frigates, including *Constitution* and *United States*, established the fledgling United States Navy.[3] They were strongly built and large, and the new ships and their crews proved themselves worthy, especially during the War of 1812.[4] However, at the outbreak of the American Civil War, the Union Navy was a relatively small force compared to the powers of Europe, consisting of only ninety vessels, including ships in and out of commission, receiving ships, and ships in ordinary.[5]

Guns designed for shipboard use followed an evolutionary path somewhat comparable to the progress in shipbuilding technology. The first effective naval guns were constructed from wrought iron segments bound together by iron hoops, not unlike the method for making wooden casks. After that, for more than four centuries armed ships mounted smoothbore cannon cast of iron or bronze.[6] First developed in the 1400s, cast gun tubes had solid breeches and were loaded from the muzzle. Cast guns were significantly stronger, more reliable, and more accurate than their wrought-iron predecessors, and within decades muzzle-loading cast bronze guns became the standard naval ordnance.[7]

As iron casting improved and iron guns became a cheaper alternative to the older bronze guns, Europe's naval powers rapidly replaced their bronze ordnance with iron. Although heavier and more prone to bursting, the cheapness of iron guns and the ability to cast larger numbers of them led to widespread adoption of cast iron guns by the end of the 1600s.[8] Cast iron guns were supplied with specialized projectiles to sever rigging, maim and kill crews, or punch through heavy wooden hulls. Constant

Replica of one of the wrought iron guns from the wreck of the Tudor warship *Mary Rose*, which sank in 1545. Courtesy Mary Rose Trust

drilling at the guns was essential to produce highly trained crews whose ability to win a battle depended on how quickly and accurately they could reload and fire their guns. This period of relative stasis ended during the middle of the nineteenth century, when the technology of naval gunnery experienced a period of rapid change unlike any before.

Arms versus Armor[9]

The Industrial Revolution brought with it significant and sometimes radical improvements and changes to weapons of war. By the middle of the nineteenth century, new weapons began to replace iron smoothbore cannons, forcing the world's navies, for the first time in centuries, to devote considerable attention to defensive strategy.

This new arms race began early in the nineteenth century with "shell" ammunition—hollow iron spheres filled with gunpowder and designed to explode at the end of their flight. Shells caused much more severe damage than solid shot.[10] This revolution in naval gunnery is generally attributed to French artillerist Henri-Joseph Paixhans (1783–1854), who described and advocated spherical shells.[11] His impressive tests in 1824 led to a recommendation that these new weapons be adopted both for coastal defense and warships.[12] However, Major George Bomford (1780–1848), chief of US Army ordnance, deserves consideration for the honor of developing the first shell gun. During the War of 1812, he placed into service the Columbiad, a very suc-

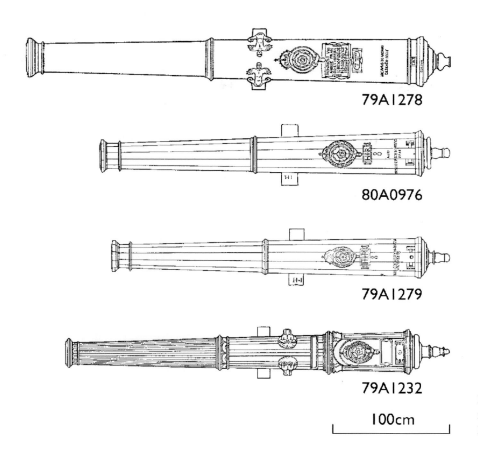

79A1278

80A0976

79A1279

79A1232

100cm

Four of the ornate cast bronze guns recovered from *Mary Rose*. Courtesy Mary Rose Trust

cessful large-bore weapon that could fire both shot and shells.[13] French naval officer Jacques Merigon de Montgéry, also credited the United States with early shell gun development. Montgéry, an expert on artillery who by the 1820s was advocating such advanced concepts as iron ships, steam power, and even ironclads, stated in an 1825 treatise, "We labour [*sic*] under a delusion if we suppose, that the introduction of hollow projectiles into our navy will prove a master stroke of policy for France; the manufacture of these projectiles, both in Great Britain and the United States, being already carried to a degree of perfection, from which the French are still very far removed."[14]

Naval authorities soon overcame their concerns over the safety of explosive shells, and shell guns became more and more common, even on large warships. In 1853, during the Crimean War, a Russian squadron effectively employed spherical shells for the destruction of a fleet of Turkish ships at Sinope in the Black Sea. This dramatic event grabbed headlines, along with the attention of the world's navies.[15]

Iron for Hulls and Armor

Naval architects also took advantage of the Industrial Revolution. Faced with extreme shortages of shipbuilding timber, European shipwrights capitalized on advances in ironworking by substituting iron for the curved wooden knees that supported ships' decks. Soon afterwards, they adopted iron framing and eventually built hulls constructed entirely of iron. By 1842, William Laird and Sons of Birkenhead, England, pioneers in this craft, had launched or were building forty-four iron vessels.[16] The US Navy launched its first iron-hulled warship, *Michigan*, in 1843. By the time of the American Civil War, the use of iron in warship construction was becoming relatively commonplace. At the same time naval constructors experimented with iron for warship armor.

One of the first applications of armor at sea was impressively demonstrated during the Crimean War. In 1855, after France and England joined Turkey in their fight against Russia, the French sent three "floating batteries"—ship-like vessels protected by

USS *Michigan,* launched in 1843, was the US Navy's first iron-hulled warship. Courtesy
The Mariners' Museum

iron plating—against Russian shore positions. The
armor effectively protected the batteries against
Russian coastal guns, and their success opened the
path toward true armored warships.[17] A British naval
commissioner, studying the Crimean battle, reportedly said that "[t]he man who goes into action in a
wooden vessel is a fool, and the man who sends him
there is a villain."[18]

By the beginning of the American Civil War,
testing of guns against iron armor in Europe and
America had produced sufficient data for determining the necessary parameters for effective naval
armor.[19] France and Britain each had built armored
warships and sent them to sea. James Ward's naval
gunnery text, revised in 1861, includes a surprisingly
comprehensive section titled "Iron and Steel-Clad
Ships." In presenting his assessment of this new arms
race, he states:

*In regarding a ship-of-war . . . the leading qualities
for consideration may be classed under two principal heads, viz., her power of offence and her means
of defence [sic]. So far as her room and displacement
are taken up by structure for mere defence, to a cor-
responding extent as a general rule is her capacity
for offence [sic] diminished. The iron-clad ships, for*
*instance, use very much of their displacement in sus-
taining enormously heavy defensive sides, and correspondingly little of the displacement for battery and
propulsion, both of which latter are, distinctively, of-
fensive. It is a great and special error to class propulsion as specially or even principally a defensive quality.*

*The long series of experiments conducted to de-
termine the resistance which iron plates will oppose
to projectiles, seem to have resulted in the following
established conclusions: 1st. A heavy cannon-ball will
pass through any practicable number of boiler-plates
riveted together. 2d. Wrought-iron 4 1/2 inches thick,
rolled in solid plates, will resist any shell or light shot,
and if backed by wood will resist any heavy solid shot
striking only once on or near the same place; and will
deflect any shot striking with much obliquity; but
a succession of very heavy solid shot (as 68-pound
balls), striking the same plate directly, will break it
in pieces, with destructive effect also upon the ship.
3d. Wooden ships plated with iron, are terribly shattered by the impact of a 68-pound shot, even when the
plates are not perforated by the balls.*[20]

Ward then describes five kinds of ironclad warships
under construction or proposed, including those like
the French *Gloire* and those following the iron de-

sign of HMS *Warrior*. A third type, proposed in England, "has the sides, from several feet below water, to recede, tumble home, 40 or 50 degrees from the perpendicular, the object being to glance the shot upwards." This concept is very much the one adopted by the Confederacy, although there is no evidence to suggest that this English design was known in America in 1861. Ward's fourth type, which he attributes to a "Captain Morrison," would simply remove the two upper decks of a three-decked seventy-four-gun wooden warship, leaving the lowest gun deck to which would be applied "as much weight in iron armor as is taken away in wood, battery, &c." The final type listed by Ward, proposed by Captain Cowper Coles, was to cut down an "old seventy-four" to the load waterline and install a sloping half-deck of heavy iron on which guns would be mounted in heavily-armored "turntables." Although Ward classifies Coles' ideas as "rather *outré*," his turntable was to become the patented "Coles turret" in England that very closely resembled *Monitor*'s rotating tower, or turret.[21]

Ward added a footnote to his description of Coles' design that gets to the heart of the nineteenth-century arms race and, indeed, seems to state a universal law of war:

In this discussion the popular sentiment, which is progressive, favors the armor ships. The general professional sentiment, on the contrary, is conservative— opposing change as at least of doubtful utility. . . . One thing however is certain, the thicker the ships the heavier the shot will be made to hammer them with. Action and reaction will go on. The thicker the sides the heavier the shot, and the heavier the shot the [thicker] the sides, and so on until some at present undefined limit is reached.[22]

The Slow Transition to Steam Power at Sea

Another warship innovation, one slow to be accepted by naval planners, was steam as a replacement for sail power. Naval authorities initially considered steam engines suitable only for auxiliary power sources, and warships fitted with steam engines continued to be fully rigged for sailing until the 1860s. The hesitant transition to steam-powered warships was not without valid reasons. Since the 1770s Europe and the United States had experimented with

steam, but a half-century later steam engines were still inefficient and unreliable propulsion devices for ships. The amount of coal they required left little room for crews, supplies, guns, and ammunition, which limited their range and fighting effectiveness. Early paddlewheels took up too much hull space normally dedicated to guns. Even worse, exposed paddlewheels and machinery could be disabled by a single shot. By the 1830s, the situation began to improve, due to innovations in steam machinery and the introduction of the practical screw propeller by John Ericsson (1803–1889).[23]

Robert Fulton's *Demologus* ("Word of the People"), with thirty-six guns, launched in 1815, is considered the world's first steam warship. *Demologus* was commissioned by the US Navy as USS *Fulton* in 1816, too late to participate in the War of 1812. In spite of these early efforts, America's early experiments with steam-powered warships failed to gain momentum, and the United States soon fell behind. Between 1815 and 1850 England "led the world in the conceptual, tactical and technical development of steam warships."[24] America's steam navy began anew in 1841 with the steam frigate USS *Mississippi*. In 1843, the Navy accepted John Ericsson's adaptation of the screw propeller for USS *Princeton*, the navy's first steam-screw warship, which was also powered by an Ericsson engine.[25]

The 3,200-ton steam frigate USS *Merrimack*,[26]

One of John Ericsson's earliest designs, this propeller is on exhibit at The Mariners' Museum. Courtesy The Mariners' Museum

THE FIRST IRONCLADS

Historians generally tend to focus on the 1860s as the beginning of the ironclad era. Surprisingly, however, the first documented armored vessels were built in Korea in the sixteenth century! *Kobukson,* or "Turtle Ships"—developed during 1592 to 1598 to repel invading Japanese fleets—featured iron spikes protruding from a strong cover, or roof that may have been armored with iron plates,[1] and there were early nineteenth-century proposals for applying iron sheathing to "floating batteries" and ships, including two American patents developed during the War of 1812.[2]

France opened the way to true armored warships with the launch in 1859 of *La Gloire,* a three-masted, full-rigged wooden warship with an auxiliary steam engine. Its protective armor consisted of iron bars bolted to its wooden sides. The following year, Britain launched HMS *Warrior,* a much more powerful and better armed vessel. In fact, *Warrior* was superior in nearly every aspect to its contemporaries. *Warrior*'s hull was constructed entirely of iron, with iron armor plating extending around its sides and below the waterline. Among its innovations was a propeller that could be raised out of the water to reduce water resistance when the engine was not in use.[3] Like *La Gloire, Warrior* was ship-rigged, but its twin-cylinder Penn steam engine was far more than an auxiliary unit. Producing 1250 horsepower, the engine could

La Gloire, built in France in 1859, was the world's first ironclad warship, with a wooden hull plated over with iron. Courtesy The Mariners' Museum

In 1860, Britain launched HMS *Warrior,* a truly modern warship, with an iron hull protected by thick iron armor. Courtesy The Mariners' Museum

drive *Warrior* at an incredible 14 knots.[4] At the time of the Battle of Hampton Roads, neither armor-clad had seen action.

Notes:

1. Baxter (1933, 6); KoreanHero.net (2009).
2. Baxter (1933, 8–9).
3. Canney (1993, 54–57); Lambert (1987).
4. Lambert (1987, 103–07).

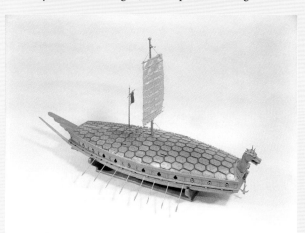

Korea must be given credit for building the first armored ships. During 1592–1598, Korea built *Kobukson,* or "Turtle Ships," to repel invading Japanese fleets. These strange craft were fitted with a strong roof, possibly plated with iron or bronze, from which iron spikes projected. Courtesy The Mariners' Museum

THE AMERICAN STEAMER, "PRINCETON."

USS *Princeton,* launched in 1843, was the US Navy's first steam-screw warship, powered by an engine and screw propeller supplied by Ericsson. A devastating gun explosion the following year was blamed on Ericsson, causing the inventor to shun navy work for years.
Courtesy The Mariners' Museum

launched in 1855, was the first of a new and im-proved class of steam-screw warships armed with shell guns.[27] *Merrimack*-class warships were still ship-rigged, wooden-hull vessels, but each was fit-ted with low-profile steam engines driving a screw propeller. The *Merrimack*-class frigates were heavily armed but their steam engines were inadequate for anything but auxiliary use. According to Rear Ad-miral Edward Simpson, the Navy planned to build these ships with no steam propulsion at all, due to what he called "the old pride in the sailing-ship, with her taut and graceful spars." As a result, he said, a compromise had to be reached, and so the ships were provided with steam engines that were adequate solely for auxiliary power.[28] *Merrimack* and two of its sister ships were destined to play an ironic and unsuspected role in the ironclad revolution.

AMERICAN IRONCLADS CAPTURE THE WORLD'S ATTENTION

The emergence of effective American ironclad war-ships on the world stage took place within the dy-namic and multifaceted technological revolution of the nineteenth century and the pressures of civil war. Less than a year after the fall of Fort Sumter, Union and Confederate navies each possessed a new and radical warship, and when they met in battle they forever changed the way war was waged at sea.

In the United States, in 1841, Robert L. and Edwin A. Stevens, the sons of Col. John Stevens of Hoboken, New Jersey, were first to develop a con-cept for a steam-powered, iron-armored warship. They proposed to the Navy Department the con-

The 3200-ton screw-steam frigate USS *Merrimack* was launched in 1855 with a powerful armament of shell guns. The frigate was to play a significant but unexpected role in the development of ironclad warships. Courtesy The Mariners' Museum

struction of an ironclad vessel of high speed, with screw propellers and all machinery below the water line. The following year the Navy contracted with the Stevens brothers for the construction of a shot- and shell-proof steamer, to be built principally of iron, with armor 4 1/2 inches thick. But subsequent experiments proved that the armor was insufficient against the newest guns, so construction was delayed. In 1854 the builders began construction of a larger, more heavily armored vessel, referred to as the "Stevens battery," but the unconventional design failed to excite naval powers in Washington and ultimately the project was abandoned.[29]

The South Takes the Initiative

On April 17, 1861, following decades of tension over slavery and states' rights, Virginia joined the rebellion of Southern states by severing all ties with the United States government. Virginia's secession prompted the resignation of hundreds of US mili-

tary officers who followed Virginia out of the Union. Virginia Governor John Letcher quickly began organizing state troops and establishing a plan of action. One of his major objectives was the Gosport Navy Yard, in Portsmouth, Virginia. He directed General William B. Taliaferro, commander of state troops, to secure all public property in Portsmouth, especially the Navy Yard and Naval Hospital.

Upon learning of Virginia's secession, and subsequent reports of planned attacks on federal positions, the Union Navy made a controversial decision to abandon the Gosport Navy Yard. On the night of April 20, troops were ordered to destroy the Navy Yard along with its ships and equipment. An eyewitness reported to the *New York Times* that marines and sailors brought down from Washington

[S]piked and disabled the guns . . . [while] a party of officers, meantime, were going through the different buildings and ships, distributing waste and turpentine, and laying a train [of gunpowder] so as to blow up the Dry Dock.[30]

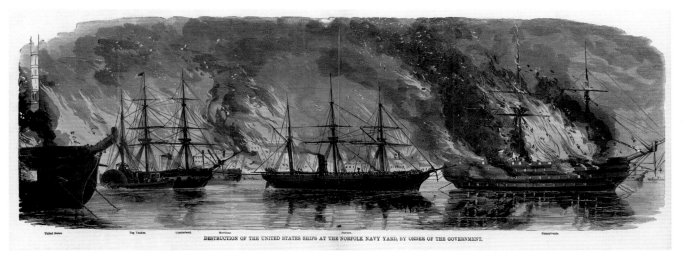

DESTRUCTION OF THE UNITED STATES SHIPS AT THE NORFOLK NAVY YARD, BY ORDER OF THE GOVERNMENT.

On the night of April 20, 1861, federal troops burned and abandoned the Gosport Navy Yard. However, Confederate forces quickly occupied the facility and saved an immense quantity of naval supplies and equipment, including the dry dock where *Merrimack*'s remains would be transformed into the South's first ironclad warship. Courtesy The Mariners' Museum

A considerable quantity of equipment was destroyed or rendered useless, and eleven Union vessels were put to the torch.[31] Virginia forces took control of the burning Navy Yard early on the morning of April 21, discovering that while many of the facility's wooden structures were destroyed, the massive stone dry dock, over a thousand cannons, and significant ship-building materials were left untouched or were easily salvageable.[32] Somehow the massive granite dry dock, one of the most valuable assets at the facility, escaped destruction.[33] Loss of the Gosport Navy Yard and its equipment, ships, and supplies was a difficult blow to the North, and it was soon proved disastrous in ways no one at that time even imagined.

On April 19, just before the fall of the Gosport facility, President Abraham Lincoln proclaimed a naval blockade of the Atlantic and Gulf coasts from South Carolina to Texas. A week later, the blockade was extended to Virginia and Union ships began taking positions near the principal southern ports. The Union strategy, which newspapers dubbed the "Anaconda Plan," was to cut off the rebel states from trade, thus preventing them from importing the manufactured goods and other materials they would need to wage war. By squeezing the Confederacy, like the constrictor squeezed its prey, the North hoped to end the war quickly.[34] The Union Navy may not have been powerful, but it dwarfed the fledgling Confed-

erate fleet, which was comprised mostly of small tugs and merchant steamers seized by the seceding states.

The Civil War and the blockade gave the Confederacy, with few warships or manufacturing facilities, a strong incentive to embrace new naval technologies. Confederate Secretary of the Navy Stephen R. Mallory quickly grasped this concept, probably with the urging of some of his naval officers, and on May 10 he wrote to the chairman of the House Committee on Naval Affairs:

I regard the possession of an iron-armored ship as a matter of the first necessity. . . . Inequality of numbers may be compensated by invulnerability; and thus not only does economy but naval success dictate the wisdom and expediency of fighting with iron against wood, without regard to first cost.[35]

Mallory requested funds be appropriated for the procurement of ironclad vessels from Europe because the South had no capabilities to build them. His argument must have been persuasive, since later that day Congress allotted $2 million for the purpose.[36]

When no European naval power agreed to sell armored ships to American secessionists, the Confederate Navy contracted for several to be built in Europe. Meanwhile, Mallory ordered Lieutenant John M. Brooke, an ordnance expert, to investigate

Confederate Secretary of the Navy Stephen Mallory was quick to realize the importance of obtaining ironclad warships to oppose the overwhelming strength of the Union Navy. Courtesy The Mariners' Museum

A photograph of Lieutenant John Brooke, a gun expert, who prepared a design for an ironclad warship. Courtesy The Mariners' Museum

options for building ironclad vessels in the South.[37] On June 23, Brooke, naval constructor John L. Porter, and chief engineer William P. Williamson met with the secretary, who inspected Brooke's drawings and a model brought by Porter. The meeting concluded with Mallory's approval of a design incorporating an armored casemate with sloping sides, and a hull with submerged ends that would provide protection from shot and shell.[38] The three naval men immediately began planning for construction of this

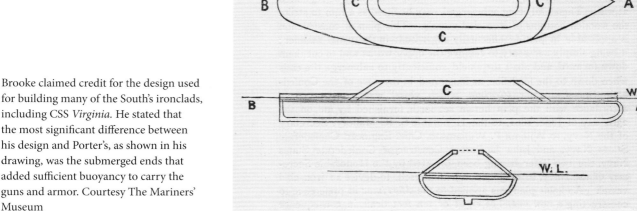

Brooke claimed credit for the design used for building many of the South's ironclads, including CSS *Virginia*. He stated that the most significant difference between his design and Porter's, as shown in his drawing, was the submerged ends that added sufficient buoyancy to carry the guns and armor. Courtesy The Mariners' Museum

John Luke Porter, a US naval constructor who resigned his commission when Virginia seceded from the Union in April 1861, was in charge of converting USS *Merrimack*'s burned hulk to the Confederate ironclad CSS *Virginia*. Courtesy The Mariners' Museum

ery from the burned hulk of USS *Merrimack*. *Merrimack* had been burned and scuttled by departing Union troops, because it was laid up for repairs and would have been difficult to move. Confederates at the yard raised *Merrimack* because it obstructed navigation. Upon inspecting the hulk, Brooke and Williamson realized *Merrimack*'s remains were sufficient to serve as the basic structure for their ironclad warship.[39] By using *Merrimack*'s lower hull and machinery, they would save months in construction time, a major consideration for the fledgling Confederate Navy.

Workers quickly moved *Merrimack*'s hulk to Gosport's Dry Dock No. One, where they trimmed its burned timbers down to the original waterline. Atop this cut-down structure, they built a deck on which was erected a massive "casemate," a superstructure 160 feet long, with sloping sides. The casemate was constructed of layers of oak and pine covered by two layers of two-inch iron plate laid at right angles to each other—in all, twenty-four inches of shielding, impervious to any known ship-borne cannon. The armor extended to the "knuckle," where the casemate was joined to the ship's hull. The knuckle and the ends of the ship that extended beyond the casemate would be submerged to protect them from shot and shell. On February 17, 1862 the Confederate Navy commissioned their new ironclad CSS *Virginia*.[40]

The Union Navy Enters the Ironclad Race

After Washington became aware that the South was building an ironclad near Norfolk, the Navy Department quickly set a high priority on the procurement

new vessel; however, a clever suggestion soon provided an opportunity to put the ironclad project on a fast track.

On June 24, Brooke and Williamson traveled to Norfolk, Virginia, to find machinery for the ironclad, while Porter worked on construction drawings. When their search failed to locate a suitable engine or boilers, Williamson suggested looking at machin-

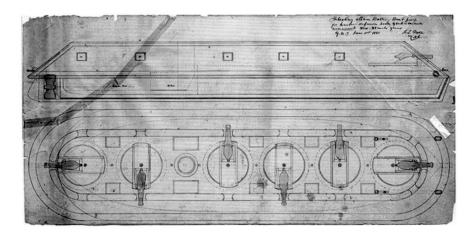

Confederate naval constructor John Porter prepared this drawing to illustrate his conceptual design for an ironclad warship. The detailed drawing, dated June 1861, is in the Collection of The Mariners' Museum. Courtesy The Mariners' Museum

A contemporary illustration of the Confederate ironclad *Virginia* within the massive Dry Dock No. 1 at the Gosport Navy Yard, Portsmouth, VA. Courtesy The Mariners' Museum

of its own ironclad, capable of successfully countering the Confederate threat. On or around August 9, 1861, the Navy Department placed notices in Northern newspapers, soliciting individuals or companies with shipbuilding experience to submit designs within twenty-five days for "Iron-Clad Steam-Vessels-of-War." Simultaneously, the Navy formed an "Ironclad Board" comprised of three senior naval officers, whose role was to review plans submitted to the Navy.[41]

Ironically, the brilliant but controversial Swedish-American engineer John Ericsson, who would eventually become famous for his ironclad designs, did not submit a proposal to the Ironclad Board, probably because of previous disputes with the US Navy. Ericsson's biographer, William Church, wrote of Ericsson's relationship with the Navy,

The difficulty was not that he was unknown, but that he was too well known—at least . . . in those bureaus of the Navy Department . . . [where] he was no favor-

ite. . . . [I]t is sufficient to say that Ericsson and the Government . . . were seldom in accord.[42]

Ericsson did not, however, ignore the call for proposals. On August 29, 1861 he bypassed the Navy, writing directly to President Abraham Lincoln, offering his services and his design for an armored "floating battery." That letter evidently went unanswered.[43] Had it not been for a very fortuitous chain of events Ericsson might be remembered today only as one of America's many prominent pioneers of the Industrial Revolution.

It was, in fact, Cornelius Bushnell, a New Haven, Connecticut, businessman whose own design for an armored vessel had been approved by the Ironclad Board, who later pressed for acceptance of Ericsson's ironclad concept. His actions make him one of the unsung heroes of the ironclad revolution. Even though the Navy accepted Bushnell's design, the Board expressed apprehension about the amount of armor the ship could safely carry. Shortly thereafter,

MERRIMAC, MERRIMACK, OR VIRGINIA?

From the time of its first launch, down through its second ig- nominious sinking, and even today, this proud warship has been referred to by various names, including USS *Merrimack*, USS *Merrimac*, "the old *Merrimac*," CSS *Virginia*, and "the Rebel Monster." The name confusion began even before the original screw-steam frigate was launched in 1855, with the labeling of some of the drawings specified "*Merrimack*" while others dropped the *k*. A 1937 memo from the Secretary of the Navy decreed that the official spelling is *Merrimack*.[1]

In only nine months, the Confederates salvaged *Merrimack's* lower hull, which had been burned and sunk at the Gosport Navy Yard, and converted it to a formidable warship unlike any other. Renamed CSS *Virginia* on February 17, 1862, its overall length was 275 feet but its ends were completely submerged, leaving only a 160-foot-long armored casemate above water. The casemate was protected by twenty-four inches of oak and pine covered by two layers of two-inch-thick wrought iron bars.

The Confederacy's entry in the ironclad race was, in many ways, as idiosyncratic as its foe, USS *Monitor*. Born of both intellect and necessity, *Virginia's* design took advantage of readily available components (*Merrimack's* hull, engines, and cannon) and applied innovative engineering to arrive at the final configuration. *Virginia* served as the prototype for all twenty-two Confederate ironclads built during the war.[2] The Union, too, adopted the sloping-sided, armored superstructure for its river ironclads. Ironically, even though *Virginia* did not contribute any of its attributes to later nineteenth-century warships, the emergence a century later of "stealth" technology has produced several designs, particularly the US Navy's *Sea Shadow*, that bear a striking resemblance to Confederate ironclads.

Notes:

1. Barthell (1959) documents the naming issue in detail.
2. Still (1971,92).

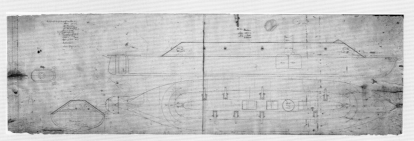

Confederate naval constructor John Porter prepared this external plan for converting *Merrimack's* salvaged hull into the ironclad warship CSS *Virginia*. Courtesy The Mariners' Museum

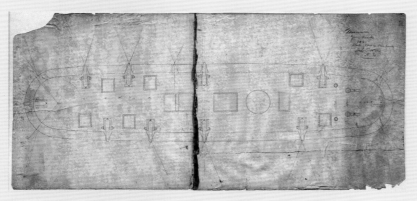

Porter also drew this plan of *Virginia's* gun deck. Courtesy The Mariners' Museum

during a chance meeting in Washington, Bushnell related the Navy's concerns to Cornelius Delamater, owner of Delamater Iron Works, who encouraged Bushnell to show his design to his longtime associate John Ericsson, whose opinion, according to Delamater, "would settle the matter definitely and with accuracy."[44]

Bushnell traveled to Ericsson's home in New York, where Ericsson worked overnight on buoyancy calculations. He assured Bushnell that his vessel, to be named USS *Galena*, would "easily carry the load you propose and stand a six-inch shot."[45] Ericsson then asked Bushnell if he had time to examine his own design for an armored warship, presented to Emperor Napoleon III in 1854 but never adopted.[46] This "sub-aquatic system of naval warfare," as

JOHN ERICSSON, *MONITOR'S* INVENTOR

John Ericsson, who designed and built *Monitor* in record time, was a brilliant engineer, inventor, and fascinating man.[1] He was born in Värmland, Sweden, on July 31, 1803. Engineering ran in the family; his father was involved in building the Göta Canal, and his brother Nils later played an instrumental role in the development of Sweden's rail system. John and Nils demonstrated potential at an early age as trainees at the canal project where their father worked. By age fourteen, John was already performing private surveys, and at seventeen he joined the Swedish army where he was soon promoted to Lieutenant.

Swedish-American John Ericsson was responsible for many innovations, including the screw propeller and USS *Monitor*. Courtesy The Mariners' Museum

In 1826, Ericsson had the opportunity to show drawings of his "flame engine" to Sweden's King Charles John, who suggested that he would find more opportunities to market his invention in England. Following the king's advice, Ericsson moved to England that year. His engine was a commercial failure due to the need to use coal, instead of wood, as its fuel. However, he remained in England and in 1829 he built a steam locomotive, Novelty, for a competition sponsored by the Liverpool and Manchester Railway. Even though mechanical problems caused Ericsson's entry to lose the competition, Novelty traveled nearly thirty-two miles an hour—faster than any vehicle ever recorded. The Times reported enthusiastically on October 8 that the Novelty "seemed, indeed, to fly, presenting one of the most sublime spectacles of human ingenuity and human daring the world ever beheld."[2]

Ericsson then turned his attention to the perfection of a hot-air (caloric) engine, which he saw as being much more efficient than steam. He invented and patented numerous other devices, the most important of which were the steam condenser and screw propeller, both of which were widely adopted. In spite of his genius, Ericsson devoted much of his energy to devices that were commercial failures. Fortunately he met an American naval captain, Robert Stockton, who convinced him to move to the United States, where his skills would be appreciated by the US Navy and American enterprise.

In 1839 Ericsson moved to New York, where he oversaw the construction of the sloop of war, USS *Princeton*, a very advanced warship. Stockton, at first a good friend, later blamed Ericsson for the failure of a cannon that he—not Ericsson—had designed. He refused to pay Ericsson for his work and, even worse, blocked his payment by the Navy. This incident resulted in a mutual resentment and distrust between Ericsson and the Navy that nearly prevented *Monitor* from being built.

Once the Navy accepted *Monitor* into service, Ericsson and his partners began developing a design for improved monitors. Ericsson continued building monitors throughout the war, always defending his original prototype and staunchly maintaining that it did not sink due to any design or construction defect.

Ericsson never abandoned his hot-air engine concept, and finally he was able to develop a caloric engine that brought him a comfortable income in his later years. John Ericsson died in New York in 1889 and his remains were returned to Stockholm aboard USS *Baltimore*. His body lies in a beautiful mausoleum in Filipstad, Värmland, near the place of his birth.

Notes:

1. Sources for this brief biography are Church (1890); Thulesius (2007); White (1960).
2. Quoted in Church (1890, vol. I. 56, 61). In 1884, it was reported that Novelty once completed a one-mile run in fifty-six seconds—over sixty-four miles per hour!

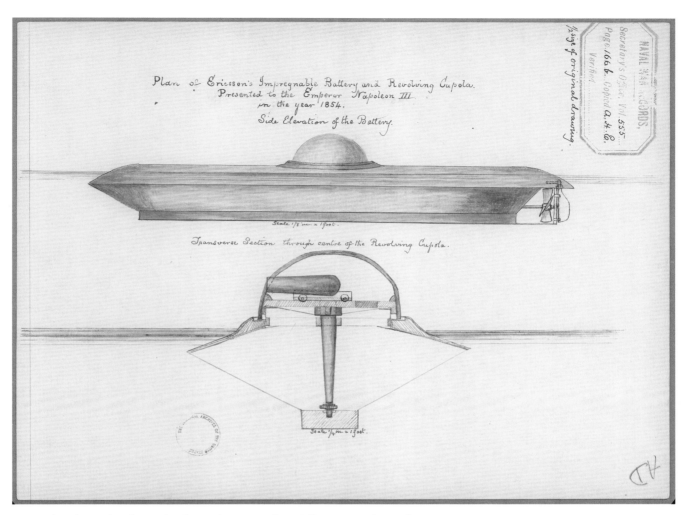

Ericsson's early warship design that featured a rotating "cupola." Ericsson submitted
the design for consideration by Emperor Napoleon III in 1854. Courtesy The Mariners'
Museum

Ericsson termed it,[47] was remarkably innovative and Bushnell was suitably impressed. He obtained Ericsson's permission to take the model with him for presentation to the Ironclad Board.[48]

Although the submission deadline had passed, Bushnell, using his business connections as well as his influence in Washington, was able to present Ericsson's design directly to President Lincoln. According to Bushnell, the president, holding Ericsson's pasteboard model of *Monitor*, commented, "All I have to say is what the girl said when she stuck her foot into the stocking, 'It strikes me there's something in it!'"[49] Lincoln encouraged Admiral Smith, senior officer of the Ironclad Board, to present Ericsson's design to the full Board. Ericsson's "floating battery" was unique in many respects, and was a striking contrast to the other designs, characteristics that were not appreciated by everyone on the Board. Commodore Charles Davis stated that it was "in the image of nothing in the heaven above or on the earth beneath or in the waters under the earth."[50]

Ericsson was eventually summoned to Washington to explain and defend his design. All agreed that Ericsson's battery was quite unlike any other vessel afloat, being almost completely submerged and with no superstructure except for its armored "tower," or gun turret, amidships and a small raised iron pilothouse forward. By the conclusion of that meeting, the Board gave Ericsson verbal approval to begin construction at once.[51] Undoubtedly, the

Board felt somewhat pressured to award Ericsson and his new partners a contract; however, they were also impressed by the applicants' guarantee to deliver in 100 days, for $275,000, an armored warship capable of countering the threat of *Virginia*, whose construction had been under way for several months.

Building the "Yankee Notion"

Monitor's construction was an impressive demonstration of organization and skill, as well as one of the earliest and most striking examples of what was a century later referred to as the "military-industrial complex." With only 100 days to build a warship unlike any before it, Ericsson and his partners had to act swiftly and wisely, and to identify and utilize virtually all major iron and machinery manufacturing facilities in the region.

On September 27, 1861, only six days after receiving written approval of his proposal, Ericsson signed a contract with Messrs. Bushnell, Griswold, and Winslow, stating that the four would share equally all net profits or losses on the new vessel.[52] Finally, on October 4, 1861, the official contract was signed for the construction of "an iron-clad shot-proof steam battery of iron and wood." Contract specifications also called for "[m]asts, spars, sails, and rigging of sufficient dimensions to drive the vessel at the rate of six knots per hour in a fair breeze," but Ericsson disregarded this item with no apparent repercussions.[53]

The partners divided responsibility for the project. Griswold and Winslow obtained the initial financial backing; Griswold handled finances; Winslow obtained all the iron, including armor plate; and Ericsson turned his conceptual sketches into detailed manufacturing drawings and supervised virtually all aspects of construction.

Ericsson wasted no time getting started on drawings and negotiating contracts for the hull, turret, and machinery. The partnership showed no hesitation in awarding contracts wherever suitable iron and components could be secured. They let contracts to a dozen or more companies, all of them in New York—close enough to allow Ericsson to inspect work in progress—except for one Baltimore, Maryland, firm. The first necessity was the hundreds of tons of iron required for the hull and armor. As Ericsson and his draftsman, C. W. MacCord,

prepared specification drawings and bills of materials, Winslow produced the necessary iron at the Troy works or ordered it from nearby suppliers.[54]

On October 25, Ericsson and his partners contracted with Thomas F. Rowland of the Continental Iron Works at Greenpoint, New York (in modern-day Brooklyn), for construction of the vessel's hull at a rate of seven and one-half cents per pound. Clearly, an agreement had already been struck, since that same day Rowland began laying the keel of this unique ship, using iron plate supplied by Winslow.[55] Ericsson selected Novelty Ironworks to build the turret, apparently because it was the only nearby facility that could bend the thick iron plates. All the major machinery, including a previously tested Ericsson vibrating-lever engine, was contracted to Delamater & Co.[56]

Work progressed remarkably well, with materials arriving at their various facilities when needed, and Ericsson issuing drawings and instructions as they were required. He inspected the ship's progress frequently, visiting Greenpoint nearly every day. The greatest obstacle to progress was the Navy itself. Commodore Smith and Engineer-in-Chief of the Navy Benjamin F. Isherwood barraged Ericsson with letters and criticism questioning one specification or another, expressing concerns about the progress of construction, stability, buoyancy, or some other factor. The Navy's delays in issuing specified partial payments caused difficulties for Ericsson and his partners in procuring necessary materials and in paying for the amount of manpower that had been planned to keep the ironclad on schedule.[57] Oddly, neither the national nor local press seemed to show much interest in the "Ericsson battery" until word arrived that on January 10, 1862, *Merrimack* had been successfully relaunched as the Confederate ironclad CSS *Virginia*.[58]

Fortunately, Ericsson's biographer William C. Church documented many facts about *Monitor*'s construction that augment the more formal records of the Navy Department and other sources. Ericsson's genius and tireless work on his "battery" are evident throughout the process. The ship employed blowers to improve the efficiency of the boilers and to ventilate all below deck spaces; the crew operated and fought the ship from within its protective hull; even the anchor could be raised and lowered from inside. Since his ironclad concept confined the officers and crew to a life below the waterline, Ericsson

MONITOR'S CONSTRUCTION

In 1887, John Ericsson addressed "the question frequently asked: What circumstances dictated [Monitor's] size and peculiar construction." He listed six very comprehensive and convincing considerations for his final design:

- Work on Virginia had progressed so far that there was not time to build a larger vessel.
- Virginia's superstructure was designed to accommodate a large battery of heavy guns while its armored sides were inclined so as to cause spherical shot to glance off with minimal damage.
- The shallow coastal waters to be encountered in the Southern states called for very light draft.
- The limited width of many Southern rivers would make it difficult or impossible to turn the ship in order to bring a fixed battery to bear.
- The ship would have to be "absolutely shot-proof" if it was to survive bombardment from Southern shore batteries in confined waters.
- Its crew must be protected against cannon fire while handling the anchor.

Ericsson described his design as follows:

[T]he hull consists of an upper and lower body joined together in the horizontal plane not far below the water-line. The length of the upper part of the hull is 172 feet, beam 41 feet; the length of the lower hull being 122 feet, beam 34 feet. The depth from the underside of deck to the keel-plate is 11 feet 2 inches, draught of water at load-line 10 feet.[1]

The Navy issued a contract for *Monitor's* construction on October 4, 1861, with the following particulars: "being almost completely submerged and with no superstructure except for its armored 'tower,' or gun turret, amidships and a small raised iron pilothouse forward."[2]

The vessel was constructed primarily of iron, although the upper deck and armor belt were made of wood plated over with iron. Wood was used in the armor belt to cushion the impact of enemy cannon fire. Extensive experimentation in the United States and Europe demonstrated the superior effectiveness of iron armor combined with wooden backing. Instead of a conventional "broadside" of cannons lined along a gun deck, Ericsson's design called for only two guns: twin eleven-inch Dahlgren smooth bore shell guns, mounted side-by-side within an armored gun turret that could be rotated to train the guns in any direction.[3]

Battle Configuration March 9, 1862

Post Battle Modifications ca. July 1862

December 1862 Configuration

Monitor was modified twice during its one-year service: (a) shows its initial configuration at the time of its battle with CSS *Virginia*; (b) shows the modified pilot house and extended vents and smoke pipes; and (c) is how *Monitor* appeared on December 31, the night it sank. Courtesy NOAA *Monitor* Collection

Notes:

1. Ericsson (1887, 730–44).
2. US Dept. of the Navy, Senate Executive Document 86, 6.
3. Peterkin (1984).

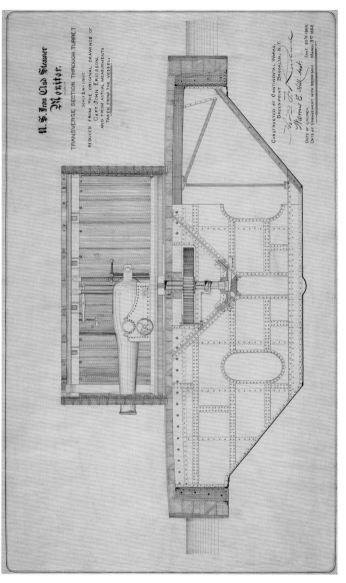

This *Monitor* drawing published in February 1862 shows a transverse section through the hull and turret. Courtesy The Mariners' Museum

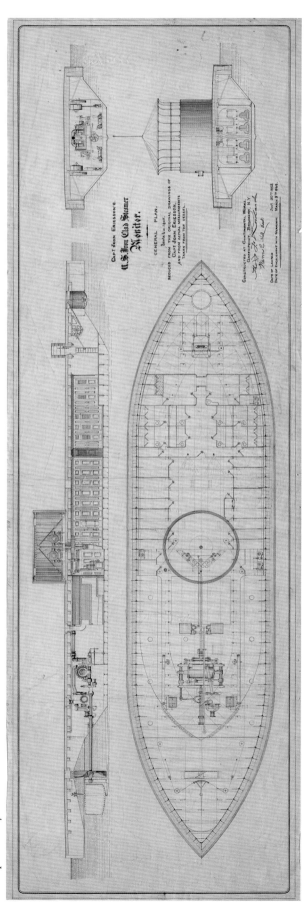

General plan and profile views of *Monitor*, showing interior features in detail. This beautiful color plan was published in February 1862, just after *Monitor*'s launch, and is believed to represent the "as-built" configuration of the ship. Courtesy The Mariners' Museum

LAUNCH OF THE MONITOR.

The launch of USS *Monitor* at the Continental Iron Works at Greenpoint, New York, as depicted in *Harper's Weekly*, September 1862. Courtesy The Mariners' Museum

supplied *Monitor* with shipboard toilets that could be flushed underwater, the world's first.

On January 11 Commodore Smith named Lieutenant John L. Worden to command the ironclad. On January 16, Worden reported for duty and began selecting his officers and crew. Four days later, as the vessel neared completion, Ericsson wrote to Gustavus V. Fox, Assistant Secretary of the Navy, to propose a name for his new warship:

The impregnable and aggressive character of this structure will admonish the leaders of the Southern Rebellion that the batteries on the banks of their rivers will no longer present barriers to the entrance of the Union forces. The iron-clad intruder will thus prove a

severe monitor to those leaders. . . . "Downing Street" will hardly view with indifference this last "Yankee notion," this monitor. . . . On these and many similar grounds, I propose to name the new battery Monitor.[59]

The Launch of "Ericsson's Folly"

The *Monitor*'s career began somewhat ignominiously, even before the ship had been launched. The Northern press tended to focus on doubts that the ironclad would float and on controversies about who deserved credit for *Monitor*'s design.[60] The nearly completed vessel was launched on January 30, 1862, 118 days after the contract was signed—a remarkable

The monitors *Passaic* (left) and *Montauk* under construction at the Continental Iron
Works, the yard that built the original *Monitor*. Courtesy The Mariners' Museum

achievement considering the obstacles faced by Ericsson and his partners. The following day, the *New York Times* reported:

On Yesterday morning, the Ericsson battery was launched from the ship-yard of Mr. T. F. ROWLAND, Greenpoint. L. I. Notwithstanding the prognostication of many that she would break her back or else swamp, she was launched successfully.[61]

A large and excited crowd gathered to watch the iron ship slide down the ways, "[n]otwithstanding the early hour, the drizzling rain, the wretched state of travelling in the streets, and the fact that no notice had been given of the intended event."[62] Many onlookers eagerly anticipated that the little "iron coffin" would continue its slide all the way to the bottom of the East River. Ericsson stood on *Monitor*'s deck during the launch, defiantly demonstrating that his

battery not only floated, but rode three feet higher than its eventual waterline, since it was not fully loaded.[63] Even though the builders were confident in their ship, they apparently took several precautions for the launch. Reports indicate that they reduced weight by not installing all of the layers of iron armor on the turret, and they temporarily chained two large wooden floatation tanks to the stern overhang to ensure that the upper hull would not dip too far into the water before the lower hull was afloat.[64]

Even after this triumphant launching, press and public sentiment had not been won over. As Charles MacCord, Ericsson's chief draftsman, later recounted, "Disappointed of this sensation [of *Monitor*'s immediate sinking], the public had manifested no little curiosity to see how the 'Ericsson Battery' would behave when she left the dock."[65] *Monitor*'s initial sea trial provided just what the critics desired; there were problems with the engine and steering,

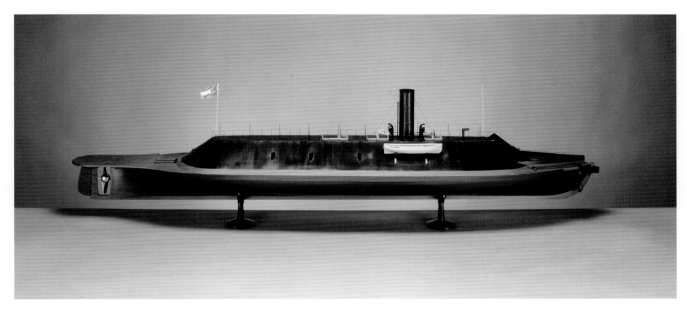

This scale model of CSS *Virginia* is on exhibit at The Mariners' Museum Newport News, Virginia. Courtesy The Mariners' Museum

and the battery had to be towed ignominiously back to the dock. The newspapers were vicious, one condemning *Monitor* and its builders under the heading "Ericsson's Folly."[66] Apparently, reporters did not remind their readers that the launch of a completely unique type of vessel, especially one created within such a compressed schedule, might be expected to encounter a few problems.

Ericsson's skills were up to the challenge, and soon *Monitor* was operating effectively and ready for action. The Navy wasted no time in ordering *Monitor* south in the hope that it would arrive in time to foil the South's ironclad. On March 6, *Monitor* departed New York under tow, endured two storms in transit, and finally arrived safely off the capes of Virginia at midday on March 8.[67]

THE ULTIMATE TEST: THE BATTLE OF HAMPTON ROADS

Day One: Wood Faces Iron[68]

Incredibly, the very day *Monitor* reached the Virginia capes, CSS *Virginia* made its initial trial run, a bold foray into Hampton Roads. Commodore Franklin Buchanan, *Virginia's* commanding officer, was eager

Tintype of Franklin Buchanan in his US Navy captain's uniform. Buchanan resigned his navy commission and was in command of CSS *Virginia* on March 8, 1862 when the Confederate ironclad destroyed two federal warships. Courtesy The Mariners' Museum

THE SINKING OF THE "CUMBERLAND" BY THE IRON CLAD "MERRIMAC", OFF NEWPORT NEWS VᴬMARCH 8ᵀᴴ1862.
The "Cumberland" went down with all her Flags flying: destroyed, but not conquered. Her gallant Commander Lieut: Morris, calling to his crew "Give them a Broadside boys, as she goes"

On March 8, 1862, CSS *Virginia* drove its iron ram into the starboard bow of the sailing
frigate USS *Cumberland*, creating a gaping hole. Courtesy The Mariners' Museum

to challenge the Union fleet. In what may have been the most incredible "shakedown cruise" in history, the hulking ironclad quickly proved that Northern fears were justified. Its menacing black armor glistening, *Virginia* steamed directly for USS *Cumberland* and drove its iron ram through the warship's starboard bow, opening a gaping hole. *Cumberland*'s valiant crew continued to man their guns and return fire until their ship sank beneath the James River. The damage inflicted on *Virginia* was little more than superficial.[69]

The ironclad then turned on USS *Congress*, running the ship aground and setting it on fire. *Virginia* continued its rout, running *Minnesota* aground and driving the steam frigates *St. Lawrence* and *Roanoke* back to the protection of the guns of Fort Monroe, while suffering minimal damage to itself. Union casualties that day were 231 men killed and more than

fifty wounded, some of whom died within days. On *Virginia*, two men were killed and eight wounded.[70] Only a receding tide and coming darkness intervened between the remaining Union ships and the Confederate ironclad.

When *Virginia* withdrew, it left behind a scene of carnage and despair for the Union Navy: of the valiant *Cumberland* nothing could be seen except for the upper sections of its masts, *Congress* was burning, and several other vessels were badly damaged. *Congress* continued to burn through the night until finally exploding around midnight when flames reached its powder magazine, the resulting concussion dramatically underscoring the day's events.

The events of March 8, 1862 at Hampton Roads constituted the worst defeat in the Navy's history up until that time. No one questioned that *Cumberland*

A photograph of John L. Worden taken by Matthew Brady in 1885. Worden is wearing the uniform of a US Navy Rear Admiral. Courtesy The Mariners' Museum

Lt. Catesby Jones assumed command of CSS *Virginia* after Buchanan was wounded on March 8, and he commanded the ironclad during its celebrated battle with *Monitor* the following day. Courtesy The Mariners' Museum

and *Congress* had fought bravely and skillfully, yet both proud warships had been completely destroyed without even the honor of having inflicted significant damage on their foe. The "Rebel Monster" became the Union's immediate concern, a concern that soon spread to wooden warship navies around the world. The ironclad era had commenced.

To those who watched, it seemed inevitable that *Virginia* would return the following day to dispatch the remaining Union vessels and shatter the blockade. That was certainly the Confederate plan. But that night, in a remarkable turn of fate, *Monitor* entered Hampton Roads, which was still illuminated by the fires burning on *Congress*. *Monitor*'s arrival buoyed Union hopes for a battle that was certain to resume the next day. Just before midnight, *Monitor* anchored next to USS *Minnesota*, which was still trapped on a sand bar, its crew await-

ing probable destruction when *Virginia* returned at first light.[71]

Day Two: Battle of the Ironclads

The naval battle of March 9 has been told and retold countless times since that first confrontation between iron-armored warships. Contributing to the fame of the battle was the fact that it was witnessed by so many combatants and civilians. Hampton Roads is a natural amphitheater that afforded spectators a magnificent view of both days' events. Hundreds of people lined the shores when *Virginia* began its assault on March 8, and many more—Northerners and Southerners alike—gathered on the ninth to cheer their ships to victory, believing that the very outcome of the war could be at stake.

FOUGHT MARCH 9TH 1862 AT HAMPTON ROADS, NEAR NORFOLK, VA.   COPYRIGHTED 1889 BY KURZ & ALLISON-CHICAGO, U.S.A.

BATTLE BETWEEN THE MONITOR AND MERRIMAC.

A Currier and Ives print depicting the Battle of Hampton Roads. The print actually incorporates elements of both days of the battle March 8 and 9, 1862. Courtesy The Mariners' Museum

A pleasant day dawned that Sunday as *Virginia* steamed back into Hampton Roads to finish off the remaining Union warships, this time under the command of Lieutenant Catesby ap Roger Jones. Jones, *Virginia*'s executive officer, relieved Commodore Buchanan the previous day after Buchanan was wounded by small arms fire while standing on deck. Jones directed his helmsman to steer straight for the grounded *Minnesota*. This time, however, the smaller *Monitor* advanced to intercept its iron counterpart, thus commencing one of the most celebrated sea battles in history. *Monitor*'s design proved to be an advantage. Its low profile was an almost impossibly small target for Confederate fire and its rotating turret allowed its two massive eleven-inch Dahlgren guns to be fired from almost any angle

without the necessity of maneuvering the ship into position.

The battle that followed, however, although dramatic, was decisive only in demonstrating the ability of two armored ships to hammer each other at close range, shot and shell bouncing off thick iron plate, as the two warships, like two heavyweight prizefighters, charged, struck, circled, feigned, and rammed, each probing for the other's weaknesses. After a time, one temporarily withdrew, then the other; each time the fight resumed. The lumbering combatants pummeled each other for nearly four hours, but failed to score a knockout. Both sides claimed victory, asserting that the other ship withdrew, but in reality the contest ended in a stalemate. In spite of the fervid desire of both fighters for a re-

MONITOR AND VIRGINIA, SIDE BY SIDE

Monitor and *Virginia* were quite different in size, shape, and configuration. Here are their respective statistics:

	USS *Monitor*[1]	CSS *Virginia*[2]
Length:	173 ft	275 ft
Beam:	41.3 ft	38.6 ft
Draft, at load line:	10 ft	21 ft (fwd), 23 ft (aft)
Displacement:	1,000 tons	4,500 tons
Armament:	two 11-inch Dahlgren smoothbore shell guns, mounted side by side in the turret	two 7-inch rifled cannons two 6.4-inch rifled cannons six 9-inch Dahlgren smoothbore shell guns (all ten guns mounted in the armored casemate) two 13-pounder howitzers (added after March 9)
Thickness of armor:	turret: 8 in	casemate: 4 in
armor belt:	5 in	
deck:	1 in	
Officers and crew:	58	260

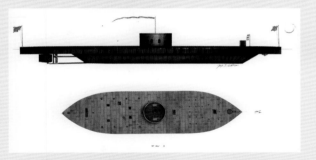

These plan and profile views of *Monitor* were drawn by the marine artist Joseph Hinds. © Joseph Hinds

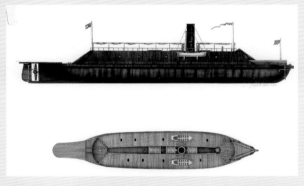

These plan and profile views of *Virginia* were drawn by the marine artist Joseph Hinds. © Joseph Hinds

Notes:

1. Peterkin (1984).
2. Still (1971); Scharf (1887).

match, such was not to be. President Lincoln ordered *Monitor* to avoid another fight with *Virginia*, since maintaining the federal blockade was the highest priority.

A century and a half later pundits are still debating the match's outcome and the significance of the battle. Historians generally agree that *Monitor* and *Virginia* fought to a virtual draw during their four-hour battle, during which the two extraordinary craft bombarded each other at close range, seeking structural weaknesses but inflicting little damage. Strategically, *Monitor* prevented *Virginia* from driving the Union Navy from Hampton Roads, thus keeping the James and York Rivers open for the

A painting by J. O. Davidson of the battle between USS *Monitor* and CSS *Virginia*.
Courtesy The Mariners' Museum

A PRESIDENTIAL VISIT

On May 5, 1862, President Abraham Lincoln departed Washington aboard the revenue cutter *Miami*, reaching Fort Monroe the following night. On May 7, after holding conferences with his officers at Fort Monroe, Lincoln paid a visit to *Monitor*. That evening, William Keeler wrote a detailed account to his wife of Lincoln's visit.[1]

We received a visit today from President Lincoln, in company with Secretaries [of the Treasury Salmon P.] Chase & [of War Edwin M.] Staunton [Stanton] & other dignitaries, attended by Gen. Wool & staff in full uniform.

Keeler noted, "Lincoln had a sad, care worn & anxious look, in strong contrast with the gay cortege by which he was surrounded." Keeler related that as Lincoln's boat pulled alongside *Monitor*, he could see the president's "lip quiver & his frame tremble with strong emotion" which Keeler attributed to Lincoln looking across Hampton Roads and imagining the terrible events of March 8 and 9.

Once aboard, Keeler wrote, Lincoln "examined everything about the vessel with care, . . . his remarks evidently shewing [sic] that he . . . was well acquainted with all the me-

chanical details of our construction." Before leaving the *Monitor*, Lincoln "had the crew mustered on the open deck & passed slowly before them hat in hand." Keeler, who opposed the consumption of alcoholic beverages aboard naval vessels, reported with delight that Lincoln "declined the invitation to whiskey but took a glass of ice water." As the president departed, *Monitor*'s officers and crew honored him with "three hearty cheers."[2]

Notes:

1. Keeler (1964), May 7, 1862.
2. Ibid.

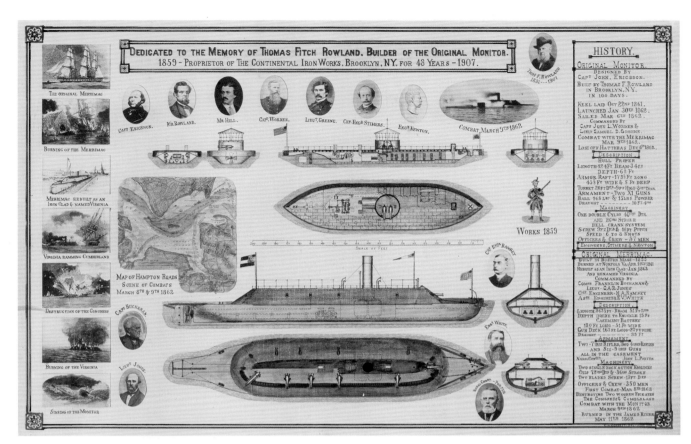

This montage print includes *Monitor* and *Virginia*, with portraits of men reponsible for building and operating them, as well as scenes from their histories. The print was dedicated to "Thomas Fitch Rowland, Builder of the Original Monitor." Drawn by Charles H. Corbett, circa 1907. Courtesy The Mariners' Museum

These sections of an engraving depict scenes from *Monitor*'s interior published in *Harper's Weekly* in April 1862. Historians believe these scenes are relatively accurate.
(1) The captain's cabin was large and impressively furnished. Courtesy The Mariners' Museum

Interior view of *Monitor*: (2) *Monitor*'s engine room is shown as if it were far more spacious than it actually was. Courtesy The Mariners' Museum

A few albumen photographs of the *Monitor* were taken on July 9, 1862 by James Gibson, providing the only actual evidence of the ironclad's appearance and crew. Some of the crew relaxing on deck. Courtesy The Mariners' Museum

Several of *Monitor*'s officers standing on deck; dents from the March 9 battle are clearly visible, as is one corner of the modified pilot house. Courtesy The Mariners' Museum

Some of *Monitor*'s crew posing on deck. Smoke from a boat stove flows across the image. Damage from a fire around the galley stove stack forced the crew to cook on deck until the damaged stove was repaired. Courtesy The Mariners' Museum

A group of *Monitor*'s officers posing in front of the gun turret. Courtesy The Mariners' Museum

LETTERS HOME

We are fortunate that the letters of several of *Monitor*'s sailors have been preserved and published, particularly the frequent correspondence of two individuals. Both men were New Yorkers, were aboard the *Monitor* nearly from launch to sinking, and both survived. *Monitor*'s acting paymaster, William Frederick Keeler, age forty, wrote frequent letters to his wife, Anna. Those letters, all of which contribute a great deal to our understanding of the Battle at Hampton Roads and life aboard *Monitor*, have been edited and published.[1]

Likewise, George Spencer Geer, age twenty-five, an enlisted man serving as a fireman, wrote nearly one hundred letters to his wife, Martha. In 1996, his letters were donated to The Mariners' Museum in Newport News, Virginia, which edited and published them,[2] providing a fascinating alternative viewpoint to that of Keeler: the view from the common sailor in the engine room as opposed to that of an officer in the wardroom. These are two examples from their letters home.

On writing home:

Geer—March 2, 1862
I will commence by telling you what I am writing on. I have for my desk a water pail turned up side down so you see we have not all the improvements of the age.

Keeler—March 4, 1862
I generally take the evenings to do my writing. Whenever I write, day or night in my state room, I have to use a candle, it is so dark. My little deck light lets in light enough for all purposes except reading & writing.

On mosquitoes:

Geer—August 3, 1862
I thought I had seen Mosquetoes [sic] and Flies that were a nuisance in NY, but I give in to Virginia. There is no use fighting. You may as well keep still and let them have their fill, because one will only tire him self out and have at last to give in to them.

Keeler—August 5, 1862
I had the forethought when at Old Point to buy me a mosquito bar [a box-framed mosquito net] (the only one on board) so that I can sleep at night undisturbed by the pestiferous vermin, that is when the heat will allow of it. Tonight we will have a scorcher.

Notes:

1. Keeler (1964).
2. Geer (2000).

Monitor's paymaster, William Keeler, wrote frequent letters to his wife, describing the battle with *Virginia*, life on board the ironclad, and a detailed account of its sinking. Courtesy The Mariners' Museum

The letters of George Geer, a fireman on *Monitor*, describe life on board the ironclad from a much different perspective than that of Keeler. Courtesy The Mariners' Museum

On August 3, 1862, George Geer wrote to his wife about mosquitoes. Courtesy The Mariners' Museum

Monitor's crew spent a miserably hot summer on patrol in the James River following its battle with CSS *Virginia*. Courtesy The Mariners' Museum

Union's planned attack on the Confederate capitol at Richmond, Virginia. Although that attack faltered, the little Union ironclad lived up to its name during the summer of 1862 by patrolling Hampton Roads and the James River, a "severe monitor," in Ericsson's words, that kept Confederate forces at bay.

The first battle between ironclad warships would have created worldwide news on its own, but the dramatic impact of the event was greatly magnified by the events of the previous day. The overwhelming victory of CSS *Virginia* over mighty Union warships left no doubt of the invincible power of iron-armored vessels, and it was actually this astonishing event that triggered global fears and attracted attention to the confrontation of March 9. Nathaniel Hawthorne, who visited Hampton Roads later in the month, expressed the significance of the events of March 8 as follows:

That last gun from the Cumberland, when her deck was half submerged, sounded the requiem of many sinking ships. Then went down all the navies of Europe,

One of *Virginia*'s damaged Dahlgren guns, its muzzle shot off on March 8, now resides at The Mariners' Museum. Courtesy The Mariners' Museum

THE OTHER FEDERAL IRONCLADS

The Navy's Ironclad Board had already accepted two proposals for ironclad warships before *Monitor*'s plans were presented. On September 27, 1861, a contract was let to C. S. Bushnell and Co., of New Haven, Connecticut, for an armored gunboat that was named *Galena*. The vessel was rated at 738 tons burthen and was powered by two Ericsson vibrating lever engines. Its sides were armored with four inches of iron bars and plates, and it was rigged as a two-masted foretopsail schooner. *Galena* was completed in April 1862 and saw its first action, along with *Monitor* and other vessels, at Drewry's Bluff, where it was severely damaged by Confederate batteries on the bluff. Although not considered successful, *Galena* remained in active service throughout the war.[1]

USS *Galena*, an armored gunboat rated at 738 tons, was badly damaged by Confederate batteries at Drewry's Bluff, but remained in active service throughout the Civil War. Courtesy The Mariners' Museum

The third ironclad, USS *New Ironsides* of 4,120 tons was described by a historian as "the finest and most formidable" warship of its day. Courtesy The Mariners' Museum

The second contract went to Merrick and Sons of Philadelphia for *New Ironsides*, a much larger ship of 4,120 tons displacement. At the end of the century, a historian wrote that when *New Ironsides* took to the sea it was "beyond question the finest and most formidable example of a battle-ship in existance."[2] With an overall length of 232 feet, the ship had a projecting ram bow and its sides for the length of the main battery were sheathed with four inches of iron plate. *New Ironsides* boasted a very heavy battery consisting of sixteen XI-inch Dahlgren guns, two 200-pdr Parrott rifles, and four 24-pdr howitzers. *New Ironsides* also served throughout the war and was said to have seen action on more days than any other vessel in the Navy.[3]

Notes:

1. Bennett (1972, 272).
2. Ibid., 272.
3. Ibid., 273.

and our own, Old Ironsides and all, and Trafalgar and a thousand other fights became only a memory, never to be acted over again. . . . There will be other battles, but no more such tests of seamanship and manhood as the battles of the past; and, moreover, the Millennium is certainly approaching, because human strife is to be transferred from the heart and personality of man into cunning contrivances of machinery, which by-and-by will fight out our wars with only the clank and smash of iron, strewing the field with broken engines, but damaging nobody's little finger except by accident. Such is obviously the tendency of modern improvement.[72]

Although no one suspected it at the time, both ironclads had seen their finest hour. Both stolidly withstood shot and shell, but neither survived the year. *Monitor* spent the weeks immediately after the Battle at Hampton Roads sitting idly near the protective guns of Fort Monroe, under orders from President Abraham Lincoln to avoid a rematch with *Virginia*. As Union troops began to occupy the Hampton Roads area, *Virginia* was stranded without a friendly port in which to take refuge. This situation left the crew with few options: the ship could not escape into the Atlantic Ocean because it would have to pass under the powerful shore batteries at Fort Monroe, and it was not designed for the open sea. Nor could *Virginia* steam up the James River to assist in the defense of Richmond because it drew too much water. On the evening of May 10, having no other options, *Virginia*'s crew drove their ship aground at Craney Island, within sight of the arena where less than two months earlier it earned everlasting fame. There, the crew set the ironclad afire and withdrew. When the fire reached its magazines, *Virginia* exploded with a roar that was heard and felt for miles. To many Southerners, that sound must have been a death knell for Confederate dreams of naval supremacy.[73]

Monitor performed blockading duty in Hampton Roads and participated in a brief, abortive attack in the upper reaches of the James River. The hot, humid Virginia summer was challenging for men in a ship of iron. The sun beat down on the black iron deck, driving inside temperatures above 100 degrees. The engine room and galley crews suffered the worst. On June 13—not even the hottest part of the summer—George Geer recorded 127 degrees Fahrenheit in the engine room, and 155 in the galley (located just forward of the boilers), even after the fire in the stove had been extinguished.[74] William Keeler summed up the situation on August 7, "Hot, hotter hottest—could stand it no longer, so last night I . . . took to our iron deck."[75]

Monitor received an overhaul at the Washington Navy Yard in November before setting out in late December from Hampton Roads on what would be its final voyage. Even after extensive preparations, *Monitor* was no match for the violent weather off Cape Hatteras, and the little ironclad foundered on December 31, 1862.

DESTRUCTION OF THE REBEL MONSTER "MERRIMAC" OFF CRANEY ISLAND MAY 11TH 1862

On May 10, 1862 *Virginia*'s crew grounded the ironclad near Norfolk and set their ship afire to prevent its capture. Sometime after midnight, *Virginia*'s powder magazine exploded. Courtesy The Mariners' Museum

LOSS OF THE "MONITOR"—GALLANT ATTEMPT OF THE OFFICERS AND CREW OF THE UNITED STATES STEAMER "RHODE ISLAND," TO RESCUE THE CREW OF THE "MONITOR," OFF CAPE HATTERAS, AT MIDNIGHT, DECEMBER 30TH, 1862.

An engraving from *Leslie's Illustrated* depicting *Monitor*'s last minutes, with USS *Rhode Island* in the background sending up distress signals. Courtesy The Mariners' Museum

The loss of these two famous vessels, on whose success so many depended, caused some naval experts to question the very viability of ironclad warships. But the confrontation between those seemingly indestructible combatants in March of 1862 set in motion a new phase of evolution of the fighting ship. By the end of the year, their progeny were already afloat, closely resembling their parents but configured to improve the war-fighting characteristics of those remarkable prototypes.

Chapter Four

—◦◦◦—

A SANCTUARY FOR AMERICA

PROTECTING *MONITOR*

Our high-quality photographs and video from the 1974 *Seaprobe* expedition clearly revealed *Monitor's* unique armor belt, anchor well, gun turret, and other distinctive features. Also clearly recognizable on the images was the camera "Doc" Edgerton lost on the wreck the previous August, confirming that the Duke team had indeed found *Monitor*. Now officials could concentrate on protecting this historic shipwreck. Many historic preservation specialists, including myself, were convinced that *Monitor* was in immediate danger of unauthorized salvage. We realized that even though the wreck lay nearly 240 feet beneath the surface, objects could be removed by divers or even grappled to the surface using equipment that could be deployed from small boats. Had we disturbed *Monitor's* resting place in order to give the proud ship a second life, or had we merely revealed its hiding place to those who would destroy it for its salvage value? We quickly learned that there were no easy answers.

Because of *Monitor's* location (sixteen miles offshore), Federal antiquities legislation did not apply, nor did the jurisdiction of the US Coast Guard. The US Navy was concerned about *Monitor's* protection, but since it had abandoned the vessel in writing in 1953, it believed it had no authority in the matter.[1] In September 1953, in a memorandum to the Secretary of the Navy, the Chief of Naval Operations reported that "a group of laymen" wished to salvage *Monitor* "for the purpose of establishing the ship as a national shrine." To perhaps assist in this quest, the CNO recommended that the Navy formally abandon *Monitor*.[2] At the end of September, the Assistant Secretary of the Navy responded, "a formal declaration of such abandonment is hereby made."[3]

Research and case law in the 1970s and 1980s determined that the US Navy's abandonment of the USS *Monitor* consisted only of striking the vessel from the Navy list, an action more accurately cast as a decision to "surplus" the ship, not a legal abandonment of the warship as an item of federal property. In fact, aside from express authority from Congress, the act of abandonment is outside the authority of any agency, including the Navy. The Navy can decommission a ship, but must follow "surplus property" procedures administered by the General Services Administration (GSA) to actually dispose of the ship.[4]

In 1974, however, it was generally, if incorrectly, assumed that if *Monitor* were discovered, the wreck would become the property of the finder. This misconception undoubtedly encouraged other private organizations to seek the ship's location. The question of ownership of sunken ships and other property has been debated for years, and court cases often become very complicated, especially when potential salvors believe they have discovered valuable treasure.

Regardless of ownership issues, quite a few organizations, governmental agencies, and individuals were determined to find ways to protect *Monitor*'s resting place. Officials at the North Carolina Division of Archives and History (NCDAH), quickly nominated the USS *Monitor* to the National Register of Historic Places, hoping that inclusion on this nationally managed list of historic properties would help protect the wreck.

Fortunately, a long-term mechanism for protecting *Monitor* was soon proposed from an unexpected source. North Carolina Congressman Walter B. Jones Sr., with the urging of members of the discovery team and others, requested that the wreck be protected through a law he had been instrumental in enacting: the Marine Protection, Research, and Sanctuaries Act of 1972.[5] This act, passed just a year before *Monitor*'s discovery, authorized the Secretary of Commerce to designate and manage marine protected areas, called National Marine Sanctuaries, based on specific qualities of the ocean areas under consideration. Of particular relevance to *Monitor*, sanctuaries could be designated within state waters or as far as the limit of the Outer Continental Shelf, 200 nautical miles from shore.

On May 13, 1974, barely a month after the *Seaprobe* expedition, the US Department of the Interior convened a national meeting to consider options for *Monitor*. Participants listened to expert reports on aspects of USS *Monitor*, ranging from its history to possible options for protecting, managing, and even salvaging the warship. Officials from the National Oceanic and Atmospheric Administration (NOAA) also participated in the May meeting, providing legal information on the ownership issue and the National Marine Sanctuary Program. Most participants quickly agreed that the National Marine Sanctuaries Act offered the most—and possibly the only—viable means for protecting *Monitor*.[6] On September 26, following up on recommendations from the May meeting, NCDAH formally nominated the USS *Monitor* to be designated a National Marine Sanctuary.[7]

Once North Carolina officially requested that *Monitor* become a sanctuary, attention turned to NOAA's Office of Coastal Zone Management, the agency to which authority was delegated for Sanctuary Act matters. On October 29, 1974, knowing that *Monitor* was scheduled for sanctuary designation in three months, NOAA and the Smithsonian Institution jointly convened a meeting of experts who could help develop management and protection regulations for the proposed *Monitor* sanctuary. Also, NOAA and NCDAH established the *Monitor* Technical Advisory Committee to provide advice and expertise for the review of proposals for research at the *Monitor* site.[8]

Monitor *National Marine Sanctuary*

On January 30, 1975, less than eighteen months since *Monitor*'s discovery and 113 years since the ship was launched, the Secretary of Commerce designated the wreck of the USS *Monitor* as the United States' first National Marine Sanctuary, to be protected and managed by the National Oceanic and Atmospheric Administration. The fact that the designation took place only four months after the nomination was submitted is a good indication of the high priority NOAA placed on *Monitor*'s protection.

At the time of *Monitor*'s designation, NOAA was in the very early stages of developing a program to oversee the new Sanctuaries Act. NOAA had anticipated that the first designations would be natural resource areas such as coral reefs, fish habitats, and other natural resources. One can only imagine the reaction when NOAA biologists learned that their first sanctuary would be a Civil War shipwreck! Nevertheless, the nascent program consulted historic preservation managers, nautical archaeologists, oceanographers, and other specialists and quickly began to formulate protection and research plans for the sanctuary.

A Description of the Monitor *Site at the Time of Designation*

Monitor lies on a relatively flat seafloor that slopes gently to the southeast for more than four nautical miles before there is an appreciable increase in the grade. The surface is composed of sand and shell hash overlying a series of nine distinct strata of sand, various clays, shell hash, and combinations of these materials.[9] Water depth varies from 220 and 235 feet, depending on the exact location and the influence of tides. The site lies southeast of Diamond Shoals,

Designation

Whereas Title III of the Marine Protection, Research, and Sanctuaries Act of 1972, Public Law 92-532, authorizes the Secretary of Commerce, with the approval of the President of the United States, to designate Marine Sanctuaries; and,

Whereas the wreckage of the U.S.S. Monitor has recently been identified; and,

Whereas it is the consensus of concerned organizations and individuals that the wreckage should be protected for its historic, cultural, and technological values; and,

Whereas the vessel has been placed on the National Register of Historic Places;

I, therefore, designate the site of the U.S.S. Monitor to be

The Monitor Marine Sanctuary

the area of which is to encompass a vertical section of the water column from the surface to the seabed and extending horizontally one mile in diameter from a center point located at 35°00'23" North Latitude and 75°24'32" West Longitude; and hereby affirm that the regulations promulgated according to the aforementioned authority will provide the necessary protection of law to preserve the esthetic values of this Historic Place.

January 30, 1975
date

Frederick B. Dent
Secretary of Commerce

The official document that designated the wreck of USS *Monitor* as America's first National Marine Sanctuary. Courtesy NOAA *Monitor* Collection

where the warm Gulf Stream, flowing northerly, collides with the southerly-flowing Labrador Current, creating constantly changing eddies and often generating sudden and intense storms. Currents at the wreck site vary significantly during a typical year, and velocities on the bottom range from zero to more than 1.5 knots, and even stronger currents have been experienced during *Monitor* expeditions. Surface currents can be even stronger. Bottom cur-

rents can flow in any direction, but because of the influence of the two principal currents, the flow is usually northeast or southwest. Temperatures at the wreck vary correspondingly. Bottom visibility also varies widely, ranging from near zero to more than 100 feet, and ambient light is generally adequate to photograph the wreck without artificial lighting.

In 1975 *Monitor*'s hull rested upside down with the port quarter armor belt supported off the bot-

NOAA'S NATIONAL MARINE SANCTUARY PROGRAM AND MARITIME HERITAGE

On January 30, 1975, the wreck of USS *Monitor* became America's first National Marine Sanctuary.[1] Today, the Office of National Marine Sanctuaries (ONMS), an agency of NOAA's National Ocean Service, manages a national system of fourteen marine protected areas—thirteen sanctuaries and a marine national monument. Ranging in size from less than one square nautical mile to 137,792 square miles, each site is a unique place with significant resources identified for special protection. The ONMS works cooperatively with the public as well as federal, state, and local officials to promote conservation while allowing compatible commercial and recreational activities. Among its goals are managing and protecting sanctuary resources, increasing public awareness of and appreciation for our natural and cultural heritage, and conducting scientific research, monitoring, exploration, educational programs, and outreach activities.

In 2002, building upon the successes of the *Monitor* expeditions and NOAA's commitment to protecting and managing nationally significant underwater resources, both natural and cultural, the ONMS gave me the opportunity to create a Maritime Heritage Program that focused more attention to these underwater resources. In its first decade, under several directors, the program has become a global leader in efforts to protect and manage underwater heritage resources.[2] The program is conducting and coordinating historical research on America's maritime heritage within the sanctuaries and beyond, locating and studying shipwrecks in sanctuary waters, and developing a comprehensive program that recognizes the significance of America's maritime past, including contributions from

The *Monitor* National Marine Sanctuary consists of a column of water one nautical mile in diameter that surrounds the wreck of USS *Monitor*. Courtesy NOAA Office of National Marine Sanctuaries

indigenous peoples. Subjects have ranged from Spanish galleons off the Florida Keys and California to passenger steamships off Cape Cod, lumber schooners at Thunder Bay in the Great Lakes to whaling ships in the remote islands and atolls of Hawaii, to traditional sailing craft and maritime fishing practices in California's Channel Islands and the coast of Washington State. Working cooperatively with other federal agencies, state and local governments, and coastal com-

munities, NOAA's Maritime Heritage Program helps connect Americans—regardless of where they live—to the precious artifacts preserved in our nation's greatest maritime museums: our coastal oceans and lakes.

Notes:

1   National Marine Sanctuary Program website: http://sanctuaries.noaa.gov/.
2   ONMS Maritime Heritage Program website: http://sanctuaries.noaa.gov/maritime.

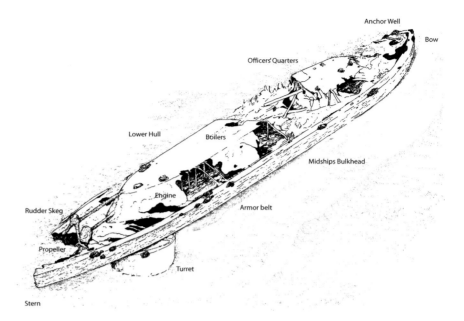

Anchor Well

Bow

Officers' Quarters

Lower Hull

Boilers

Midships Bulkhead

Engine

Armor belt

Rudder Skeg

Propeller

Turret

Stern

An isometric line drawing of *Monitor*, based upon the Navy photomosaic; it identifies key hull elements and clearly shows the relationship between the hull and turret. Courtesy NOAA *Monitor* Collection

tom by the displaced and inverted turret, creating a starboard list of approximately 19 degrees. The longitudinal axis of the hull lies nearly east-west, with the bow pointing approximately 290 degrees. The Gulf Stream has scoured the north side of the wreck, while depositing sediment within the hull, covering the starboard (south) armor belt. This scouring has created pockets that sometimes extend deeper than 230 feet.

The port armor belt was intact all the way from the bow to twenty-four feet past the turret, at which point the entire stern was badly damaged and the armor belt disintegrated. The aft end of the propeller shaft was no longer seated in its bushing on the skeg, and the hull beneath the skeg was too badly damaged to support the two legs of the skeg. The propeller appeared to be resting on the damaged hull and was heavily shrouded in corrosion products and marine organisms. The lower (or displacement) hull was constructed of iron plating riveted to iron frames. Preservation of the lower hull differed significantly between bow and stern. Frames and bottom plating were relatively intact aft of the amidships bulkhead, but forward of that point the hull had completely collapsed. Side plating on the lower hull had separated from the frames except for a section near the machinery spaces, aft. The turret appeared to be

relatively intact, although about two-thirds of it was obscured from view by the overlying armor belt.

The *Seaprobe* Expedition and subsequent pre-designation investigations provided a great deal of information about the *Monitor* and its environs; however, many important questions related to site preservation and structural integrity remained to be answered by future research.

Post-Designation Protection, Preservation, and Research Planning

Once the designation was official, NOAA moved quickly to implement a protection framework. Interim regulations for protecting *Monitor* were published in the *Federal Register* on February 5, 1975, inviting public comment until March 7, 1975. Following review and revisions, Final Regulations for the *Monitor* National Marine Sanctuary were published in the *Federal Register* on May 19, 1975.[10] This schedule seems incredibly compressed by today's standards, but the *Monitor* regulations were expedited in order to ensure protection of the wreck.

Several academic scholars involved with the original discovery of *Monitor* were so interested in *Monitor*'s future that they established an independent, not-for-profit research organization named the *Monitor* Research and Recovery Foundation (MRRF). The founders' goal was to play a role in the development of plans for *Monitor* and to ensure that excitement and momentum were maintained. Soon after its formation MRRF requested that another national *Monitor* conference be convened so that the foundation could present its proposal and seek consensus on a direction for preservation, research, and possible recovery.

The Smithsonian Institution convened a fourth national conference on *Monitor* during January 15–16, 1976, two weeks shy of the first anniversary of *Monitor*'s designation as a marine sanctuary. This conference was notable for the intensity of deliberations, both general and specific, concerning *Monitor*'s future. The MRRF presented its plan for total recovery and display of *Monitor*. Some of the attendees stated that the MRRF proposal was well thought out and viable, while others insisted that talk of recovery was premature until much more information had been gathered from the site. The participants did not reach consensus but the conference recommended that NOAA establish an advisory council to assist with the critical task of developing a detailed management strategy.[11]

Through all the meetings and deliberations, I was in almost complete agreement with Gordon Watts, co-discoverer and principal consulting archaeologist on all things *Monitor*. We were not opposed to recovering *Monitor*, but we sided with those who felt that more engineering and archaeological data collection should be the first priority. Some salvage and conservation experts had warned that successful recovery of the hull would be difficult if not impossible and that the recovery costs—in the millions or tens of millions of dollars—would be eclipsed by conservation costs. Also, we were reminded that previous recovery projects had often ended in disaster, even when conducted by skilled and well-meaning people. A well-known case was cited: the attempted recovery of the Union ironclad USS *Cairo*, which lay in only a few feet of water. The well-intentioned salvors inadvertently ripped *Cairo*'s hull into pieces and scattered its contents.[12]

NOAA and the state of North Carolina soon formalized an agreement to officially collaborate to develop research and management plans and review proposals for research within the sanctuary. This federal-state partnership was an essential ingredient in the evolution of a comprehensive plan for managing all phases of research and protection. Under the NOAA/NC agreement, the North Carolina Department of Cultural Resources prepared a research and development concept for the *Monitor* sanctuary.[13] This plan discussed the significance and condition of the site, proposed research and development goals, and outlined research and development phases.

INVESTIGATING *MONITOR*

Throughout the long period of conferences and planning, NOAA and others actively sought to obtain data from the site that would establish a baseline condition for *Monitor* and provide the information necessary for developing long-range management and research plans.

While NOAA resource managers worked with interested parties to develop a management plan, others gathered as much background information as possible on *Monitor*'s history, construction, discovery, and current condition. Working primarily with North Carolina state underwater archaeologist Gordon Watts, NOAA began developing a research plan for the sanctuary. By this time, my partners and I had dissolved our consulting company, Marine Archaeological Research Services Inc., and I had taken a job in Richmond, Virginia. Even though I was no longer working for Watts, I kept in touch, especially on *Monitor* research, and managed to remain involved as a volunteer advisor.

Site reports described the *Monitor* site as an iron-and-wood shipwreck lying upside down, well offshore and nearly 240 feet beneath the surface in an area known for treacherous storms and difficult working conditions. Beginning with the available information, NOAA planners developed a preliminary research plan. They temporarily set aside the insistent calls for *Monitor*'s immediate and total salvage, instead concentrating on gathering more data on the wreck and its environment. Even before *Monitor* became a sanctuary, several organizations conducted research expeditions to the site. Then in February 1977 NOAA issued the first permit for research at the sanctuary to the *Monitor* Research and Recovery Foundation (MRRF). Two months later, MRRF conducted an environmental assessment aboard the University of Delaware's new research vessel *Cape Henlopen*. Robert Sheridan recovered a twenty-foot

Over the years, researchers have employed an impressive array of sophisticated, state-of-the-art marine science equipment at the *Monitor* sanctuary. Three deep submergence vehicles have participated in the research, along with several types of remotely operated vehicles and autonomous underwater vehicles. Numerous sonars and magnetometers have mapped the site, along with still and video cameras and laser scanning systems. Military and civilian dive systems have been used, including mixed-gas scuba, surface-supplied diving, saturation diving, and mixed-gas rebreathers.

The versatile *Johnson-Sea-Link* submersibles supported *Monitor* research from 1977 to 2002. Courtesy NOAA *Monitor* Collection

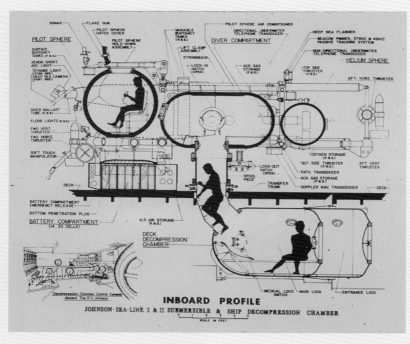

A cutaway view of the 3-person *Johnson-Sea-Link* submersible showing how its dive chamber mated with the decompression chamber within the support ship. Courtesy NOAA *Monitor* Collection

JOHNSON-SEA-LINK SUBMERSIBLES

During 1977 to 1983, Harbor Branch Foundation's two *Johnson-Sea-Link* (*J-S-L*) research submersibles were at the heart of *Monitor* research. Each submersible is twenty-seven feet long, 10.9 feet high, and 8.3 feet wide, and at the time could descend to 1,000 feet.[1] The *J-S-Ls* are fitted with an array of thrusters (small motors with propellers aligned in different axes) that make them extremely maneuverable. Each sub contains two pressure hulls, each capable of carrying two persons: a pilot and passenger in the front sphere and two passengers in the smaller aft chamber. The subs were not tethered to the surface ship, thus they were free to move slowly and deliberately over *Monitor* on specific headings and fixed distances above the wreck. These capabilities made it possible to record excellent still and video imagery of the wreck and to explore areas close to and beneath the hull for several hours each dive.

These remarkable subs have played major roles in an impressive range of undersea research, including assisting NASA with locating the wreckage of the space shuttle *Challenger* in 1986. After nearly four decades of usage, upgrades, and 9,000 dives, the *J-S-Ls* are the "workhorses" of Harbor Branch's submersible fleet.[2]

CLELIA SUBMERSIBLE

Harbor Branch also brought their research submersible *Clelia* to *Monitor*

(*continued*)

Harbor Branch's 3-person *Clelia* submersible was utilized on several *Monitor* expeditions. Courtesy NOAA *Monitor* Collection

several times. *Clelia* is a three-person sub with a large spherical viewport at the bow that affords scientists and observers a spectacular view of *Monitor*. This sub was once fitted with an experimental laser line scanner during a *Monitor* imaging survey. *Clelia* has since been deactivated.

MIXED-GAS DIVE SYSTEM

J-S-L submersible dives could be lockout or nonlockout, depending on whether or not divers exited the sub. On each *Monitor* lockout dive, *J-S-L* was configured to deploy a diver for a working dive of up to 60 minutes, while a second diver remained in the dive chamber as a tender and rescue diver. During ascent, a dive officer in the forward compartment reduced pressure in the dive compartment according to a professional decompression schedule, which allowed the divers to complete the first portion of their decompression in the sub. Once on the ship the divers transferred from

the sub to a larger decompression chamber to complete their slow return to surface pressure.

Most of the divers wore conventional wet suits, even though water temperature was often in the mid-to-high sixties Fahrenheit, and Kirby-

Morgan KMB-10 band masks to which "heliox," a gas mixture of 10 percent oxygen and 90 percent helium, was supplied through umbilicals.[3] Each umbilical provided a diver with a direct connection to the submersible that supplied breathing gas, a depth-measuring tube, and two-way communications between divers and the sub's pilot sphere. In turn, the sub communicated with the surface vessel via a two-way hydrophone link.

REMOTELY OPERATED VEHICLES AND AUTONOMOUS UNDERSEA VEHICLES

Remotely operated vehicles (ROVs) played a major role in *Monitor* research, beginning in 1977 with the Cabled Observation and Rescue Device (CORD), designed, built, and operated by Harbor Branch, which recorded some of the first video of *Monitor* from seabed level. The Navy's ROV *Deep Drone* was used in 1987 to recover a variety of data. This much larger ROV had a heavy frame, powerful thrusters, and a manipulator arm

(continued)

The US Navy's *Deep Drone* is a large ROV that can be fitted with a variety of research tools, as it demonstrated during the 1987 sonar and corrosion studies. Courtesy NOAA *Monitor* Collection

Harbor Branch's CORD ROV recorded the first images of *Monitor* from seafloor level. Courtesy NOAA *Monitor* Collection

with navigation data such as depth, heading, survey track lines, and so forth before being released to carry out its instructions. Once its tasks are complete, it surfaces, is recovered, and its data downloaded. These clever robots, which are similar to NASA spacecraft like the Mars Rovers, can survey large areas, carry a variety of equipment, and operate more inexpensively and from a smaller research vessel than other similar instruments.[6]

Notes:

1. The *J-S-Ls* were eventually capable of descending to 3,000 feet. Complete descriptions of these remarkable vehicles can be found at the Harbor Branch website: http://www.fau.edu /hboi/OceanTechnology/OTsubops .php (accessed September 7, 2011).
2. Ibid. The subs no longer have lockout capability, since scientists can efficiently conduct most tasks from inside or by using ROVs.
3. The ratio of gasses is determined by the deepest depth to be encountered.
4. http://www.supsalv.org/00c2_deep Drone7200Rov.asp
5. http://www.benthos.com/rov- unmanned-underwater-vehicle-mini rover.asp
6. http://www.whoi.edu/page.do?pid =10078

that offered mission planners a wide range of research options. *Deep Drone* was fitted with video and still cameras, a precise navigation system, and the instrumentation necessary for making corrosion readings, using the agile manipulator arm to control the instrument probe. *Deep Drone* is similar to the "work class" ROVs seen on television during the Deepwater Horizon spill in 2010.[4]

Both the Navy and *National Geographic* employed Benthos MiniROVERs, small but versatile craft weighing slightly more than fifty pounds and capable of carrying high resolution still and video cameras and lights.[5]

More recently, the development of autonomous underwater vehicles (AUVs) has flourished, and NOAA has employed these free-swimming, pilotless craft for various types of research, including mapping the *Monitor* sanctuary and other areas off North Carolina. An AUV is programmed

piston core from an area just southeast of *Monitor* and Harold "Doc" Edgerton used his new camera system to record the first video and still images of *Monitor* from a horizontal view near the bottom. From the sediment core, Sheridan and his students documented the stratigraphy of the seafloor in the vicinity of the *Monitor* and made predictions on how that stratigraphy might affect *Monitor*'s preservation and efforts to recover the wreck.[14]

In July 1977 NOAA conducted its first *Monitor* expedition, the first major site investigation since the 1974 *Seaprobe* survey. The expedition utilized research submersibles—small research submarines—to obtain high-quality video and deploy scientific divers. The sanctuary program within NOAA's Office of Coastal Zone Management developed a cooperative agreement with the Harbor Branch Foundation (HBF), a respected marine research organization possessing specialized oceanographic equipment and divers. The two joined with the North Carolina Division of Archives and History to plan and conduct *Monitor* research. Gordon Watts, head of the state's Underwater Archaeology Branch, and his staff provided most of the archaeological advice for the

Harbor Branch's R/V *Johnson* launching the *Johnson-Sea-Link* submersible over *Monitor* in 1977. Courtesy NOAA *Monitor* Collection

expedition. Each of Harbor Branch's two submersibles, *Johnson-Sea-Link I* and *II*, could transport as many as four people safely and effectively to depths of 1,000 feet, and deliver divers to *Monitor*. The expedition was conducted from a surface vessel with the capability to launch and recover a submersible and to complete diver decompression in an on-board chamber facility. All operations were conducted in a "live boat" mode; that is, there was no need for the surface vessels to anchor, thus avoiding any anchoring threat to the wreck site.

Harbor Branch Foundation (HBF) employed both its *J-S-L* submersibles, which were supported by the HBF research vessels *Johnson* and *Sea Diver*.[15] Planners divided the project into two phases: during the first phase, scientists conducted a reconnaissance and fact-gathering effort, then, during the second phase, divers performed a hands-on inspection of *Monitor*. First, the wreck and adjacent seabed were mapped during an extensive side-scan sonar survey, followed by deployment of a remotely operated vehicle (ROV)—the Cabled Observation and Rescue Device (CORD)—equipment designed, built, and operated by Harbor Branch. The CORD gave researchers the first views of *Monitor* from a seafloor

perspective, documenting the area beneath the inverted hull.

On this expedition, Commander Floyd Childress represented NOAA's Sanctuaries Programs Office and Ted Lillestolen was the NOAA representative; Roger Cook was HBF operations director and Gordon Watts was archaeological advisor. On the very first dive, the team discovered a signal lantern lying partially buried in the sand, not far from *Monitor*'s turret. Watts concluded that this almost had to be the lantern that signaled *Monitor*'s distress on the night the ship went down. Everyone also agreed that the lantern was in danger of being swept away by currents or damaged in some other way. By radio, the team conducted consultations with state and federal officials, receiving concurrence with Watts' recommendation that the lantern be recovered. The lantern was brought to the surface without damage on the next dive.

Thanks to Don Rosencrantz, a friend who was consulting with NOAA on the *Monitor* project, I was able to visit the expedition on July 26. I was astounded by the complexity and productivity of the HBF equipment and the enthusiasm of the entire research team. I was also able to observe a lockout

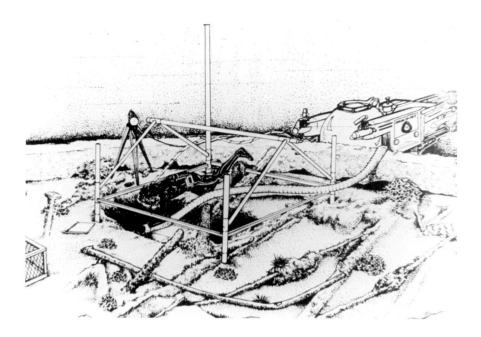

During the 1979 *Monitor* expedition, archaeologists conducted an excavation in the captain's stateroom with the aid of an aluminum grid and a suction dredge. Courtesy NOAA *Monitor* Collection

dive from the R/V *Johnson*. Two divers descended in *J-S-L II's* aft compartment, the dive compartment, which was sealed and maintained at surface pressure (one atmosphere) until the divers were ready to exit. Forward, in the acrylic sphere, one person piloted the sub while the other supervised all aspects of dive operations. Once the sub was lowered into the water, I climbed to the bridge where the sub communications station was located. From there we could listen to the dive supervisor talk to the sub crew. We could also watch a tracking screen that displayed the position of the sub relative to the research vessel and the *Monitor*.

Once the sub reached the designated work area, the divers pressurized the aft compartment to ambient external pressure and one diver exited the sub for a period of nearly sixty minutes. As we listened to the dive supervisor in front of us talking to the sub, all I could think of was, *I wish I were that diver right now*! When the working diver reentered the sub, the hatch was sealed and the dive supervisor in the pilot sphere took control of the dive compartment pressure, commencing the first phase of decompression. The sub then left the sea floor and soon it bobbed to the surface amid a huge swirl of bubbles, as excess air escaped from its ballast tank vents.

In a well-rehearsed procedure, the research vessel eased alongside the *Sea-Link* and a swimmer dove in and swam a line to the sub. The swimmer climbed aboard the sub and waited while it was winched in close to the stern, where a much heavier wire rope from the purpose-built "Hydro-Crane" was lowered to the swimmer's waiting hands. The swimmer attached the locking mechanism then dived off the sub to a rope trailing in the water; he was then quickly hauled on board. The intricate recovery mechanism then engaged and the *J-S-L* was winched from the water and gently placed on the deck, where it was mated to a pressure trunk leading down to the four-person, double-lock decompression chamber. There, the divers completed their decompression in relative comfort. We were very impressed with Harbor Branch's entire operation. They were seasoned professionals, and everything was done with speed and precision.

The pioneering 1977 *Monitor* expedition was extremely successful, despite some adverse weather and mechanical difficulties, inherent in at-sea operations. Weather and other conditions permitting, the sub made three dives each day: two lockout dives with an observation-only dive between. Between them, the two subs obtained more than 4,000 black-and-white and color 35-mm stereo images, in both vertical and oblique views, under controlled navigation conditions, for use in developing a detailed site assessment and possible photomosaic. They also recorded many hours of videotape and placed scientific divers on the site for the first time.

MONITOR'S DISTRESS SIGNAL

On July 25, on the first submersible dive of the 1977 *Monitor* expedition, the team made an exciting and significant discovery. Pilot Tim Askew and archaeologist Gordon Watts were in *Johnson-Sea-Link II*'s pilot sphere. As the sub approached *Monitor*'s hull, Askew and Watts spotted a small object lying

Harbor Branch's Tim Askew examines *Monitor*'s signal lantern just after its recovery during the 1977 expedition. Courtesy NOAA *Monitor* Collection

partially buried in the sand. On closer inspection, the two could see that the object appeared to be a ship's lantern, lying only about fifty feet from *Monitor*, not far from the turret. After consulting the National Park Service, the US Navy, and the Advisory Council on Historic Preservation, NOAA approved recovery of the lantern. All parties were in agreement that the lantern was in danger of being damaged or swept away by currents. On the subsequent dive, HBF diver Richard Roesch carefully freed and recovered the object without damage. The team got a big morale boost when they saw the lantern's red lens.

Conservators discovered that the signal lantern's thin brass base was badly corroded, and its red lens was cracked. They were able to determine that the type of break exhibited by the lens was not caused by impact with a hard surface but, rather, was typical of a break that results when hot glass suddenly comes in contact with water. Given its type and location, coupled with the fact that the lantern must have landed in the water while still lit, essentially confirmed that this is the lantern hung from *Monitor*'s turret as

This red-lens signal lantern was discovered on the first submersible dive to the *Monitor*; ironically, its light was the last thing seen before the ironclad sank on New Year's Eve, 1862. Courtesy The Mariners' Museum

a distress signal on the night the ship sank. If so, the lantern's story is even more incredible: its light was the last evidence of *Monitor* on the night it sank in 1862, then was the first object discovered on NOAA's first dive to the site!

Divers captured additional images using a diver-held camera system.

The expedition produced significant data on the condition of the *Monitor*'s hull and artifacts, and demonstrated that submersible-based scientific diving operations at *Monitor*'s depth were feasible, safe, and productive. The expedition also generated a flood of public excitement by documenting and recovering the signal lantern, a fragment of iron hull plating, and the Duke University camera system that was snagged in the wreck during the 1973 *Eastward* cruise. Moreover, the scientific recovery of artifacts offered

encouragement to those who wanted to see more recovery efforts—and even salvage of the entire ship.[16]

Detailed analysis of the wrought-iron hull plate by Huntington Alloys Inc. showed the quality of the metal to be "very good" and superior to the quality of iron from the hulls of two British-built vessels from the same period. Nevertheless, all the plates exhibited varying degrees of damage from corrosion, and most researchers did not consider data from a single *Monitor* hull plate fragment to be sufficient for an accurate prediction of the overall rate of corrosive degradation of *Monitor*'s structure.[17]

MONITOR: MEANING AND FUTURE

Possibly the most significant *Monitor* conference took place in April 1978, when participants from the United States and overseas gathered in Raleigh, North Carolina, to discuss *Monitor*'s meaning and future. By this time more was known about *Monitor*, thanks to a 1977 expedition that placed divers and archaeologists on the site, documented the wreck with still and video photography, and recovered a lantern and hull plate for conservation and analysis.

In his opening statement of purpose, Dr. Larry E. Tise, director of the North Carolina Division of Archives and History, remarked that "all of the previous national meetings on the *Monitor* have occurred with the implicit assumption that the *Monitor* would be recovered . . . as soon as technology and resources made it possible," whereas this conference addressed "the question of 'should'" *Monitor* be recovered.[18] He concluded with this vision for the conference:

In my mind it is crucially important that we deal here with the "should" questions relating to the future of the Monitor. *What should be the future of the* Monitor? *Given its importance, how should it be treated? . . . And I hope that when we have departed, leaving a written record of our deliberations, we shall share a sense of what the final answers . . . ought to be.*[19]

In his conference remarks, NOAA's Lieutenant Commander Floyd Childress outlined a new approach to ocean management.[20] Considering that NOAA was a very new agency (formed in 1970) and that the sanctuary program was even newer, Childress' presentation demonstrated NOAA's effectiveness in applying a scientific approach to ocean management regardless of the type of resource to be managed. He said,

The effort to preserve the U.S.S. Monitor *is a small part of a much larger national concern about managing our offshore resources. There is a significant effort afoot within the federal government to implement a new, more effective policy on the way we manage the oceans. . . .*

What we seek is a new approach to ocean management—one based on planning, analysis and decision making that recognizes the interplay of human activities and the natural environment. . . . NOAA has taken a first step toward developing this new approach. . . . [T]he Office of Ocean Management . . .

will evaluate existing and projected demands on ocean resources in terms of use levels, resource availability, and environmental and socioeconomic impacts.

One of the presenters was Robert Sheridan, co-discoverer of *Monitor* and president of the *Monitor* Research and Recovery Foundation (MRRF). His paper began with a summary of his environmental studies of the area in which *Monitor* lies. He then presented a remarkable proposal to recover *Monitor* using the MV *Hughes Glomar Explorer*, the giant drillship that in August 1974 had recovered part of the Russian nuclear submarine *K-129* from a depth of 16,500 feet.[21] The recovery proposal was based on a plan submitted to MRRF in 1976 by Global Marine Development Inc. (GMDI), which owned the drillship.[22] The plan proposed for *Glomar Explorer* to lower a "special submarine vehicle" over *Monitor*'s hull, actuate hydraulic doors on the vehicle that would scoop up the wreck and fifteen feet of seabed sediments beneath it, then raise the contents, turret and all, into the drillship's 200-foot-long center well.[23]

The proposal struck many of us as mind-blowingly complex, expensive, and improbable. As an archaeologist with an engineering background, I thought it unlikely that *Monitor* would survive the scoop-and-lift operation without severe damage. I had read about *Glomar Explorer*'s recovery effort that apparently resulted in ripping the bow off the Russian sub's hull. All I could think of was that GMDI was proposing to use a system on *Monitor*'s fragile, century-old iron hull that had just torn apart a modern submarine made of titanium. For some of us, the concept seemed like too much, too soon, and we could not even guess at the final cost for recovery and conservation. Still, the idea was intriguing, and I have not been able to determine if the proposal was given serious consideration.

The conference concluded with approval of the following resolution:

Steps should be taken by all agencies and interested parties to proceed with all necessary operations to determine the full nature of the environment and material condition of the Monitor, *and any decision relative to the recovery or eventual disposition of the* Monitor *should be deferred until these studies are completed . . . Americans should realize that the* Monitor *will not be raised in the near future, if it is*

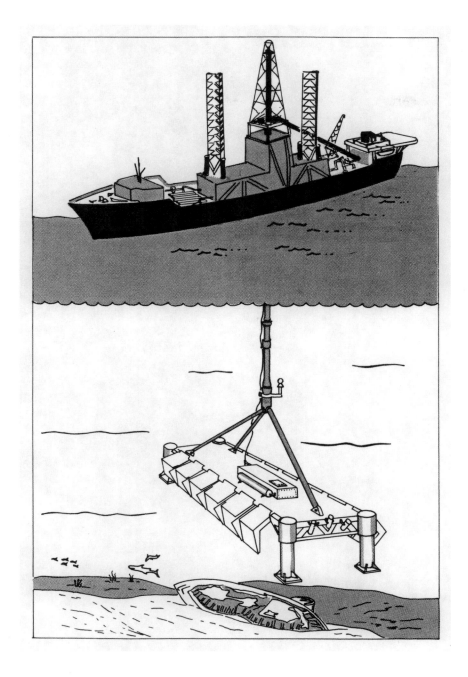

A drawing based on a Global Marine Development, Inc., proposal for recovering *Monitor*'s entire hull using the famous *Glomar Explorer* and a "special submarine vehicle." Courtesy Robert Sheridan

to be treated in a scientific and technologically sound manner.[24]

The resolution did not set well with MRRF and others, who felt that the government should arrange for *Glomar Explorer* to recover *Monitor* within the next year or two, before the wreck suffered further deterioration. Public information about the drillship was still sketchy at the time of the conference, but at least some of the attendees were aware of the ship's capabilities and that it very likely could be made operational.[25] In fact, although few of us knew about it, two months after the conference an article in the Navy's *NAVSEA Journal* stated that GMDI had signed a charter agreement with the Navy, leasing the ship for a thirteen-month charter with four six-month options. According to the article, activation and minor modifications began in June 1978, with at-sea testing to begin that winter.[26] That would mean that GMDI did, indeed, expect to have a fully functional ship that could be further modified for the proposed *Monitor* recovery. All we know for certain is that no action was taken on the GMDI proposal, and some of the researchers that were involved at that time still wonder "what if."

The April 1978 *Monitor* Conference disseminated a great deal of valuable and relevant information concerning *Monitor*'s future. The publication documenting the proceedings of the conference is one of the most valuable early milestones in the history of the *Monitor* sanctuary and also for the history of ocean resource protection and management strategies, research methodologies, and recovery and conservation technologies. Today, we more or less routinely deal with management issues regarding submerged cultural resources; however, in the 1970s there was far less information available on which to rely, and far less was known about the natural factors that acted on shipwrecks. The conference was a landmark event.

A Formal Management Plan Is Implemented

Early on, NOAA established a cooperative agreement with the state of North Carolina for developing management and research guidelines for the new sanctuary. In October 1978 NOAA reviewed a draft management plan proposed by the State of North Carolina. Widespread support for the plan led NOAA to implement it, with minor changes, almost immediately, even though it was not published until three years later. The plan paved the way for three principal partners, the US Government, US Navy, and state of North Carolina, to work together with a *Monitor* Federal Review Committee.[27] NOAA and the state of North Carolina would cooperatively manage the site, through an agreement that designated the NC Department of Cultural Resources, Division of Archives and History as onsite manager. Gordon P. Watts Jr., North Carolina's Underwater Archaeologist, directed the state's activities related to the *Monitor* agreement.

NOAA's primary management option for *Monitor* at that time was to protect the resource in its current location so that it could be preserved and enjoyed now and in the future. This policy of in situ (in place) preservation is adhered to by nearly all international preservation agencies and organi-

zations, and has been endorsed by the UNESCO (United Nations Educational, Scientific, and Cultural Organization) Convention on the Protection of Underwater Cultural Heritage. It is important to point out, however, that in situ preservation is the first—but by no means the only—option for managing an archaeological site. Cases are usually decided on an individual basis, taking into consideration such factors as site threats (erosion, channel dredging, or other factors); significance (state, national, or international); and condition (well-preserved, partially preserved, badly deteriorated, and scattered).

For those who want things to move quickly, the in situ preservation policy frequently creates frustration, often leading to accusations about do-nothing bureaucrats and sluggish government action. Nevertheless, there is an important consideration that must guide all decisions: shipwrecks and other cultural resources are unique and nonrenewable, unlike living resources that, given time and care, can regenerate. Additionally, a shipwreck is often referred to as a "time capsule" because when it sank, its hull and contents, representing a microcosm of its society, were captured at a precise moment of time. If those remains are disturbed before they can be documented in place, much of the information the site contained will be lost. As we proceeded in the years that followed, we kept all of these principles in mind and carefully weighed the options before deciding on a staged series of recoveries that were backed by science and archaeology. Our decision making and actions were conducted in the public interest, based on applicable law, with public review and expert consultation.

A Celebrity Visit

In June, a dive team from the Cousteau Society made a series of dives from the R/V *Calypso* in an attempt to film *Monitor* for a planned television special on shipwrecks. Heavy seas and strong currents limited their diving, and poor bottom visibility thwarted their efforts to obtain usable footage. The Cousteau team reported their entire expedition had resulted in only twelve minutes of poor-quality film. However, the Cousteau divers became the first to make untethered scuba dives on *Monitor*.[28]

RESEARCH EXPEDITIONS TO THE *MONITOR* NATIONAL MARINE SANCTUARY[1]

Date		Sponsor	Accomplishments
1973	August	DUML	R/V *Eastward*—discovered USS *Monitor*
1974	April	USN, NCDAH, NGS	R/V *Alcoa Seaprobe*—made photomosaic of *Monitor*
	May	DUML, UD	R/V *Eastward*—dredged near *Monitor* for bottom samples
	August	DUML, USCG	USCGC *Chilula*—recorded *Monitor* on sonar
	August	DUML	R/V *Beveridge*—imaged *Monitor* with u/w television system
1976	June	MRRF, UD	R/V *Eastward*—surveyed with magnetometer and sub-bottom profiler
1977	April	MRRF, UD	Collected environmental data, recovered a 6m bottom core, imaged on closed-circuit TV
	July	NOAA, NCDAH, USN, HBOI	First NOAA expedition, used submersibles for photogrammetric mapping, videography, diving, and limited artifact retrieval
1979	June	the Cousteau Society	R/V *Calypso*—attempts to film *Monitor for television special on historic wrecks; only twelve minutes of film obtained*
	August	NOAA, NCDAH, HBF	Submersibles support archaeological investigation and test excavation within *Monitor*'s hull; still and video coverage of site
1983	August	NOAA, ECU, HBF	General site investigations, stabilization assessment, and recovery of *Monitor*'s main anchor
1985	August	Eastport, Ocean Search International	Conducting of physical and bathymetric testing to create an electronic grid across the entirety of the wreck site
	August	NOAA, USN	Bathymetric, subbottom, and magnetic composition of seafloor within sanctuary boundaries; installed meters to record ongoing current and water conditions
1987	May	NOAA, USN	Accurately locate and photograph all archaeological artifacts/features within the site boundaries, perform corrosion and structural surveys
1990	June	NOAA, HBOI	Begin a series of systematic surveys, establish permanent site datums, further video and photographic documentation, biological survey
	June	Farb *Monitor* Expedition 1990	First NOAA-permitted dives on *Monitor* by private recreational divers; acquired high-quality film footage and video
		Gary Gentile Expedition	Second NOAA-permitted dives on *Monitor* by private recreational divers; acquired high-quality images
	July	NOAA, HBOI	Continued datum placement, still and visual site photography, artifact recovery
1991	June	NOAA, HBOI	Emergency investigation following report of unauthorized anchoring incident; found evidence of recent impact on turret, armor belt, skeg; recovered a recording thermograph;
	October	NOAA, HBOI	visual inspection and videography; documented additional deterioration of skeg and propeller assembly
1993	July	NOAA, NOAA EDU, HBOI	(MARSS'93) Conduct first NOAA bell dives, deploy 4,000-lb. clump anchor for permanent mooring, conduct test excavation within turret to determine fill composition, record site with high-res video

(continued)

[1] *Note*: Not all private dives are listed after 1990.

Date		Sponsor	Accomplishments
1994	Sept.–Oct.	Atlantic Wreck Diving	First private, nonresearch dives to the *Monitor* National Marine Sanctuary, conducted under the first Special Use Permit issued by the *Monitor National Marine Sanctuary*
1995	August–Oct.	NOAA, USN, TMM, UNC-W, Key West Diver	(MARRS'95) Navy divers aboard USS *Edenton* (ATS-1) prepare *Monitor*'s propeller for recovery, conducted first NOAA-sponsored "technical" dives on *Monitor* using self-contained mixed-gas diving gear
	Aug.–Sept.	Atlantic Wreck Diving	Private, nonresearch dives to the *Monitor* National Marine Sanctuary continued, conducted under a NOAA three-year Special Use Permit
	October	NOAA, USN, HOBI, Raytheon Electronics	*Clelia*: Prototype laser line scanner was used to create high-resolution "near-photographic" images of the wreck
1997	June	NOAA, SAIC	NOAA Ship Ferrel: Image *Monitor* with Northrop Grumman laser line-scanner mounted inside a tow vehicle; poor weather prevented data collection
1998	May–June	NOAA, USN, UNC-W, CF, TMM	*Monitor*'s propeller raised on June 5, taken to Mariners' Museum for preservation; recovered wood and metal samples, other items
1999	June	NOAA, USN, TMM, UNC-W, Key West Diver	Data gathering expedition in prep for hull stabilization and engine recovery; survey made of engine and beneath port armor belt
	Aug.	NOAA, UNC-W, CF	Continued survey and assessment of engine room, artifact recovery, and excavations in turret; data used to finalize long-range plan
2000	Apr.	NOAA, UNC-W, CF	Recovered artifacts, cleared silt and debris from in and around engine room, recorded several hours of video
	May	NOAA, USN, HBOI	Collected last-minute data prior to beginning stabilization and engine recovery operations
	June	NOAA, USN, UNC-W, CF	Engine Recovery System (ERS) lowered over the wreck; grout bags placed under port armor belt; recovered floor plate sample, white ironstone pitcher, propeller shaft segment, stuffing box, and rudder support skeg
	July	NOAA, NURC, ECU, CF	Recorded engine area in prep for recovery, surveyed area for threatened artifacts
2001	March–April	NOAA, UNC-W, ECU, CF	Inspected ERS, mapped position of Engine Lifting Frame (ELF) relative to engine room, remeasured areas where grout bags were to be installed
	April-May	NOAA, USN	USS *Grapple*: Install final components of Engine Recovery System; ELF lowered into position above engine
	June–July	NOAA, USN	*Wotan* Barge: Grout bags installed, *Monitor*'s engine recovered, along with numerous components and artifacts, preparations made for raising turret
	August	NOAA, MIT, UNC-W	Use custom MIT sub bottom profiler to survey inside and outside of turret to look for guns and hidden obstructions
2002	March	NOAA, USN	US Navy research submarine *NR-1* images *Monitor* with sidescan and multibeam sonar
2002	June–July	NOAA, USN, TMM, UNC-W, ECU, HBOI	*Wotan* Barge: *Monitor*'s gun turret safely recovered on August 5; NOAA team conducts postrecovery survey and stabilization
2003	May	NOAA, MIT/WHOI	MIT/WHOI deployed SeaBED AUV
		NOAA, UNC-W, ECU	Postrecovery site survey, site mapping, photomosaics

(continued)

Date	Sponsor	Accomplishments
2004	NOAA/USN	Site Cleanup
2006	NOAA/URI	Sonar and high-definition video survey
2009	NOAA/RU	Diving and AUV Survey

KEY: CF = Cambrian Foundation
DUML = Duke University Marine Laboratory
ECU = East Carolina University UNC-W = Univ. of North Carolina at Wilmington
HBOI = Harbor Branch Foundation/Harbor Branch Oceanographic Institution
KWD = Key West Divers
MIT= Massachusetts Institute of Technology
NCDAH = North Carolina Division of Archives and History
NGS = National Geographic Society
NOAA EDU = NOAA Experimental Diving Unit
NURC = National Undersea Research Center at the University of North Carolina at Wilmington
RU = Rutgers University
SAIC = Science Applications International Corporation
TMM = The Mariners' Museum
UD = University of Delaware
URI = University of Rhode Island
USCG = US Coast Guard
USN = US Navy
WHOI = Woods Hole Oceanographic Institution

ADDITIONAL NOAA/HARBOR BRANCH SITE ASSESSMENTS

In April 1978, through a fortuitous chain of events, I became Virginia's first state underwater archaeologist, hired to direct a survey for British ships sunk in 1781 during the Battle of Yorktown.[29] One of my collateral duties was to cooperate with archaeology programs in neighboring states, which soon gave me an opportunity to rejoin the *Monitor* team. Not long after starting my new job, I received a phone call from Gordon Watts. He explained that he was planning another *Monitor* expedition with NOAA and Harbor Branch, and this time he hoped to get approval for a small team of archaeologists to conduct an excavation inside *Monitor*'s hull. He was phoning to invite me to be on his *Monitor* dive team. I immediately said "Yes!" Fortunately, my employer, the Virginia Historic Landmarks Commission,[30] granted approval for me to participate in the 1979 *Monitor* expedition and Virginia Sea Grant provided funds to support my participation.

I worked closely with Watts, his assistant, Richard Lawrence, and the Underwater Archaeology Branch staff as they developed the expedition research plan. The three principal agencies that participated in the 1977 expedition agreed to team up again in 1979. This time, however, the objectives were even more ambitious: I would join Gordon and Richard on the archaeology team to conduct hands-on investigations at the *Monitor* sanctuary at a working bottom depth of 240 feet. We would each be paired up with an experienced Harbor Branch diver who would serve as dive tender and safety backup. In order to qualify for *Monitor* dives, we would have to pass a medical examination and complete extensive training.

In spring 1979 we underwent a week of extensive medical testing at the Duke Center for Hyperbaric Medicine and Environmental Physiology in Durham, North Carolina, followed by classroom and diving training at Harbor Branch's Fort Pierce, Florida, facility. We conducted open-water "lockout" dive training at West End, Grand Bahama Island.

"LOCKOUT" DIVE TRAINING

In 1979, with approval from the Virginia Historic Landmarks Commission, I participated in diving investigations on the *Monitor* with Gordon Watts and his assistant, Richard Lawrence. In spring 1979 the training began. First, we underwent a week of medical testing at the Duke Center for Hyperbaric Medicine and Environmental Physiology in Durham, North Carolina. We were tested, poked, prodded, examined, and x-rayed. We were paraded around the facility as a group and had begun to feel a bit like NASA astronauts getting ready to blast off into space. It was during this week of medical testing that we began to realize that a month-long series of deep dives was not a common scientific diving scenario. Most deep scientific dives were brief, and not repeated frequently; in fact, Harbor Branch had one of the very few noncommercial programs capable of conducting deep, mixed-gas dives. Fortunately, we passed all the tests and were certified to begin dive training.

Training began in a classroom at Harbor Branch's Fort Pierce, Florida, facility, known at that time as "Link Port" (for Edwin Link, who had designed and built the *J-S-L* submersibles). As we stuffed our heads with facts about the subs, formulae, and calculations on mixed-gas diving physiology and other topics, my euphoria was suddenly punctured from an unexpected source. The first night at Link Port, as I lay in bed thinking about the upcoming mission, my lifelong claustrophobia began to seep out. I visualized myself climbing inside the decidedly tiny dive compartment and watching my dive tender dog the hatch closed as we began to descend to where the water pressed on our little refuge at nearly 110 pounds per square inch.

Suddenly, I broke out in a cold sweat! Even though I had been in the sub once before, I was certain that I couldn't force myself into that dive compartment. The next day, during a break, I pulled Gordon off to the side and confessed my phobia and my certainty that I would let him down when the time came for me to make my first dive. He tried to convince me that I would be fine once the time came and, besides, we had plenty of training days ahead to get used to the sub. I was so concerned I offered to withdraw from the project so he would have time to train someone to take my place, but he wouldn't hear of it.

"Just wait," he insisted. "Just think about climbing inside the *Monitor*'s hull and uncovering all those secrets that lie inside, waiting for us."

After several more days of classroom work and equipment familiarity dives at dockside, we headed for West End,

Grand Bahama Island, for lockout training. That night, aboard the research vessel, I sneaked away from the rest of the team, most of whom were watching a video in the crew lounge. Quietly, with a small flashlight, I crept onto the stern, where the submarine, safely secured to the deck, stood waiting. I stooped and reached beneath the dive compartment, pulling out a large hose that ran from a below-deck air source through the compartment opening to reduce humidity inside. Taking a deep breath and turning on my flashlight, I slowly stood up, letting my head and shoulders enter the open hatch.

My apprehension rose and sweat beaded on my forehead and ran down onto my T-shirt. While I took more deep breaths, I shone the light around the compartment, concentrating on recalling the names and functions of all the gauges, switches, and pipes as they came into view. With another deep breath I pulled myself up into the compartment. Although I'm somewhat short, I could barely sit inside, my knees pulled up to my chin, my head bumping into something near the top of the compartment. I forced myself to sit there for a few minutes without moving. My heart rate began to slow and I tried to visualize the hatch dropping open on the seabed, letting me scramble out to see *Monitor*. By the next day, when I made my first training dive, I was okay—still apprehensive, but too excited about the mission to panic. When the time came for my first actual dive on *Monitor*, my excitement almost completely overwhelmed my phobias, and I launched my dive without hesitation.

The author "locked out" of the *Johnson-Sea-Link* submersible during a training dive in the Bahamas. Courtesy NOAA *Monitor* Collection

With the help of Harbor Branch's excellent team of scientific divers, we were soon confident of our abilities and ready for the fall expedition.

Archaeological Excavation and Assessment Expedition — August 1–26, 1979

On August 1, we arrived at the *Monitor* sanctuary aboard R/V *Johnson*, which was carrying the submersible *Johnson-Sea-Link I.* Floyd Childress and Ted Lillestolen were again the NOAA representatives, Roger Cook was HBF operations director, and Gordon Watts was archaeological advisor. Weather and equipment were cooperative, and most days we were able to conduct three dives, lockout dives in morning and afternoon with a brief midday observation dive. The midday dives provided an opportunity to collect still and video imagery and to assess results from the morning dive. These nonlockout dives also let us send down VIPs, including engineers, salvors, and others, to observe the site firsthand and to formulate options for future work.

On my first dive, my excitement overwhelmed my phobias, and I quickly walked to *Monitor*'s turret, where (after a reverent moment) I went about my assigned task of installing reference pipes that would provide a framework for our mapping activities. This fairly simple procedure would have been impossible without the battery-powered water pump

on *J-S-L I.* We quickly verified Robert Sheridan's geological report since, as he predicted, we encountered a hard, nearly impenetrable substrate three to six feet beneath the seafloor. This layer prevented us from jetting all four reference pipes a full five feet into the seabed, as we had hoped.

Once the reference datums were installed, Gordon inspected the forward hull area, looking for an area free of iron hull plates where we could conduct our excavation. Everywhere he looked he saw collapsed beams and hull plates, cemented together by iron corrosion products and marine organisms. Finally, he located a small clear area and marked the location with colored surveyor's tape. He then made a series of measurements to pinpoint the spot. When he plotted his measurements on a large drawing of *Monitor*'s hull, he found that the chosen excavation site was over the captain's cabin. The next divers installed an aluminum grid over the area to serve both as a reference and a scaffold, to simplify measurements and to prevent us from damaging any fragile objects as we worked.

The expedition soon fell into a rhythm of two lockout dives per day, separated by a midday nonlockout dive for observation and videography, interrupted, of course, by an occasional equipment issue or weather problem. We began with an operations plan containing a list of planned dives, each with specific goals and designated personnel. Almost immediately we had to modify the plan, since some of

Gordon Watts moves away from the *Johnson-Sea-Link* on a research dive on *Monitor* in 1979. Courtesy NOAA *Monitor* Collection

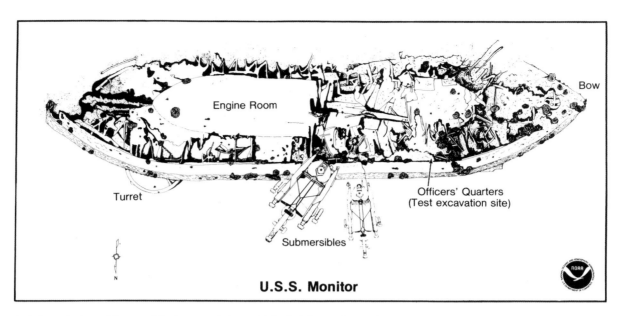

Artist's rendering of the 1979 *Monitor* expedition, with both *Johnson-Sea-Link* submersibles diving simultaneously at the site. Courtesy NOAA *Monitor* Collection

our dive tasks required more time than expected, while others were modified or deleted as our knowledge of the site increased. We attempted to keep the sequence of goals intact, however, since individual dive tasks were scheduled so as to accomplish progressively larger goals.

Almost immediately we had to modify out dive plans because of an unforeseen obstacle: "Sam the Grouper," five feet of giant puppy-dog energy! He followed us everywhere we went, often stirring up silt and getting in the way of our camera. Things only got worse when my dive tender, Mike Mitchell, sneaked Sam a hot dog from the galley. When the hatch opened on the next sub dive, Sam stuck his big head up into the dive chamber, ready for his next meal!

Dive safety was also a factor in the dive plan, scheduling each archaeologist/tender team for one dive every three dives. This precaution gave each diver about thirty-six hours between dives, which was sufficient for us to rest and eliminate all the gasses that had dissolved in our tissues during our time under pressure. While topside, we had time to catch up on our archaeological record-keeping and trying to contact our offices and families. In those pre-cellular and pre-Facebook dark ages, our only electronic link with the rest of the world was the ship's radio or a very expensive satellite phone.

We based our dive plan on years of research and thousands of hours of testing and operational dives by military and commercial divers. As a result, we had very few dive-related problems. I suffered my first-ever ear infection (apparently caused by high humidity in the decompression chamber) and Gordon was stricken with decompression sickness—a painful case of the "bends." He was successfully treated in the on-board chamber. Fortunately, since

A resident grouper at the *Monitor* site, whom we named "Sam," seemed completely unafraid and followed us around the wreck, as seen in this image pulled from a videotape. Courtesy NOAA *Monitor* Collection

Gordon Watts (right) and Richard Roesch waiting in the deck decompression chamber following a *Monitor* dive in 1979. Courtesy NOAA *Monitor* Collection

it was his last scheduled dive, he lost no time on the site.

The only other notable problem was communicating underwater. We had to speak in a helium atmosphere with our faces scrunched up in a rubber mask. The Harbor Branch tenders had a difficult time understanding all of us, even though the communications equipment contained a "helium unscrambler" designed to readjust our "chipmunk" voices back to normal. That worked well enough that Richard and I could be understood if we spoke slowly enough, but no one was able to understand Gordon's southern drawl. Roger Cook concluded that they were going to have to fit out the comms with a "Carolina unscrambler."

Overall, the 1979 expedition was a tremendous success. Having adequate dive time and excellent mobility made it possible for us to thoroughly inspect *Monitor*'s hull and exposed artifacts, including areas beneath and inside the hull that had not been seen before. During one phase of the expedition, both *J-S-L*s were onsite, which provided the opportunity for one sub to conduct lockout dives while the other filmed the dive activities and documented other portions of the wreck. Robotic vehicles are very effective, but sometimes nothing beats what scientists like to call "The Mark One Eyeball."

Our test excavation within the captain's cabin gave us new insights into the wreck's condition and the dynamics of the environment in which it lies. We encountered three distinct stratigraphic levels inside

the hull before reaching intact deck structure. The oak deck beams and pine deck planking felt solid when probed, suggesting that the deck may still be relatively intact and helping to maintain the structural integrity of the deck and armor belt—referred to as the "upper hull." The presence of modern plastic material more than a foot down confirmed our suspicion that deep running currents frequently disturb the upper sediments inside and beneath the wreck. We observed a concentration of artifacts lying against the forward sides of the oak deck beams. That, along with previously documented damage to the stern, suggested that the ship sank stern first, the aft end of the armor belt striking the seafloor with considerable force.

At this point, it might be helpful to define our terminology for the wreck. Since the hull and turret lie upside down, terms can be confusing. However, the key fact is that port and starboard—unlike right and left—are always the same, even if a ship is inverted. Therefore, it is the port armor belt that rests on the turret, while the starboard belt is almost completely buried. On our site drawings, depending on the purpose, directions may be noted with a north arrow or there might be a symbol indicating fore-aft and port-starboard.

The state of preservation varied within the test area and elsewhere. We found intact glass bottles and jars, wood and leather items, and other well-preserved artifacts that offered the promise of a wide range of artifacts to help us fill in minute details of

Harbor Branch diver Richard Roesch carefully placing *Monitor*'s signal lantern in a padded plastic bucket for recovery. Courtesy NOAA *Monitor* Collection

Monitor's story. However, we also encountered two large holes in the deck, forward of the amidships bulkhead, where cultural material and hull components had spilled onto the sand beneath. The deck had also ruptured in the area where the rim of the turret contacted the deck. The contact surface was remarkably small, due to the angle between the rim of the turret and the sloping deck, a situation that created very high stress loading on that portion of the deck. Over the years, the stern, which we believe was damaged at the time of sinking, began to deteriorate as corrosion and shipworms weakened the structure. This deterioration resulted in a partial collapse of the deck where it made contact with the turret. No evidence of *Monitor*'s shot and shell were located, even though dozens of eleven-inch-diameter iron spheres—larger than bowling balls—should have been easy to spot.

One of the most striking features of the site, observable only from the seafloor, was the large portion of *Monitor*'s deck that was not supported from below. We estimated that as much as 50 percent of the hull was unsupported, due to its position on top of the turret. Forward of the pilot house, currents scoured around the bow, leaving a void beneath. Following the port armor belt aft, the distance between hull and sand increased, reaching a height of ten feet at the aft

preserved extent of the armor belt. The weight of the engine, boilers, auxiliary machinery, and tons of coal and accumulated silt were combining in an attempt to collapse the entire hull.

Forward of the amidships bulkhead, the lower hull (the highest part of the inverted hull) had almost completely collapsed. Aft of the bulkhead the lower hull was more intact, but still showed signs of weakening, especially the side plating, which bore the full force of bottom currents. Measurements with a simple diver-held inclinometer suggested that *Monitor*'s bow lay nearly flat on the seafloor, with an increasing "twist" toward the stern, due to the hull's position atop the turret. From the amidships bulkhead aft, the list to starboard was approximately 19 degrees, with a 2 1/2 degree bow-down slope along the armor belt.

While preservation within the test excavation area suggested intact deck structure in the bow, our observations and measurements clearly demonstrated that *Monitor*'s hull was weakened or collapsed in many areas and we concluded that very little overall structural integrity remained.

The wealth of recovered data provided valuable insight into the archaeological and engineering aspects of *Monitor*'s condition, and broadened the knowledge base upon which future sanctuary management deci-

At "Level 4" the excavation in the captain's stateroom reached the deck beams and planking, where several artifacts were found. Courtesy NOAA *Monitor* Collection

sions would depend. However, we recommended that additional engineering data was needed before a viable recovery plan could be developed.[31]

Site Assessment and Anchor Recovery Expedition—August 1983

By 1982, Nancy M. Foster, chief of the Sanctuary Programs Division (SPD), was anxious to resume research at the *Monitor* sanctuary. Fact finding and planning had continued, but no expeditions had been conducted since 1979. Gordon Watts, who had led NOAA's *Monitor* field research up until this time, was now with the Maritime Studies Program at East Carolina University (ECU). The Sanctuaries and Reserves Division (SRD) and ECU developed plans for an expedition in 1983 to be cosponsored by NOAA, the Harbor Branch Foundation, and ECU. Goals were to continue the site assessment performed

DIVING MILESTONES — 1977 AND 1979

The 1977 *Monitor* expedition utilized equipment that was relatively commonplace in the scientific and commercial diving arenas, but rarely available to archaeologists. Harbor Branch scientific divers conducted all the dives, which were observed by an archaeologist from within the submersible (see second sidebar in this chapter, "Undersea Research Systems Used on *Monitor*"). The expedition produced significant data on the condition of *Monitor*'s hull and artifacts, and demonstrated that submersible-based scientific diving operations at *Monitor*'s depth were feasible, safe, and productive. Today, this accomplishment may seem trivial, but in the 1970s deep archaeological dives were extremely rare. Only military and commercial divers worked at *Monitor*'s depth on a regular basis.

Dives in 1979 were even more groundbreaking, since most of the diving was done by the archaeologists with training and support from Harbor Branch. An excavation conducted inside the captain's stateroom was considered a milestone in the relatively new field of underwater archaeology. In fact, as far as we know this remains the deepest hands-on archaeological excavation ever conducted by trained archaeologists. The success of these dives, along with dives during the 1983 anchor recovery, paved the way for NOAA to eventually conduct its own dives on *Monitor*.

during 1977 and 1979 and to determine the team's ability to locate, map, and recover a large iron object from *Monitor*. As before, archaeologists and Harbor Branch divers shared the diving tasks, supported by a *J-S-L* submersible. Once again, I joined the archaeology team, this time with Gordon Watts and Wesley K. Hall, a graduate student in ECU's maritime program. Also participating in the expedition was Edward M. Miller, who edited the "Project Cheesebox" publication and in 1978 published a book based on that report.[32]

We chose *Monitor*'s iron, four-fluked anchor as an ideal object to recover. First of all, we predicted it would be partially exposed on the seafloor, where it might be snagged by trawl nets or the anchor of a ship illegally moored in the sanctuary. We knew the anchor should be easy to locate, relatively straightforward to recover, and made of wrought iron so it would be sturdy enough to recover without concern for damage. Another plus was that the anchor was composed of large, thick iron components that would give conservators the opportunity to compare its state of preservation with that of the hull plate recovered in 1977. Such comparisons, we hoped, would help us develop predictive models to estimate the overall extent of preservation of *Monitor*'s hull and to refine conservation plans for future recoveries.

The anchor also had special historical significance. It was unlike conventional ship anchors, having been designed by Ericsson specifically for *Monitor*. Ericsson designed the anchor and its handling system so that the anchor could be raised and lowered from inside the hull, without the crew being exposed to enemy guns. Once everyone agreed to recover the anchor, we developed a detailed recovery and conservation plan, secured the resources for conservation treatment, and arranged for public display. With such a high level of public interest in *Monitor*, we felt that the anchor was just the type of artifact to represent the ironclad. Unlike the hull plate, pipe, davit, and other hull components we had previously recovered, the anchor would be readily identified as a part of a ship, which would draw attention and interest to the associated interpretive captions and exhibits that would tell the bigger story of *Monitor*.

Although no one had actually seen the anchor, we were confident we could locate it. One evening during the 1979 expedition, we had met on board the research vessel with retired Navy Captain Ernest Peterkin, a *Monitor* expert. We began to discuss the an-

chor and soon we had agreed on a probable heading and distance the sub should follow from the *Monitor*'s bow in order to locate the anchor. We assumed the anchor would still be attached to its chain and that it would not be completely buried, thanks to the hard substrate we encountered around the wreck.

During a late afternoon sub dive on August 21, pilot Tim Askew and observer Edward Miller located the anchor without much difficulty. As predicted, it was lying partially exposed in the sand approximately 450 feet south-southwest of *Monitor*'s bow. The following morning, near-zero visibility resulted in an early termination of the first dive. That afternoon, with visibility still poor, the sub was launched for a dive to prepare the anchor for recovery. I was the working diver for this task. When the *J-S-L* reached *Monitor*, visibility was less than ten feet and it was very dark. As I watched live video on a small video screen in the dive compartment, the sub eased up to the anchor. Two flukes were exposed, but heavily encrusted with corrosion products and marine organisms, all wrapped in a jumble of modern rope that had snagged on the flukes. The sub's manipulator cut away most of the obstructions and I got the word to prepare to dive.

My task was to attach a large fixed-volume salvage bag to the anchor and, time permitting, expose a section of chain to be cut later by a Harbor Branch diver. When the hatch opened I scrambled out of the sub, grabbed the bag from the sub's forward basket, and turned toward the anchor, illuminated in the sub's powerful lights. Suddenly, a bright object streaked past, startling me. Darting in and out of the light beams were a dozen or more large amberjack that had followed us here from the wreck. Literally hundreds of tiny creatures joined them, flitting around the sub's lights like moths on a summer night.

I walked to the anchor and took out my knife. After cutting away the remaining modern lines, I secured a nylon strap around the flukes. I then attached the lift bag to the ends of the strap and began filling it with gas from a small probe attached to my band mask. As we planned, I added sufficient gas to keep the bag upright, but not enough to lift the anchor. I then cleared sand from a section of chain next to the anchor and used a small hammer to beat off the corrosion products that would have prevented the electric "Broco" cutting torch from functioning. There were shiny spots on the chain when I got the call to return to the sub.

The author, diving from the *Johnson-Sea-Link* submersible, attached a lifting sling and salvage bag to the anchor. Courtesy NOAA *Monitor* Collection

The next morning Craig Caddigan cut the chain and the lift bag was filled from inside the sub. Even when the lift bag was nearly full, the anchor did not budge. This was puzzling, since we estimated the anchor would weigh less than half the bag's 3,000-pound lift capacity. As it turned out, we were right on target: the anchor, with its concreted surface and five feet of chain weighed 1,450 pounds. However, there was another factor in play. The anchor had lain on the seabed for more than a century, eventually becoming partially buried. Corrosion slowly formed a huge conglomerate of sand and shell that added considerable weight to the anchor. When the lift bag filled to capacity, the extra pull broke the anchor free, and it accelerated off the bottom in a cloud of silt like a rocket blasting off.

As soon as the sub reported that the anchor was on its way up, nearly everyone on the ship ran to the rail to watch the big yellow salvage bag break the surface. Soon a cheer went up as a huge mass of bubbles spread across the surface, letting us know that the salvage bag was venting the excess air created as the pressure decreased on the way up. But the cheering died off when nothing else happened. The flow of bubbles subsided, but no bag appeared. We looked on all sides of the ship. We waited. The sub was contacted, but all they could report was that their visibility was completely blacked out by the anchor's silt cloud.

While the sub was being recovered, our team speculated on what could have happened. The anchor had definitely left the bottom but had not made it to the surface. Even though the salvage bag was new and was a brand known for its strength and reliability, we couldn't help but conclude that the bag had ruptured during the ascent, sending the anchor back to the bottom. We considered that to be merely a temporary setback, since Harbor Branch had attached an electronic beacon to the nylon sling, and that would lead us back to the anchor.

On the next dive, the sub quickly picked up the regular "ping" of the beacon and even though visibility was only a few feet, it navigated straight to the beacon. It was lying in the sand, not attached to anything! That report sent a shock through the team. Even worse, someone suggested an alternative explanation for the missing anchor. What if the combined lift weight of the anchor, chain, and attached concretion roughly equaled the lift capacity of the salvage bag? If so, the bag may have lifted the anchor toward the surface until the lift and weight exactly canceled each other, leaving the anchor suspended somewhere in the water column as the Gulf Stream carried it steadily northward.

We were still pondering that terrible scenario when the weather began to worsen. The HBF was as determined to recover the anchor as was our archaeology team. They suggested that we temporar-

Monitor's anchor being lifted out of the water in 1983; the salvage bag is still attached. Courtesy NOAA *Monitor* Collection

ily suspend operations while they conducted another project nearby, then resume the recovery effort when the weather improved. At this point I had to leave the ship and return to my real job, where I anxiously awaited news from the site. On July 29 I received a call from Gordon Watts. Good news: the first sub team experienced excellent visibility and they quickly located the anchor.

What Watts said next, however, prickled the hair on my neck: the anchor was lying only a few feet from where the sub was sitting when it inflated the lift bag. The only explanation was that when the anchor broke free it rose so rapidly the heavy bag ruptured, sending the anchor crashing back into the sand not far from the sub. Had luck really been against us, the anchor could have come crashing down onto the sub. This was a reminder to all of us that conducting research at sea is more than an adventure; it involves real danger that cannot be completely eliminated by careful planning and skilled personnel.

Fortunately, the anchor was recovered without incident, using two lift bags for extra security. Once ashore, the archaeologists trucked the 1,300-pound anchor to East Carolina University where it began a lengthy process of conservation by Curtiss Peterson. That process involved careful desalinization of the metal which removed salts that, over more than a century of immersion in seawater, had permeated its structure. This is basically the treatment used on all metal objects recovered from shipwrecks, and is absolutely essential to the survival of the artifacts. Left untreated, drying would have allowed the imbedded salts to crystallize, creating internal pressures that would have caused the anchor to gradually split apart and disintegrate.

The Harbor Branch *Sea-Link* submersibles proved excellent for collecting visual data from *Monitor*. The subs are stable, highly maneuverable, and equipped with high-quality still and video cameras, high-intensity lights, and a laser measurement reference system. The subs can also recover samples and perform other tasks with their manipulator arms. The subs' ability to remain on the bottom for three hours or more provides scientists with an excellent opportunity to make observations, select areas to examine, and recover materials, all without the need for diving.

The submersible lockout method of diving on *Monitor* was ideal in many ways. It allowed a diver to spend up to an hour directly on the wreck—with no

Following conservation, *Monitor*'s anchor was placed on exhibit at The Mariners'
Museum, where it has been prominently displayed in a series of ever-expanding *Monitor*
exhibits. Courtesy The Mariners' Museum

need to descend through the water column or ascend slowly while conducting essential decompression stops. The system was far safer and more effective than surface-supplied or scuba diving. There were also several drawbacks. For safety reasons, decompression, and submersible systems recharge, only one diver could work outside on each dive, and only two dives could be made each day. Each one-hour dive required approximately 4 1/2 hours of decompression. No dives could be made during that time because the chamber would not be available in case of an accident. Therefore, the maximum daily diver onsite work time was two hours, regardless of the number of available personnel. Overall, the *J-S-Ls* offered scientists the opportunity to safely conduct hands-on investigations in environments that could not be accessed using conventional scuba or surface-supplied diving techniques. Even though robotic vehicles can now accomplish many of those same scientific tasks, the *J-S-Ls* filled a niche that no other system has fully satisfied.[33]

Although this expedition was hampered by adverse weather conditions, the results contributed to the growing body of data on *Monitor*'s condition. In addition, the discovery and recovery of the anchor verified the researchers' ability to locate and recover an object weighing nearly a ton.[34] We had learned a great deal more about the wreck and about working on a deep, exposed site. At the time we were conducting these investigations, underwater archaeology was conducted primarily within scuba diving limits and closer to shore. Our work on *Monitor* was a pioneering effort that extended both science and historic preservation into a new level beneath the sea.

The USS Monitor *Project*

The NCDAH continued to assist NOAA with *Monitor* research and management through 1982. At that time, NOAA began to transfer part of the responsibility to ECU, where Gordon Watts and William N. Still Jr. had established the Program in Maritime History and Underwater Research. NOAA awarded a grant to ECU for several *Monitor*-related projects, including the publication and distribution of a periodic activities report titled *Cheesebox*, a tip of the hat to one of *Monitor*'s nicknames, the "Little Cheesebox on a Raft." The ECU, with leadership from Gordon Watts, played a leading role in the development of *Monitor* research plans.

In December 1983, NOAA hired Edward M. Miller as project manager for *Monitor*. Miller, who had maintained a strong interest in *Monitor* since Project Cheesebox, and who had participated in NOAA's 1983 expedition, worked closely with Nancy Foster, SPD director, to refine long-range management plans and goals for *Monitor*. On January 30, 1985, NOAA, the US Navy, and the National Trust for Historic Preservation held a ceremony at the US Naval Academy to mark the tenth anniversary of *Monitor*'s designation as a National Marine Sanctuary. *Monitor*'s signal lantern, recovered in 1977, was displayed for the first time. Dr. Foster used this opportunity to announce a partnership with the National Trust for the establishment of the USS *Monitor* Project. Foster told the gathering that the National Trust would provide NOAA with the means to raise

private funds and promote the participation of public and private organizations. Those of us who had been following the *Monitor* situation closely were encouraged by Dr. Foster's announcement and many of us volunteered to assist.

The USS *Monitor* Project launched a multi-pronged approach to management and research, creating a Project Planning Committee to recommend policy and priorities. Six subcommittees would provide additional expertise to the planning committee on historical and archaeological documentation, architectural and engineering documentation, site documentation, museum and conservation issues, and fund-raising.

NOAA ASSESSMENT SURVEYS

The NOAA/Harbor Branch expeditions had contributed significant information on the condition of *Monitor* and its contents. However, the Project Planning Committee felt that additional data was required before any decision was reached on *Monitor*'s fate. Under Miller's guidance, NOAA conducted complex survey expeditions at the site in 1985 and 1987 using remote-sensing equipment and robotic vehicles, but no human divers. The general objective

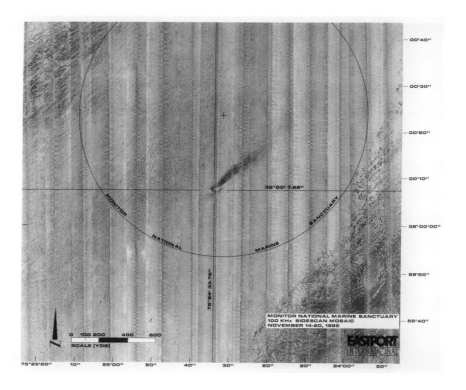

A mosaic of sonar images that shows bottom features in all but the northern section of the *Monitor* National Marine Sanctuary. The distinct scour trail that extends northeast from the wreck is caused by the powerful Gulf Stream. Courtesy NOAA *Monitor* Collection

for these expeditions was to collect additional data identified by experts as essential for a more complete understanding of *Monitor*'s condition and the natural forces acting on the site. Although I didn't participate in either expedition, I followed their progress closely.

Site Assessment and Documentation Survey—1985

During August and November 1985, NOAA, the National Trust for Historic Preservation, and Eastport International Inc. (of Upper Marlboro, Maryland, a Navy search and recovery contractor founded by Craig Mullen), conducted surveys utilizing the Environmental Protection Agency Research Vessel *Peter W. Anderson*, which was equipped with an accurate microwave navigation system. In order to reference the survey instruments directly with *Monitor* itself, the survey team deployed a system of acoustic transponders on the seabed around the wreck site.

A side scan sonar survey covering the entire sanctuary revealed that the wreck lies in an essentially featureless, silty plain that extends over most of the sanctuary. This survey confirmed other findings that *Monitor* itself has contributed to alteration of surrounding landforms: a prominent northeast-to-southwest scour trail extends from the wreck on its lee or northeast side, formed by the passage of the northerly-flowing Gulf Stream over the wreck. The scour is visible because the silty surface material has been eroded away, exposing larger shell fragments and stone. A second survey, utilizing higher frequency sonar, was also conducted close in and over the wreck, revealing additional detail on the orientation and condition of *Monitor*'s hull. The sonar imagery provided a strong reminder of the powerful natural forces that are always at work reducing the wreck to eventual rubble. Our challenge was to attempt to quantify the effect of these forces in our attempt to predict when *Monitor* would begin to collapse.

The expedition also conducted a magnetometer survey around the wreck in an effort to detect ship debris either lost at the time of sinking or possibly thrown clear during World War II if *Monitor*'s hull had been mistaken for a German submarine and damaged by depth charges.[35] Unfortunately, either the magnetic signature of any scattered material was too low or the resolution of the sensor was insufficient to detect any significant debris outside the immediate area of the wreck.

Further Development of the Monitor *Project Infrastructure*

In April 1986, I was invited to become a member of the *Monitor* Archaeological Documentation Subcommittee and on April 4, I attended their first meeting, where we reviewed available *Monitor* data and listed information we felt was still needed from the site.

During this period of change it was becoming apparent that NOAA needed a partner organization to provide a secure, publicly accessible archive for the rapidly-growing collection of documents, photographs, archival material, and artifacts related to the *Monitor*. As a result, in September 1986, with assistance from the Council of American Maritime Museums, NOAA issued a formal request for proposals for a principal museum desiring to provide the required archival services and, in addition, develop an interpretive exhibit to tell *Monitor*'s story and display the artifacts recovered from the wreck.[36]

On March 9, 1987, a national commemoration of the 125th anniversary of the *Monitor*'s Battle at Hampton Roads was held at The Mariners' Museum, Newport News, Virginia. This event was significant for several reasons besides the anniversary celebration. First, NOAA formally announced the designation of The Mariners' Museum as the principal museum for management and curation of *Monitor*-related materials. NOAA and the museum then formally designated this material "the National Collection of *Monitor* Artifacts and Papers." Finally, a representative from the Department of the Interior's National Park Service (NPS) formally announced that *Monitor* had been designated a National Historic Landmark (NHL) on June 23, 1986. *Monitor* was only the second shipwreck to receive this recognition.[37]

All of us who were associated with the *Monitor* Project were justifiably proud of this achievement, because the Landmark designation was more than a status symbol. Rather, it reflected careful study of the factors that made *Monitor* so exceptionally significant in American history and archaeology and helped guide future management decisions about the wreck. The National Park Service had joined the *Monitor* Project to provide historical expertise

MONITOR AND MERRIMAC

"BATTLE OF THE MONITOR AND MERRIMACK (C.S.S. VIRGINIA)" BY CARL EVERS

125TH COMMEMORATION OF THE FIRST BATTLE OF THE IRONCLADS

MARCH 9, 1862 — MARCH 9, 1987

"Their names are for history; and so long as we remain a people, so long will the work of the Monitor be remembered, and her story told to our children's children...the "little cheesebox on a raft" has made herself a name which will not soon be forgotten by the American people."

GRENVILLE WEEKS Surgeon, U.S.S. Monitor

★

MONITOR NATIONAL MARINE SANCTUARY
NATIONAL MARINE SANCTUARY PROGRAM
NATIONAL OCEANIC AND ATMOSPHERIC ADMINISTRATION

A poster commemorating the 125th anniversary of *Monitor*'s battle with CSS *Virginia*.
Courtesy NOAA *Monitor* Collection

and to conduct a series of historical and archaeological context studies that led to the National Historic Landmark designation by the Secretary of the Interior.

Under the leadership of the NPS' Chief Historian Edwin C. Bearss, an NPS *Monitor* initiative was conducted by historian James P. Delgado, who authored *Monitor*'s excellent NHL study. One of the significant results of the initiative was the creation, in 1987, of the US Government's first maritime preservation program, which Delgado was selected to lead. This was also the beginning of a long-term collaboration between NPS and NOAA on *Monitor* that continues to this day and that now includes cooperative research in national marine sanctuaries and national parks around the nation.

The Battle of Hampton Roads 125th Anniversary Celebration, March 1987, at The Mariners' Museum, which had just been selected as NOAA's principal museum partner for the *Monitor* Project. In this photo Dr. Nancy Foster, chief of the Sanctuary Programs Division, and Virginia Senator Paul S. Trible Jr. unveil the plaque confirming that USS *Monitor* had been designated a National Historic Landmark. Courtesy NOAA *Monitor* Collection

Site Assessment and Documentation Survey—1987

During May 25 through June 9, 1987, NOAA, the US Navy, and Eastport International conducted extensive research made possible through an interagency agreement between NOAA and the US Navy Office of the Supervisor of Salvage and Diving. Primary objectives included determining the extent of cultural material lying outside the wreck, evaluating the level of corrosion activity, conducting a structural survey, and conducting a three-dimensional sonar survey of the wreck. The sponsors selected a principal investigator for each of the four primary studies, and obtained the necessary support equipment and personnel.

The expedition relied on a Navy-owned, remotely operated vehicle, *Deep Drone*, for data recovery. *Deep Drone*, weighing more than two tons and equipped with powerful thrusters and a precise navigation system, was the first large ROV to be deployed on *Monitor*. All operations were conducted from the US Navy's 226-foot oceangoing tug USNS *Apache* (TATF172), which was anchored over the wreck on a four-point moor. Previous expeditions

had been, for the most part, "live boat" operations; that is, the support vessel did not anchor during submersible diving or remote sensing activities. In order for *Deep Drone* to maneuver accurately around the site, however, it was essential that the support ship remain in a fixed position so the ROV's cable could be tended. A very accurate navigation system was established for *Apache* and *Deep Drone* to ensure that all data would include precise coordinates to enhance later analysis.

The first task was for personnel from Corrpro Companies Inc. to conduct a corrosion investigation on *Monitor*'s hull using techniques developed for the offshore oil industry. They measured the electric field gradient at approximately 100 locations using a sensor mounted on *Deep Drone*. Then direct potential measurements were recorded at various locations using a metallic contact probe. To obtain these measurements, *Deep Drone*'s manipulator arm was used to "stab" the probe against surfaces on *Monitor*'s hull and turret. Although this technique caused much gnashing of teeth among the archaeologists, it is the industry standard method for obtaining essential corrosion data. The probe was small and the

In 1987 the Navy's *Deep Drone* remotely-operated vehicle (ROV) conducted a corrosion investigation and high-resolution sonar survey of *Monitor*'s hull. Courtesy NOAA *Monitor* Collection

investigators agreed that any slight damage it caused was mitigated by the value of the information obtained.

Results, conclusions, and recommendations were published in the expedition report, and proved useful in planning for additional corrosion studies and for considering the possibility of protecting *Monitor*'s structure on the seabed using the same type of corrosion protection methods used routinely on such structures as oil platforms.[38]

The next task, directed by J. Barto Arnold III, expedition consulting archaeologist, was to conduct a systematic intensive surface survey of a 300-by-500 foot expanse containing *Monitor*'s hull and the sur-

rounding area predicted to contain all artifacts from the wreck. The survey collected hundreds of still photos and more than fifty hours of video during this survey. During the surface survey a downward-looking profiling sonar, mounted on *Deep Drone* along with the still and video cameras, scanned *Monitor*'s hull in order to produce a three-dimensional sonar image from which quantitative measurements could be extracted. The Deep Submergence Laboratory of the Woods Hole Oceanographic Institution provided the equipment and conducted the sonar research.

Both the photographic and sonar surveys were hampered by problems with the navigation, primarily related to the geometry of the navigation setup.

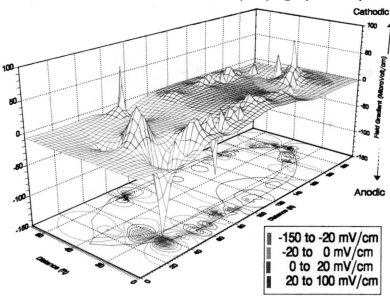

Electric Field Gradient - Surface/Topographic Map

Cathodic

Anodic

▮	-150 to -20 mV/cm
▮	-20 to 0 mV/cm
▮	0 to 20 mV/cm
▮	20 to 100 mV/cm

Graph showing surface and topographic maps of *Monitor*'s electric field gradient, based on the 1987 *Deep Drone* data. Note: upward spikes indicate hull areas that are cathodic (protective). Courtesy NOAA *Monitor* Collection

The transducer mounted on top of *Deep Drone* sometimes could not receive signals from all the reference transducers anchored to the seabed due to "shadowing" effects caused by the wreck or the ROV itself. As a result, positioning information to the sonar was not adequate to produce the high accuracy three-dimensional model of the wreck that researchers had anticipated. After sophisticated post-processing, however, Woods Hole produced some striking three-dimensional images of the wreck from various viewpoints, along with an animated "fly-over."

In spite of a few difficulties with equipment, visibility, and subsurface currents, the 1987 expedition produced a wide range of important data on the configuration and condition of the *Monitor* and the immediate surrounding area. Results and conclusions from the survey were alarming. Barto Arnold, the expedition's consulting archaeologist, and Gordon Watts, who assessed the structural survey data, concluded in the expedition's final report that there had been significant changes to the site since 1983 and that the rate of deterioration seemed to be accelerating.[39] Arnold concluded that the fragile condition of *Monitor*'s hull suggested that if no efforts were made to stabilize the site, *Monitor* could deteriorate to the point that it would be unrecognizable within five to ten years.[40] Gordon Watts, the researcher with the

most knowledge of the wreck, analyzed the expedition photographs and reported numerous areas where the hull structure was further degraded since 1979.

This bleak report seemed to confirm the concerns raised by Newton and Sheridan in the 1970s. However, those concerns, and even the predictions in the 1987 report—which were based on more than a decade of additional observations and measurements—all depended upon very limited scientific knowledge. No one had conducted major studies on the corrosion of iron ships in salt water under differing environmental conditions and our accumulated data on *Monitor*, though extensive, was not sufficient to predict with certainty when *Monitor*'s hull would collapse. When I discussed the condition of *Monitor*'s hull I often used the analogy of an old barn. When I was a boy, my family would drive several times a year to visit my grandparents in southwestern Virginia. Each time, I looked forward to seeing an old barn that sat near the highway and that always seemed ready to collapse. Parts of its roof and siding were missing and vines twisted in and out of gaps between boards. The entire structure leaned ominously to one side, yet the barn persisted for years until finally we were saddened by the sight of a crumpled pile of scraps where the barn had stood against the elements for so long. A carpenter might have exam-

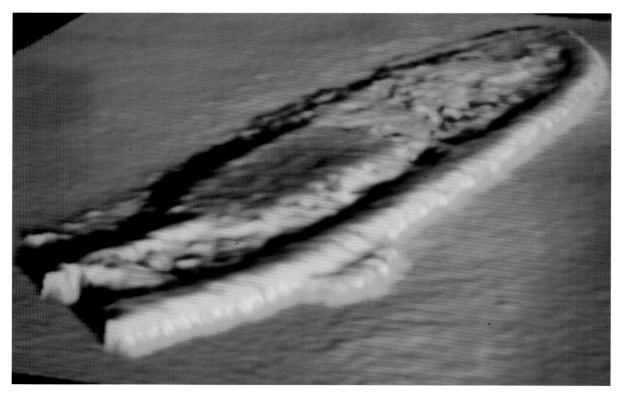

Sonar data from the 1987 survey were used to generate a three-dimensional image of *Monitor*. Courtesy NOAA *Monitor* Collection

ined the posts and roof beams and nails to determine the barn's condition, but nothing would have determined exactly when the final collapse would occur. The end could have resulted from exceptional wind from a thunderstorm or the weight of a heavy snowfall. To me, the *Monitor* was very much like the old barn. Its collapse was inevitable, but no one knew when or how it would happen. This was our frustration in attempting to determine how to deal with *Monitor*'s deteriorating condition. All we could say with certainty was that the *Monitor* was disintegrating at a much faster rate than we had expected and that if we did not act quickly to save the ship we may be too late.

The report recommended that NOAA revisit the *Monitor* management plan in light of the latest site information. It also recommended that NOAA increase site surveillance, acquire additional site data, compare photographic and video data from all expeditions to further quantify the types and rates of deterioration, consider applying corrosion protection to the wreck, and, most significantly, give consideration to a plan for recovery, conservation, curation, and display of the turret and other objects of special interest.

AN APPROACHING CRISIS

During the first decade since *Monitor*'s discovery, an impressive number of accomplishments had been achieved. *Monitor* had been added to the National Register of Historic Places, then designated a National Marine Sanctuary and a National Historic Landmark, which was a careful assessment of the ship's national and international historical significance; regulations had been promulgated to protect the site and establish a process for site access and research; a management plan had been implemented; and periodic inspection and research expeditions were being conducted.

The second decade brought progress as well, with new plans, studies, and expeditions to the site, along with expansion of the *Monitor* Collection. In 1987 the National Park Service, in cooperation with NOAA, developed the *USS Monitor National Marine Sanctu-*

ary Research Management Plan as a guide for future research by NOAA and others.[41] NOAA contracted with experts for a series of historical and technical studies designed to gather and interpret available data, including a compendium of *Monitor*'s drawings and plans, a report on companies that contributed to its construction, biographies of all its commanding officers, and a detailed list of all the ship's expected contents, including provisions.[42] In 1988 and 1989, NOAA and the state of Maryland cooperated in the development of a US national preservation policy for *Monitor* and other submerged cultural resources.[43] In the late 1980s, NOAA's Marine and Estuarine Management Division (MEMD) assumed full responsibility for management of the *Monitor* sanctuary.

By the time the 1987 expedition report was received, MEMD was already well aware of the basic situation at the sanctuary: *Monitor* was almost completely exposed on the seabed, subject to the ravages of currents, corrosion, and human activities; *Monitor*'s hull was under extraordinary stresses due to the configuration of the wreck on the seabed; the hull could collapse at any time, an event that would result in severe damage to hull components and artifacts,

and destruction of much of the site's archaeological record. However, NOAA did not have the funds or in-house capability to attempt any corrective action at the site.

A 1989 reorganization resulted in MEMD becoming the Sanctuaries and Reserves Division (SRD), part of NOAA's Office of Ocean and Coastal Resource Management. NOAA Corps officer Lt. Ilene Byron was selected to serve as manager of the *Monitor* National Marine Sanctuary. Byron continued NOAA's practice of inspecting *Monitor* at every opportunity until she returned to sea duty in late 1990. The purpose of these inspection surveys was to look for and document any additional changes at the site. In 1990, exceptional visibility in excess of 100 feet resulted in some of the most spectacular video ever recorded at the site, which produced an excellent record of *Monitor*'s condition at that time.

As the *Monitor* National Marine Sanctuary approached its fifteenth anniversary, its future was uncertain. Even as NOAA tenaciously attempted to protect and preserve *Monitor* on the seafloor, it began seeking to determine the best course of action for the near future.

Chapter Five

CHARTING A NEW COURSE

FOR *MONITOR*

By the end of the second decade after *Monitor*'s discovery, NOAA faced a decision on how best to manage the wreck for the American public. Simply stated, the key issue was to whether to leave *Monitor* where it was found, on the seabed, or to recover all or parts of the ship. This was an important question for a variety of reasons, and not just cost. Excavation and recovery of the wreck, even portions of it, would add to our knowledge of the ship—particularly of the ship's officers and crew and the conditions of their life and service not otherwise recorded—despite the surviving logbooks and the letters and accounts of survivors. Recovery might also answer questions concerning how the ship perished that night, and perhaps the fate of some of the lost crew. Archaeology adds to, refines, and at times corrects written history. It could do so (and ultimately did) for *Monitor*. There was also the extraordinary significance of the *Monitor*'s technological innovations and the ship's watershed place in naval history.

Another primary consideration was that our various expeditions had collected ample evidence that *Monitor* was deteriorating rapidly. We faced ongoing changes that would continue to transform *Monitor* from a relatively intact ship into a degraded archaeological site. Deterioration and change are not, by themselves, compelling arguments for recov-

ery to prevent loss of data, because archaeologists can and do extract remarkable amounts of information from sites hundreds and thousands of years old. However, we had to take into account the potential value of sharing the ship as it was, in an arrested state of change, if we recovered all or portions of it for the public to see and interact with in a museum setting, rather than an occasional video glimpse of the wreck on the bottom of the sea.

While deterioration of shipwrecks may not always be justification for recovery in and of itself, we began to perceive, especially in the face of repeated public requests to see more of this particular wreck, that we should consider raising *Monitor*. While in situ (in place) preservation is the preferred option for managing underwater archaeological sites, there have always been cases where exceptional significance, potential for learning important new information, intense public interest, and the ability of a raised wreck or its excavated artifacts to educate and inspire have led to full excavation, recovery, conservation, and exhibition of significant sites. Among these are ships as diverse as the world's oldest wreck, the 3,300-year-old Ulu Burun ship in Turkey, Viking ships and the Swedish Warship *Vasa* in Scandinavia, Henry VIII's *Mary Rose* in England, and the Confederate submarine *H. L. Hunley* in the United States.

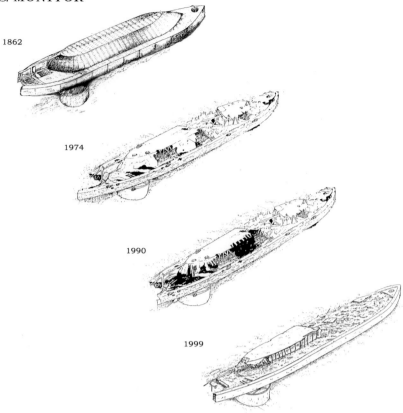

1862

1974

1990

1999

Monitor's hull began to deteriorate at an accelerating rate during the 1980s and 1990s. Archaeologists believe that the stern was damaged at the time of sinking. Courtesy NOAA *Monitor* Collection

That these recovered and preserved vessels have been well received by the public is exemplified by the nearly intact *Vasa*, which has, since its recovery in 1961, been one of the most popular tourist attractions in all of Scandinavia.

By the mid-1990s, we believed that we had accumulated sufficient data for determining NOAA's management policy for *Monitor*'s future. We could point to documentation of a known process of slow, regular transformation by deterioration, the possibility of accelerated change or inadvertent damage because the site's location was widely known, the incredible technological value and historical and archaeological significance of *Monitor*, as well as the ability through archaeology to offer something of educational value to the public. We also had consulted with experts about the engineering and marine salvage feasibility of recovering all or part of the site with a high level of confidence that we would succeed. After years of research, we realized over time that for our "preferred option," there are cases where excavation and recovery is the correct response. *Monitor* was one of them.

Scientific expeditions conducted by NOAA and other agencies during the 1980s generated considerable evidence that *Monitor*'s hull was less stable than had been assumed in the sanctuary management plan. The 1987 survey report went so far as to recommend that NOAA consider options for stabilization and recovery. This same recommendation had been made in the 1970s by several individuals concerned about *Monitor*, particularly Newton, Sheridan, and Edgerton, whose *Monitor* Research and Recovery Foundation had argued strenuously in the 1970s for recovery. In spite of their enthusiastic urging and fund-raising, however, the foundation was unable to raise sufficient funds to pursue its goal or to foster a federal appropriation for a government-led recovery effort.

NOAA had learned from experience that conducting operations at the sanctuary was difficult and expensive, even just for ROV surveys. Experts could not provide accurate estimates for a recovery mission because it was impossible to determine the structural integrity of *Monitor*'s hull. Most salvors who studied the site data expressed doubts that *Monitor* could be recovered intact, that is, the entire hull in one piece. Conservators who treated artifacts from underwater sites declined to even attempt to estimate the cost of conservation of the entire wreck. They pointed out that *Monitor*'s hull was a huge "composite artifact"; that is, composed of wood, iron, and other materials. Because the treatment methods for different materials are not always compatible, the hull, they said, would have to be completely disassembled and the contents removed and separated by type of material.

As if these issues were not enough for NOAA to wrestle with, new developments opened the site to increased visitation by the diving public.

ESCALATING MANAGEMENT ISSUES

Pressure from Recreational Divers for Site Access

In the late 1980s, a new issue emerged. In 1984 Gary Gentile, a recreational diver, submitted a request to the state of North Carolina for a permit to dive on the *Monitor*. On December 4, the North Carolina Division of Archives and History responded that the state "has no authority to grant permits for activities in the *Monitor* National Marine Sanctuary" and suggested that the applicant contact NOAA.[1] Gentile subsequently submitted a request to NOAA for a permit to dive at the *Monitor* sanctuary. The sanctuary program initially denied the request primarily on human safety grounds, because the divers planned to dive to *Monitor*'s 240-foot depth using compressed-air scuba diving gear. NOAA considered such dives to be unsafe, and with good reason. The *US Navy Diving Manual*, the *NOAA Diving Manual*, and the leading recreational scuba certifying organizations recommend that for safety reasons recreational scuba divers breathing compressed air should not descend below 130 feet.[2] One danger is that breathing compressed air at *Monitor*'s depth causes a debilitating condition known as *nitrogen narcosis*. This condition of impairment causes loss of coordination and judgment similar to that of drunkenness. Another danger is that under extreme pressure, oxygen can be toxic, causing convulsions.

The petitioning divers countered, arguing that a newly emerging scuba technique known as "technical diving" made it possible for divers with advanced training to safely breathe air at *Monitor*'s depth.

Eventually Gentile, assisted by attorney Peter Hess, sued NOAA, claiming that the *Monitor* sanctuary belongs to the public and therefore the public has a right to access the sanctuary. They cited provisions of the National Marine Sanctuaries Act that requires NOAA to facilitate public access consistent with NOAA's primary responsibility to protect sanctuary resources. In 1989, Administrative Law Judge Hugh Dolan ruled that NOAA's basis for denying the permit was improperly based on diving standards that applied to employees of NOAA and the US Navy, which had not been incorporated into NOAA sanctuary regulations. Judge Dolan directed NOAA to reconsider the application within the framework of its regulations.

Because of *Monitor*'s exceptional historical and archaeological significance, sanctuary regulations had been written to limit public access to scientific research. NOAA worked with Gentile and other groups to revise their applications to come within the meaning of scientific research expeditions. As a result, limited private research diving began at the *Monitor* sanctuary in 1990. The divers adhered to the permit conditions, made numerous safe dives, and reportedly did not make contact with the wreck. (NOAA's own diving regulations prohibited NOAA from sending an observer down with the divers.)[3]

Gentile and Hess subsequently challenged the NOAA regulation limiting public access to scientific research. Although their challenge was unsuccessful, NOAA ultimately agreed, after observing several seasons of private expeditions, that limited public access for recreational diving was reasonable and appropriate, provided there was no contact with the wreck. Therefore, we developed a Special Use Permit for nonresearch expeditions and, through a competitive bidding process, selected Atlantic Wreck Divers to plan and conduct the dives under the Special Use Permit. During the summer of 1984, Captain Art Kirchner, Atlantic Wreck Divers, took several groups of divers to the sanctuary. Participants expressed their excitement and encouraged us to renew the permit. The following year, Atlantic Wreck Divers successfully obtained a three-year Special Use Permit and nonresearch *Monitor* dives became an annual event until major NOAA/US Navy recovery expeditions commenced.

Once it was clear that we were going to see increasing numbers of divers at the sanctuary, we became concerned that large numbers of divers might

RECREATIONAL DIVERS AT THE *MONITOR* SANCTUARY

In 1990, NOAA awarded the first two nondisturbance research permits to private dive groups, subsequently making possible the first "technical" scuba dives on *Monitor*. Dive teams headed by Roderick M. Farb and Gary Gentile conducted their dives during the summer of 1990 and submitted written reports along with useful video and still imagery of the site to NOAA, opening the door for numerous additional private dives on *Monitor*.

During June 5–13, 1990, the Rod Farb *Monitor* Expedition conducted the first NOAA-permitted open-circuit "technical" scuba dives on *Monitor*. North Carolinian Farb made his first dive to the *Monitor* on his fortieth birthday. The expedition demonstrated that scuba diving to *Monitor*'s depth breathing self-contained air

was a viable method for observing and documenting the wreck. The team, which conducted additional dives during June 18–22, retrieved high-quality still and video images of the site using hand-held cameras. Farb applied computer-aided mapping techniques to the resulting imagery in order to document the wreck more accurately and to identify changes to the site.[1] He also produced a video of the expedition that aired on North Carolina television and at major US dive conferences.

The Gary Gentile *Monitor* Expedition conducted similar technical diving during June 30–July 11, 1990. Most of the Gentile team utilized specially mixed breathing gas, rather than air. This team, too, produced high-quality still and video imagery of the wreck.[2]

Following these two pioneering expeditions, numerous technical diving groups obtained NOAA research permits for the *Monitor* sanctuary, all providing copies of imagery, observations, and measurements that contributed to the growing volume of

Terrence Tysall (center, blue top) briefs Cambrian Foundation team members before a *Monitor* dive. Courtesy Cambrian Foundation

data on the wreck. Of all groups that dove *Monitor*, none provided as much valuable assistance as the Cambrian Foundation, a not-for-profit organization dedicated to utilizing their diving skills for science.[3] These skilled and dedicated divers planned their expeditions around NOAA's stated data needs, resulting in the acquisition of essential data ranging from precise measurements and site sketches to high-quality video and still imagery.

The level of cooperation between NOAA and private dive groups grew during the 1990s, and the contributions those divers made to NOAA's efforts to document and preserve *Monitor* should not be underestimated. Eventually, private "technical" divers not only helped train some members of our NOAA team, they also participated in several NOAA dives at the *Monitor* sanctuary and elsewhere.

In 1990 Rod Farb and his team of "technical" divers conducted the first successful private dives on *Monitor*. Courtesy Joe Poe

Farb used measurements and videotape of key elements of *Monitor*'s hull to establish baseline data from which future changes could be determined. Courtesy Joe Poe

Notes:

1. Farb (1998, 397–402).
2. Gentile (1993).
3. http://www.cambrianfoundation.org /category/uss-monitor/

cause an increased rate of deterioration of *Monitor* and its contents, despite their high skill level, through inadvertent or even intentional disturbance of the wreck. While I have dived with many wreck divers who are highly skilled and in control of their actions, I have witnessed others becoming disoriented or panicky and banging into fragile objects or disturbing artifacts from their resting places. Similarly, I believe that most of today's divers are conscientious, mindful of fragile sites, and aware that wrecks like *Monitor* are essentially a museum beneath the sea with a "take only pictures, leave only bubbles" rule. However, I also knew from firsthand experience that some "old school" wreck divers just can't resist a souvenir, even if it comes from a site protected by law for everyone to enjoy and appreciate. Far too many historic objects end up in divers' trophy cases where very few people will ever see or appreciate them.

Public access is an issue for managers of all public lands, dry or submerged. Sometimes there is a fine balance between allowing access to public resources and protecting those resources for future generations. Given *Monitor*'s significance and a body of evidence suggesting that its hull and contents were fragile and unstable, we found it difficult to determine an appropriate set of access rules. On the one hand, divers might damage the *Monitor*, and on the other, divers might be injured or killed by entrapment or collapsing structure. We needed to ensure that we could maintain the proper balance between protection and access. Difficulty notwithstanding, NOAA developed access rules that made it possible for a small but dedicated segment of the public to share the experience of visiting *Monitor* in person.

Damage from Fishing Activities

In 1991, the US Coast Guard discovered a recreational fishing boat from Hatteras anchored within the *Monitor* sanctuary. Subsequent inspections by NOAA produced evidence that a boat, presumably the one apprehended, had damaged *Monitor*'s stern. Video collected by a *Johnson-Sea-Link* submersible clearly showed areas on the armor belt where corrosion and marine life had been scraped away, exposing the metal to fresh corrosion and loss. More alarming, however, was video showing that the boat's anchor had snagged *Monitor*'s skeg—the heavy beam that supported the propeller and rudder—ripping it loose from the lower hull. The fact that a small boat could do such substantial damage heightened NOAA's concerns about the fragile nature of *Monitor*'s hull.

REASSESSMENT OF NOAA'S *MONITOR* MANAGEMENT STRATEGY

In April 1992, I was hired as the new manager of the *Monitor* National Marine Sanctuary. I attributed my selection to my long relationship with North Carolina's Underwater Archaeology Branch and my participation in NOAA *Monitor* expeditions and advisory committees. I was intimately familiar with the site and with the threats to *Monitor*'s hull and contents, but I needed to learn more about how NOAA and SRD operated and what options might be available for dealing with the *Monitor* crisis.

I immediately sought advice from NOAA personnel, especially Bruce Terrell, SRD maritime historian, and Dina Hill, the only other *Monitor* sanctuary staff member. Hill had been directly involved with the *Monitor* since its discovery in 1973, and had been serving as acting manager for nearly a year. She was an indispensable source of institutional knowledge and advice concerning the development of sanctuary policy and research. I also relied heavily on outside advice from *Monitor* experts at ECU, Harbor Branch, and other agencies and organizations, especially Gordon Watts, who had remained involved in *Monitor* research and whom I considered to be the leading expert on the ship and its current condition.

We quickly developed a list of data needs, based partly on recommendations from previous researchers. Most of the data would have to be collected at the sanctuary, which meant we needed to schedule another expedition. I soon discovered that my budget was not nearly sufficient to conduct a meaningful site visit in 1992 or 1993. Fortunately, the SRD staff helped me write and submit a grant proposal to the University National Oceanographic Laboratory System (UNOLS) program that resulted in the *Monitor* sanctuary receiving sufficient grant funds to lease a vessel for the conduct of a *Monitor* expedition sometime during 1993. We immediately began outlining an operations plan employing diving archaeologists to collect data.

Private research divers examine the gaping tear in *Monitor*'s stern caused by a fishing boat that snagged its anchor on *Monitor*'s skeg. Photo by Rod Farb, Courtesy NOAA *Monitor* Collection

NOAA MARSS Expedition, 1993

Our expedition, which we designated the *Monitor* Archaeological Research and Structural Survey (MARSS), would be sponsored by NOAA's Sanctuaries and Reserves Division (SRD) and the UNOLS grant, with limited assistance from the US Coast Guard. We designed our operations plan based on the amount of available funding and our desire for a close-up inspection of *Monitor*. We felt that the best way to assess the condition of the wreck was through submersible lockout diving operations.

The Harbor Branch Oceanographic Institution (formerly the Harbor Branch Foundation, NOAA's partner for three previous *Monitor* expeditions) submitted the successful competitive bid to supply support equipment and personnel for the expedition. I was delighted with our rapid progress except for one major problem. Because of the very limited demand for lockout capabilities, Harbor Branch had reconfig-

ured their ships and *Johnson-Sea-Link* submersibles for one-atmosphere dives only—no lockout diving. We had not been able to locate any companies offering lockout subs, so we sought a plan B.

Conducting our own dives on *Monitor* was a problem. The wreck lies at a water depth that is a bit too deep for conventional scuba and NOAA did not allow its divers to descend below the no-decompression, compressed air limits. However, fortune smiled once again. I was able to convince Dr. Morgan Wells, director of NOAA's Experimental Diving Unit, of the importance of getting diving archaeologists on *Monitor*. Wells offered for the NOAA Diving Program and the NOAA Experimental Diving Unit to develop a dive plan and to supervise the training and onsite dives. This was excellent news, since Wells was well-known and respected in the military and scientific dive communities. In the 1970s, he was largely responsible for the acceptance and popularity of "Nitrox," a blend of nitrogen and oxygen that is now in widespread use. He developed a method for mixing the gas, and then published decompression tables for two mixes, NOAA Nitrox I and II.[4] These two mixes, along with the well-proven tables, are still popular in recreational and scientific diving. Wells often promoted the use of Nitrox by telling divers, "Nitrox is as good as air, only better."[5]

Wells built the dive plan around a NOAA open diving bell and a breathing gas suitable for *Monitor*'s depth. We would not breathe heliox, as before, but instead would use a mixture of oxygen, helium, and nitrogen generally referred to as "tri-mix." Since Wells optimized the proportion of gasses for *Monitor*'s depth, we soon began referring to the formula as "*Monitor* Mix."[6]

Because NOAA had not previously conducted mixed gas dives, we assembled a scientific dive team composed of NOAA divers and experienced university and private divers. We invited Roderick Farb, who had conducted the first private dives on *Monitor*, to join the team as a technical advisor. He accepted, and we relied heavily on his skills and experience during dive training and at the sanctuary. Rod's role underscored the new relationship we developed with divers who were not only interested in seeing history underwater, but in helping to learn more about it.

Dr. Wells took the lead on dive procedures and safety, with support from the NOAA Diving Pro-gram, headed by Cliff Newell. The dive program also supplied personnel and equipment. In the spring of 1993 we assembled our dive team at Harbor Branch's facility in Fort Pierce, Florida, where we rigged the NOAA open bell on the deck of the R/V *Edwin Link*, the vessel we would be using onsite. We conducted a week of training that included classroom and diving exercises.

Our dive procedure required the surface vessel to remain stationary over the site during diving operations, a duty for which the *Link* was not designed. The US Navy came to our rescue, tasking the Submarine Rescue Ship USS *Ortolan* (ASR-22), stationed at Little Creek, Virginia, with installing a temporary four-point mooring for our use. Once *Edwin Link* was secured in the mooring, its position was adjusted on the four mooring lines so that the diving bell would descend precisely to a predetermined position near *Monitor*'s hull. This process involved having *J-S-L II* place a sonar beacon on the wreck, then aligning the vessel to the correct position using the ship's integrated navigational system.

Unfortunately, the MARSS expedition suffered one of the worst extended periods of bad weather ever encountered in the sanctuary. Not long after *Ortolan* disappeared over the horizon, the wind shifted, straining our bow mooring lines. With great difficulty, since *Link* was not designed for moored operations, we rotated the ship 90 degrees to bring its

Harbor Branch's R/V *Edwin Link* and the *Johnson-Sea-Link II* submersible supported NOAA's 1993 *Monitor* Expedition. Courtesy NOAA *Monitor* Collection

bow into the wind. Just after dark the wind strengthened and swung back to where it was when we first moored.

Before we could react, our port bow mooring line—a thick, double-braided nylon rope that I kept as a reminder—chafed against the ship and parted with a loud bang. Crew and scientists responded to the emergency as *Link* swung to starboard, where the huge waves crashed against its side, causing it to jerk and roll violently. A crisis quickly developed in the stern, as *Link* drifted dangerously close to one of *Ortolan*'s huge steel mooring buoys. Had they collided, waves may have lifted the buoy onto Link's low stern and into the submersible. One can only guess what damage the ship would have suffered. By this time, nonessential personnel were gathering at their lifeboat stations while the rest of us ran around the deck, trying to follow orders from the ship's officers and otherwise stay out of the way.

In the stern, several turns of the port mooring line were wrapped around the small steel winch drum used for the sub. The strain from the mooring line was so immense the drum imploded, throwing a spray of shrapnel that penetrated the steel side of the ship and peppered the superstructure where Bruce Terrell and my boss, Randy Schneider, were standing. An alert crewman lashed his knife to a boathook and cut the line, which let the ship drift away from the menacing buoy. We were safe, but we had to leave the mooring and transit to Morehead City, North Carolina, to repair the mooring lines. Someone tried to joke that we must have been trying to reenact the sinking of *Monitor*, but not many of us found humor there. (A crew member, shooting video for the National Geographic Society, brilliantly captured most of the action and our ordeal later aired on National Geographic Explorer.)

I hoped that we had paid our dues to the sea gods and that the rest of the expedition would be straightforward. After all, this was my first expedition as sanctuary manager and I wanted to produce results. Unfortunately, the sea gods were not yet finished with us. (Or was it the "Curse of the *Monitor*," well-known to insiders?) We suffered rough seas, frequent squalls, waterspouts, and poor bottom conditions throughout our time onsite. In spite of these setbacks, we conducted nine submersible dives and three dives with the diving bell. We managed to achieve several of our primary goals, including placement of a 1,000-pound concrete mooring block near the wreck for use on future expeditions. We designed the mooring to provide a fixed location for divers to descend and then conduct in-water decompression during ascent. We hoped this mooring would provide safe access for NOAA and the private divers who had begun to conduct annual research at the sanctuary.

We also conducted a small test excavation inside the turret using a thruster mounted on the front of the submersible to "fan" silt from the turret. Seated in the pilot sphere, only a few feet from the thruster, I was able to direct the fanning operation so that we did not displace any cultural material. We saw no evidence of the turret's deck, even though Watts reported encountering decking in 1979. Apparently, at least some of the wooden deck planks were destroyed by *Teredo navalis* (commonly called shipworms) soon after *Monitor* sank. No artifacts were encountered.

The MARSS documented new evidence of hull

The NOAA open diving bell being readied for use during the 1993 *Monitor* Expedition. Courtesy NOAA *Monitor* Collection

In 1993, Morgan Wells (right) and Cliff Newell of the NOAA Diving Program developed and supervised the first NOAA dives on *Monitor*; those dives were the first deep mixed-gas dives ever conducted by NOAA divers. Courtesy NOAA *Monitor* Collection

deterioration and learned more about the contents of the turret. We also recorded approximately sixteen hours of high-resolution videotape. Even though our diving had been severely curtailed, NOAA was satisfied with our results. The NOAA Dive Program accepted tri-mix as a viable option for limited scientific diving to a maximum depth of 300 feet, and the gas mixture became known as "NOAA Tri-Mix." The associated dive tables have been used on several NOAA-sponsored research projects.

We had confirmed for ourselves that the rate of deterioration of *Monitor*'s hull had increased and it

was clear that the hull could not remain intact much longer. The weight of the engine and boilers was constantly pressing down on a part of the hull that was suspended above the bottom by the turret. The armored deck had already partially caved in at the point where it made contact with the turret. As a result of these findings, I set a high priority on re-evaluating *Monitor* management options, and assessing the possible need for large-scale recovery.

NOAA MARRS Expedition, 1995

Two years later, we conducted the *Monitor* Archaeological Research, Recovery, and Stabilization Expedition (MARRS'95) consisting of two segments: one, a NOAA diving reconnaissance operation, and two, a major effort to help stabilize *Monitor*'s stern by recovering its propeller. We had previously documented that the 1991 anchoring incident initiated an ongoing chain reaction of deterioration and collapse in the stern. The massive iron skeg that formerly supported the propeller and rudder had been pulled loose from the lower hull, causing it to shift off to the starboard side. The remaining stern structure in the vicinity of the propeller and shaft appeared to be badly deteriorated. We were afraid that the skeg's shift would place the considerable weight of the propeller and shaft on the lowest propeller blade and on the engine itself. Therefore, we hoped that removal

The author (left, with back to camera) and Rod Farb preparing for a *Monitor* dive in 1993. Courtesy NOAA *Monitor* Collection

A Navy dive team assigned to the salvage ship USS *Edenton* attempted to recover *Monitor*'s propeller in 1995. Courtesy NOAA *Monitor* Collection

of the propeller and shaft would lessen the strain on the damaged stern and also help stabilize the engine.

This was the first large-scale collaborative effort between NOAA and the US Navy. The Navy had not agreed to fully support NOAA's request for long-term assistance with *Monitor*. However, USS *Edenton* (ATS-1), the US Navy's only ship in the Atlantic Fleet at that time that was capable of mixed-gas diving, was given approval to conduct a dive training exercise at the *Monitor* sanctuary in order to increase the mixed-gas diving capabilities of Navy salvage divers.

Our NOAA team, including the R/V *Elusive*, from the University of North Carolina at Wilmington, assembled at Hatteras on August 13 for briefings and equipment preparation. By the next morning, Hatteras was experiencing heavy surf from Hurricane Felix, which was threatening us from the south. We learned that all Navy vessels in Hampton Roads were on alert for a possible "hurricane sortie," which would send many of the warships to preassigned stations until the hurricane had passed. At the US Coast Guard Station at Hatteras Inlet, we unpacked all our dive gear, and set up the gas mixing equipment in preparation for our training dives.

We awoke the next morning to the wail of evac-

uation sirens! A mandatory hurricane evacuation order had been issued for the entire Outer Banks, so we had to quickly pack our personal effects, vacate our housing units, load up all the dive gear that we had laboriously set up the previous day, and get in the long line of cars seeking safety on the mainland. Hurricane Felix had disrupted everything. *Edenton* sortied out to sea, *Elusive* returned to Wilmington, and our team collected at my office at Fort Eustis, near Newport News, Virginia. Everyone was discussing options and scrambling to adjust their schedules for the delay. The Outer Banks finally reopened on August 18, and we left for Hatteras the next day. Fortunately, everyone was able to return, and we were able to conduct successful training dives. With Commander John Paul Johnston as the commanding officer, *Edenton* departed its homeport of Little Creek, Virginia, on August 22 and was moored over *Monitor* the next day. However, currents were too strong for diving.

Finally, on August 24–25 we conducted the first NOAA self-contained (untethered) dives on *Monitor*. Our dives were only possible because *Edenton* was onsite and capable of treating a dive emergency, should we have problems. We prepared extensively

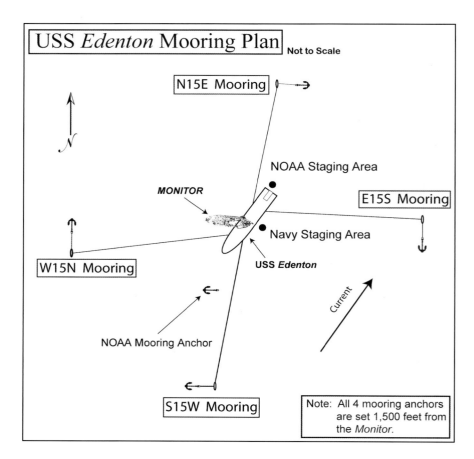

USS *Edenton* Mooring Plan Not to Scale

N15E Mooring

NOAA Staging Area

MONITOR

E15S Mooring

Navy Staging Area

W15N Mooring

USS *Edenton*

Current

NOAA Mooring Anchor

S15W Mooring

Note: All 4 mooring anchors are set 1,500 feet from the *Monitor*.

USS *Edenton* carried all the gear necessary for positioning itself over *Monitor*'s hull on a four-point mooring. This mooring system, used by almost all the ships and barges at the *Monitor* site, allowed the vessel's position to be adjusted, as necessary, to permit diving and recovery at specific points on *Monitor*'s hull. Courtesy NOAA *Monitor* Collection

for those dives, getting our training from Key West Divers, a facility respected for its attention to safety. The highlight of the dives occurred on August 25 when Navy divers, walking on the seabed wearing helmets and breathing surface-supplied gas, met our NOAA dive team—swimming overhead in a self-contained mode—at *Monitor*'s stern. For my dive buddy Craig McLean and me, this was an important and enjoyable new milestone in the history of NOAA diving.

NOAA made two dives and the Navy made seventeen before operations were halted by the threat of Hurricanes Humberto and Iris. Divers wrapped a Kevlar strap around the propeller and shaft and inspected the propeller blades. They discovered that large concentrations of encrustation and marine growth cemented three of the four blades to the hull, adding yet another task to be accomplished before the propeller could be removed. They chipped all of the encrustation from the section of shaft where the cut would be made. They had just prepared to cut when, on September 2, severe storms forced *Edenton* to disconnect from their mooring buoys and return to Little Creek.

On October 2, I boarded *Edenton* at Little Creek for a return to Hatteras. This time I took a NOAA video camera and a special bracket made by The Mariners' Museum that would let us lower the camera down a weighted line to check bottom conditions before sending divers down. The following day we checked bottom conditions with the video camera, then Navy divers descended to the wreck and connected a specially made grounding plate to the propeller shaft. On the next dive, at 4:34 p.m., divers began cutting the shaft, using a Broco underwater cutting unit with high-temperature exothermic rods. On the next dive, the exothermic rod encountered an imperfection in the metal, causing a small explosion that shattered the diver's welding visor, and terminating the dive. By the next morning, heavy seas forced *Edenton* to leave the mooring again. Undaunted, *Edenton* returned again on October 17, but strong currents and building seas forced the crew to recover the moorings and terminate the expedition for the season. The power of Hatteras had thwarted human intervention once again.

The research vessel *Elusive* was used to deploy NOAA divers on *Monitor* while Navy divers were descending to the wreck from USS *Edenton*. Courtesy NOAA *Monitor* Collection

A LONG-RANGE, COMPREHENSIVE PRESERVATION PLAN FOR *MONITOR*

By 1995 concern over the *Monitor* crisis had become widespread, due to consistent reports that the *Monitor*'s hull was on the verge of collapse. That year NOAA Administrator D. James Baker stated, "Stabilizing the USS *Monitor* is one of the more important maritime archaeological expeditions of this decade.

It is critical that we work to preserve the integrity of this National Historic Landmark."[7]

As part of the National Marine Sanctuary Program's annual report to Congress, it was my job to present a yearly update on NOAA's progress at the *Monitor* sanctuary and any new changes in *Monitor*'s condition. In 1996, Congress responded to my report of *Monitor*'s worsening condition by mandating that the secretary of commerce produce "a long-range,

NOAA diving history was made when Navy and NOAA divers met at *Monitor*'s stern during the 1995 expedition. Here, the author (left) joins a Navy diver in examining *Monitor*'s propeller. Courtesy NOAA *Monitor* Collection

comprehensive plan for the management, stabilization, preservation, and recovery of artifacts and materials of the U.S.S. MONITOR."[8] The secretary was also directed, "to the extent feasible utilize the resources of other Federal and private entities with expertise and capabilities that are helpful" and to submit the plan within twelve months of the date of enactment of the Act, which was October 11, 1996.[9] Unfortunately, no funding was allocated for producing the report.

Development of the Monitor Preservation Plan

NOAA's National Marine Sanctuary Program, primarily the *Monitor* National Marine Sanctuary staff, was responsible for developing the *Monitor* comprehensive plan. Even though no funding had been appropriated for plan preparation, we were well positioned to respond rapidly to this requirement for several reasons. First, research data we had collected over more than twenty years had already alerted NOAA that a critical situation was developing at the *Monitor* site; second, based on that knowledge, we had already been exploring options for action; and finally, we had already enlisted numerous outside agencies and organizations in the effort to find acceptable solutions to the *Monitor* crisis.

We quickly determined that the *Monitor* comprehensive plan must contain certain essential elements, including present and predicted conditions of the wreck and its contents; a list of options for recovery, including the feasibility and estimated costs for each option; along with proposed methodologies and costs for conservation and exhibition. We were also determined to ensure that the plan adhered to cultural resource management best practices, as defined by the Federal Archaeological Program.

Almost immediately, we began seeking internal funding and support while, at the same, identifying interested outside parties that might be willing to assist with various aspects of the plan. Based on its previous research and planning, we were aware that we must get input from experts in salvage, diving, engineering, archaeology, geology, biology, and conservation, as well as additional detailed information on *Monitor*'s construction. We also were certain we needed additional site data in order to develop detailed engineering recommendations.

For the engineering and salvage plans, I knew we needed someone on staff with an intimate knowledge of *Monitor*'s construction, right down to the rivets, and I knew just the man for the job. *Monitor* sanctuary contractor Jeffrey Johnston, a historian who had built operating models of *Monitor* and other ships as a hobby, already possessed a great deal of knowledge about the ship. I asked Jeff to study all existing plans and construction details of *Monitor*, as well as data accumulated by NOAA researchers, and then develop a compendium of construction information that we could provide to engineering and salvage experts. Jeff quickly became the "go-to guy" for details related to *Monitor*'s size, weight, machinery, crew, or anything else related to the ship. His expertise proved indispensable throughout planning and implementation. Dina Hill, the only other permanent member of the staff, was our "corporate memory." When we needed information from an earlier site report or policy memo, all we had to do was give Dina a general description and she would magically produce one or more relevant documents.

During plan development in 1997, the US Navy provided advice and expertise on a not-to-interfere basis, but we quickly realized that we needed additional assistance on engineering and salvage issues. Fortunately, Craig Mullen, president of Eastport International Inc., the Navy's Undersea Operations contractor at the time, offered, with approval from the Navy, to develop a preliminary *Monitor* "trade-off study" at no cost to the government.[10] Mullen had assisted the Navy and NOAA during previous *Monitor* expeditions and had developed a strong interest in this historic ship and the engineering challenges the site presented. Shortly thereafter, Eastport was acquired by Oceaneering International Inc., a major international marine services company, and Oceaneering honored the agreement to prepare the *Monitor* study.

Oceaneering's objective in this preliminary proposal was to provide a top level concept of operation for the emergency recovery, stabilization, and preservation of the *Monitor*; and to provide an initial plan for state and federal Section 106 review, a predisturbance requirement for historic properties.[11] Oceaneering told us that given the voluminous amount of information generated during previous expeditions and research, they felt they could perform a series of trade-off studies using the more viable concepts to determine the best combined approach for providing for the long-term preservation of the *Monitor* and associated historic material. The objective of these studies, they said, was to select a single approach or "Concept of Operation" that would lead to a successful outcome.

A "trade-off study" identifies options for action, comparing the pros and cons of those options, and choosing the best option based on "trade-offs" within specified parameters, such as feasibility, safety, cost, and so forth. Oceaneering identified six key trade studies and defined an objective for each. The Oceaneering team selected methodologies to be evaluated for each study, and then listed major advantages and disadvantages for each selected methodology. Oceaneering evaluated each selected methodology based on a set of criteria, weighted on a 1 to 10 scale based on the team's judgment of the overall relevance and value of each. Finally, each trade-off was studied by the team and validated by a separate panel consisting of three individuals outside of the proposal team.[12]

On April 25, 1997, Oceaneering submitted the study to the Navy's Supervisor of Salvage, Diving, and Ocean Engineering (SUPSALV). Oceaneering's study formed a solid basis for decision making and planning for the *Monitor* comprehensive plan. We included a summary of the Oceaneering study in the plan.[13]

On November 6, 1997—just within the congressionally mandated one-year time frame—NOAA submitted the *Monitor* comprehensive plan to Congress on behalf of the secretary of commerce. The plan, *Charting a New Course for the Monitor*, described the extent of deterioration, outlined a variety of possible options for the stabilization and preservation, and discussed advantages, disadvantages, and costs for each option.

Because of *Monitor*'s exceptional historical significance and the severity of the perceived threat to its hull and contents, NOAA first released the plan in draft form in order to permit a NOAA-created panel of experts and the public at large to review it and provide comments. We received nearly 100 written comments, all but two expressing support or strong support for the recommended option. We took all comments, general and technical, into account and in April 1998 published the final preservation plan and submitted it to Congress.

Summary of NOAA's Final Long-Range, Comprehensive Preservation Plan for Monitor

We included six options in the plan, ranging from a "no-action" option to full recovery of *Monitor* and all its contents; we also listed two combined options. We selected and recommended shoring combined with selective recovery as our preferred option (see sidebar).

Our decision was based on the conclusion that it was not feasible to recover the entire ship and its contents because the hull was too badly deteriorated to survive a salvage attempt. Given that assumption, we reasoned that recovery of some of *Monitor*'s most important and recognizable components was not only feasible, but would provide new information on the ship and, very likely, clues to why it sank. The second part of this option was stabilization of the remaining portion of the hull by shoring up the portion of deck raised above the seabed. This option also argued that it was in the best interests of the nation to preserve key parts of *Monitor* for future generations. Although we had no accurate cost estimate, our best guess was that this option would cost at least $20 to 22 million, including conservation.

After presenting all options and recommending a combination of shoring followed by selective recovery, the plan proposed a six-phase approach for implementation that included a detailed predisturbance survey, hull stabilization, component removal in a predetermined sequence, and a postremoval survey and additional stabilization as required. In 1997, even as the draft plan was being written, *Monitor* NMS staff was actively conducting research and planning in support of whatever option would be chosen. Working closely with the US Navy's Office of Supervisor of Salvage, Diving, and Ocean Engineering; Oceaneering International; the Navy's diving, search, and undersea operations contractor; and others, NOAA began considering how the various options might be funded and implemented.

Considerations for Implementing the Recommended Option

In order to develop detailed implementation plans, we had to consider the complex nature of deepwater recovery operations, the adverse environmental

MONITOR PRESERVATION PLAN—OPTIONS AND PHASED IMPLEMENTATION

In developing options for the *Monitor* Comprehensive, Long-Range Preservation Plan requested by Congress, NOAA relied heavily on the Oceaneering International trade study. In addition, *Monitor* sanctuary staff reviewed all previous reports and proposals for onsite activities, including previous archaeological, engineering, and corrosion reports; current and draft revised *Monitor* management plans; and other documents. The Mariners' Museum provided expertise on conservation and curation needs, as well as options for exhibition. NOAA also held informal discussions with scores of engineers, archaeologists, and other specialists in order to identify potential new technology and funding sources that could be applied to the *Monitor* situation. The resulting plan identified a range of options for stabilizing and/or preserving *Monitor*.

Option 1 was to continue managing the *Monitor* as before, with no onsite intervention, a continuation of NOAA's preferred option when it was assumed that *Monitor* was stable. The advantage was that no changes in budget or management strategy would be required; the obvious disadvantage was *Monitor*'s continued and unchecked disintegration and its inac-

cessibility to all but a very few people. Options 2 through 4 considered in situ preservation through shoring up or burying the hull, or by installing cathodic protection to slow the rate of deterioration. Expert opinion was that none of these methods would prevent the continued deterioration of *Monitor*'s hull and contents, even though the process might be slowed. Even complete encapsulation of the hull by bottom sediments would be subject to constant erosion that would reexpose parts of the wreck and, in addition, burial would not stop all of the processes that caused deterioration.

Option 5 proposed recovering only specific components and artifacts that had been determined by NOAA and others to possess exceptional historic value, such as the propeller, engine, turret, guns, and small artifacts (these items represented approximately 20 percent of the total weight of *Monitor* and its contents). Option 6, the final option, examined the possibilities for full recovery of *Monitor* and all its contents. Several combined options were also considered, including shoring plus cathodic protection or shoring plus partial recovery.

NOAA determined that stabilization options could be achieved with

less technological difficulty, lower cost, and less risk to the resource than recovery options, but that stabilization would, at best, only delay the inevitable collapse of *Monitor*'s hull. Eventually, NOAA would still have to decide if major components of the ship would be recovered for preservation and exhibition. Input from experts in engineering, salvage, chemistry, and conservation all suggested that an attempt to recover the entire hull and its contents would be incredibly expensive, likely to fail, and even if successful would produce a conservation nightmare that would likely cost in excess of $100 million. Therefore, NOAA concluded that the best and most achievable option was option 8: first shore up *Monitor*'s hull and then recover the components and artifacts that represent the ironclad's most significant features and historic characteristics.

Once NOAA made that decision, the agency began working closely with the US Navy, the Navy's salvage contractor, Oceaneering International, The Mariners' Museum, and others to develop a detailed implementation plan. The resulting plan consisted of six major phases, to be conducted, if possible, in the sequence presented.

(continued)

conditions at the sanctuary, and the fragile nature of *Monitor* and its contents. One of the most important factors we had to bear in mind was the severity and unpredictability of the site environment. The most favorable weather window is historically June through September. Unfortunately that window overlaps the annual hurricane season. When we reviewed all NOAA and private expeditions to the sanctuary since 1990 we found that, on average, we were only able to dive one day out of three. That

estimate included expeditions staged from large research vessels and US Navy salvage ships as well as from small craft. Therefore, planning had to include a generous allocation of "lay-by days" to account for adverse weather.

We also had to keep in mind that *Monitor* is a highly significant, yet fragile, historical resource, and, in addition, might contain human remains. Stabilization options, including cathodic protection, shoring by mechanical supports, and shoring with

PHASE I: PREDISTURBANCE ARCHAEOLOGICAL SURVEY, MAPPING, AND RECOVERY

A NOAA archaeological survey team would closely survey, map, and recover exposed artifacts in areas likely to be impacted by the planned stabilization and recovery. Special attention would be paid to mapping beneath the elevated port side of the hull, from the bow to aft of the turret, where shoring was to take place. All work was to be accomplished without divers venturing beneath the hull.

PHASE II: SHORING BENEATH THE HULL

US Navy divers would develop a shoring plan based on a Navy determination of the most appropriate and safe method that could be installed by divers. Consideration would be given to pumped sand, prefilled sandbags, pumped "grout" (pumping a type of cement into preinstalled bags), mechanical jacks or supports, or a combination of methods. Special consideration was to be given to supporting the area beneath the boilers and engine, whose weight was exerting considerable downward stress on the hull. The plan specified that shoring had to be completed before engine or turret recovery commenced.

PHASE III: REMOVAL OF DRIVE TRAIN (SKEG, PROPELLER, LOWER HULL, AND ENGINE)

Navy divers would remove the skeg (an iron support for the rudder and propeller), which was already partially separated from the hull, and place it on the seabed to the south of the wreck. Then the propeller shaft would be cut and the propeller and shaft lifted to the surface. The lower hull over the engine room would be cut away and placed on the seabed near the skeg. The engine would then be disconnected and raised to the surface. (Note: planners developed this phase so that if onsite time and equipment were not available to accomplish all work at the same time, the skeg, propeller/shaft, and engine could be recovered in one, two, or three site visits.)

PHASE IV: REMOVAL OF THE ARMOR BELT AND HULL SECTION ABOVE THE TURRET

After considering several possible methods for gaining access to the turret, it was determined that the best approach for avoiding damage to the turret—the most significant object to be recovered—was to remove the damaged hull and armor belt section directly above the turret to provide a clear work area above and around the turret. With the hull shored up from beneath (phase II) and the drive train—engine, shaft, propeller, and skeg—removed (phase III), planners believed that the removal of the hull and armor belt from above the turret would not create significant new stresses on the hull.

PHASE V: REMOVAL OF THE TURRET

With the turret cleared of overhead obstructions during phase IV, it would now be rigged and raised. A specially designed support cradle would be attached to the turret by Navy divers and rigged to a lifting crane on a surface barge. The cradle would support the turret on all sides and, to the fullest extent possible, from beneath, before the lift to the surface.

PHASE VI: POSTRECOVERY SURVEY AND STABILIZATION

Following completion of all recovery operations, an archaeological and engineering survey would assess the condition of the remaining hull and contents to determine if the hull was adequately shored up and stabilized. The survey would also note, and possibly recover, exposed artifacts that could be damaged if left on the site.

(continued)

---

sand, sandbags, or grout bags, posed their own potential damage to hull and contents. If not carried out properly, the process of installing mechanical shoring material might itself cause significant damage to the wreck.

Recovery methodology required even more precautions, since the most dangerous phase of any recovery operation is raising large objects through the air-water interface. There are countless instances of recovery operations that successfully rigged and raised large objects from the seabed, only to have them dashed to pieces against the side of a barge or torn apart by gravity when they were raised from the water, causing all of their weight to be concentrated on a few cables or straps.

NOAA considered proper archaeological control of all onsite activities to be of paramount importance. We recognized that the operations plan had to clearly delineate the responsibilities of all key personnel and provide guidelines and thresholds for

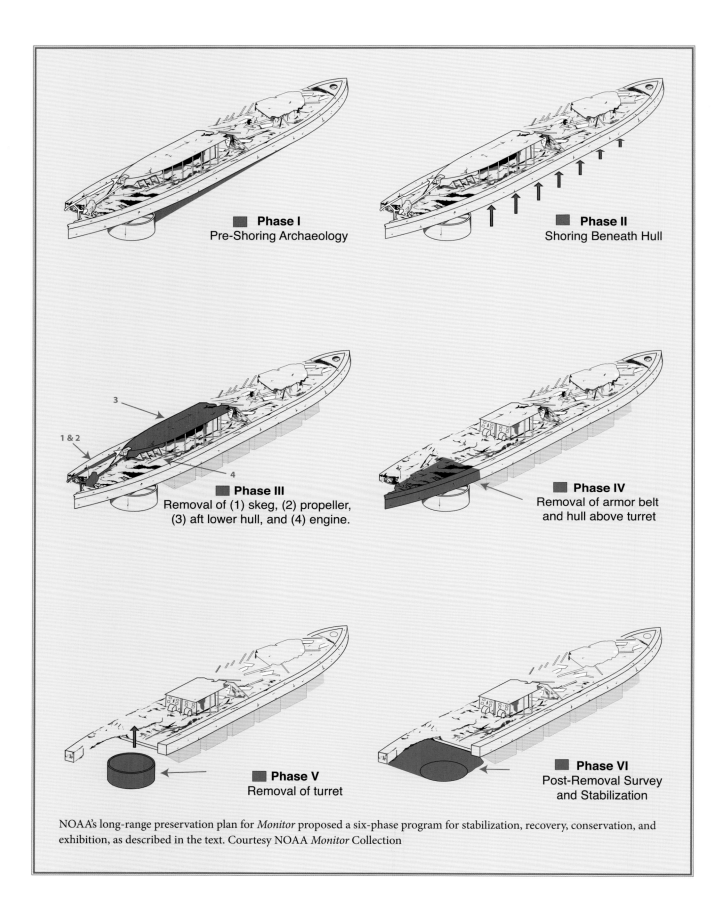

Phase I
Pre-Shoring Archaeology

Phase II
Shoring Beneath Hull

Phase III
Removal of (1) skeg, (2) propeller,
(3) aft lower hull, and (4) engine.

Phase IV
Removal of armor belt
and hull above turret

Phase V
Removal of turret

Phase VI
Post-Removal Survey
and Stabilization

NOAA's long-range preservation plan for *Monitor* proposed a six-phase program for stabilization, recovery, conservation, and exhibition, as described in the text. Courtesy NOAA *Monitor* Collection

possible cessation or termination of onsite activities due to weather, technological problems, or other factors. The plan had to require that all onsite operations be conducted under the close scrutiny of a qualified archaeologist familiar with *Monitor* and the surrounding environment. The project archaeologist needed the authority to halt operations if continuing might damage *Monitor* beyond acceptable limits.

Archaeological survey, mapping, and small-object recovery operations had to take place before any large-scale stabilization or recovery operations commenced. The predisturbance activities needed to provide for mapping, documentation, and recovery of artifacts likely to be moved, damaged, or destroyed during stabilization/recovery operations.

Conservation of the finds is always a major consideration on any underwater project when planning archaeological recovery. We expected the *Monitor* site to yield cultural objects consisting of a wide variety of materials, including iron, brass, copper, wood, hemp, ceramics, and glass. Some objects would be constructed from a variety of materials, which would make them more difficult to treat. Initially, onsite conservation would consist primarily of ensuring that recovered objects were stabilized and protected from damage until they could be transferred to a laboratory for treatment. Laboratory conservation would be a major effort and would require a sizable facility and staff.

The comprehensive plan also included provisions for developing a major public exhibition that would incorporate many of the artifacts recovered from *Monitor*. Some of the objects might not be suitable for exhibition because of poor condition, unwieldy size, or other factors. However, those objects still required conservation before being placed into secure storage to be maintained in a stable condition for future study and inspection.

NOAA understood at the outset that implementation costs would run into tens of millions of dollars. In the year we spent preparing the comprehensive plan, however, we did not have sufficient information or resources to prepare a detailed budget or list of possible funding sources. Except for initial mapping and small-scale artifact recovery, we were determined that no onsite intervention should take place until adequate funding was committed for completion of all phases of the project, including conservation. Fortunately, we were able to establish an alliance of federal, state, and private organizations with an in-terest in preserving *Monitor*, and the resulting partnership—primarily NOAA, the US Navy, and The Mariners' Museum—was able to attract additional partners and generate the support necessary to carry out the recommendations of the *Monitor* plan.

Federal law provides that sites listed on the National Register of Historic Places are subject to protection, and proposed activities that might result in potential adverse effects to the resource must be reviewed. Since *Monitor* was a National Historic Landmark, the new plan had to be reviewed by state and federal officials, in compliance with the law.

Because of the predicted disintegration of *Monitor*, we proposed that *Monitor* be classified as a threatened site. Federal law contains special provisions for threatened sites, with consideration being given to the relative impact to a threatened resource if left undisturbed versus taking positive action to preserve as much of the resource as possible. We argued that in *Monitor*'s case, if positive action were not taken to stabilize the hull and/or recover some of the material, the entire site would be irreparably damaged by continued deterioration, possibly within five years. Therefore, the risk of collateral damage during shoring and recovery operations was somewhat mitigated, especially when considering that recovered portions of the *Monitor* would be preserved in perpetuity. The significance of this particular wreck, coupled with intense public interest, also contributed to NOAA's decision to raise parts of the wreck, thus arresting the changes wrought by time and environment and preserving *Monitor*'s essence for public display and education.

FINAL RECOMMENDATIONS

Stabilization combined with selective recovery offered an approach that conformed to NOAA's long-range strategic objectives and offered the best possible prospects for preservation of *Monitor*. NOAA and its partners were confident that the priority assigned to this project would be in proportion to both the documented and perceived significance of this historic ship, its value to the public, and the long-range goals of the National Marine Sanctuary Program. The admiration and attention afforded the USS *Monitor* over more than a century and the sustained high level of public interest and excitement about the wreck since its discovery suggested that the site has iconic significance to the American public that transcends federal guidelines and National Historic Landmark criteria.

Our narrative clearly explained that implementation would require extensive planning, broad-based funding, and numerous site visits over a period of at least three years. The first steps, scheduled to take place during 1998 and 1999, would provide data needed to flesh out the plan. We also had to prepare and submit an environmental assessment and a financial plan.

In deciding what, if any, large components should be recovered from *Monitor*, we considered several critical factors, especially technological feasibility, conservation and curation facilities, and financial capability. The decision to recover, conserve, and curate (retain and care for in perpetuity) large objects that had been deteriorating in seawater represented a major long-term commitment of resources. We had to weigh the historical and archaeological significance of each major object against factors such as condition, diagnostic importance, size and weight, engineering difficulties, exhibit potential, and available and projected curation resources.

INITIAL PLANNING AND IMPLEMENTATION

Even before NOAA and congressional approval, we began preparing implementation plans. We quickly developed a list of artifacts and hull components to be recovered. We assigned the propeller, engine, turret, and guns highest priority, but included a list of associated equipment and artifacts, most of which had been suggested in the *Monitor* comprehensive plan. We also made plans for initial onsite diving activities to survey and map the site and recover small artifacts that might be damaged by the major site activities. *Monitor* sanctuary staff worked closely with engineers and salvors to ensure that site activities would have minimal negative impact on *Monitor*'s hull and contents.

We determined that the desired onsite shoring and recovery operations could be completed in six major phases, depending on the availability of adequate equipment, personnel, and funding (see sidebar). We believed that phase I and part of phase II could be accomplished during 1998 and 1999, which would reduce the number of tasks to be accomplished during the large-scale recovery expeditions. However, we had to move carefully, since even after NOAA and Congress approved the plan we had no specific authorization for implementation and the Navy had not yet committed resources.

In early 1998, as we made the final revisions to the *Monitor* Comprehensive Preservation Plan, we were not certain when—or even if—the plan would be approved. However, by that time a new opportunity had presented itself, one that might let us conduct some of the necessary site activities without waiting for final approval.

Chapter Six

IMPLEMENTING THE
RECOVERY PLAN

By fall 1997, we had completed the draft of the *Monitor* Comprehensive Plan required by Congress, but so far Congress had not appropriated funds nor had the Navy committed to a multiyear recovery effort. Without Navy support, I didn't think the plan could succeed. Recovery would require massive equipment, skilled personnel, and tens of millions of dollars that NOAA did not have. NOAA is a science agency with limited capabilities or expertise in salvage. We have ships and divers, but the closest we ever get to salvage is periodic recovery of environmental monitoring equipment. With only enough funding for a small NOAA expedition in 1998, I assumed that the most we could accomplish would be acquiring the measurements and photographs we needed to develop a more detailed recovery plan. Then I received a phone call that changed everything.

HELP FROM A NEW SOURCE

The caller was Commander Christopher Murray, Commanding Officer of the US Navy's Mobile Diving and Salvage Unit TWO (MDSU TWO). I was very familiar with MDSU TWO. Their divers helped me on a shipwreck excavation in Yorktown, Virginia, during the 1980s. Headquartered in nearby Nor-folk, Virginia, MDSU TWO is part of Naval Surface Forces, Atlantic Fleet, and is responsible for Navy salvage in the Atlantic Ocean and Gulf of Mexico. Commander Murray explained that he wanted to conduct a realistic training exercise utilizing their new deepwater dive system, and he had been told that I might be able to provide a suitable test site. I was speechless, which was unusual for me. Was someone playing a prank? Or had our prayers been answered? I recovered sufficiently to assure Murray that I had just the site he was looking for. I believed that if MDSU TWO could help us salvage *Monitor*'s propeller, it would demonstrate the viability of our long-range recovery plan and generate the support we needed.

After some additional discussion, we agreed that a *Monitor* expedition in 1998 would benefit both parties. I quickly arranged for NOAA to submit a written request for MDSU assistance, and the Navy quickly authorized MDSU TWO to conduct training operations at the sanctuary in order to apply lessons learned during the 1995 attempted propeller recovery and to evaluate their new diving system. The MDSU TWO funded most of the cost from their annual training budget, while NOAA's Sanctuaries and Reserves Division (SRD) paid for breathing gas and some of the specialized equipment and supplies the Navy needed. The SRD also allocated funds for additional NOAA untethered, mixed-gas dives on *Monitor*.

PROPELLER RECOVERY EXPEDITION, 1998

"Getting to Know You"—Initial Planning

Even before we submitted a formal request, we were already planning the 1998 expedition with Commander Murray and his divers. One of NOAA's initial concerns was that Navy salvage divers might not be capable of shifting their orientation from modern salvage to careful archaeological mapping and recovery. Commander Murray was very aware of this issue as well. He told us, "Navy salvage divers are trained to dive to the bottom, find the biggest pieces, rig them, and yank them to the surface." He added with a sheepish grin that he assumed archaeologists tended to use a more delicate approach. We agreed to deal with this issue during the planning stage in order to minimize the potential for onsite disputes.

The dive coordination plan we developed required a high level of mutual trust and cooperation between NOAA and MDSU TWO. *Monitor* sanctuary staff would participate in each briefing; we would use a wreck model to show Navy divers where their work areas were located; then MDSU TWO dive supervisors would conduct their standard safety briefing and tell the divers what tasks they were to carry out. During each dive, either Jeff Johnston, *Monitor* program specialist and historian, or I would stand at the dive station where we could watch the live video image from the diver's hand-held camera, listen to communications between both divers and their surface tender, and talk to the divers if necessary. This cooperative plan ensured best archaeological practices during all expedition activities.[1]

We were determined to make this expedition a success, so we focused on a series of tasks that would provide essential engineering and archaeological data for hull stabilization and recovery of major hull components. The major goals of the expedition were to map and document specific areas of *Monitor*'s hull, recover exposed artifacts, and assess Navy deepwater diving methodology and equipment. The MDSU TWO was confident that they could also recover *Monitor*'s propeller, so we added an option for recovery of the propeller if both parties agreed at the time that we could get the prop without damaging it.

Our *Monitor* National Marine Sanctuary office is located at The Mariners' Museum in Newport News, Virginia, less than an hour's drive from MDSU TWO's facility at the Naval Amphibious Base, Little Creek, Virginia. This proximity made it possible for us to meet frequently and work closely for planning. The Mariners' Museum is NOAA's partner for conservation and exhibition, so being near the conservation lab was ideal for planning how best to recover artifacts and transport them to the museum.

To prepare for the expedition, we developed detailed goals and objectives, then converted them into a list of specific dive tasks listed in the order they needed to be accomplished. We also listed dive tasks that could be carried out whenever time permitted. The MDSU TWO had conducted countless operations at sea, so their plan stressed safety and took into account factors beyond their control, including inclement weather, equipment breakdown, and diver illness. We also discussed the possibility that archaeological requirements might create delays, since this project would require more caution than normal. This is where the whole NOAA/Navy partnership might have broken down: the Navy was determined to get the prop on deck and we archaeologists were equally determined to see that the propeller suffered no serious damage. Fortunately, Commander Murray and his senior staff understood that success did not mean just recovering the propeller, but recovering it intact. He constantly reminded his divers of this important distinction. In turn, I assured MDSU that Jeff and I would be as flexible as possible, and that we would provide extensive information on site conditions and *Monitor*'s construction.

Early in the planning process, MDSU TWO realized that their deck space requirements exceeded the capabilities of available Navy vessels. They needed extensive space for their new Fly-Away Mixed-Gas Diving System (FMGS) that included a recompression chamber, numerous large flasks of breathing gas, and additional personnel and equipment, along with a suitable location for storing the propeller after recovery. To resolve this issue, Commander Murray requested the Deep Submergence Elevator Support Ship (DSESS) *Kellie Chouest*, a 320-foot research vessel under lease to the US Navy from the Edison Chouest Offshore Company. *Kellie Chouest* had a wide range of capabilities and its stern was fitted with a massive elevator system designed for launch and recovery of the Deep Submergence Rescue Vehicles (DSRVs) for NATO submarine rescue and unmanned deep submergence vehicle operations.

Murray knew *Kellie*'s deck would accommodate MDSU's needs with space left over, so he pulled me aside at a planning meeting with a suggestion. He was wearing a grin that I had come to recognize; it meant something interesting was in store. His news, however, was much more than interesting: Murray told me that since there was extra deck space aboard *Kellie Chouest*, he had requested authorization for a NOAA team to stage dive operations in an unused deck location during the *Monitor* expedition. I was delighted with the concept, but asked how that was possible since none of us was certified to dive with the Navy. The grin was back, this time with a twinkle in the eye.

"Ah, but John," he said, "You won't be diving *with* Navy divers, you'll just be diving off the same ship." After a pause he added, "Now, if my divers and yours happen to descend on *Monitor* at the same time, well, we're still not diving *together*."

What a great opportunity for our NOAA dive team—if I could convince NOAA to go along with the plan. As soon as I got back to my office I phoned David Dinsmore, director of the NOAA Diving Program, and presented my arguments. First, we would have a much better dive platform than in 1995, plus we would have access to the Navy's decompression chamber, medical personnel, and trained operators—all at no cost to NOAA—and finally, we would be able to observe and assist Navy divers on the wreck. Dave was surprisingly easy to convince, since he was interested in supporting the growing number of requests from NOAA scientists for diving projects in the 130- to 300-foot range.

We agreed on a plan that included divers from the *Monitor* National Marine Sanctuary, NOAA Diving Program, University of North Carolina at Wilmington, and a new partner, the Cambrian Foundation. We were familiar with this not-for-profit group through their NOAA-permitted *Monitor* research. Headed by former Navy diver Terrence Tysall, the Cambrian Foundation is made up of enthusiastic divers willing to volunteer their skills on science projects ranging from caves to shipwrecks. Before the expedition, our diverse team would train at facilities in NOAA's Florida Keys National Marine Sanctuary. Tysall, an experienced technical diving

instructor, would plan and teach the course in consultation with Dave Dinsmore.

Jeff and I spent most of the spring of 1998 coordinating plans and developing an expedition operations manual. Commander Murray would be in charge of all at-sea operations aboard the DSESS *Kellie Chouest*, but he would coordinate closely with me in my role as NOAA's Expedition Chief Scientist and On-Site Archaeologist. In that capacity, I could suspend operations if I believed that a continuation was likely to cause significant adverse effects to *Monitor*.

On our NOAA dive team, Tysall served as Expedition Diving Supervisor and was responsible for diving procedures and equipment along with day-to-day diving. Dinsmore was Expedition Diving Coordinator. In that capacity he was responsible for overseeing all NOAA dive operations and dive safety and had authority to halt dive operations if, in his opinion, the diving conditions or planned activities constituted a hazard to any member of the team.

During March 16–23, the Cambrian Foundation trained our team in the skills of technical, mixed-gas diving. That training in the Florida Keys National Marine Sanctuary was followed in June by additional training dives at Hatteras, using the R/V *Cape Fear*, from the University of North Carolina at Wilmington (UNC-W).

Propeller Recovery—May 26–June 11, 1998

At 7:00 p.m. on May 25, following a week of loading and preparations, *Kellie Chouest* departed Little Creek Naval Amphibious Base. Arriving at the *Monitor* National Marine Sanctuary at noon the next day, we were greeted by what we had come to think of as "typical Hatteras" conditions: four- to six-foot seas, and a forecast calling for things to get worse. That's not what happened, and by 7:30 on the morning of May 27, the seas had calmed and *Kellie Chouest*'s crew began the difficult mooring evolution that placed the ship in a stationary position directly above *Monitor*. The mooring consisted of four huge anchors, each weighing ten tons, positioned approximately 90 degrees apart, to hold the ship securely over the wreck. This made it possible for us to position *Kellie* over *Monitor*'s port quarter, where Navy divers could descend within easy reach of the umbilicals that tethered them to the surface.

Establishing a four-point mooring is a difficult

The US Navy's research vessel *Kellie Chouest* positioned over *Monitor* on a four-point moor during the 1998 anchor recovery expedition. Courtesy NOAA *Monitor* Collection

task under ideal conditions, and this project was made more difficult because the ship had to place moorings on four sides of *Monitor* without allowing any of the mooring cables (which weighed ten pounds per foot) to come in contact with the wreck. Our concerns, however, were unfounded. *Kellie*'s crew hailed from "Cajun country," where they spent

most of their days performing complex work in Gulf of Mexico offshore oil fields. To them, this was just another day at sea. Within two hours all four anchors had been set and the crew had begun to winch the mooring cables in and out until *Kellie* was at the correct position and heading.

The *Kellie Chouest* was an ideal vessel for this ap-

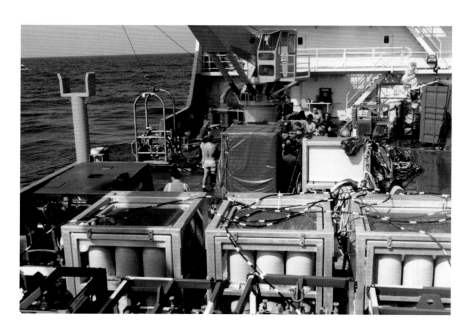

MDSU TWO installed its flyaway mixed-gas dive system on the center of *Kellie Chouest*'s weather deck, leaving room for large flasks of breathing gas and a NOAA dive station aft. Courtesy NOAA *Monitor* Collection

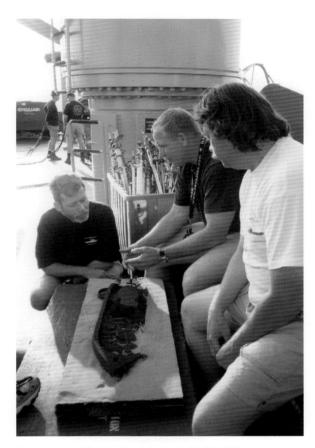

Commander Christopher Murray, MDSU TWO commanding officer, explains his plan for an upcoming *Monitor* dive to NOAA's John Broadwater (left), and Jeff Johnston, using a model of *Monitor* made by Johnston for use on the expedition. Courtesy NOAA *Monitor* Collection

plication, having adequate deck space for both dive stations and associated equipment, plus berthing and eating facilities for the expedition team, which included the Navy and NOAA teams in addition to the vessel crew. There were also capabilities for lifting and storing the *Monitor*'s propeller and shaft.

Since the Navy divers were not familiar with the dive site, *Monitor* staff participated in each dive briefing, using a scale model of the *Monitor* wreck as a visual aid. Throughout each dive, the dive supervisor and either Jeff Johnston or I monitored the video from a diver-held camera and listened to communications between both divers and the surface. All video was recorded for later review and archiving. In a break with standard procedures, Commander Murray told his divers that at times they would be talking through their communication gear directly

to NOAA personnel, and that they were to follow their directions unless ordered otherwise by the dive supervisor. Jeff and I considered that to be a remarkable demonstration of the mutual trust and cooperative attitude we had developed. At 2:00 that afternoon the dive platform, or *stage*, was lowered with the Diver Underwater Color Television System (DUCTS) camera attached, giving us our first view of the bottom. The underwater video made it possible to set the stage "clump" without damaging the wreck. The clump was a 2,000-pound weight attached to a steel cable for the purpose of stabilizing the dive stage and guiding it up and down the water column like an elevator in a twenty-five-story building. Without the clump and cable, currents would spin the stage and drag it away from the intended dive site.

At 1515 hours (3:15 p.m.), MDSU launched the first dive of the expedition, a general reconnaissance dive. A second dive followed, during which *Kellie* was repositioned slightly to move the dive clump closer to *Monitor*'s port stern. Each time the clump descended, Jeff and I held our breath, hoping the clump would not become a shipwreck pile driver. The MDSU TWO, realizing the danger, began lowering the clump to 200 feet, then lowering the stage to the clump so the divers could guide the clump and stage during the final descent.

Just after noon the following day, our team made its first dive. It was one of the most surreal dives any of us had ever experienced. *Kellie*'s sides were too high above the water for us to jump in or climb out with our dive gear. *Kellie*'s captain had the solution: he had us step onto the DSRV elevator platform and don our gear, whereupon he lowered us into the water. At the end of our dive, we swam into the lowered elevator and sat around at ten feet below the surface while completing our final decompression stop. When our decompression was finished, our dive supervisor gave a signal and we were raised to the deck on our own seventy-five-ton capacity elevator! We soon developed a daily rhythm. Weather permitting, both dive teams conducted dives. Our team took a lot of ribbing from Navy divers, who thought we were foolhardy to dive in the open sea with no tether or communications. But after a few days the MDSU divers, encumbered by heavy suits and weights, and with the current tugging on their umbilicals, began to notice how easily our divers glided over the wreck, making measurements and

US NAVY SURFACE SUPPLIED DIVE EQUIPMENT AND PROCEDURES

The Navy's dive station was located amidships on the port side of *Kellie Chouest*, with the helium and oxygen breathing gasses stored nearby in large pressure cylinders. This expedition was the first to deploy MDSU TWO's new Fly-Away Mixed-Gas Diving System (FMGS), a completely portable, self-contained system that can be quickly mobilized, transported by road, air, or sea, and deployed on a vessel of opportunity. The FMGS consists of racks of large high-pressure cylinders containing helium, oxygen, and air, and a control console for mixing and distributing gasses, along with associated equipment, piping, and hoses.

Navy divers wore the MK 21, Mod 1 diving helmet, which was adapted from the popular commercial Kirby-Morgan Superlite 17. The helmet weighs approximately twenty-seven pounds dry but is neutrally buoyant in water. A diving umbilical supplies the helmet with gas and provides for two-way communication with the dive supervisor on the surface and the other diver. Divers wore hot-water suits, which are similar to conventional wet suits, except they are equipped to supply hot water to the divers to maintain their bodies in an adequate temperature range. Although summer water temperatures at the *Monitor* sanctuary were normally 68°F or above, breathing helium removes body heat much faster than air, so most of the divers used the hot water.

On each dive, two divers—designated "Red" and "Green" for communications purposes—descended to the site on a dive stage, or platform, suspended from a special winch. A third diver, "Yellow," sat on a bench at the surface, suited up and ready to deploy at a moment's notice in case of an emergency. A major innovation in 1998 was to coil seventy-five feet of each diver's umbilical and secure

Navy surface-supplied divers descend to *Monitor* in the two-diver stage. A white tool bucket hangs on the outside. Courtesy NOAA *Monitor* Collection

the coils on the dive stage, making it easier for the divers to move out from the stage when on the bottom. To reduce the drag of the umbilical in the water column on the divers on the bottom, the umbilical was shackled to the descent line with spinnaker shackles every fifty to seventy-five feet, thus significantly reducing the catenary (bow) in the umbilical.

The "bottom mix" used on *Monitor* was a mixture of 85 percent helium and 15 percent oxygen, while the gas for decompression was 50 percent helium and 50 percent oxygen. Decompression during all Navy dives followed standard surface decompression (SUR-D) tables. In this procedure, the divers returned to the dive stage at the end of their specified dive time and were slowly raised to the surface in steps, or stops, according to tested and published Navy Diving Tables.

(*continued*)

Navy divers receiving a pre-dive briefing before descending to the *Monitor* site. Courtesy NOAA *Monitor* Collection

Navy divers filled out a NOAA post-dive debriefing form after every dive while completing their decompression in the deck chamber. Courtesy NOAA *Monitor* Collection

ber. Just as with scuba diving, "bottom time" begins when the divers leave the surface and ends when they start their ascent. On a typical forty-minute *Monitor* dive, two divers descend on the stage, which stops ten to fifteen feet off the bottom. As soon as they get clearance from the dive supervisor they release their seventy-five feet of coiled umbilical, jump off the stage, then have to drag their umbilicals first to the wreck and then to their work site. They have to leave their task in time to get back to the stage, climb up their umbilicals back onto the stage, clear their umbilicals, and begin their ascent—all before forty minutes have elapsed, which means that actual time spent on the task is usually twenty minutes or less.

After arriving at their final in-water decompression stop at a depth of fifty feet, the divers' helium-oxygen gas was switched to pure oxygen and the divers were raised directly to the surface and onto the *Kellie*'s deck.[1] Once on their dive benches, they were quickly helped out of their equipment and rushed into the deck decompression chamber (DDC) where they completed their decompression in safety and relative comfort. For a dive to a maximum depth of 230 feet, divers can spend up to forty minutes underwater, after which they would need about three and a half hours of total decompression, with two and a half hours of that spent in the decompression cham-

Note:

1. As a result of the extensive Navy diving conducted on *Monitor* in 1998, the official US Navy helium decompression tables were modified so that the divers were raised to forty feet, where they continued to breathe the fifty/fifty mix until being raised to the surface for final decompression.

shooting video. That seemed to soften their opinions somewhat. Before long, MDSU TWO divers began visiting the NOAA dive station on deck with suggestions such as, "Hey, if you guys happen to be in the stern next dive, could you maybe shoot some video around the propeller blades and see if you can tell where the blades are touching the hull?" We considered those "casual" requests to be testimonies to our value and, on the other hand, we respected the Navy's skills in conducting all the heavy work. We were bonding into a single team.

Both dive teams conducted numerous reconnaissance dives, documenting key areas with still and video photography. As our understanding of the site increased, we found it easier to develop effective plans for future dives and for the eventual propeller

recovery (all of us were expecting to return to Little Creek with the prop on board!). Every diver, Navy and NOAA, completed a Diver Debriefing Form after each dive in order to capture as many observations and activities as possible. Jeff and I collected and filed those logs and maintained a daily journal and artifact catalog.

The MDSU TWO had fabricated an *eduction* dredge to conduct test excavations. This clever device consisted of a hydraulically powered water pump that drew water through a long flexible hose, creating an "underwater vacuum cleaner." During excavation, a Navy diver operated the dredge while a NOAA archaeologist observed or helped guide the dredge head. Inside the inverted turret, the dredge penetrated through more than a half meter of sand,

CDR Murray suiting up for a dive to inspect *Monitor*'s propeller and shaft. Courtesy NOAA *Monitor* Collection

Two MDSU TWO divers on the stage being deployed over the side for a dive on *Monitor*. The closest diver's coiled-up umbilical can be seen just inside the stage. Courtesy NOAA *Monitor* Collection

shell, and dead coral without encountering any deck structure or any evidence of the cannon and carriages.

Outside, at the base of the turret, the dredge penetrated into the seabed nearly a meter before being halted by what appeared to be an iron concretion (a conglomeration of iron and corrosion products) at the lip of the turret. This was helpful, since we guessed that the concretion was an awning stanchion or part of the rifle shield, which told us that we were likely to encounter more obstructions when attempting to raise the turret.

Using a hole-cutting saw and a special wood corer, Navy divers extracted a slender core of oak from inside the port armor belt. They then sealed the resulting hole with marine epoxy to prevent further deterioration. The wood core would give us more information on the condition of armor belt, which we needed for formulating plans to stabilize the armor belt and eventually remove a portion of the belt in order to gain access to the turret.

While NOAA divers continued with site documentation and small artifact recovery, the Navy divers closely inspected the area around the propeller. Beneath the collapsed stern they encountered deck plates, plate fragments, and other structural debris. This area had to be cleared in preparation for shoring the propeller shaft and stabilizing the stern.

Initially, the propeller was almost unrecognizable because of a thick covering of concretion, sponges, and soft corals. Once Navy divers cleared away most of the soft marine growth, we could see that the skeg, the heavy beam intended to support the propeller shaft and rudder, had dropped down against the shaft—evidence of damage by a fishing boat anchor in 1991. As more soft marine growth was removed from the propeller, we discovered that three of its four blades had suffered significant damage. This raised additional concern, since the propeller was made of cast iron, which is relatively brittle and prone to breakage. A close inspection of the blades showed that concretion and marine growth

NOAA's Broadwater (center) and Johnston (standing, far right) stood at the "comms box" during Navy dives, where they could watch and listen to the divers. Courtesy NOAA *Monitor* Collection

appeared to be just as thick in the damaged areas as elsewhere, which meant the breaks must have occurred while *Monitor* was afloat or during the sinking. I recorded that fact in my journal. I didn't want our expedition to get blamed for the damage!

The least damaged of the four blades extended down into the wreck where iron concretions "cemented" it to the hull. Divers tried unsuccessfully to free the concreted blade with hand tools. We considered the use of hydraulic impact tools but decided that was too risky. At that point a MDSU diver suggested a cable saw—using a length of steel cable to cut through metal by pulling it back and forth while holding pressure against the surface to be cut. Several experienced Navy divers assured us they could separate the blade from the bulkhead without damage, so we agreed to give it a try. The first diver inserted a six-foot length of steel cable between the blade and the bulkhead and began pulling it back and forth, applying pressure against the concretion. The technique worked extremely well, and soon all the blades were free.

We decided the best place to cut the shaft was about four feet aft of where it passed through the hull, because of a structural beam that seemed to be providing support for the shaft. This spot was not far from the ragged groove where we began to cut the shaft in 1995. Because conventional underwater cutting methods had not worked well then, MDSU researched possible alternatives, eventually selecting a *guillotine saw*. This was a hydraulically powered

reciprocating device like a hacksaw on steroids. The manufacturer's representative guaranteed it would do the job with ease—but, then, the cutting torch company representative had told us the same thing about his product in 1995. As a little added insurance, MDSU TWO divers had trained with the saw by cutting a nine-inch piece of metal round stock, the same diameter as *Monitor*'s shaft, first on the surface and then underwater at pier side.

In 1998, a NOAA team made their *Monitor* dives from *Kellie Chouest*'s stern, entering and leaving the water on a massive elevator designed for a submarine rescue vehicle. Courtesy NOAA *Monitor* Collection

Curious amberjack and black sea bass often followed NOAA and Navy divers around the wreck. Courtesy NOAA *Monitor* Collection

NOAA divers took advantage of especially good visibility to survey and videotape *Monitor*'s hull. Courtesy NOAA *Monitor* Collection

NOAA divers conducted their decompression by ascending up a line in the water column. On days when the current was strong, they decompressed on an unanchored line that drifted with the current, thus minimizing current stress during ascent. Courtesy NOAA *Monitor* Collection

NOAA "TECHNICAL" DIVE PROCEDURES

During the 1998 *Monitor* expedition NOAA conducted their first full-scale "technical" trimix dives. NOAA dives were conducted by a small team of NOAA and Cambrian Foundation divers following provisional procedures and protocols established by the NOAA Diving Program, NOAA's National Undersea Research Center at the University of North Carolina at Wilmington, and the Cambrian Foundation. The NOAA Diving Safety Board granted approval for the team to conduct untethered, self-contained mixed-gas diving techniques at the *Monitor* as a proof of concept project. The dive plan, developed with input from numerous proponents of technical diving, utilized the same basic mixed-gas equipment and procedures as in 1995.

The NOAA dive team breathed a gas mix that was a blend of 18 percent oxygen, 32 percent nitrogen, and 50 percent helium that was initially called "*Monitor* Mix." Decompression tables were developed in 1993 and used successfully on the 1993 and later expeditions.

The use of mixed gas, rather than compressed air, greatly improved divers' effectiveness and ability to deal with possible emergencies due to minimization of nitrogen narcosis and oxygen toxicity, both potential hazards when breathing air at the *Monitor*'s maximum depth of 240 feet. NOAA and Cambrian Foundation personnel conducted all gas mixing and testing activities. The Navy's deck decompression chamber (DDC) and diving medical technicians on board the *Kellie Chouest* were available in case of a diving emergency.

For diver deployment and recovery, NOAA divers were treated to one of the most unique but effective systems ever utilized. Due to the *Kellie Chouest*'s high freeboard and the need to avoid interfering with the Navy dive station, NOAA divers were launched and recovered on the huge

steel elevator that was designed for a thirty-eight-ton rescue submersible. A rigid-floor inflatable boat was available in the event that a diver was adrift and had to be recovered.

NOAA divers, wearing open-circuit mixed-gas diving equipment, prepare to dive to *Monitor*. Courtesy NOAA *Monitor* Collection

A special "guilloutine saw" was used to cut through *Monitor*'s solid 9-inch-diameter iron propeller shaft. Courtesy NOAA *Monitor* Collection

We sat down after dinner on May 31 to review our progress. Work was progressing well in the stern, many of the survey and documentation tasks on our list were already complete, and the weather had been cooperating. Even as we were meeting, however, the wind began strengthening, as if to remind us that out here the sea gods still made all final decisions. That evening, waves broke over the side and roiled across the deck; the bottom section of the Navy's heavy grade aluminum ladder carried away.

The following day, the seas were too rough for diving, so MDSU used the time to fabricate a metal cradle for the prop and shaft out of the angle iron that had been taken aboard for that purpose. They also developed a clever and efficient plan for moving the skeg out of the way. When diving resumed on June 2, the skeg was rigged before bad weather forced us to call a halt to operations again. The next day surface conditions were much improved, but the first pair of divers reported less than one foot of visibility on the bottom and a current estimated at 5 knots, which was pulling the dive stage more than 35 degrees off its optimal vertical position! The MDSU enlisted every available hand on deck, including archaeologists, to help tend the divers' umbilicals and video cables. Finally, on June 4, conditions improved and the skeg was quickly lifted away from the wreck without incident, leaving the propeller and shaft clear for recovery.

That afternoon, we met to review the Navy's recovery plan. They laid out a detailed step-by-step plan for supporting the propeller and rigging the shaft, then cutting the shaft to free the propeller.

The MDSU team had borrowed Jeff's wreck model and had rigged miniature lifting straps and spreader bars to the shaft. The riggers proposed using a large salvage lift bag to support the lift straps until it was time to connect the harness to the crane's hook, so they had "simulated" the lift bag with a condom inflated with helium, which caused it to "float" over the propeller assembly just as the lift bag was supposed to do. When the model was presented to the gathered team, it broke the tension but created a potential censorship situation for the production team that was filming our meeting for inclusion in a NOVA documentary on the expedition.

We spent the next hour or so trying to detect any fatal flaws in the plan. Based on the known density of wrought iron, we calculated that the cast iron propeller should weigh no more than 3,500 pounds and the solid nine-inch diameter wrought iron shaft about 200 pounds per running foot. This meant that the total lift weight should not exceed 6,000 pounds, well below the capacity of *Kellie*'s crane. The obstructions were clear, the guillotine saw was securely attached to the shaft, and so both teams gave the thumbs up. Sleep did not come easily for me that night, but Commander Murray was confidently snoring before my teeth were brushed.

Early on the morning of Friday, June 5 we received predictions of rapidly deteriorating weather. Once we began cutting the shaft, it would need to be supported by a cable from *Kellie*'s crane; but once the cable was attached, the propeller and shaft would be subjected to forces transmitted down the cable from the sea's actions on *Kellie*'s hull. If the waves and swells became more severe, as predicted, safe recovery would be impossible. We only had a few days remaining onsite, so we were faced with the realization that today probably was our last chance for recovery. We agreed to begin and continue until the prop was on deck. I was very nervous about this decision—which was essentially irreversible once the cutting commenced—but by his time I was confident in MDSU TWO's capabilities.

The first divers rigged three heavy Kevlar straps to the shaft, bringing the three free ends together in a sling and suspending them above the wreck with a large salvage bag that would maintain a slight strain on the sling. *Kellie*'s crew repositioned the ship so the lifting cable hung directly above the shaft. The second pair of divers attached the cable to the sling, leaving enough slack to prevent surface motion from

A MDSU TWO diver guides the guilloutine saw during the propeller shaft cut. Courtesy NOAA *Monitor* Collection

pulling on the shaft. The third pair of divers connected hydraulic hoses to the guillotine saw and began cutting. Everything was proceeding as planned.

The saw worked smoothly at first, but as the blade cut deeper it began to bind and snag on the tough wrought iron, which caused the saw to loosen on the shaft. Divers had to retighten the saw without misaligning the blade. As the cut deepened, several blades broke and had to be replaced underwater, slowing the process even more. Further complicating the situation, we lost the video signal, leaving us without a view of the cutting effort. I left Jeff in charge topside while I joined several NOAA divers for a close-up view of the cutting operation.

The position of the lifting cable looked perfect, but the seas were building, causing the cable to periodically come taut. To compensate, the crane operator let out more slack. The diver operating the saw was struggling. I could see that as the diver tightened the saw on the shaft, the pressure was cracking the concretion layer, which, in turn, loosened the saw even more. All we could do was watch and hope for the best.

By late afternoon, Commander Murray and his team were running out of saw blades—and divers. For safety reasons, divers were prohibited from making a repeat dive for twelve hours, and MDSU was down to its last two dive teams. The MDSU TWO's

Master Diver Donnie Dennis went down next, determined to complete the cut. He attacked the shaft with all the energy he could muster, but with only an inch to go, the blade snapped. Murray had been holding back, hoping his divers would finish the job, but now it was up to him. He was on the last available dive team.

The sun was setting when Murray and Petty Officer Honsberger entered the water for one last attempt. If they were unsuccessful, they would try to disconnect the lifting cable, but that would leave the propeller with no support; if the cable remained connected, the propeller would likely be damaged when *Kellie Chouest* was forced to ride out the squalls that were headed our way. For those of us nervously watching from the deck, the suspense was intense. Adding to our concern and frustration was the fact that a connector on the DUCTS camera had failed, leaving us with no visual image of what was happening down below.

A heavy swell was building, and with it the amplitude of *Kellie*'s rising and falling increased. At 7:35 p.m. a particularly large swell lifted *Kellie* until the mooring cables began to strain. Suddenly, a shrill, helium-induced voice spat from the communication box, "It's free! It's free!" The swell had produced a slight upward strain on the lifting sling, just enough to part the remaining metal to be cut. With a snap the propeller and shaft lifted up and aft, clear of the stern, just as the Navy riggers had planned.

The alert topside crew quickly ordered the cable to be taken in twenty feet to prevent the shaft from swinging back and hitting the wreck or, even worse, one of the divers. Once the divers were back on the stage they were raised fifty feet off the bottom, where they could make certain that the prop and shaft stayed clear of the wreck. As they watched the propeller lift from the wreck, scores of *Monitor*'s resident amberjack rushed up and began swirling around the rising propeller and shaft as if bidding it farewell, or perhaps honoring the divers who had finally triumphed in their quest. The divers watched in awe as the setting sun bathed propeller and amberjack in a warm glow.

The crane operator winched the propeller and shaft up to a depth of one hundred feet before pausing while sailors cleared the deck for recovery. At 10:28 p.m., *Monitor*'s four-bladed iron propeller finally broke the surface without damage, still attached to eleven feet of shaft. And none too soon, the seas had already become rough, making it difficult for the crane operator to time his lift with the ship's rolls. With skill born of experience, the operator swung the prop across the deck where a score of divers helped guide it onto its new cradle.

On June 7, the seas subsided enough for us to resume diving. All the divers enjoyed inspecting the end of the shaft, which flash rust had turned bright orange. The MDSU recovered three deck plates for analysis and comparison with one recovered in 1977. We hoped those bits of iron would help us estimate the amount of deterioration since then. The following day MDSU recovered core samples from the seabed to determine its load-bearing capability. One of our final tasks was to excavate a small test hole inside the turret to look for evidence of wooden deck and guns. For that dive, I arranged to meet a MDSU diver at the turret. He would operate the eductor dredge while I helped guide the dredge head and watched for artifacts and features. The dive went well and afterward I completed the required in-water decompression with my two NOAA dive partners.

I had stored my gear and was headed for a shower when I began to feel slightly nauseous. While talking to a diver on deck, I suddenly felt dizzy and had to sit down. Before I could move, I found myself surrounded by a swarm of Diving-Certified EMTs, Chief Master Divers, and Diving Medical Officers. It was

Monitor's propeller and a section of the shaft broke the surface on the evening of June 5, 1998. Courtesy NOAA *Monitor* Collection

diagnosis by committee; I answered the same questions over and over until my dizziness became more severe. Before I could protest I was rushed into the recompression chamber, where I underwent treatment for decompression sickness—the "bends." Later, I learned that I had damaged my inner ear, a permanent injury that would prevent further deep diving.

On June 10, *Kellie Chouest* retrieved its moorings and transited to Newport News Shipbuilding, where the propeller was offloaded onto a truck and transported to The Mariners' Museum to begin conservation.

Phase 2—NOAA Dives, June 9–26

As *Kellie* departed, a NOAA team moved in to conduct additional survey dives. This phase 2 expedition involved NOAA's National Marine Sanctuary Program, the NOAA Diving Program, the National

Research Vessel *Cape Fear*, from the University of North Carolina at Wilmington. Courtesy NOAA *Monitor* Collection

The NOAA Ship *Ferrel* supported NOAA's *Monitor* dives following the Navy's departure. Courtesy NOAA *Monitor* Collection

Undersea Research Center/University of North Carolina at Wilmington, the Cambrian Foundation, and The Mariners' Museum. Once again, most of the personnel were the same as the previous year. We conducted all diving operations from the UNC-Wilmington vessel *Cape Fear*, with a double-lock hyperbaric chamber and qualified operators available aboard the NOAA ship *Ferrel*, which stood faithfully by during dive operations.

1998 Accomplishments

The 1998 expedition was extremely successful. We conducted dives on twenty-seven of thirty possible days, for a total of ninety dives—fifty-five by the Navy and thirty-five by NOAA. We logged a total of 106 hours cumulative bottom time, nearly twice the total (fifty-five hours) of all five previous NOAA diving expeditions to *Monitor*. Counting the lengthy decompression times, our cumulative total dive time was 625 hours. In addition to much-needed measurements, observations, and video, we recovered thirty artifacts and samples plus, of course, the propeller and shaft.

Among the recovered objects was an iron deck plate measuring ten feet by three feet. Although this plate had completely separated from the deck it was remarkably intact. We also recovered part of a small steam engine, an unidentified object made of iron and brass or bronze, a bottle fragment similar to one recovered during the 1979 *Monitor* expedition, and a portion of a small tureen lid—a nice find that matched a fragment recovered on a Cambrian

Foundation research expedition several years earlier. For the participants, our main accomplishment was demonstrating that Navy salvage divers could safely recover a large, yet fragile, object made of brittle cast iron. This gave us the confidence to begin discussing next steps.

On June 12, The Mariners' Museum held a media event to unveil the propeller and announce that it would be conserved in a tank designed by Newport News Shipbuilding that would be available to the public throughout the treatment process. Commander Murray and his divers, looking impressive in their dress whites, pulled a plastic sheet from the propeller to reveal it to the gathered onlookers.

Media coverage of the expedition was extensive, including a NOVA documentary that aired on the Public Broadcasting Network, footage on the National Geographic Channel, news coverage by affiliates of all three major networks, and news stories on CNN, Fox, and The Learning Channel. We were even visited by a news team from Swedish Television, reminding us that *Monitor*'s inventor, John Ericsson, is viewed by the Swedish people as one of their most prominent figures. We were encouraged by the enthusiastic and positive public response to our success, and hoped that funding for the recovery would follow.

DATA COLLECTION EXPEDITION, 1999

Although *Monitor*'s friends in NOAA, the Navy, and Congress were seeking funding for the recovery

Monitor's propeller was unveiled at The
Mariners' Museum on June 12, 1998.
Courtesy The Mariners' Museum

A crowd gathered in the makeshift conservation area behind The Mariners' Museum
to watch *Monitor*'s propeller being installed in a specially-fabricated conservation tank.
Courtesy The Mariners' Museum

Following nearly 3 years in conservation, *Monitor*'s propeller was placed on exhibition inside The Mariners' Museum. Courtesy The Mariners' Museum

operations, we began the year 1999 with no significant budget. Therefore, we built our plans for 1999 around another Navy training mission, focused on retrieving additional site information we needed for recovery of the engine and turret.[2] The 1999 expedition consisted of two phases: a Navy expedition in June, followed by a NOAA expedition in July/ August.

Navy Operations, June 14–28, 1999

Participants and methodologies for 1999 remained essentially the same as before, with two significant exceptions. First, all Navy operations were conducted from USS *Grasp* (ARS-51), based at Little Creek Naval Amphibious Base, utilizing divers assigned to the ship and from MDSU TWO. *Grasp*'s commanding officer was Lieutenant Commander Eric Anderson; Commander Philip Beierl was now the commanding officer of MDSU TWO, which supplied additional divers for the expedition. Jeff Johnston and I were once again the NOAA representatives for the expedition.

Grasp departed Little Creek on Monday, June 14, passing Diamond Shoals at sunrise the next morn-

ing. *Grasp*'s deck space was limited, so the entire fantail was covered by huge loops of heavy steel mooring cables, chain, and anchors required for the four moorings that would hold us in position over *Monitor*. While final preparations were being made on deck, Anderson located the *Monitor* on his fathometer and set that location into his navigation system. The mooring plan was simple in concept, but required skill and precision to carry out safely. Each mooring leg would be set 800 feet from the wreck at ninety-degree intervals.

Just after 11:00 a.m. *Grasp* began the first mooring evolution, and all four moorings were in place and adjusted by 3:30 p.m. Then we headed south to Morehead City, North Carolina, where MDSU TWO's flyaway mixed-gas dive system and divers were waiting. We had to wait for the mooring gear to be deployed in order to make room for the dive system and extra divers. Jeff and I quickly learned that there were serious fishermen aboard *Grasp*, including the captain, who caught a big Mahi Mahi around 5:30. While he was posing for photos, the fish managed to flap its way to a scupper and over the side.

We were alongside the Morehead City State Port by 8:00 a.m. and were under way again by 10:00 with divers and equipment aboard. We were back at *Monitor* by 5:00 p.m. and secured in the mooring by 7:00. We had been alerted to the possibility that Tropical Storm Arlene—the first arrival of the Atlantic hurricane season—might be a threat, but it had turned north while still east of Bermuda, so we dodged that bullet.

The Navy made one dive on June 17 before heavy seas set in. Conditions improved by June 20, and the Navy resumed diving, investigating *Monitor*'s engineering spaces, galley, amidships, and stern. They also dug a small test hole outside the base of the turret, once again exposing what we believed to be evidence of the iron stanchions and rifle shield that would likely make turret recovery more difficult.

At sea, one never knows what the next day will bring. Although we felt prepared for almost any contingency, June 24 brought us a visitor that no one could have anticipated. As several of us stood on the fantail watching the Navy prepare for another dive, I heard a sound like a sea lion barking. I paid no attention, having long ago learned that horsing around during idle time is a Navy diver specialty. When the bark came again, however, it sounded authentic, so I turned to see who was so talented. Unbelievably,

Since 1987, NOAA had been attempting to acquire a new image of *Monitor*'s entire hull to supersede the 1974 *Seaprobe* photomosaic as the current representation of the site. The 1987 sonar documentation was useful, but did not produce a detailed site map. By the mid-1990s we began seeking help in earnest, knowing that *Monitor*'s hull was changing rapidly and that recovery operations were likely.

Finally, in 1995, we were offered a very promising opportunity. Michael Strand, from the US Navy's Coastal Systems Station, Dahlgren Division, Naval Surface Warfare Center, in Panama City, Florida, and Brian Coles, from Raytheon Electronic Systems, Tewksbury, Massachusetts, offered to document *Monitor* using a prototype laser line-scanning system (LLS) being developed primarily for mine countermeasures. The four-channel system they proposed to use was capable of generating full-color photographic-quality imagery of underwater objects from as far away as ten to fifteen feet or more, depending upon water turbidity.[1] NOAA contracted the Harbor Branch Oceanographic Institution to mount the large LLS unit on their submersible, *Clelia*. During October 9–15, 1996, we attempted to image *Monitor* on numerous dives, but bad surface weather, coupled with strong bottom currents and very poor visibility, limited data collection to two dives of approximately one hour each. The resulting imagery was both dramatic and disappointing. Strong currents

(continued)

An experimental Navy laser line scanner was installed on the Harbor Branch submersible *Clelia* for an operational test designed to image *Monitor*'s hull in high definition. Courtesy NOAA *Monitor* Collection

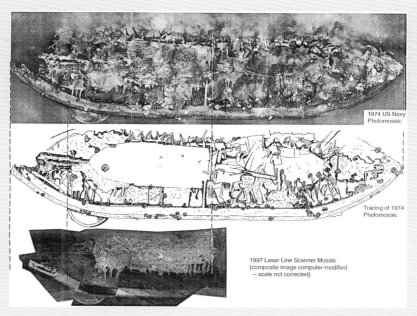

1974 US Navy Photomosaic

Tracing of 1974 Photomosaic

1997 Laser Line Scanner Mosaic (composite image computer-modified -- scale not corrected)

Results from the laser line scanner expedition aligned with the 1974 *Monitor* photomosaic. Courtesy NOAA *Monitor* Collection

A laser line scanner (top), operated by the Science Applications International Corporation (SAIC), is tested on board the NOAA Ship *Ferrel* before being installed in its tow housing for an attempt to image *Monitor* in high definition. Courtesy NOAA *Monitor* Collection

caused *Clelia* to follow arcing paths, instead of straight-line passes over the wreck, which resulted in banana-shaped images that were so distorted that no amount of post-processing could correct them. However, the few images that resulted from relatively straight passes over portions of the wreck were very detailed and impressive.[2]

In June of the following year we were able to conduct another laser line-scanner survey of *Monitor*, this one a towed-sensor built by Northrop Grumman Oceanic Systems and operated by Science Applications International Corporation (SAIC). We arranged for the NOAA ship *Ferrel* to support the mission, which was conducted during June 11–15, 1997. The laser system was operated by Jeff Chu, of Northrop Grumman, and Jan Vlcek, SAIC, was in charge of overall towing operations. Lieutenant Ilene Byron was commanding officer of *Ferrel*. Once again, bad weather and subsurface currents thwarted our attempts to obtain suitable laser imagery of *Monitor*'s hull.

Even when we were able to apply cutting-edge technology to the task of imaging *Monitor*, environmental conditions at the site prevented us from obtaining the desired results. Fortunately, many hours of high-quality videotape and still images provided us with a detailed and permanent record of the site almost on a yearly basis.

Notes:

1. Mazel et al. (2003, 522–34).
2. Jaffe et al. (2001, 70–72).

standing not ten feet behind me was a huge, real-life sea lion! Sea lions are not native to this coast, especially twenty miles offshore, which made this apparition even more surreal. The beast just stood there, looking around, seeming quite comfortable around the growing crowd of awestruck divers.

Once I recovered somewhat from my shock, I realized that this was a marine mammal, and therefore subject to the Marine Mammal Protection Act that NOAA enforced. I knew that people were prohibited from approaching, feeding, or in any way harassing such creatures. I quickly climbed to the bridge to make my report to NOAA and to ask for instructions, but Commander Beierl, phone in hand, asked me to clear the bridge for a few minutes. In a couple of minutes Beierl opened the door on the bridge wing and invited me in. With only the hint of a smile he informed me that he knew where the sea lion had come from and that "someone" would be here by tomorrow to pick him up.

Both Beierl and I received instructions to keep everyone away from the sea lion and to prohibit the release of any photographs until further notice. By this time everyone had figured out that the animal must be part of a Navy program that used marine mammals to recover items from the ocean floor, and probably other tasks. Not long afterwards, we learned that his name was Gremlin, and he had been "AWOL" for two months after going missing during training operations on Virginia's Eastern Shore, hundreds of miles north of us. He must have seen *Grasp*'s gray hull, we reasoned, and decided to see if we would take him aboard and feed him. When he reached the ship, he found a large opening in the stern for the port stern mooring cable, through which he was able to leap aboard.

Gremlin's handlers from the Navy's EOD Unit Three arrived the next day. Gremlin was returned to the West Coast where, ironically, his training facility was within sight of the office of Donald Rosencrantz, an engineer and NOAA *Monitor* consultant. Don and I had been friends for years and it was he who arranged for me to accompany him to the 1977 *Monitor* expedition. Don sent an amusing e-mail telling me that Gremlin said "hi," but leaving me to sort out later how he could have known. A news story quipped, "In keeping with an old Navy tradition for sailors separated from their unit, Gremlin reported

The salvage ship USS *Grasp* participated in several important *Monitor* expeditions.
Courtesy NOAA *Monitor* Collection

During the 1999 *Monitor* expedition, *Grasp* hosted an unexpected visit from "Gremlin," a Navy-trained sea lion.
Courtesy NOAA *Monitor* Collection

to the nearest Navy unit and could be considered AWOL no longer."[3]

Humorous respites were rare at the sanctuary. It is impossible to accurately convey the day-to-day difficulties we encountered on these *Monitor* expeditions. Nothing is ever routine or "normal" out there. Winds and waves are almost constantly changing in direction and intensity, as are subsurface currents. These factors cause the surface vessel to shift on its mooring, which, in turn, shifts the dive clump. Sometimes the divers reached the bottom only to realize that *Grasp* had shifted too far away from *Monitor* for their umbilicals to extend. On June 24, our NOAA subsurface buoy, usually a safe distance away, had been pulled laterally by strong currents and twisted around the clump cable, requiring the Navy to expend a dive to clear the lines.

June 26 was another frustrating day. We awoke

to excellent weather and cobalt blue water indicating that we were now surrounded by the warm, northerly-flowing Gulf Stream. As the first divers descended, they discovered that the change in current had shifted *Grasp*'s position, causing the clump to come in contact with the turret, dislodging a large section of protective concretion. Fortunately, we had brought with us several large aluminum anodes, donated by corrosion specialists at Corrpro Inc., and after consulting with Curtiss Peterson, conservator at The Mariners' Museum, we decided to attach an anode to the turret to help prevent further corrosion of the exposed section. We hoped the anode would have the same effect as "sacrificial anodes" that boaters attached to metal hulls and outboard motors to prevent saltwater corrosion. On June 27, the Navy attached the anode using a large C-clamp.

Later that day, on dive number twenty-five, the Navy placed a time capsule in the captain's stateroom near *Monitor*'s bow. The capsule, made from a watertight PVC canister designed for sample storage, contained memorabilia from the participants and their parent organizations, along with personal notes from NOAA and Navy personnel. My own

A "CP gun" was used to make corrosion measurements on *Monitor*'s turret and hull components. Courtesy NOAA *Monitor* Collection

contribution was a note on the back of my business card pledging "to make every effort to ensure that the *Monitor*'s turret is raised, conserved and placed on exhibit so that the world will never forget this magnificent ship and its men."

On June 28, the Navy conducted two final dives before departing the sanctuary. We left after a total of twenty-nine dives, with all primary objec-

NOAA installed sacrificial anodes, mounted on PVC frames, to provide temporary corrosion protection for *Monitor* while recovery planning was underway. Courtesy NOAA *Monitor* Collection

tives completed. Six artifacts were recovered: four twenty-five-pound circular lead weights, possibly counter weights for *Monitor*'s engine, a copper oil cup or can, and an eighteen-inch section of copper pipe with a threaded flange on one end that may have been part of *Monitor*'s radiator system. More important for future planning, Navy combat photographers recorded unprecedented video and still photographic images of areas exhibiting dramatic deterioration: the stern, engineering spaces, and other areas aft of the amidships bulkhead.

Phase 2 (NOAA Operations): August 3–25

The second phase of research got under way on August 3 with training dives for an expedition sponsored by NOAA, the Cambrian Foundation, the National Undersea Research Center/University of North Carolina at Wilmington, and The Mariners' Museum. Each day we provided a brief report to be posted on the NOAA and Mariners' Museum websites and also in the *Monitor* "Clash of Armor" exhibit at the museum. With each site update we posted an 1862 event that affected *Monitor*'s crew that same day.

Our expedition was conducted entirely from the R/V *Cape Fear*, with an onshore recompression chamber and a crew of qualified personnel at the US Coast Guard's Hatteras Inlet Station. NOAA preferred to have a chamber onsite, but the shore location was close enough to serve in a dive emergency. Jeff and I represented the Marine Sanctuary Program, David Dinsmore was the NOAA Diving Program representative, Doug Kesling and Terrence Tysall directed the diving operations, and Dr. Michael Ott was our volunteer diving medical officer.

Following training and preparatory "work-up" dives, we made our first *Monitor* dives on August 10. On August 14, our divers anchored a current meter just off *Monitor*'s bow to give us a continuous record of water temperature and current direction and velocity over successive months. On August 16, we

tested a portable airlift consisting of a ten-foot-long section of four-inch diameter PVC pipe powered by air from a standard scuba cylinder, to create suction at the bottom of the pipe. The airlift worked surprisingly well. Two days later we used the airlift, with an extended length of twenty feet, to deepen the Navy's test hole at the base of the turret. We encountered the same obstruction and followed it down at least 1.5 feet below the edge of the turret wall—a feature we would need to take into account when developing our plan for raising the turret.

Also on August 18, a "CP Gun" (a hand-held underwater corrosion potential measurement device) was used to record seven voltage potential readings near the turret. This information was given to engineers at Corrpro, who reported that the sacrificial anode seemed to be protecting the turret from more corrosion. During August 22–23, our divers placed two cylindrical aluminum alloy anodes (each measuring three feet long by three inches in diameter) near the base of the turret and connected them to the turret wall with heavy-gauge wire and specially-fabricated C-clamps. Our corrosion experts told us these larger anodes would protect the turret for several years.

NOAA's phase 2 expedition conducted dives on eighteen of twenty-three possible dive days. A total of 130 person-dives were made, logging a total of 72.3 hours cumulative bottom time. We obtained excellent digital video of the engine and fire-room, the area of deck that contacted the turret, and the gap between the armor belt and seabed along the port side. Accurate documentation of these areas was critical for planning the next recovery missions; between the Navy video and our video and stills, we had what we needed. Both the Navy and NOAA had logged enough dives to become familiar with the site, make adjustments to our dive procedures, and improve dive efficiency. We also installed sacrificial anodes designed to protect the turret until time for its recovery. It had been a productive year, but without major funding we would not be able to take the next steps to save more of *Monitor*.

Chapter Seven

————⊷∞⊶————

ENGINEERING THE RECOVERY OF *MONITOR*'S MACHINERY

While we were planning and conducting research at the *Monitor* sanctuary in 1999, others were trying to secure funding for the upcoming recovery missions. The MDSU TWO, working closely with Commander Murray, who was now Naval Sea Systems Command's Supervisor of Diving, had submitted a request for support to the Legacy Resource Management Program, a Department of Defense program that funds historic preservation projects in all branches of the military. We knew our request would be up against scores of proposals for surveys, historic building renovations, and at least two very significant historic shipwreck projects, the Confederate submarine *Hunley* and the Confederate Raider *Alabama*.

Congressman Herbert H. Bateman, who represented Virginia's First District, had been working for years to ensure that *Monitor* would be protected for future generations. He strongly supported the request for Legacy funding. Bateman had sponsored the original request to the House Resource Committee to require NOAA to submit a "long-range, comprehensive plan for the management, stabilization, preservation, and recovery of artifacts and materials of the U.S.S. MONITOR."[1] John Rayfield, Professional Staff on the House Resources Commit-

tee, helped draft the report requirement and closely followed the progress of the *Monitor* project.

One morning in spring of 2000, Murray phoned to tell me he had to appear that afternoon in Virginia Senator John Warner's office to respond to concerns about the legality of Legacy Program support for *Monitor*. Murray said he would address the Navy issues, but asked me to be there to answer questions about archaeological aspects of the proposal. I quickly drove home, changed into a suit, and made the three-hour drive to DC. I arrived in Senator Warner's office just in time to hear an attorney from the Navy Office of the Judge Advocate General stating that the Legacy program could not provide funding for the *Monitor* since NOAA's preservation plan made it clear that the Navy had abandoned the ship in the 1950s. Legacy funds, he explained, could only be used for property owned by the Department of Defense.

As I sat there in shock and disbelief, Murray responded that as he read the Legacy requirements, projects were eligible for funding if they involved DOD property *or if the proposed project activities would demonstrably benefit the military*. He then described numerous examples where Navy experience on *Monitor* had improved his divers' skills, giving them realistic training that prepared them for submarine rescue, aircraft recoveries, and other marine disasters. The JAG officers and Senate staffers listened intently to Murray's argument until he sat down. The room was quiet for a minute, as everyone in the room looked at everyone else. Then the JAG attorney nodded his head and said he thought that might resolve the issue. I had a feeling that he had been looking for a way out of this impasse, especially since Senator Warner and Congressman Bateman—who held senior positions on House and Senate Committees on Armed Services—made it clear they expected DOD cooperation. Murray and I left the meeting convinced that *Monitor* remained in the running.

With immense relief, we soon received word that the Legacy Program had awarded the Navy a grant for an expedition in 2000. This was the break we had been waiting for, and additional support quickly followed. NOAA provided direct matching funding and additional support; The Mariners' Museum, our third principal partner, contributed the services of a skilled conservator, conservation equipment, and other staff; and Newport News Shipbuilding offered in-kind support for fabricating conservation tanks. With only a few months to prepare, we began developing detailed plans.

HULL STABILIZATION AND DEPLOYMENT OF THE ENGINE RECOVERY STRUCTURE, 2000

Expedition Planning

The Office of the Supervisor of Salvage, Mobile Diving, and Salvage Unit TWO, and Oceaneering International Inc., the Navy's salvage contractor, bore the bulk of responsibility for developing plans for stabilizing *Monitor*'s hull and recovering its steam engine. The *Monitor* National Marine Sanctuary staff provided detailed information on engine and hull construction, with an emphasis on how the engine and its associated condenser and piping were attached. We also provided drawings showing the large, unsupported gap beneath the hull created when the hull came to rest on the turret. The Mariners' Museum drew up a plan for transport, storage, and conservation of the engine and associated components.

Each year, we took on bigger tasks and this was our most complex project to date. Therefore we were encouraged to learn that MDSU TWO commanding officer Philip Beierl held an engineering degree from the Massachusetts Institute of Technology.

Engineers and archaeologists agreed that *Monitor*'s hull must be shored up from beneath in order to prevent possible collapse during or after the planned recovery operations. Stabilizing the hull was relatively straightforward. We had carefully mapped the exposed, unsupported area along the port side where the turret held the hull above the seafloor. Using those measurements, MDSU TWO and Oceaneering fabricated a set of wedge-shaped canvas bags supported by aluminum frames. The size and shape of each bag was based on its intended location, so that its base would rest on the seafloor, its top against *Monitor*'s inverted deck. Once installed, the bags would be filled with *grout* (cement), which would harden to create concrete support pillars beneath the hull.

The engine recovery plan, however, was not at all straightforward. *Monitor* lay upside down, and the engine was inside the most intact portion of the lower hull. We estimated that it would take Navy divers at least two to three weeks to dismantle the iron plating and frames comprising the hull surrounding the engine. Even worse, once they began to remove the heavy engine room frames, the engine would be unsupported, which meant it would drop onto the weakened deck beams, possibly collapsing the entire hull in that area. Carrying out that plan would be dangerous for the divers and possibly catastrophic for *Monitor*'s engine and hull.

Jeff Johnston suggested a different approach. Instead of removing the hull, we could recover the engine with its associated hull section still attached, which would significantly reduce the amount of cutting and, at the same time, provide support for the engine. As Jeff pointed out on the drawings spread across the table, the strongest section of lower hull was the segment that supported the engine. We pursued Jeff's idea, but still encountered two major obstacles. First, we would eventually have to cut the engine and its surrounding hull section free, which would still require some type of support to prevent its crashing down onto—and probably through—the inverted deck. Second, it would be impossible to support the engine from a ship or barge on the surface during the cutting operation. We had courted disaster in 1998 by attaching the propeller shaft to a cable from *Kellie Chouest*'s crane for the few hours required to cut the shaft; separating the engine from *Monitor*'s hull would take days, if not weeks. Over such a long time period, heavy waves and swells would undoubtedly cause irreparable damage to *Monitor* and, even worse, would create totally unsafe diving conditions.

Eventually, Oceaneering came up with a workable solution that I dubbed "the good ole boys' engine lifter." Back in the hills of Kentucky where I grew up, if you want to remove a truck engine, you simply take off the hood, slide a steel frame that looks like a beefed-up children's swing set astraddle the fenders, and raise the engine with a chain fall. Our Engine Recovery System (ERS) was essentially the same device, only many times larger and stronger. We would rig *Monitor*'s engine to the ERS, which, since its legs were solidly embedded in the seafloor, was not affected by currents or waves. Then all we needed to do was wait for a calm day to lift the entire assembly—ERS with engine securely attached—to the surface.

With the basic decisions made, our plan for 2000 began to take shape. Oceaneering would design and fabricate the ERS. The Navy would procure a large derrick barge in order to lift and deploy the massive ERS. We would also need a barge's deck space to house all mission personnel and equipment for diving and grouting. We would install and fill nine grout bags to support *Monitor*'s hull; then we would carefully lower the ERS down over the wreck, directly over the engine room, and onto the seafloor. Depending on the time remaining, we would begin preparations for engine removal.

The *Monitor* 2000 expedition was shaping up to be the most complex and difficult mission to date. However, NOAA and the Navy had developed an excellent working relationship during the previous two expeditions and we were confident we could satisfactorily resolve any onsite issues and make alterations to the operations plan as required. NOAA planned to conduct dives both before and after the Navy expedition, hoping we could complete some of the simpler tasks in order to maximize the Navy's time onsite. By mid-April 2000, we had completed most of the planning and procurement and it was time to put our plans to the test. NOAA's team would open this busy season with an expedition designed to inspect the engine room area and collect data the Navy would need.

2000 Monitor *Expedition, Phase 1: April 25–May 13*

Operating from the R/V *Cape Fear*, our NOAA team conducted technical dives on the *Monitor* from April 25–May 13, accomplishing most of our intended tasks. As before, the NOAA team consisted of divers from NURC/UNC-Wilmington and the Cambrian Foundation, along with a new partner, the Maritime Studies Program at East Carolina University.

We concentrated our documentation and photography on the space beneath the hull where Navy divers would install grout bags, and the engine room section that the Navy would remove as a single unit. I wanted accurate depth measurements around the hull so we could draw up an accurate three-dimensional site plan, but the only available instruments were our diving depth gauges, which recorded to the nearest foot. While pondering that limitation it occurred to me that most of our divers were wearing high-end gauges, all of them manufactured for a global market.

"Can't these gauges be programmed to read in metric?" I asked.

Getting an affirmative answer, I instructed the measurement team to program their depth gauges to read metric, since that setting displayed depth in tenths of meters—about four inches, or roughly three times as precise. This trick worked well, and by repeating the measurements at specific points over the course of two days we were able to obtain some very accurate depths for our site plan.

We mapped and recovered a few loose artifacts and hull samples. We also found that the anodes we attached to the turret and armor belt the previous year had decreased in size, solid evidence that they were protecting *Monitor*. These heavy aluminum-alloy pigs work in the same manner as sacrificial anodes on a small boat: due to careful selection of the molecular properties, corrosion consumes the anodes instead of *Monitor*'s hull. Finally, we tested several rivet heads and lower hull plates over the engine room, all of which were remarkably still quite sound. That made the Navy team a bit apprehensive.

HEAVY METAL, PART 1: ENGINE RECOVERY STRUCTURE

The structure for raising *Monitor*'s steam engine was designed by Oceaneering International Inc. (OII), and constructed in New Orleans under OII's supervision. Designated the engine recovery system (ERS), the structure consisted of three parts: a four-legged *bridge* to span the hull, a *trolley* designed to slide across the bridge to align with the engine room, and the *engine lifting frame* (ELF), to which the engine and surrounding structure would be attached.

The bridge structure measured 100 feet by fifty-seven feet and thirty-nine feet high, because it had to be wide enough to straddle the *Monitor*'s hull and tall enough for the engine and attached hull framing to be lifted clear of the wreck. The trolley was a rectan-

The Engine Recovery Structure being assembled in Louisiana. Courtesy NOAA *Monitor* Collection

gular steel frame, sixty by twenty-six feet, that was placed across the bridge where it could slide port or starboard and forward or aft so as to align itself over the engine room. The ELF was a twenty-five-foot-square reinforced steel frame designed to be suspended from the trolley and positioned directly over the hull/engine section to be lifted. All rigging was between the hull and ELF. The three-component engine recovery system weighed eighty-five tons, more than twice the estimated weight of the engine itself.

This drawing shows the three major components of the engine recovery structure (ERS) and how it was positioned over *Monitor*'s engine room. Courtesy NOAA *Monitor* Collection

2000 Monitor *Expedition, Phase 2: June 30–July 31*

In mid-June, a tug from Louisiana entered the Little Creek Naval Amphibious Base lashed close alongside the Weeks 526 barge, a 292 by 82-foot derrick barge equipped with a 350-ton crane. This was to be our home for the month of July. In less than a week Chris Little, Oceaneering's expedition superintendent, and MDSU TWO erected a small city on the barge's deck, including special vans containing crew berthing, full galley, water purification and sewage treatment plants, and a grouting plant. The MDSU TWO added the Navy's Fly-Away Mixed-Gas Div-

ing System, two recompression chambers, hydraulic power units, generators, and office and repair vans. The most impressive deck cargo, however, was the Engine Recovery Structure (ERS), which arrived in Norfolk just in time to be placed aboard one end of the Weeks barge. Jeff took one look at this barge, laden with a huge crane, dozens of steel containers and, now, the 39-foot-tall ERS, and christened it "Bargezilla."

On June 30, we arrived at the *Monitor* sanctuary aboard the barge which, with its crane arm boomed up, was imposing enough to be seen sixteen miles away in the Outer Banks town of Buxton. The MDSU TWO was in charge, supported by the Naval

Barge with Engine Recovery Structure (ERS) on deck, 2000. Courtesy NOAA *Monitor* Collection

Sea Systems Command and NOAA. The tug captain coordinated with Beierl, and the barge was quickly moored over *Monitor* on eight anchors, whose cable lengths could be adjusted to position the barge very precisely. The MDSU quickly set up their dive station. Further along the barge's side they readied the grouting plant. On the opposite end of the deck was the dive station for a modified SeaROVER remotely operated vehicle (ROV) provided, with an operator, by the National Geographic Society. With its ability to function in strong currents, and its excellent still and video cameras, the SeaROVER gave us a valuable live view of diving operations.

The Navy's diving methodology was the same as in previous years, except that this year the Navy decompressed their divers using a provisional revised schedule designed to reduce the incidence of oxygen toxicity—the first revision in many years. The principal modification was the use of a 50 percent helium/50 percent oxygen mixture instead of pure oxygen during the late stages of in-water decompression. The long-standing decompression table was modified after repeated reports of oxygen toxicity incidents during previous *Monitor* dives. When Navy divers entered the water to dive on *Monitor* this year, they would be the conducting the first at-sea dives using these new decompression tables. This was another example we could report to the Legacy Program of how *Monitor* dives were benefiting the Navy.

Harbor Branch Oceanographic Institution's submersible, *Clelia*, was onsite for two weeks, giving expedition leaders an opportunity to inspect the site in much more detail than the ROV—or even diving—permitted. Since I was unable to dive, watching

operations from *Clelia* was especially helpful, and quite a treat.

The Navy's first goal was hull stabilization. On July 12, MDSU TWO divers placed the seven canvas grout bags at predetermined intervals beneath the port hull. Each of the bags was supported by an aluminum tubing frame fabricated to fit a specific location. Each grout bag consisted of five separate chambers, the largest at the base, each fitted with a filling tube. The largest bag, placed just forward of the turret, had a base of eight by fifteen feet and a filled height of five feet. Some of the MDSU TWO divers had learned to operate the grout plant, where the grout, in powder form, was mixed with water before being pumped down to the bags.

The plan was to fill each chamber of each bag, beginning at the bottom level, until the top of each bag was in contact with *Monitor*'s inverted deck. Navy divers would insert the grout hose into a bag's filling tube, then notify the barge crew to begin pumping grout down the hose. We quickly encountered a serious problem: the twenty-minute time limit for each dive was not sufficient to fill an entire chamber. The MDSU adjusted the plan so that each dive team ended its dive by inserting the hose into a new fill tube. Then grout was pumped while the next team prepared to dive. The next pair of divers checked the bag, then flushed the hose and moved to a new fill tube. This method worked well unless equipment or weather issues interrupted the timing, which would result in a clogged hose that required time to clear. The ROV allowed us to watch the bag filling from the barge, which helped coordinate the grout pumping operation.

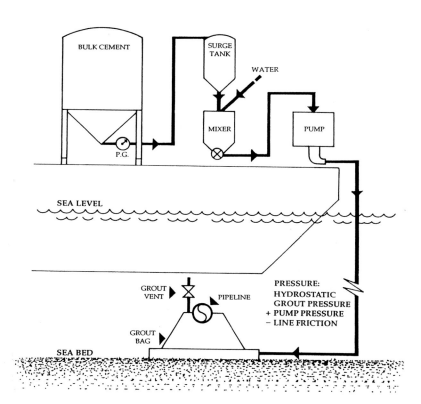

Schematic of the system used to mix grout and pump it down into custom fabricated bags to support *Monitor*'s hull.

Wreck of the
USS *Monitor*

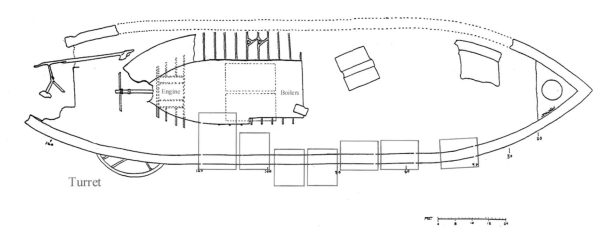

Turret

Seven grout bags (red rectangles) were placed beneath *Monitor*'s hull to support the inverted deck and help prevent additional hull sagging or collapse. Courtesy NOAA *Monitor* Collection

A Navy diver installing a grout bag beneath *Monitor*'s raised hull. Below, a filled grout bag. Courtesy NOAA *Monitor* Collection

As bag filling continued, we prepared to lower the bridge component of the ERS as soon as a calm day presented itself. First, divers placed large targets on *Monitor*'s hull, just above the engine room section that we planned to recover. We then secured fixed, downward-facing cameras on the bridge, aligned so as to home in on the targets, similar to a spacecraft docking guide.

On the morning of July 14, there was a slight swell from the southwest, with seas of three to four feet. At 6:30 a.m. we decided to deploy the bridge.

Conditions were not ideal, but we knew we might not get a better day. While one team made final preparations to the bridge, another was repositioning the barge so the crane would be aligned properly. We used the ROV to confirm that we were in the correct position. By early afternoon, everything was ready and the weather was holding.

At 1:45 p.m. we held a final safety briefing, then commenced the deployment evolution. The crane did not have enough cable to lower the bridge all the way to the bottom, so we had to use a two-stage

Commander Beierl using a handheld GPS unit to align the barge precisely with *Monitor*'s hull. Courtesy NOAA *Monitor* Collection

process. By 3:50 p.m. the eighty-five-ton bridge was hanging beneath the barge and the final lowering operation began. In the control van, we stared intently at the small video screen on which Beierl had drawn target marks with a grease pencil. At 4:08 p.m. the targets on *Monitor*'s hull appeared on the screen. The ROV had the bridge in sight and by panning its camera up and down we could guide the crane operator to make minor adjustments to align the bridge. Our "docking" system worked so well that at 5:30 p.m. the ERS touched down within one foot of its intended lo-

cation—well within limits. Someone shouted, "The bridge has landed!" We all breathed a big sigh of relief, since we had no contingency for running out of time before we could deploy the bridge.

On July 21 we finally completed the shoring operation. All the grout bags were filled, and most of them made direct contact with *Monitor*'s deck. The second NOAA team had arrived onsite and they began carefully videotaping the positions of the grout bags and the ERS. Navy divers now turned their efforts to the lower hull, using a hydraulic chisel to begin separating the hull section to be lifted. The topside crew began preparing the trolley and engine lifting frame to be lowered onto the bridge. Since we were making good progress, we contacted The Mariners' Museum to ask if their conservation facility could accommodate the skeg and another section of propeller shaft. The skeg lay beside the hull where we had placed it two years earlier. We cut the propeller shaft as close to the engine as possible, since leaving a long section of shaft attached would make engine recovery more difficult and may well have damaged the engine. On July 26 the museum responded that they would make arrangements to accept and conserve both items. That same day, Navy divers, using the guillotine saw that detached the shaft in 1998, cut a ten-foot shaft section on four dives.

The following afternoon, we raised the shaft,

NOAA divers place "targets" on *Monitor*'s lower hull to help guide the "bridge" into position. Courtesy NOAA *Monitor* Collection

The "bridge," being lowered over the side of the Weeks barge to be placed over *Monitor*'s engine room. Courtesy NOAA *Monitor* Collection

The engine recovery structure in place over *Monitor*'s engine room; the square engine lifting frame is suspended just above the engine. Courtesy NOAA *Monitor* Collection

Commander Beierl inspects the engine room in preparation for engine recovery being planned for the following year. Courtesy NOAA *Monitor* Collection

still attached to the "stuffing box" where it passed through the hull. At 8:25 p.m., the crane operator deftly placed the trolley and ELF at the center of the bridge, directly above the engine room. Now the entire engine recovery structure was in place, where it would remain until we returned for the engine in 2001.

On the morning of July 28, Commander Beierl and Master Diver Robertson made the last Navy dive of the expedition, attaching lifting slings to the skeg. At 11:00 a.m. the skeg was lowered to the barge deck and everyone began preparing for departure. By 8:00 p.m. the mooring anchors and cables were on deck and the barge and its new cargo headed for Little Creek. The artifacts were offloaded at Little Creek and transported to The Mariners' Museum by the Ft. Eustis Army Transportation Unit.

2000 Monitor *Expedition, Phase 3: July 17–August 10*

When the barge left the sanctuary on July 28, I hitched a ride aboard the Navy's chartered shuttle boat, *Christine J.*, which took me to Hatteras where I rejoined the NOAA dive team to acquire more data needed for planning the eventual recovery of *Monitor*'s guns and turret. Once again, I was frustrated that my 1998 bends incident was still preventing me from diving. Fortunately, we had a skilled and enthusiastic research team that included divers from ECU and the Cambrian Foundation.

One of our primary goals was to examine and document the "fire room," a space between the engine and boilers where coal heavers fed coal to the twin boilers while engineers operated the engine. The fire room is open on both sides due to disintegration of lower hull plates. Terrence Tysall and Kyle Creamer used a diver propulsion vehicle (DPV), a torpedo-shaped, battery-powered device designed to pull a diver through the water, to excavate a small test hole beneath the engine. Kyle directed the DPV downward while Terrence braced them both against the little scooter's thrust. The divers eventually washed out a small hole through which they could feel what they believed was a deck beam and probably the main steam pipe from the boilers to the engine. That seemed to confirm our hypothesis that due to the collapse of the lower hull the engine now rested directly on *Monitor*'s inverted deck. If so, Navy divers would not have to worry about the engine falling but they would probably find it difficult to rig lifting slings beneath the engine.

I asked Terrence, an outstanding diver and excellent sketch artist, to draw the face of the engine, noting locations of fragile controls, gauges, and pipes to be avoided during the engine rigging operation in 2001. The team also documented that same area with still and video cameras. When we examined the sketches and imagery, we could see that the configuration of the engine face and gauges matched the *Monitor* "as-built" drawings. Among the fragile items were glass tubes, thin brass tubing, clock, engine revolutions counter, and steam pressure gauge.

Another team, headed by ECU archaeology graduate students Tane Casserley and Gary Byrd, wrestled our "deepwater airlift" to the bottom and excavated a small test hole inside the turret. Airlifts are the "underwater vacuum cleaners" of maritime archaeology, but because of *Monitor*'s depth and strong currents, ours had to function without a supply of air from the surface. Our simple airlift consisted of a ten-foot section of plastic home plumbing pipe through which we injected air from a large cylinder. The system was very portable and functioned better than expected.

The excavators exposed lots of small pieces of Ivory Tree coral, *Oculina varicosa*, embedded in tightly packed sediment. *Oculina* grows in abundance on *Monitor*'s hull, and when it dies, its branches litter the wreck and surrounding seabed. Inside the turret, it seemed to have formed a hard layer that prevented currents from scouring out the interior sediments. On subsequent dives, Casserley reached a depth of three feet, where the sediment changed to a fine, clay-like material that is commonly encountered in underwater "digs." He did not locate *Monitor*'s Dahlgren guns, but did expose the iron beams on which the gun carriages rolled. We also learned that once the *Oculina* layer was penetrated, the tur-

Fire Room Components

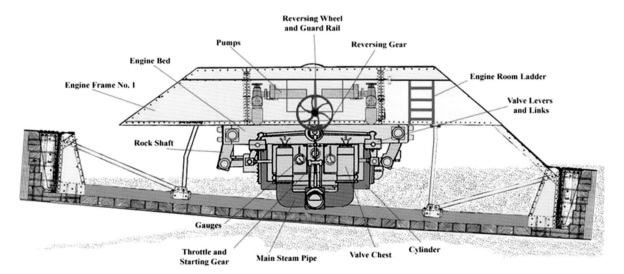

Monitor Collection, NOAA

A cross section through *Monitor*'s fire room, facing aft, showing how the lower hull has collapsed, causing the engine to fall onto the inverted main deck. Courtesy NOAA *Monitor* Collection

A mosaic showing the face of *Monitor*'s engine. The reversing wheel (left) is still in place, as are the bilge pumps (top) and stairs to engine level (right). Courtesy NOAA *Monitor* Collection

ret seemed to be filled with a soft layer that could be easily removed.

NOAA divers also secured the trolley to the bridge with chains. We didn't think the Gulf Stream could move a steel truss, but we weren't willing to chance having an ocean trawler accidentally drag the trolley onto the wreck. Our team made its last dive on August 10, recovering an intact ironstone pitcher and several other exposed objects from the area forward of the amidships bulkhead.

Site Preparations Completed

The *Monitor* 2000 expedition stabilized *Monitor*'s hull with grout bags, installed the eighty-five-ton, three-part Engine Recovery Structure, began dismantlement of the engine compartment, and recovered two major components from the historic ironclad's propulsion system. Navy divers completed 168 dives, logging eighty-two hours and twenty-nine minutes of bottom time. NOAA's team added at least

A photograph of the engine of the monitor USS *Commanche*, which was very similar to the original *Monitor* engine. Courtesy The Mariners' Museum

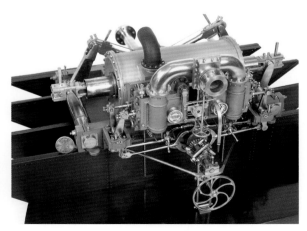

A very accurate scale model of *Monitor*'s engine by Richard Carlstedt, based on both historical drawings and the recovered engine itself. Photo by Ron Erickson, courtesy Richard Carlstedt

Objects recovered in 2001: (a) ironstone pitcher; (b) brass sconce that once held a lantern; (c) an oilcan; (d) the engine register recorded the number of revolutions made by *Monitor*'s engine; it is the only object recovered to date that bears the ship's name; and (e) this wheel was used to reverse the direction of rotation of the engine. All Courtesy NOAA *Monitor* Collection

the same amount. We had convincingly demonstrated our ability to place the huge steel bridge precisely in position to raise the engine. We were now one step closer to recovering *Monitor*'s steam engine and turret. But, again, we had no promises of future funding.

STEAM ENGINE RECOVERY, 2001

Fortune smiled again on the sunken *Monitor*, when the Legacy Program awarded another grant for recovery of the engine during the summer of 2001. NOAA, The Mariners' Museum, and Newport News

Shipbuilding all provided cash and in-kind matching.[2] We now felt confident that if engine recovery were successful, funding for turret recovery would be almost automatic.

Expedition Planning

When we received the news, we were already deeply involved in recovery planning for both the engine and the turret. The Navy had selected a new salvage contractor, Phoenix International Inc., who worked with us on planning and who would participate in the work onsite. Phoenix designated Tom Bailey as their Project Officer and Jim Kelly as Project Engineer. There were changes in the Navy personnel as well. Christopher Murray, now a captain, was Program Manager for the Chief of Naval Operations (CNO), and official representative of the Office of the Supervisor of Salvage and Diving (SUPSALV). Commander Barbara "Bobbie" Scholley, the new C.O. of MDSU TWO, was the Navy's On-Scene Commander.

Jim Kelly worked for weeks with Jeff Johnston to develop a detailed computer-aided drawing (CAD), 3-D solid model of *Monitor*'s engine and the surrounding hull structure, based on the best available historical drawings and descriptions. Kelly then placed the engine/hull section into a general model of the wreck as it lay on the seabed. From this, he

calculated that the slope and list of the wreck caused a shift of the center of gravity of the engine/hull section of approximately 3.5 feet. Navy planners factored this estimate into their plan for positioning the ELF. Jeff Johnston generated additional graphics to help guide the planning and orient the divers.

We developed a detailed list of tasks, estimated the time required to complete them, and quickly realized that it would be impossible to complete all the tasks. Our funds gave us forty-five days onsite with a barge and dive systems, plus two weeks for mobilization, and another two weeks for demobilization. We concluded that, if we were to give ourselves the best odds for success, we needed to conduct some of the preparatory activities before the barge arrived. As we sought other options and assets, both NOAA and the Navy responded.

We determined that engine recovery would require four separate expeditions. We knew that would tax our capabilities to the limit, but we had no choice. First, NOAA would conduct dives in late spring to inspect the Engine Recovery Structure, then recover exposed artifacts near the engine room that might be damaged during recovery operations. The Navy would send a salvage ship and MDSU TWO dive team to prepare the ERS and begin cutting free the section to be lifted. During the primary expedition, a large derrick barge would support engine recov-

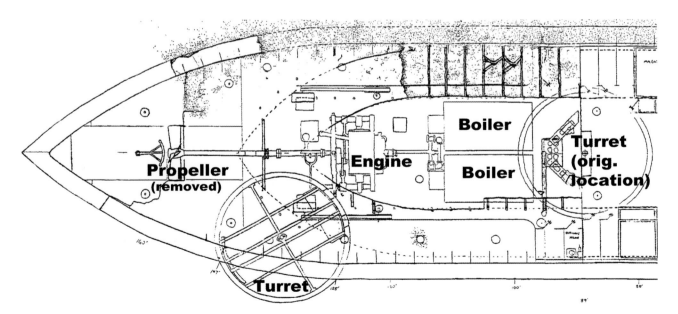

A plan view showing the exact location of *Monitor*'s engine, fire room and boilers.
Courtesy NOAA *Monitor* Collection

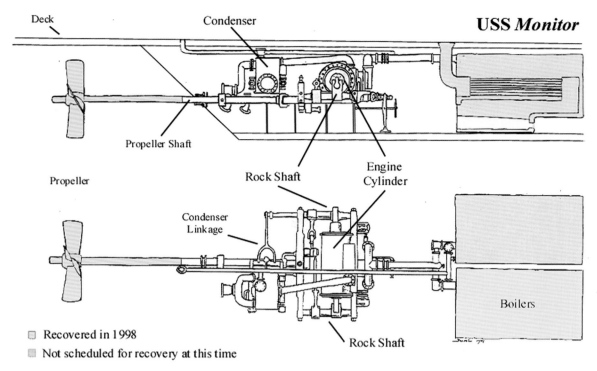

Deck   Condenser

Propeller Shaft

Propeller

Rock Shaft

Engine
Cylinder

Condenser
Linkage

Boilers

Rock Shaft

☐ Recovered in 1998
☐ Not scheduled for recovery at this time

Plan and profile drawings of *Monitor*'s complete drive train. Courtesy NOAA *Monitor*
Collection

ery. Finally, NOAA would conduct postrecovery site clean-up and documentation dives.

Each year our mission objectives had become more difficult, and this year was no exception, both because of the volume of work to be accomplished and the weight of the object to be lifted. We needed a bigger platform than the Weeks barge. Phoenix would arrange a suitable lease, probably from one of the companies operating in the Gulf of Mexico

oil fields. We also needed much more time for the divers to work.

Dive Planning

During early planning for engine and turret recovery Commander Murray realized that saturation diving capability would be essential. One of the many lessons he and other US Navy Divers learned during the propeller recovery in 1998 was that they could not assume any task would be easy while working at the *Monitor* sanctuary. A combination of environmental factors—frequent and often sudden storms, strong currents, and deep water—made Hatteras one of the most difficult sites they had encountered. Additionally, recovery of such large, heavy objects as the engine and turret would require much more time on the bottom to complete literally hundreds of tasks including assessment, disassembly, digging, cutting, removal, rigging, and other complex, potentially dangerous activities.

Even experienced surface supplied divers were limited to roughly thirty minutes actual working time, followed by about three and a half hours of de-

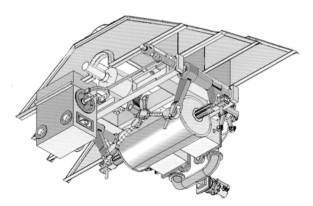

Computer-aided design solid model showing *Monitor*'s engine and the associated engine bed and frames that were removed as one unit. Courtesy NOAA *Monitor* Collection

compression, during which time diving ceased until the divers had successfully completed their return to surface pressure. The MDSU TWO improved efficiency considerably by adding a second decompression chamber, but surface supplied diving just was not capable of providing the necessary bottom time for the complex tasks that lay ahead. Another consideration was fatigue, since diving was being conducted around the clock, seven days a week, weather permitting, which was very strenuous for the divers who, following their dive, remained on duty to support subsequent dives.

Saturation diving would be more complex, but would allow divers to remain on the bottom for routinely up to five and a half hours and occasionally up to seven. The same divers would dive every day, which would give them the opportunity to become familiar with the wreck and be able to complete assigned tasks quickly and effectively. Murray easily convinced us that saturation diving was the way to go. There was only one small problem: at the time the Navy did not have a surface vessel with saturation diving capability. Fortunately, when the need arose, Murray was in a position to help.

With the support of the Navy's Supervisor of Diving and Salvage and the Chief of Naval Operations (CNO), Director of Deep Submergence Vehicles, Commander Murray set out with Master Diver Chuck Young to propose a proof of concept to use Navy personnel and a commercial saturation (SAT) system to conduct deep water salvage. This would be a first for Navy Diving. A commercial system would be selected and then thoroughly inspected by Navy divers and a certification team from the Navy's Supervisor of Diving and Salvage. The system would then be tested, followed by training of Navy divers and, if everything went according to plan, a CNO Waiver that would allow us to use the system for *Monitor* recovery expeditions. Once Murray had approval to proceed, he worked hurriedly with Tom Bailey to develop detailed plans and locate a suitable system. In early 2001, while Navy preparations continued at a furious pace, NOAA sent its first dive team to the sanctuary.

2001 Monitor *Expedition, Phase 1:*
March 25 to April 11

In late March, when cold water, strong winds, and frequent storms are typical, our NOAA team ar-

rived at the *Monitor* Sanctuary aboard the UNC-Wilmington research vessel *Cape Fear*. Jeff and I directed operations from the boat, while Tane Casserley headed up the NOAA dive team.

Our team made its first dive on March 28. Water temperature was chilly and the waves were high. Despite only having 30-foot visibility on the bottom, the divers had no difficulty locating *Monitor*, thanks to the huge ERS sitting above the wreck. After ten days on site, we had only made two dives as a result of high winds. We also faced huge challenges due to cold and dark water, thanks to a shift in the Gulf Stream's currents. We pressed on, battling the weather, and completed our goals despite having only half of our planned time to finish the job. The ERS was in good condition, despite light rust and scattered barnacles. We mapped the position of the engine lifting frame relative to the engine room and recorded video of the entire area. We mapped and recovered sixteen artifacts, including a bayonet hilt, glass lantern chimneys, and several US Navy condiment bottles. The glass whale-oil lamp chimneys were recovered from the sand, where they apparently fell from a storage area in the deck near the turret. Amazingly, one was completely intact and the others were only chipped. Once again, we checked our measurements of the space where grout bags would be installed, making note of any possible obstructions to report to MDSU and Phoenix.

2001 Monitor *Expedition, Phase 2:*
April 21 to May 6

USS *Grapple* (ARS 53) supported dive operations at *Monitor* from April 26 to May 12, 2001. After the salvage ship was secured in a four-point moor, *Grapple*'s divers conducted thirty-two dives, logging more than thirty hours of dive time preparing the engine recovery system for the upcoming recovery expedition. While inclement weather hampered dive operations, MDSU completed their tasks. Everything was now ready for the main event.

2001 Monitor *Expedition, Phase 3:*
June 3 to July 25

The goal for phase 3 was simply stated: recover *Monitor*'s steam engine. Our detailed task list was much

USS *Grapple*, like its sister ship *Grasp*, participated in several *Monitor* expeditions. Courtesy NOAA *Monitor* Collection

more complicated. Phoenix leased the derrick barge *Wotan* from Manson Gulf Inc., of Houma, Louisiana. *Wotan* supported a 500-ton crane and a 100-ton mobile "deck crawler" crane. It was more than that, however; it was large enough to be configured as a floating city that could support 108 personnel for sixty days—at least forty-five of which would be at *Monitor*—operating twenty-four hours a day, seven days a week.

Wotan carried two separate Navy diving stations, fifty feet apart, and an ROV station. One station consisted of Navy surface supplied mixed gas divers. The second station was a saturation dive station using a leased civilian saturation system. Both

For recovery of *Monitor*'s engine and turret, the larger crane-barge *Wotan* was leased by the Navy. Courtesy NOAA *Monitor* Collection

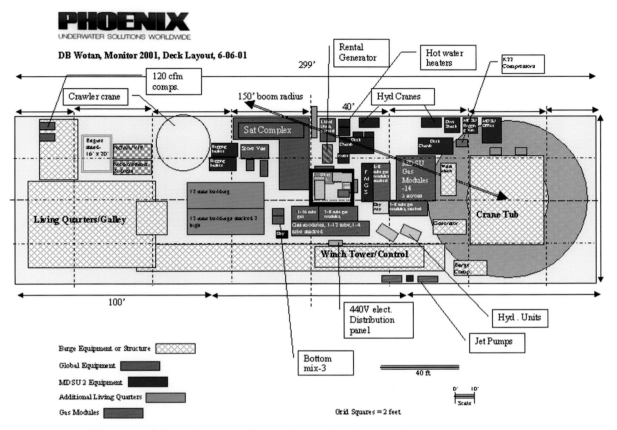

Wotan became a "floating city" during the 2001 and 2002 *Monitor* Expeditions, with complete working, eating and sleeping arrangements for more than 100 personnel.
Courtesy NOAA *Monitor* Collection

stations operated on two twelve-hour shifts a day for round-the-clock diving. Using a leased Global Industries 1504 saturation system that had virtually been rebuilt by Navy divers during the previous six months, Navy divers could conduct dive excursions of up to six hours at a time (compared to forty minutes a dive, maximum) with the surface-supplied system.

For cutting the engine/hull assembly free of the wreck, MDSU collected some impressive equipment. There was a Broco cutting torch, several types of hydraulic cutting tools, including a vicious-looking "nibbler," several jackhammers, and a "hydro-blaster" capable of pumping water through a nozzle at pressures up to 20,000 pounds per square inch, creating a high-pressure water jet to slice through thick steel.

Mobilization. Phase 3 actually began in Houma, Louisiana, in mid-May. An advance team from MDSU TWO, the Navy Experimental Diving Unit,

and Phoenix loaded all of the equipment, including the saturation diving system. On June 3 the tug *Arapahoe Chief* took *Wotan* under tow. All twenty-one saturation divers sailed with the barge, where they trained for the next fourteen days while en route to Hatteras. Captain Murray was aboard to oversee final preparation and final inspection of the "SAT" system; Jeff rode the barge on its long transit, too, teaching the divers as much as possible about the construction of *Monitor*'s lower hull and the engine attachment.

On the first leg, across the Gulf of Mexico, Tropical Storm Allison hampered *Wotan*'s progress, slowing it to only 4 knots for much of the time. Conditions improved as they began traveling up the coast of Florida, but Tropical Storm Allison threatened to overtake them, so tug and barge diverted to Morehead City, North Carolina, arriving on June 13. The following day, I joined the MDSU TWO divers at Little Creek and we drove to Morehead City to

SATURATION DIVING SYSTEM USED BY THE US NAVY

An overall view of the saturation diving system used at the *Monitor* site during 2001 and 2002. Courtesy NOAA *Monitor* Collection

Without saturation diving capability, the complex recovery operations conducted during 2001 and 2002 would not have been possible. The saturation system used for *Monitor* recovery operations was the Global 1504 Portable SAT System, leased from Global Industries. It is a twelve-person, two-chamber system with a two-person bell that is launched and recovered using an A-frame. The bottom of the bell mates with the top of a transfer trunk that connects to both of the two six-person deck chambers. The system can operate as deep as 1,500 feet. The SAT divers wore a helmet similar to the MK 21 worn by Navy surface supplied divers, but modified for long-duration saturation diving with a gas reclamation system that conserves breathing gas. Their hot-water diving suits were also similar to those worn by surface supplied divers.

On *Monitor* saturation dives, a "dive" actually began when four divers entered one of the deck chambers and were pressurized to a "working pressure" of 180 feet of seawater (fsw), which was sufficient for them to reach *Monitor* at a maximum working depth of 240 feet. As the divers remained in the pressurized chamber, their bodies eventually absorbed as much dissolved gas as possible at that pressure, at which point their bodies were "saturated." The primary advantage of saturation diving is that as long as the divers remain under pressure, they do not need to spend hours decompressing after each dive. At the end of their saturation interval, which could be as

(continued)

A schematic diagram showing the major components of the saturation diving system. Courtesy NOAA *Monitor* Collection

Navy saturation divers looking out of one of the two "SAT" chambers in which they will spend up to two weeks under pressure while working on *Monitor*. Courtesy NOAA *Monitor* Collection

SAT system control station. Courtesy NOAA *Monitor* Collection

long as two weeks or more, the divers would undergo a single decompression of approximately seventy hours (nearly three days). This means that our saturation divers were no longer limited to the twenty- to twenty-five-minute dive times of surface supplied diving, and so they were able to spend considerably more time working at the site.

A typical dive consisted of sending two divers from the deck chamber into the bell. Once the bell was sealed, still at the working pressure of the deck chamber, it was lifted over the side of the barge and lowered to a position just above the *Monitor*, where the pressures inside and out were equal, at which point the divers could open their hatch. Each bell excursion was planned for ten to eleven hours, with two excursions scheduled for each twenty-four-hour period. One diver would deploy while the second diver remained inside as bell operator and standby diver. The first diver completed a four to five hour excursion (dive outside the bell), then exchanged position with the standby diver. At the end of the excursion, the bell was raised and mated with the transfer trunk. The dive teams then rotated for the next excursion.

An advantage of the Global 1504 system is that its two independent deck chambers permitted one team to be pressurized and ready before decompression began on the previous team. This minimized downtime between teams.

load the remaining equipment and join *Wotan* for the final transit to the sanctuary.

At 2:00 p.m. we met with members of the press before beginning a series of planning meetings aboard the barge while loading continued. After the evening meal, I moved into the steel box that was to be my home for the next six weeks. My address was "S6-LB8"—starboard box number 6, left bottom bunk, number 8. At noon on Saturday, June 16, we departed Morehead City bound for *Monitor*. We divided our team into two watches, or shifts: I would work the day watch (6:00 a.m. to 6:00 p.m.) with Captain Murray, and Jeff—a night-owl—volunteered to join Commander Scholley on the night watch.

On the morning of June 17 we arrived at the sanctuary and took advantage of the beautiful, calm morning to begin the mooring operation. At 7:50 a.m. *Arapahoe Chief* placed the first anchor up current, followed quickly by a second to hold *Wotan* roughly in position. By 10:10 all eight anchors were set, and *Wotan* was sitting above *Monitor*, roughly on an east-west orientation. By this time, I had witnessed numerous ships and barges performing this "mooring evolution" but I was still amazed at how quickly and efficiently *Arapahoe Chief*'s crew set the anchors and the barge crew adjusted the heavy steel wire-rope cables—each 1,900 feet long—with giant winches, positioning the barge exactly where it was wanted. I also marveled at our ability to pinpoint our position relative to the *Monitor*. Using Differential Global Positioning System (DGPS) satellite receivers and specialized navigation software, we could adjust the barge while watching a display that indicated the positions of the barge, wreck, and ERS relative to one another. We made the final position adjustment by sending down the empty dive stage with a downward-pointing camera that let us align the dive station to within a few feet. By 10:43, less than three hours after we began, we were exactly in position to begin diving.

In the afternoon, we launched Phoenix's Benthos MiniROVER ROV, which gave us a quick look around the site. At 11:00 p.m., the surface-supplied divers conducted the expedition's first dive, setting up a hydraulic ram for positioning the ELF. By morning, all the rams were in place and the divers were installing the hydraulic hoses and manifolds that will operate the rams.

At 1:15 p.m. the saturation bell was lowered into the water, with most of us crowded around the ROV display to watch the bell descend. Surface-supplied diving continued through the day and night, and at 8:55 the next morning our SAT system was officially certified after completing a checkout dive to depth. With the checkout dive completed under the watchful eye of NAVSEA's Supervisor of Salvage and Diving's certification team, the final authorization for use of the civilian SAT system was received from the Office of the CNO. Now we could ramp up diving operations. Wasting no time, the Navy put the bell back in the water at 10:15 a.m. with the first two working SAT divers. They logged nearly eight hours on this first dive, getting the ERS hydraulics almost ready to operate.

While divers continued aligning the ELF, encountering annoying problems with lifting chains, several of us continued to review and refine the recovery plan. By June 21, divers had conducted reconnaissance dives around the perimeter of the section to be recovered, and had inspected the large steam condenser that was still connected to the engine by mechanical linkage and steam piping. The divers found numerous artifacts and began recovering them or moving them out of the work area. Weather was generally good, but heavy seas and strong currents sometimes slowed dive operations. Fortunately the SAT system was virtually immune to seas and currents. As long as the bell could be launched, it

The saturation diving bell is lowered over *Wotan*'s side with two Navy divers who will continue preparing *Monitor*'s engine for recovery. Courtesy NOAA *Monitor* Collection

was suspended just above the work area for each ten hour-long (or more) dive. It was the tender diver who suffered most, having to sit inside the bell as the pressure rose and fell in rhythm with the swells and waves.

Cutting and Rigging. In order to recover the engine, Navy divers first removed lower hull plating around the engineering spaces (engine room) in order to gain access to the engine. The SAT divers used the Broco cutting torch to burn off the rivet heads holding the plating onto the frames. This was slow because of the heavy layers of marine growth and corrosion that prevented the torch from operating. On June 24, a lower hull plate was removed from the starboard side of the engine. Later, the ELF was finally positioned directly above the center of gravity of the engine section and lowered to within three feet of the hull.

Just before midnight, Jeff woke Murray and me to report that divers had encountered possible human remains inside the engine room. We threw on our clothes and rushed to the SAT diver's video display. All work had ceased. The diver, who had been dredging silt out of the engine compartment, was standing by for instructions. When he moved his helmet camera closer to the "remains" we soon realized he had discovered the bones and shell plates from a sizable sea turtle! We had a good laugh (mostly at the SAT diver's expense) and work resumed.

Surface-supplied divers were focusing on removal of the condenser, which was proving to be more challenging than we had anticipated. They removed quite a bit of metal debris, mostly from deteriorated hull beams and plating, then dredged the looser silt away, stopping frequently to deal with artifacts. As if that was not enough hindrance, as they progressed deeper into the silt they exposed large lumps of coal that had become chemically bonded to each other and to surrounding objects. Surface-supplied diving is strenuous under the best of conditions, and these teams were going up and down as often as decompression requirements permitted. The work had become so slow and repetitive; the divers were referring to each day as "Groundhog Day," after the movie in which Bill Murray wakes up every morning to discover that it is still Groundhog Day.

Meanwhile, SAT divers worked around the

Photomosaic of the intact aft portion of *Monitor*'s lower hull. The engine room is at the far left. Courtesy NOAA *Monitor* Collection

clock to secure the thirty-five-ton engine to the ELF. After they had removed enough hull plating to get access to the engine, they had to expose the engine foundation plate by digging through the same type of cemented coal that covered the base of the condenser. This slow process required more than a week of backbreaking work by SAT divers laboring up to four hours at a time with chipping hammers in confined spaces. We had to get access to the foundation plate, the two-inch thick iron casting to which the engine was securely bolted. Jeff had showed us on the drawings and the 3-D CAD model that the foundation plate was probably going to be the strongest object to which we could rig the four lifting chains from the ELF.

As an interim measure, SAT divers rigged wire-rope cables and nylon lifting straps from the engine to the ELF. This supported the engine from the ELF that, in turn, was firmly suspended from the bridge system. The SAT divers could now proceed with excavating and cutting with no fear of the engine shifting or dropping. By June 28 divers had begun to excavate around and beneath the engine. This required digging as deep as three feet in some areas, using chipping hammers, jackhammers, and the hydro-blaster. The concreted coal was so difficult to remove that only the hydro-blaster was successful in dislodging the lumps.

We were making excellent progress until the night of June 28, when SAT diving was halted because several of the divers reported flu-like symptoms and

one had an ear infection. The SAT divers and chamber operators were familiar with these issues, which are not uncommon with saturation diving. The divers must live for weeks at a time in close confinement in a humid steel chamber, under six times the

A Navy diver clears sediment using a "hydro-blaster," a device that generates a very high-pressure stream of water at the nozzle. Courtesy NOAA *Monitor* Collection

Navy team leaders Scholley (left) and Murray prepare for a dive to inspect the progress of work. Courtesy NOAA *Monitor* Collection

surface pressure and breathing a helium-oxygen gas mix. Fortunately, the situation improved rapidly and diving resumed. Then, early in the morning of July 2, the wind shifted and increased, causing one of the mooring cables to part. The barge had then swung more than 100 feet away from the wreck. Very fortunately, the SAT bell and surface-supplied stage were on deck, along with most of the hydraulic tool hoses, so very little damage was done.

By dawn, the wind had shifted to northeast and built to around 20 knots, creating seven- to nine-foot seas that slammed against *Wotan*'s north side, from which we staged all our dive and ROV operations. Later, the seas subsided and we moved the barge back into position. The following morning we had to hold dive operations until the parted mooring line was replaced. During this lull in diving operations, a team was busy fabricating two steel "T-beams" that would support the engine. We had already decided that the best way to lift the engine was to cut holes in the foundation plate and then place steel beams underneath the plate to spread the load and serve as rigging points.

Later, on July 3 diving resumed and that evening the SAT diver drilled a pilot hole in the foundation plate. During the night watch, the Broco cutting torch removed an iron cylinder two inches thick and six inches in diameter. To our amazement and delight, the exposed surface of this iron cylinder was as shiny as modern steel. Nevertheless, we knew

that cast iron that has been immersed in saltwater for more than a century is brittle and cannot be counted on to provide support, so we continued preparing the steel beams.

The rest of July 4 was business as usual, with only passing references to Independence Day, although that evening we could see fireworks bursting over several Outer Banks communities. At noon a boat arrived from Beaufort, North Carolina, with a new, more powerful hydro blaster—this one capable of producing a 20,000 psi jet—to help dislodge the concreted coal from the engine. Divers measured the four hull frames that supported the *Monitor*'s engineering space, since they were part of the hull assembly that would be raised with the engine. They, too, would be supported with steel beams. Divers used our old friend the guillotine saw to cut the large steam pipe that ran from the engine to the condenser. By July 8, all six main engine lift points had been rigged, the mechanical linkage arm between the engine and condenser had been cut, the connecting steam pipe had been cut, and hydro blasting and condenser rigging were under way. The further we excavated the more we exposed engine parts that required support or artifacts and auxiliary machinery that needed to be removed or recovered. The task list seemed to grow rather than shrink!

Once the engine was freed and completely exposed, divers attached additional chains, wire-ropes,

This graphic shows how the engine and its frames were attached to the "engine lifting frame," which was in turn connected by adjustable cables to the spreader and bridge. Courtesy NOAA *Monitor* Collection

and nylon straps to further spread the lifting load and secure the steam engine to the lifting frame. As a final step to ensure that no small parts would be dislodged and lost, divers wrapped the entire engine in strong cargo netting that, in turn, was secured to the ELF.

By July 14 we were very nearly ready for the recovery. Bailey notified Lockwood Brothers, in Hampton Roads, to be on thirty-six-hour notice to get under way with the barge that would transport the engine to Newport News. On *Wotan*, excitement was building, but so, too, was the level of fatigue. The divers had been working nonstop for weeks, encountering and overcoming problems with nearly every dive. The divers did not talk about fatigue— Navy divers would not admit to that—but their dive supervisors kept a close eye on dive operations and repeatedly reminded each dive team that safety was the top priority. We kept a constant watch on the calendar and the weather forecasts, never forgetting

that we had to recover the engine before time and funding ran out.

At 7:40 p.m. on July 14, we were in position for the initial lift. A SAT diver was on the bottom near the engine room, two surface-supplied divers were on top of the bridge, waiting to operate the hydraulic lifting rams, and the ROV was roaming around giving topside a view of the scene. Once we agreed that everything was ready, the hydraulic pump was energized and at 7:55 *Monitor*'s engine was raised off the hull. The lift was only a few feet, to provide enough space beneath the engine/hull assembly for divers to add the final supporting straps and cargo nets. Divers completed the final tasks, made another inspection, and reported that the engine was ready to lift. Another team of divers raised the engine assembly higher, toward the top of the bridge. The final step attached cables from the ELF to the bridge to stabilize the engine and prevent it from swinging during recovery.

SUMMARY OF NAVY DIVING—2001

Approximately 150 Navy divers from twenty-six different commands participated in the engine recovery expedition in 2001, logging a total of 665 hours working bottom time in depths down to 238 feet. Navy divers rarely accumulate so much mixed-gas dive time. Mixed-gas diving is very expensive, and so most training is done on air at shallow depths. Also, although saturation diving has many advantages, especially for providing greatly increased bottom times at deeper depths, there have been few opportunities in recent years for Navy salvage divers to obtain or retain proficiency in saturation diving. Therefore, the *Moni-*

tor expedition provided them with an unprecedented training opportunity.

- Surface supplied diving
  - Surface supplied HEO2 dives completed: 429
  - Total hours of working bottom time: 201

- Saturation diving
  - Total number of bell excursions: 45
  - Total hours of working bottom time: 465
  - Total days in saturation: 416 man-days in saturation

A Navy diver stands atop *Monitor*'s engine frames, while connecting support straps from the engine to the engine lifting frame. The engine and frames can be seen hanging by numerous cables and straps just below the engine lifting frame. Courtesy NOAA *Monitor* Collection

On July 16, at 4:30 in the morning, everyone was up and ready to go. Weather conditions were excellent, with small waves and no current. Lockwood's barge had arrived just after midnight and was tied alongside *Wotan*. At 7:30, Master Diver Chuck Young, the SAT diver, placed the lifting bridle in position for the lift. At 9:50 two surface-supplied divers had joined Young and were helping secure the heavy shackles to the padeyes at the four corners atop the bridge.

At 10:45 a.m., we all gave the "thumbs up" and the engine, still attached to the lower hull, lifted cleanly off the bottom. Because of the water depth, the engine was first lifted about halfway up, where the crane's cable was reattached to a lower attachment point for the final lift. Anticipation kept building throughout this evolution. Everything proceeded smoothly and at 11:56 the engine appeared at the surface, to the enthusiastic shouts and cheers from everyone on the barge. The combined weight of the engine, hull, and ERS was an amazing 135 tons, but the crane did its work, quickly placing the entire assembly on the deck of the smaller barge. Another major piece of *Monitor*, and a unique and important one representing the engineering genius of its inventor and builders, had returned to the surface.

Now that the engine was exposed to air and sunlight, we had to keep it wet at all times to prevent rapid disintegration. We were prepared for this. Curtiss Peterson, The Mariners' Museum conservator, quickly recruited volunteers and rigged a prefabricated sprinkler system to keep the engine wet until it could be placed in a permanent conservation tank. With the ERS secured, and with pumps spraying water over the engine, the barge departed for the slow transit to Newport News Shipbuilding.

On *Wotan*, our job was not done. Saturation divers continued working in the area where the engine had been removed and where the condenser still sat, surrounded by pipes, coal and other debris. The dive teams were ready to begin freeing the condenser by July 18. The iron was in such good shape, the divers were able to use a wrench to back out the large bolts holding the condenser to the hull frame! At 3:30 in the morning of July 19, the condenser came out of the sea and onto the deck of *Wotan*. This was the last operation of the 2001 expedition.

Back at Newport News Shipbuilding, skilled riggers removed the ELF, with the engine still attached, from the ERS, and placed it in a specially built transportation cradle. The shipyard used their 310-ton gantry crane to lift the engine and lifting cradle back onto the Lockwood Brothers barge. On August 7, the barge was towed up the James River and beached at a preselected spot on the shore across from The Mariners' Museum. Once the barge was secure, a temporary ramp was set up, and a massive fifty-six-wheel trailer was rolled up the ramp and under the cradle. The cradle was then lowered onto the trailer, which rolled down the ramp and up to the road. After a brief ceremony the trailer transported its engine and cradle payload up to the museum's conservation yard and to a waiting 32,000-gallon conservation tank. The process went smoothly, giving us renewed confidence that we could repeat the same process the following year with *Monitor*'s gun turret.

This had been an amazing year. We had re-

During August 2–4, 2001, we teamed up with the Deep Sea Archaeology Research Group (DeepArch) at the Massachusetts Institute of Technology for a survey of *Monitor*'s turret to see if we could determine whether the two guns were still inside. A secondary goal was to attempt to document any obstructions around the base of the turret that might impede recovery operations. For these tasks, David Mindell and Brian Bingham brought their portable high frequency (150 kHz) sub-bottom profiler. The profiler was mounted inside a waterproof case designed to be carried and positioned by two divers. This survey was supported by the R/V *Cape Fear*, from the University of North Carolina at Wilmington (UNC-W), and a team of divers from NOAA, East Carolina University, and the National Undersea Research Program at UNC-W. Although results were not conclusive, significant echoes from inside the turret suggested that the guns were still inside.[1]

With each expedition, we recorded changes to the site in as much detail as possible. Realizing that the 2002 expedition was going to alter the *Monitor*'s hull almost beyond recognition, we requested survey time from the Navy's nuclear-powered ocean engineering and research submarine *NR-1* to document the site before the turret recovery. The project was approved, and on March 23, 2002, Jeff Johnston and I boarded the sub off Hatteras and spent the night on board as *NR-1* made repeated passes over *Monitor* with video cameras and sonar recording every detail. This survey gave us a permanent record of *Monitor* as it existed before we attacked its armor belt and made off with its gun turret. The *NR-1* was the most sophisticated underwater vehicle to visit *Monitor* and Jeff and I felt privileged to have the opportunity

NOAA divers scanning the turret using a portable subbottom profiler designed and built at MIT. Courtesy NOAA *Monitor* Collection

The US Navy research submarine *NR-1* conducted a remote-sensing survey of *Monitor* in March 2002, successfully imaging the site before the turret and a segment of armor belt were removed. Courtesy NOAA *Monitor* Collection

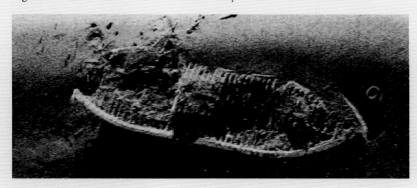

NR-1 generated several excellent sidescan sonar images of *Monitor*, including this full-length view. Courtesy NOAA *Monitor* Collection

to work with the outstanding crew of Navy scientists. Launched in 1969, *NR-1* was never officially commissioned; the sub conducted hundreds of scientific research missions, most of them classified, and was finally deactivated in 2008.[2]

Notes:

1. Mindell and Bingham (2001).
2. http://www.Navy.mil/navydata/cno /n87/usw/issue_14/nr1.html (retrieved February 8, 2010).

On July 16, 2001, *Monitor*'s engine, secured within the ERS, emerged from the water.
Courtesy NOAA *Monitor* Collection

The engine was held securely to the lifting
frame by a network of cables and lifting
straps. As a final step, cargo netting was
suspended below the engine in case any
parts should dislodge during recovery.
Courtesy NOAA *Monitor* Collection

Once the engine arrived at The Mariners' Museum, it was placed in a specially-built conservation tank adjacent to the propeller tank. Courtesy NOAA *Monitor* Collection

covered approximately 250 artifacts, including the thirty-ton engine and associated equipment, the steam condenser, a forced-air blower, leather belt, and auxiliary steam engine, two Worthington steam-powered bilge pumps, and other assorted auxiliary machinery and equipment. Our next target, the turret, now awaited us. With the turret's recovery, the last of *Monitor*'s major equipment and, arguably, the most significant part of the lost warship's revolutionary technology, would be returned to the nation from the depths of the sea. We turned our attention to the task of lifting the massive wrought iron turret. We knew it would be our greatest challenge, and our greatest triumph. Little did we know that it would also bring us face to face with some of *Monitor*'s lost crew.

Chapter Eight

⟶⟩●⟨⟵

MONITOR COMPLETES ITS FINAL VOYAGE

TURRET RECOVERY PLANNING

Monitor Expedition 2002 was our last scheduled recovery mission to fulfill the objectives of the comprehensive, long-range *Monitor* preservation plan. In 1998, Navy divers recovered *Monitor*'s propeller, which reduced stresses on the hull. NOAA and the Navy conducted additional survey and site preparation work in 1999 and 2000, and deployed the Engine Recovery Structure over *Monitor*'s hull. In 2001, we successfully recovered the engine and began preparing the armor belt and turret for the final season. Now it was time to put our skills and experience to work on the most challenging expedition yet.

The Legacy Program came through for us once again, awarding the funds requested for turret recovery during the summer of 2002. NOAA's National Marine Sanctuary Program and Office of Ocean Exploration contributed significant matching funds and The Mariners' Museum provided conservation staff, Curtiss Peterson and Gary Paden, who were already tending the artifacts previously recovered. The Apprentice School at Newport News Shipbuilding fabricated a conservation tank of sufficient size to contain the turret. Other organizations and individuals provided additional support. Before the expedition began, we had obtained adequate fund-

ing and assets to conduct the mission, to house and conserve all recovered cultural material securely, and to analyze and report on expedition results.

Expedition Planning

The sequence of events for 2002 included removing a section of armor belt and hull from atop the turret, partially excavating the turret, then rigging and recovering the turret and all its remaining contents. The key partners remained the same: NOAA's National Marine Sanctuary Program; the US Navy Supervisor of Salvage (SUPSALV), Naval Sea Systems Command; US Navy, Mobile Diving and Salvage Unit TWO; Phoenix International Inc., the Navy salvage contractor; and The Mariners' Museum. Newport News Shipbuilding and the US Coast Guard provided additional support.

The decision to cut and remove the section of armor belt and decking that blocked access to the turret was not without controversy. Years before, NOAA received several proposals for raising the turret. One called for supporting the armor belt with steel jacks, then digging a deep pit into which the turret would slide, leaving it clear of the armor belt. Another recommended using heavy cables and pulleys to pull the turret out from under the armor belt. There were other, less feasible proposals as well.

From the beginning, however, I argued that we should remove the obstructions rather than try to move the turret laterally. My reasoning was simple: the turret was constructed from 192 individual iron plates, riveted and bolted together to form a cylinder almost twenty-two feet in diameter. Now, the turret was displaced and inverted; we had no way of knowing how much deterioration those rivets and bolts had suffered over the years, but we had already observed that some of the large bolt heads on the turret wall had disintegrated. Attempting to pull the turret sideways would place tremendous stresses on the fasteners, which could cause the plates to pull apart, leaving the turret and contents strewn on the seabed. (My greatest fear was that we would recover a "turret kit"—some assembly required!)

Another fact that supported the removal of the armor belt and hull atop the turret was that the structure was already badly deteriorated, so damage would be relatively insignificant. It was the turret, after all, that was *Monitor*'s most iconic feature, and

we were certain it contained the guns and other artifacts that would reveal important details about the ship and its crew in their final hours.

None of us wanted to damage any part of this historic site, but in the end we had rejected all other proposals as unsatisfactory. Therefore, we developed a recovery plan specifying removing a section of armor belt and overlying structure followed by lifting the turret directly to the surface. We submitted our plan to the scrutiny of state and federal authorities and received approval to proceed.

With that decision behind us, we now turned our attention to "how" we would raise the turret. Thanks to the removal of several plates from the armor belt during 2001 we had a clear plan for completing that task, but recovering the turret presented new challenges. The most obvious suggestion was to place the Engine Recovery Structure back over the wreck and use it to rig and raise the turret. Jim Kelly, our Phoenix engineer, explained that unfortunately the ERS could not support the much larger weight of the turret and contents, which was three to four times as heavy as the engine. Even with more steel added to

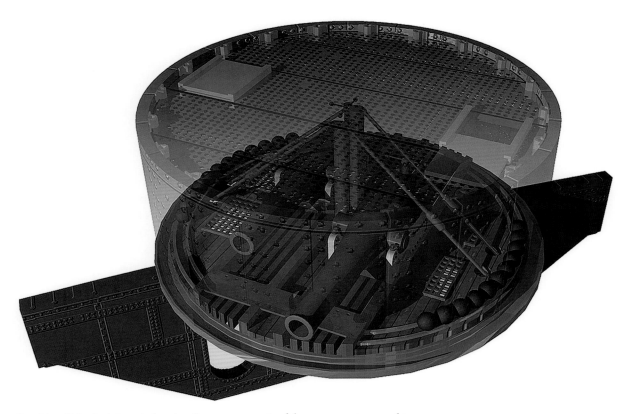

Graphic of *Monitor*'s turret, showing the arrangements of the guns, carriages and inner structure. Courtesy © Bill Pitzer

the structure, there were other problems that could not be overcome. We needed an entirely new solution.

Kelly and Johnston developed a detailed computer model of the turret structure and added the guns and carriages. From the model, Kelly estimated the weight of the turret, contents, and silt at 185 tons! That weight, plus the added weight of lifting cables and supports, would tax the capacity of *Wotan*'s derrick crane. In addition, as the turret came out of the water and lost the buoyant force due to the displaced volume of water, the load would surge to over 200 tons. We all had a vision of the turret breaking the surface and being so tantalizingly close and then breaking apart and crashing back into the sea. The crane was rated at 500 tons, but that value had to be reduced by the angle at which the boom was extended, with additional allowances for dynamic loading caused by sea motion. Given our time and funding limitations, we could not consider leasing a larger barge and crane.

We met frequently, reviewing and debating numerous proposals. Phoenix brought in a consultant who suggested some unique and imaginative recovery plans, but one by one, we rejected them. Finally, on March 26, 2002, Kelly proposed a design that met all our criteria; he called it "the Spider." Kelly presented a sketch showing a strong steel frame with eight legs forming an open cylinder. The legs could be pushed out fifteen degrees from vertical to form a huge "claw" that would be lowered over the turret on a calm day. Then, divers would actuate hydraulic cylinders that would pull the legs inward until they rested beneath the base of the turret. Inner projections at the base of each leg would support the turret evenly at eight points, distributing the load and capturing the turret roof to prevent it from falling out.

All of the planners liked the idea at once, but we had several reservations. Could we lower the Spider over the turret without fear of serious damage to the turret structure? Could the legs be secured in place beneath the turret in spite of the obstructions we had encountered in our test excavations? And would the turret roof (if, in fact, it was still in place) be secure for the long lift to the surface? The salvage experts and divers were confident that we could accomplish the first two objectives, but Jeff and I were less willing to agree that the turret roof would remain in place, particularly as the turret first rose out of the water. We felt that issue might be a deal-breaker.

Kelly listened to the comments, then sketched a new structure on a white board: a steel platform. We would use the Spider to capture the turret and lift it a few feet above the seabed. Then the crane would swing slightly, moving the turret to a circular steel platform that had previously been placed on the seabed. The Spider would be lowered onto the platform and secured there by divers, thus supporting the turret roof from underneath for the lift to the surface. Everyone agreed that the entire plan would require incredibly calm seas and exceptional skill on the part of the crane operator. After much more discussion, we concurred that the "Spider and Platform" was the breakthrough we had been searching for. The device was approved.

Phoenix immediately began drafting construction drawings for the lifting structures while arrangements were being made for the other equipment. We planned for forty-five days onsite, plus approximately four weeks mobilization and three weeks demobilization, counting approximately two weeks barge transit each way between Louisiana and the sanctuary. A NOAA scientific dive team would overlap the Navy expedition by a week or more, to assist Navy divers as requested and to record the Navy expedition on videotape. Once again, the derrick barge *Wotan* would be leased from Manson Gulf and the saturation system from Global Industries.

2002 *MONITOR* EXPEDITION

On June 7, *Wotan* departed Houma, Louisiana, loaded with essentially the same personnel facilities and equipment as 2001, except the completed Spider and Platform were part of this year's deck cargo. Jeff was aboard to conduct diver briefings, since there were new faces on the dive teams and the plan was unusually complex. Ten days later, *Wotan* paused off Morehead City, North Carolina, to take advantage of calm seas to prepare the mooring anchors. Unfortunately, the shaft that rotates *Wotan*'s crane turret snapped, causing a detour past *Monitor* and up to Norfolk, Virginia, for repairs. Finally, at 5:30 p.m. on June 24, we pulled out of Norfolk, arriving at the sanctuary at 3:15 a.m. on June 26.

Supervisory personnel and command structure were similar to 2001, giving us an incredibly strong and experienced team. Captain Chris Murray was

HEAVY METAL, PART 2: "SPIDER" AND PLATFORM

After much discussion and debate NOAA, the US Navy, and Phoenix International (the Navy's new salvage contractor) finally agreed on a method for lifting

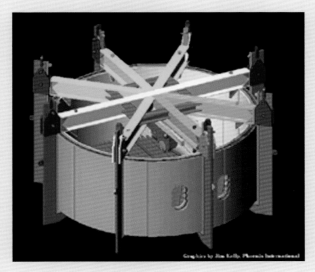

The Spider supported the turret evenly at eight points on the bottom lip and also provided a strong structure from which additional rigging was attached to the guns and roof structure. Courtesy NOAA *Monitor* Collection

The last step before turret recovery was to place the Spider, with the turret inside, onto a steel platform that would ensure that the roof did not fall out during recovery. Courtesy NOAA *Monitor* Collection

Monitor's gun turret. Various ideas for reusing the engine recovery system were considered, but the turret was too heavy for the ERS, even if reinforced. The new concept, called "the Spider," would be just wide enough to fit down over the turret and "grasp" it securely. The twenty-five-ton Spider, or "claw" as it was interchangeably referred to, consisted of a steel frame with eight horizontal arms, each supporting a pivoting steel leg capable of swinging out 15 degrees from vertical to enable them to clear the exterior wall of the turret. The base of each leg had an inward-reaching shelf on which the rim of the turret would sit during recovery. The plan was to slowly lower the Spider, with all eight legs pivoted out in the "open" position, until the legs rested on the seafloor with the turret inside its grasp. Then Navy divers would use hydraulic rams to push the legs up under the rim of the turret, whereupon the legs would be locked in the "closed" position.

A circular steel platform was constructed to the same diameter as the Spider. Once the Spider was in place, the platform would be lowered to the seabed, approximately twenty feet from the turret. The turret would be lifted a few feet off the bottom and swung away from the wreck and over the platform, where the Spider would be carefully placed onto the platform. The exact alignment would be accomplished by a clever system of two tapered "cups" fitted to opposing legs of the turret that would mate with two "stabbing guides" of different heights, as shown in the illustration. One of the tapered cups would mate with the taller stabbing guide, and then the crane would slowly rotate the Spider/turret until the cup on the leg on the opposite side of the Spider aligned and mated with the shorter stabbing guide. Once both stabbing guides engaged, the entire spider assembly would be lowered onto the platform. Once aligned and lowered, padeyes on each of the spider legs would be aligned with padeyes on the platform, and divers would attach turnbuckles to firmly affix the spider to the platform. The platform was fitted with truck tires to act as "springs" to provide support between the platform and the roof panels of the turret, which were recessed beneath the turret rim. This unique invention ensured the safe recovery of *Monitor*'s famous gun turret and the preservation of the archaeological record it contained.

once again the SUPSALV representative and CNO Program Manager. Bobbie Scholley, recently selected for promotion to Captain, was still MDSU TWO's C.O., and was again serving as On-Scene Commander and Salvage Officer, responsible for overall planning and execution of Navy activities onsite. Tom Bailey returned as Phoenix Project Officer and Jim Kelly was Phoenix's onsite engineer, to advise on the turret lift and keep a watchful eye on the lift weight. Jeff and I each headed up a watch for NOAA's Archaeology Team, assisted by Tane Casserley and Eric Emery, a forensic archaeologist with the US Army Central Identification Laboratory in Hawaii (CILHI), who would oversee the recovery of any human remains that we encountered.

As in previous years, we conducted activities 24/7, on two watches: midnight to noon and noon to midnight. The surface-supplied and saturation dive teams, the NOAA Archaeology Team, and almost all other personnel followed this schedule. During each twelve-hour shift, two saturation divers descended to the wreck in the transfer bell, from which they each spent four to six work hours outside the bell, while the other diver tended from within the bell. Several surface-supplied dives were usually conducted on each shift. In order to ensure efficiency and continuity of work tasks, we held a "handover" briefing thirty minutes before each shift, during which the oncoming team was briefed by the previous shift on work progress, potential problems, and recommendations. Dive stations also remained the same.

The mooring operation proceeded quickly, and at 9:27 a.m., Navy surface-supplied divers conducted the first dive of the expedition. At 1:00 p.m., the saturation team launched the bell on a working dive that also served as the SAT certification dive for this year. The divers wasted no time in getting down to business, using a high-volume stream of water to clear silt and debris from *Monitor*'s stern deck. On the next surface-supplied dive, Captain Scholley and Master Diver Scott Heineman conducted a quick reconnaissance and began placing objects from the stern into a large salvage basket for later recovery. The Navy was working extra hard to make up for the time lost during the unplanned diversion to Norfolk.

SUMMARY OF NAVY DIVING—2002[1]

Approximately 142 Navy divers from twenty-five different commands participated in the turret recovery expedition in 2002, logging a remarkable 928 hours of total working bottom time in depths down to 238 feet. As stated in the previous chapter, Navy divers rarely accumulate so much mixed-gas dive time, and almost no saturation dive time. During the period of 1995 to 2004, Navy dives at the *Monitor* sanctuary accumulated valuable data that resulted in a modification to the Navy's mixed gas decompression tables and eventually led to the Navy's purchase of its own saturation diving system.

- Surface supplied diving
  - Surface supplied HEO2 dives completed: 507 dives
  - Total hours of working bottom time: 286 hours, 31 minutes
  - Total dive time, including decompression: 1,858 hours, 34 minutes

- Saturation diving
  - Total number of bell excursions: 154 dives
  - Total hours of working bottom time: 641 hours, 37 minutes
  - Total diver-days in saturation: 650.75 diver-days

Note:

1. US Navy reports to the Office of the Supervisor of Diving and Salvage and to the Legacy Resource Management Program; expedition field data.

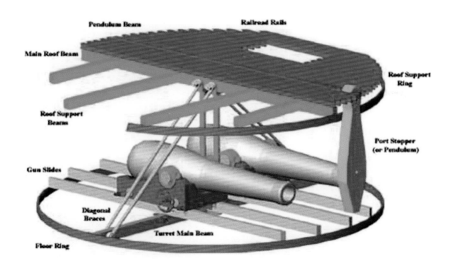

Labels on diagram:
Pendulum Beam · Railroad Rails · Main Roof Beam · Roof Support Ring · Roof Support Beams · Port Stopper (or Pendulum) · Gun Slides · Diagonal Braces · Turret Main Beam · Floor Ring

Phoenix engineer Jim Kelly generated a computer solid model of *Monitor*'s turret from which he computed an accurate estimated weight for the turret, guns and sediment. Courtesy NOAA *Monitor* Collection

The sea had other plans. Winds and seas built throughout the night, and by our 11:30 a.m. shift briefing, six- to eight-foot seas out of the southwest had pushed the barge out of position. By midafternoon we had to reposition the barge so it would ride better in the heavy seas. We soon discovered that at least two of the massive mooring anchors were dragging. Through all of this, the SAT divers continued to work and even the surface-supplied divers managed to get in a couple of dives. The weather remained bad on the twenty-eighth, and we had to suspend all diving when the barge shifted so far the SAT diver was pulled off the wreck. After an evening thunderstorm passed through, creating winds over 50 knots, the seas began to calm and diving resumed. The night shift concentrated on removal of the armor belt. Our plan was to cut the belt at two places and move each section off the wreck. Jeff prepared detailed graphics showing how the armor belt was put together, and he used his graphics, plus some of the surviving *Monitor* drawings, to brief the divers on what they were up against.

The armor belt proved more difficult to cut than expected. Divers from both teams used every tool at their disposal trying to find something that would work. We knew that the belt was well made—Jeff had developed a series of drawings showing its construction—but we thought that the cutting torch and hydro-blaster would cut through the iron and wood without difficulty. The one-inch plates were cut in two locations and then placed on the seabed, thus exposing the plate beneath it. This continued until all had been removed, exposing the thirty-inch wood core and angle-iron frame. The wood was a problem.

It had been impregnated by iron oxide until it was the consistency of petrified wood. The cutting torch could not burn it—it would not conduct electricity—an underwater chain saw could not be used due to the numerous metal spikes that criss-crossed the wood core and the hydro-blaster jet could not cut through it as easily as first predicted from early tests on land. Eventually, Navy determination and persistence won out, but the process took much longer than we had predicted.

On July 2 the hydro-blaster stopped working. Apparently, the around-the-clock strain of battling the armor belt took its toll. Another unit was immediately ordered and, to my amazement, arrived on the Fourth of July. Independence Day was no holiday on the barge, but the day was not without a few displays of patriotism, including a few mysterious pops and bangs during the night watch.

The following day, after what seemed like months of daily labor, divers connected the crane's

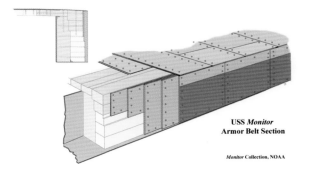

USS *Monitor*
Armor Belt Section

Monitor Collection, NOAA

Among the graphics constructed by Jeff Johnston were several showing the inner construction details of the armor belt. Courtesy NOAA *Monitor* Collection

Just aft of the turret several fallen and partially seperated deck plates (far left) indicated the advanced state of deterioration of *Monitor*'s hull. Courtesy NOAA *Monitor* Collection

Saturation divers spent many hours cutting through the armor belt using a variety of tools, most successfully the high-pressure hydro-blaster. Courtesy NOAA *Monitor* Collection

lifting hook to the sling on the armor belt. Finally, at 7:57 p.m., the armor belt, with remnants of the deck still attached, rose off the hull in one thirty-ton, forty-one-foot long section. The crane swung the load away from the wreck and deposited it nearby in a predetermined location. For the first time, we could see the entire turret. The first thing I noticed was that the turret was full to the rim with silt, coal, and debris, much of which would have to be removed to reduce weight before the lift. Our Navy divers were about to get some additional archaeological training, and I doubted they would be able to muster much enthusiasm for removing silt while Jeff and I hovered over them at the communications station, asking for measurements and cautioning them about going too fast.

As turret excavation began, at least one member of the NOAA Archaeology Team remained on duty in the saturation control van around the clock, so we could watch and document the excavation as seen from the SAT diver's helmet camera. We also videotaped all the excavation dives. On Sunday, July 7, SAT divers began removing the upper debris layer from the turret, some of which fell into the turret when the armor belt and hull section was removed. I designated this mixture of concretion fragments and coal "Layer A." Just beneath, Layer B consisted primarily of silt and dead coral, with bits of coal and concretion mixed in. In one area the dead coral was as deep as eighteen inches. While SAT divers excavated inside the turret, surface-supplied divers labored to clear the area around the turret base where the legs of the Spider would land.

At this point in the expedition, our days generally consisted of repetitive tasks—cutting, clearing, excavating—punctuated by the occasional problem to be solved. Inevitably, someone periodically relieved the tension and monotony with a prank, and the archaeologists were not infrequently targeted. On every expedition, I carried a standard federal-issue green-cover log book that served as my field journal. In it, I recorded times and activities, special accomplishments, meeting/discussion notes, scheduled visitors, all punctuated with crude sketches. The journal was my "security blanket" (not to mention my auxiliary memory) and I kept it close at all times. Once in a while, when I took a break to get coffee or visit the head, a Navy guy would yield to the temptation to see what I was writing. The next logical step was to contribute notes of their own, but usually written as if I had penned the comments. An example, recorded sometime after 7:00 p.m. on July 7, was, "These Navy guys really know what they're doing! CAPT Murray has mellowed out significantly from last year's expedition." As might be

Saturation and surface-supplied divers worked around the clock to meet the tight schedule. Courtesy NOAA *Monitor* Collection

Working at night, with only helmet lights for illumination, often made activities more difficult. Here, a saturation diver (blue helmet) walks over to help a surface-supplied diver. Courtesy NOAA *Monitor* Collection

Even holidays were work days, but the barge team demonstrated their resourcefulness to acknowledge America's Independence Day. Courtesy NOAA *Monitor* Collection

On July 5, a 41-foot section of armor belt was lifted away from *Monitor*'s hull and placed alongside the wreck. A Navy photographer was dispatched to document the turret, visible for the first time since the ship sank. Courtesy NOAA *Monitor* Collection

anticipated, some of the Navy contributions to my journal could not be quoted!

I spent most of my watch in the SAT van or the ROV van where, when bottom conditions were good, the MiniROVER's camera provided a useful view of the site and excavation. Jeff had become a proficient pilot, and he and I both enjoyed our "stick time" on the Rover. By July 13, turret excavation had exposed both guns and carriages and the massive port stoppers that sat directly behind the gunports. Each port stopper had been secured for sea by push-

Monitor Collection, NOAA

The turret was completely filled with silt, debris, and—unexpectedly—tons of coal. Courtesy NOAA *Monitor* Collection

Navy divers quickly surveyed the exposed turret, then set up dredges to begin removing part of the contents so that lifting straps could be attached to the guns and interior structure. Courtesy NOAA *Monitor* Collection

Dive teams took turns excavating the turret while NOAA archaeologists watched and recorded their progress via helmet-mounted cameras and the ROV. Courtesy NOAA *Monitor* Collection

Captain Murray and Captain (select) Scholley share a minute of relaxation during a brief lull in recovery operations. Courtesy NOAA *Monitor* Collection

On July 17 the "spider" was lowered over the side and down to the turret. Courtesy NOAA *Monitor* Collection

Jeff Johnston (left), the author, and other members of the NOAA team documented *Monitor* artifacts as they came to the surface during preparations for turret recovery. Courtesy NOAA *Monitor* Collection

The saturation diver stood on the armor belt and helped guide the spider into place around the turret. Nearby, the *Johnson-Sea-Link* (right) videotaped the placement, while the ROV videotaped the whole scene. Courtesy NOAA *Monitor* Collection

ing a two-inch-diameter threaded rod through a small hole in the stopper and securing it inside and out with wooden "bucklers" that were destroyed by *Teredo* soon after *Monitor* sank. The rods were still in place, but were not designed to hold the two-ton stoppers in place, so divers replaced them with new steel rods, which were secured with wood and steel.

On July 14, our supply boat, *Emmanuel*, brought conservators Curtiss Peterson and Wayne Lusardi out to transport more than eighty artifacts back to The Mariners' Museum. The following day, Harbor Branch's research vessel *Seward Johnson* arrived with the *Johnson-Sea-Link II* submersible. For the next few days, we observed and videotaped the dive op-

erations from the sub. We also provided observation dives to several members of the press.

The weather on July 17 was excellent, and we took advantage of the calm seas by deploying the Spider. The SAT diver, stationed safely off to the side, helped guide the Spider into position, and Oren "Bubby" Haydel, our crane operator, lowered it slowly to the bottom. At 12:30 p.m. the Spider touched down on the seabed with only a slight kiss of one leg against the turret wall. This was the first task that rated a high "pucker factor" and it had been accomplished with near perfection. Or so we thought.

On close inspection, we discovered that several of the legs had encountered buried obstruc-

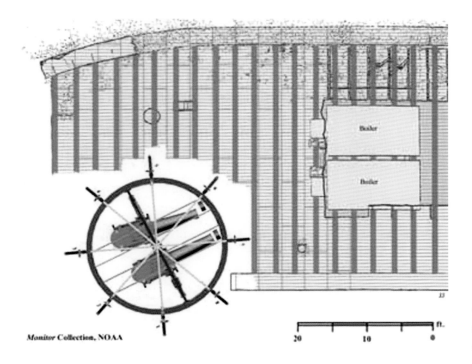

Monitor Collection, NOAA

20   10   0   ft.

This diagram illustrates the placement of the spider over the turret. Courtesy NOAA *Monitor* Collection

tions that were preventing the Spider from seating properly around the turret. The hydro-blaster, hoses, and airlift were moved into position for use in breaking loose the obstructions—a mix of concretions, sand, shell, and coal—that were preventing the legs from settling to their required positions around the turret. Divers used high-pressure water hoses fitted with special nozzles for jetting around

the legs, hoping to clear the obstructions. When a leg reached the necessary depth, a diver would connect the hydraulic hand pump to the actuating ram and attempt to push the leg beneath the lip of the turret.

The SAT and surface-supplied divers worked with the hydro-blaster, airlifts, and crowbars to get the legs seated, and they made slow progress. On

The saturation diver inspected the positions of the spider's legs and discovered that several had landed on obstructions. Courtesy NOAA *Monitor* Collection

With the ROV hovering nearby, a diver (right) works to clear obstructions while another tries to seat one of the Spider's legs. Courtesy NOAA *Monitor* Collection

July 20 a new team of four SAT divers entered the chamber; the Spider was beginning to level out and its legs were moving into position. That night we were entertained by a spectacular electrical storm that sent huge bolts of lightning from clouds to water, creating huge red-orange fireballs. It was very impressive and very intimidating, since our barge was the tallest object within twenty miles! Captain Murray was working on the wreck that night; he later told us, "There is nothing more spectacular than observing an electrical storm in the middle of the night through 238 feet of crystal clear water! Unbelievable!"

On July 21—our twenty-seventh day onsite—Navy divers were still trying to seat the Spider. Robert Schwemmer, from our Channel Islands National Marine Sanctuary, reported on board, and Wayne Lusardi, Mariners' Museum conservator, arrived to oversee the documentation and temporary storage of recovered artifacts. Our NOAA dive team arrived at Hatteras and planned to begin diving as soon as the Navy granted permission. The following day our director, Daniel J. Basta, came aboard for a visit, along with several other VIPs. Since the weather was good, the Navy placed the Spider Platform on the bottom, just aft of the turret.

As work continued to seat the Spider, excavation resumed inside the turret. Jeff was guiding the excavation toward one of the roof hatches and we were waiting for confirmation that the roof panels were still in place. On July 23, SAT divers Chris Murray and Mitch Pierce excavated and probed, reporting they believed the roof was in place, but may have dropped a foot or so from its original position. The next day, SAT divers visually confirmed the presence of roof beams, which meant the turret still contained all or most of the material that was inside when *Monitor* sank. Jeff and I were delighted.

Things seemed to be moving along well, but at

As each of the spider's legs was lowered into position, it was pushed beneath the lip of the turret using a hand-operated hydraulic system. Courtesy NOAA *Monitor* Collection

about 9:00 a.m. on July 26, Senior Chief Wade Bingham, the SAT diver working inside the turret, uncovered a bone that glowed white in the glare of his helmet light. I soon joined the growing crowd in the SAT van, where Jeff and Eric Emery were helping the diver make initial measurements of the location of the possible human remains. Eric soon confirmed that the bones were human. The discovery of human remains changed the dynamic on *Wotan*. Prior to this discovery, some of the tough, brazen Navy sailors considered the expedition a salvage job with the goal of getting iron on deck. Finding the remains changed this to an expedition to bring home one of their own, a Navy sailor not too unlike any of the Navy sailors working on this expedition. We decided at the morning briefing that it was essential for the SAT and surface-supplied divers to work together until the Spider was in place before proceeding with excavation of the human remains. In the afternoon, all diving concentrated on the Spider.

By Sunday, July 28, with time running out, four of the Spider's eight legs had been pinned in place, their bases snugly beneath the lip of the turret. At 6:00 p.m. the next day, Vernon Malone, the SAT diver, secured the pin in leg no. 4, the final one. The Spider was locked in place! We were scheduled to

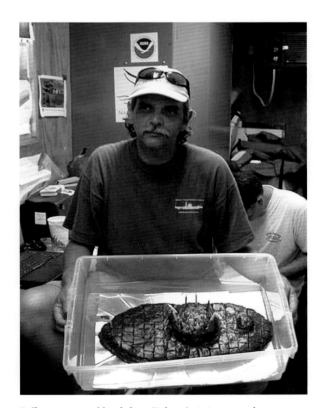

Jeff spent several birthdays (July 25) sitting over the *Monitor*, but this year the support team brought him a custom-made cake. Courtesy NOAA *Monitor* Collection

On July 21 the NOAA dive team arrived and began documenting progress on the turret excavation. Courtesy NOAA *Monitor* Collection

complete our work and leave the site by August 7, but we still had quite a bit of work to do. And there was the issue of weather—*always* the issue of weather. With each passing day, we lost one more chance to raise the turret.

On July 30, the SAT diver completely uncovered one of the two roof hatches, and through the hatch he saw Spider leg no. 1. This was a morale booster, and it gave us more options for rigging the roof to make sure it would not collapse during recovery. That night, Eric worked with the SAT diver to map and remove the human remains. They removed the skull, mandible, vertebrae, and other bones, but some were solidly concreted to the turret roof. Eric carefully examined, cataloged, and stored all human remains in a locked building.

The noon briefing on August 1 revealed growing discontent among team members. Removal of the human remains had been slow, painstaking work, which had interfered with final preparations for the lift. Many of the divers were frustrated by the slow progress and were convinced that we should raise the turret at the first opportunity while the weather was cooperating. This type of frustration is typical of the late stages of an expedition, and although Jeff and I were also anxious to recover, we were determined to see that everything possible had been done to secure the turret roof and stabilize the human remains and artifacts inside. Excellent weather on August 2 created even more grumbling about NOAA archaeologists jeopardizing the entire expedition by insisting on more rigging.

In spite of differences of opinion, Navy divers worked feverishly and invented ways to install ad-

ditional support. The guns were supported by Kevlar straps attached atop the Spider; special braces were fabricated and installed around the outside of the turret to support the roof; and finally, a steel beam was worked underneath the turret so that support cables could be rigged from the beam, up through the two hatches, and secured to the top of the Spider. Jeff and I agreed that the braces and beam should be sufficient. Besides, we knew that those dedicated men and women had done all that could be done. As a last step, divers placed plastic sheets over the sediment inside the turret and secured them in place with sandbags.

By August 3, Eric and the SAT divers had removed as much of the skeleton as possible, but both legs and the right arm were firmly cemented in place and would have to come up with the turret. Turret rigging was complete, riggers were preparing the massive lifting bridle, and everything was in readiness for the lift.

At 4:00 a.m. on Sunday, August 4, seas were four to five feet, with a moderate swell—not ideal conditions for the lift. Even worse, the bottom current was so strong it had dragged the ROV out to the end of its tether. The current was estimated to be approaching 3 knots, too strong for diving. By evening, seas were still running southeast at five feet, and bottom current was still in excess of 2 knots. *Wotan* had been repositioned twice but was still riding poorly, with strain on the cables. At 7:30 p.m., the tug moved several of the anchors and repositioned the barge so it was nearly meeting the seas head-on. We made the decision to stand down until 6:00 a.m. The weather forecast was not promising, and we were down to three days.

At 6:15 on the morning of Monday, August 5, conditions were marginal, but might not improve. NOAA's National Hurricane Center was tracking a tropical depression that was moving north off the South Carolina coast, probably only a day away from us.[1] Scholley consulted Chief Warrant Officer Rick Cavey and others on her team; Jeff and I huddled to compare notes. At this point, NOAA, the Navy, Phoenix, and Manson Gulf all needed to approve the turret lift. We had to be confident that we could perform the lift without injuring a diver or damaging the turret. We soon agreed that sea conditions were within acceptable parameters, but just barely. The consensus was to proceed with preparations, but to reassess the situation throughout the morning. Jeff

Frequent periods of high winds and waves hampered recovery operations throughout the expedition. Courtesy NOAA *Monitor* Collection

headed for the galley to refill his coffee mug. "Bubby" Haydel, the crane operator, saw the look of concern on Jeff's face and said cheerfully, "Don't worry, Jeff, I won't break your turret!" Bubby may have been the only calm person on board that day.

Just before 7:00 a.m., Bubby's crane roared to life and lowered the lifting sling into the water. Chief Petty Officer Steve Janek, a veteran of previous *Monitor* expeditions, volunteered to descend twenty-five feet to the lifting frame and free the eight lifting straps that had to be attached to the Spider's legs. He encountered a current so strong that he was barely able to cut the restraining lines that allowed the heavy shackles to pull the straps down to their full length. When Janek was pulled back to the barge, he reported, "It's ripping down there!"

The lifting frame, with its eight straps dangling beneath, was lowered to the bottom. By the time the straps reached SAT diver Chief Boatswain's Mate Keith Nelson, however, they were tangled so badly that we doubted he could clear them. But "Nelly" was one of the best and most determined of the divers, and he insisted he could connect the straps. If he had connected part of them, but not the rest, we would have been in big trouble, since the barge would have been attached directly to the turret, but not adequately attached for a successful lift. I'd seen what these guys could do, so I told Cavey to let Nelly go for it. What followed was a frustrating dance of strength and endurance, with Nelly pulling and twisting the straps and wrestling the 135-pound shackles, while

Cavey relayed orders to Bubby for minute crane adjustments calculated to make Nelly's job easier. As if the scenario had been scripted by Clive Cussler, the final strap was the most difficult to connect. Finally, at 11:15 a.m., Nelly slid the pin into the eighth shackle, generating cheers and "Hoo-Yahs" on deck. The turret was rigged!

At that point, we were committed. We had

Master Diver Jim Mariano and Chief Warrant Officer Rick Cavey carefully watched every step of recovery preparations, along with many other key personnel from the Navy, NOAA, Phoenix, and Manson Gulf. Courtesy NOAA *Monitor* Collection

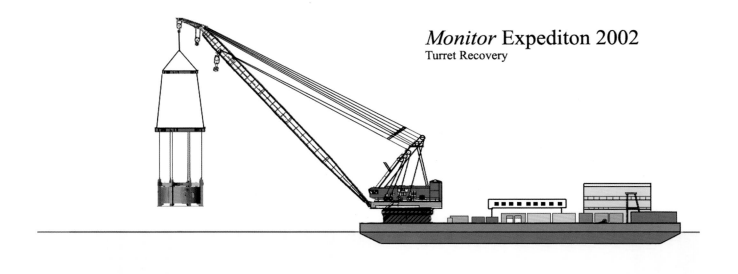

Monitor Expediton 2002
Turret Recovery

Johnston

This graphic shows the complex turret lifting system: a 500-ton crane is attached to a series of cables and spreaders, which in turn are attached to the spider and platform, within which the turret is securely cradled. Courtesy NOAA *Monitor* Collection

agreed at the final briefing that all key personnel had to approve the lift. All stations were asked to report their status, and everyone responded, "Ready." After one last exchange of nods with Cavey, Scholley asked me for permission to lift and I quickly gave the thumbs-up. On command, Bubby began taking up slack on the cable, making tiny adjustments on the boom position to keep the cable tending as vertical as possible. I watched the image from Nelly's helmet camera as the turret began to move. At 1:17 p.m. Cavey announced that the turret had cleared the bottom.

My cheer caught in my throat as I saw huge clouds of silt roiling up as the turret rose and fell with the roll of the barge. I was afraid that in spite of our precautions, the roof had collapsed. When the silt began to clear we could see the turret, suspended a few feet off the bottom, just outside the wreck. We paused to check status again, then Cavey relayed orders to the crane and the turret began to swing toward the platform. At 2:36, after a harrowing struggle, the divers coaxed the turret onto Jim Kelly's clever stabbing guides, which aligned and mated the Spider with the platform. The two were secured to each other, and the whole assembly was ready for the lift. Once again, not only was history about to be recovered—it was about to be made.

Chapter Nine

IN *MONITOR*'S TURRET

ENTERING A TOMB

At just past 5:30 p.m., the lip of the turret broke the surface to the cheers of everyone on *Wotan* and also on the R/V *Cape Fear* and several charter boats that had come out from Hatteras. Someone shouted and pointed to dark shapes darting around the turret. Our resident school of amberjack had escorted the turret all the way to the surface, just as it had done for the propeller and engine, to say goodbye one last time. We continued to hold our collective breaths until the turret, after making a few frightening swings at the end of the long lifting bridle, settled gently onto the deck at exactly 5:47 p.m. Only then could we relax and begin to revel in our triumph. Amid all the shouting, high-fiving, and yes, tears, an impromptu ceremony took place. Cavey, with a huge grin, walked up to Scholley and announced, "Ma'am, I'd like to present you the *Monitor* turret."

Bobbie laughed, then seeing me standing nearby, turned and said, "John, on behalf of the entire US Navy I'd like to present *you* the *Monitor* turret!"

I doubt that any of us could adequately describe our feelings that afternoon. For me, there was an almost overwhelming sense of relief, a relaxing of tension and anxiety that had been building for months. We had done it! We had saved *Monitor*'s turret, and a quick look inside confirmed that we had also saved its contents. Everyone was taking pictures, congratu-

lating one another, taking more pictures. Even with all the celebrating, work continued. Within hours of recovery, Wayne had erected a sprinkler system that sprayed water down and around the turret to keep the huge artifact and its contents wet during the long transit to The Mariners' Museum. That accomplished, he covered the exposed human remains with wet towels and a POW/MIA (Prisoner of War/Missing in Action) flag, then exited the turret through the ceiling hatch—the first person to pass through that portal since the *Monitor*'s officers and crew abandoned their ship on that cold, stormy New Year's Eve, 140 years ago. The story had not ended; the rest of the story was inside, waiting to be uncovered.

The next morning we discovered that our decision to lift on the fifth was well justified. Not only was Tropical Storm Cristobal headed our way, but also the Navy divers discovered that the bottom current was too strong for them to conduct any work. They had to leave an assortment of tools and equipment on the bottom for later retrieval. Had we delayed the turret lift just one day, we would have missed our last chance at success. Was this good luck, or had we finally figured out how to beat Mother Nature? I like to think that it was a little of both. After all these years we were certainly more experienced at reading the weather, and we were more effective at working in the marginal conditions that Hatteras so often handed us. In the end, though, we all knew

On August 5, 2002, *Monitor*'s gun turret was successfully raised from the seafloor.
Courtesy NOAA *Monitor* Collection

The author (left) and Captain (sel.) Scholley cheer as *Monitor*'s turret emerges from the water. Courtesy NOAA *Monitor* Collection

Cheering and congratulations continued as the turret was raised and carefully placed on the barge's deck. Courtesy NOAA *Monitor* Collection

how close we had come to failure. We had no funds to wait for good weather. We were lucky.

That afternoon, as our tug *Delta Force* was trying to recover *Wotan*'s mooring anchors, one of its propellers became entangled in a cable. Divers had to remove the cable before the barge began dragging its anchors—possibly snagging *Monitor*'s hull in the process. This could have been a disastrous scenario but, lucky for us—and *Monitor*—the crisis was handled with customary calm and skill by our live-aboard salvage team. Later that night, every-

thing was safely secured and *Wotan* was under way for Newport News.

By sunrise on August 7, the seas had calmed a little, but *Delta Force* was struggling against seas as high as six feet, rolling out of the northeast. To the south, Tropical Storm Cristobal was turning more

The NOAA team poses proudly in front of the turret: (left to right) Bob Schwemmer, Wayne Lusardi, Jeff Johnston, Michelle Fox, and the author. The NOAA dive team were cheering from the nearby R/V *Cape Fear*. Courtesy NOAA *Monitor* Collection

The *Monitor* 2002 expedition team gathered in front of the turret for a group photo soon after the turret was safely secured on deck. (Because divers were rotated on and off the barge throughout the expedition, this photo represents only the ones who were on board at the time of recovery.) Courtesy NOAA *Monitor* Collection

to the east and was no longer predicted to overtake us. As *Wotan* began to ride more easily, I decided we should get into the turret to assess the condition of the human remains and other exposed objects. I hoped it would be possible to remove the rest of the skeleton before we reached Hampton Roads. We felt it would not be appropriate to participate in a cheerful celebration with a *Monitor* sailor still entombed in the turret. At this point, Jeff, Wayne, and I were among the few expedition members who had not been inside the turret. Almost all the Navy and NOAA divers had worked inside the turret or had at least peered into it. Now it was our turn to assess the situation.

At 1:45 p.m., the three of us donned coveralls and kneepads, gathered up a few archaeological tools, and ducked underneath the turret. I led the way,

slowly raising my head and shoulders through the hatch. Directly in front of me, at eye level, were the remaining bones of a sailor who had not escaped. All sensations of the barge's motion disappeared, along with all thoughts about the two people behind me. A flood of emotions and questions filled my head. Even as I contemplated this sailor's fate, another part of my mind absorbed the sights and sounds around me. Water dripped from beams, guns, and cables, its sounds echoing off the iron walls as if I were in a cave, or a damp tomb. I recalled a vivid memory. It was 1979 and I was standing on the seabed just outside the turret, my hand lightly touching its crusty surface, wondering if I would ever know what secrets lay on the other side of that armored wall. Now, twenty-three years later, almost to the day, I was inside. Just then, Jeff tapped me and asked if I was go-

When NOAA archaeologists first entered the turret on the barge, the most impressive objects were the two massive Dahlgren guns, upside down, but still attached to their carriages. Courtesy NOAA *Monitor* Collection

ing to let anyone else in. The spell was broken; it was time to get to work.

We carefully crawled on all fours, keeping to exposed roof beams wherever possible. One of the most satisfying aspects of archaeology is discovering and understanding evidence from the past. The *Monitor*'s turret was literally filled with clues to what happened on the night *Monitor* sank. All around us, recognizable objects were imbedded in the sediment, which was still quite deep in some areas. Most prominent, of course, were the twin Dahlgrens, lying upside down, still firmly attached to their carriages. When the turret turned over, the huge guns had crashed down against the diagonal braces with enough force to bend them, but the braces held, preventing the guns from bursting through the turret roof. I was still amazed that the roof remained in place through the entire sinking process. *Monitor* builder John Ericsson had described fastening the two roof panels only lightly, since gravity would hold them in place and since it might be necessary to remove the pan-

els to service the guns. Whatever the reason, I was thankful that the roof held, since it captured all the objects inside and, along with them, the preserved glimpses into that tragic night off Hatteras.

Clearly visible, too, were the two teardrop-shaped iron port stoppers, still held in place behind the gunports by corrosion and the Navy's supports. In addition to the two pairs of diagonal turret braces that appeared on *Monitor* drawings, I now got my first close-up look at the previously undocumented braces. The first set of braces consisted of two pairs of thick iron rods, running perpendicular to the guns, fitted with turnbuckles so they could be adjusted as necessary to square up the base of the turret. The second set of braces was made up of two strong iron bars running fore-and-aft, between the guns, at right angles to the other set of diagonal braces. We assumed this second set of braces was added to help support the tremendous weight of the turret structure and guns, and probably to keep the turret base as level as possible. The turret could not be rotated if the base sagged even a fraction of an inch, so the extra diagonal braces, which ran from top to bottom, may have been necessary for proper turret operation.

While Jeff and I continued to look, Wayne crawled to the skeleton, designated "Individual Number One." Wayne had experience excavating human remains, and he was anxious to complete the bone recovery. While he carefully excavated with small tools, I began measuring and recording exposed features. The leg bones extended over an iron roof beam, where the feet, toes pointing downward, were still clad in leather boots. Wayne had been excavating for a while when suddenly he mumbled, "Uh-oh!" I looked down to see him sliding his finger along a muddy bone that did not line up with the others. He said that either this bone represented a yet-uncovered break, or we were looking at Individual Number Two.

We soon confirmed that a second individual lay

Wayne Lusardi (left) and the author began excavating human remains while the turret was still en route to Hampton Roads. Courtesy NOAA *Monitor* Collection

underneath and nearly perpendicular to the first. He lay with his feet close to the turret wall and his head beneath the breech of the Dahlgren. His bones were imbedded in clay and concretion, so we knew that excavation would be a lengthy process. As Wayne and I discussed the new find, Jeff shouted for us to have a look at what he had uncovered. Draped across several roof beams was what Jeff identified as a woolen overcoat, with what looked very much like a human bone protruding from underneath. Faced with the possibility of a third body, and maybe more, we told Scholley of our finds and that it was impossible for us to remove the human remains before we docked in Newport News.

We continued to excavate and map throughout the afternoon, stopping periodically to let Schwemmer spray saltwater into the turret's interior from above to make certain everything remained wet. As we worked, faces would appear around the lip of the turret as divers, barge crew, and media representatives took turns peering down to watch our progress. We explained that many of the remains were firmly cemented to the turret, making removal a slow, painstaking process. We worked with trowels when possible, but more often with knife points, dental tools, and jets of water from squeeze bottles.

We recovered a large, black, hard rubber button bearing the familiar image of an anchor and the letters "U.S.N." Although everyone knew quite well that these were Navy sailors, the button seemed to snap the personal side of this tragedy back into focus, especially for the Navy divers. Seeing the bones, coat, and button affected Master Diver Scott Heineman, a veteran of numerous body recoveries, including dozens of corpses from downed airliners and sunken vessels. "It wasn't until I saw the remnants of their uniforms that I gave them more than a passing thought," he later said. "That's when I started thinking they were real."

Heineman was not alone. The mood on board *Wotan* seemed to become more solemn with each new discovery. The senior leaders held an informal discussion about the homecoming ceremony. Some felt it was inappropriate to conduct any type of celebration until the remains had been removed. Others disagreed. Senior Chief Petty Officer Larry Fahey best expressed the alternative viewpoint. "In my opinion, we should be proud," he said. "One of MDSU TWO's duties is body recovery, and here we've recovered two sailors who've been missing in action for a long time and we're bringing them back to their families."

Petty Officer First Class Ken Riendeau, who had listened quietly to the discussion, added, "These guys are like our shipmates. We should be happy to have the honor of bringing them home."[1] Around the group, heads began to nod, and it seemed we had reached consensus. Jeff and I exchanged smiles. We both agreed with Fahey and Riendeau, but we had been careful to stay out of the discussion, knowing the Navy should make the decision.

Scholley conveyed our feelings to those ashore. Apparently, a similar discussion had taken place there among NOAA, Navy, and museum officials, and they had reached a similar conclusion. The ceremony would be held as scheduled, but would be modified to include a memorial for the sailors inside the turret.

MONITOR COMPLETES ITS FINAL VOYAGE

At 6:30 on the morning of Friday, August 9, everyone was on deck enjoying a beautiful sunrise and anticipating our entrance into Hampton Roads. USS *Chinook*, the NOAA ship *Ronald H. Brown*, and dozens of private boats escorted us into the Capes of Virginia. At 7:35 a.m., Fort Monroe, where *Monitor* found refuge in 1862, was just off our starboard beam. There was a flash, followed by a deep boom, as a battery of Army howitzers fired the first of a twenty-one-gun salute. It was a moving experience—one that transported me back in time to that December day in 1862 when *Monitor* passed this same fort, outward bound for enemy waters it never reached. Now, thanks to the men and women on this barge, Fort Monroe was given the opportunity to welcome the little ironclad's most iconic component home, after an interrupted mission that spanned more than a century.

We passed *Monitor*'s old anchorage near Fort Monroe and over that span of Hampton Roads where the first two ironclads in the New World had fought each other in one of history's most famous sea battles. Johnston waved his arm across the scene. "Can you believe it?" he said, with uncharacteristic emotion, "She's home now. She's really home. When she passed through that imaginary line between Fort Wool and Fort Monroe, she came back to her old

battleground."[2] We looked out over the water without talking, each of us deep in his own thoughts.

Newport News was ready for our arrival. Hundreds of people, some with flags and banners, lined the waterfront. As we approached the staging area, we strained to recognize our friends and loved ones. Most of us were trying to contact them by cell phone. Next to me, a sailor was trying to tell his wife how to spot him, standing among scores of his fellow divers. Johnston leaned over toward him and said, "Just tell her you're the one with the blue shirt and green shorts!" It was one of Jeff's favorite jokes, since all Navy personnel and most civilians were dressed in identical blue project t-shirts and Navy-issue green shorts.

The day was hot, especially on *Wotan*'s steel deck. Master Diver Jim Mariano moved among the divers, offering bottled water and exchanging celebratory "Hoo-Yahs." Mark Erickson, one of our most faithful newspaper reporters, asked Mariano if he could define the term. He paused for a moment, as if trying to decide how to best respond, then said, "It can mean pretty much everything we want it to mean. . . . You can ask a question with it; you can *answer* a question with it. . . . You can motivate with it. You can use it as an expletive. It's 'Hoo-Yah!'" On this day, for Navy, NOAA, and The Mariners' Museum, "Hoo-Yah" meant "We did it!" Quite a few television and print media representatives attended the ceremony, augmenting the limited number of press visitors and film crews we carried on the barge.

Wotan rounded Newport News Point and soon *Delta Force* and another tug nudged the barge and its precious cargo gently up against a seawall adjacent to the Herbert Bateman Virginia Advanced Shipbuilding and Carrier Integration Center at Newport News Shipbuilding. This was a meaningful location, since the late Congressman Bateman had been instrumental in obtaining funding for the *Monitor* recovery expeditions. After a series of welcome home speeches and a prayer for the *Monitor* sailors, we all stood at attention as Riendeau and Nelson, representing the surface-supplied and saturation diving teams, respectively, lowered the American flag from the side of the turret. They folded it into a tight triangle in the traditional manner, then passed it on to the master divers, who turned and presented it to Cavey. Cradling the flag, Cavey walked across the gangway and up to the speakers' platform, where he passed the flag to Scholley with a salute.

Monitor's turret arrived in Newport News on August 9 to a 21-gun salute from Fort Monroe and an enthusiastic crowd at the waterfront. Courtesy The Mariners' Museum

At that point, Scholley turned to me and held out the flag. Our eyes met, and we experienced a moment of shared pride and respect that could never be expressed in words. We shook hands and as I took the flag, I realized that this brief exchange would always be one of the most memorable events of my life. I then completed the ceremony by presenting the flag to Timothy Keeney, NOAA's Deputy Assistant Secretary for Oceans and Atmosphere.

The crowd's applause was overshadowed by Master Diver Heineman's shout of "Hoo-Yah, Navy deep sea divers!" More than one hundred sailors echoed the shout, which was followed by Heineman's second call, "Hoo-Yah, America!", to which the entire crowd responded with gusto.

THE TURRET'S FINAL JOURNEY

With the ceremony concluded, the crowd began to disperse and we turned once again to the turret, which still had to complete the brief final leg of its

journey. Bubby returned to his station high on the crane while Navy riggers checked the lifting bridle. Only a few minutes later the turret, still secured within the Spider, was lifted off *Wotan*'s deck and gently placed onto a barge for the short voyage up the James River. This was the same barge that a year earlier had delivered *Monitor*'s steam engine to The Mariners' Museum. Curtiss Peterson, Wayne Lusardi, and others from The Mariners' Museum kept watch during the transfer, making sure the turret was periodically sprayed with water. Museum conservators maintained an all-night vigil to ensure that the turret and its contents were kept wet.

The next morning there was an air of excitement around the museum. By midmorning a crowd that eventually swelled to more than 2,000 had gathered at the museum's James River entrance to welcome the turret to its new permanent home. I was there, along with NOAA and museum staff, family and friends, news media, Civil War buffs, and other enthusiastic onlookers. Among them were a few people who, like myself, had been involved in *Monitor* research for

A folded American flag was passed from Navy divers to their commanding officer who passed the flag to the author (left) for presentation to NOAA. Watching this solemn ceremony were numerous dignitaries. Courtesy NOAA *Monitor* Collection

three decades. I spotted a beaming Ed Miller, NOAA's lead on the USS *Monitor* Project in the 1980s.

We soon got our first look at the turret, sitting on wooden blocks at the center of the barge, as it passed beneath the James River Bridge. As the barge drew closer, I was impressed with how much it looked like *Monitor* may have appeared from CSS *Virginia*'s pilot house: a low, flat platform with a turret at the center.

As the crowd watched in amazement, the little Lockwood tug shoved the barge directly onto the shore, just below Lion's Bridge, near the back entrance to the museum. With the tug holding the barge in place, several men placed steel ramps between the barge deck and the beach. The Lockwood Brothers' massive eighty-eight-wheel flatbed transporter then began to roll up the ramp and beneath the blocked-up turret. After what seemed like hours (but was only a few minutes), the barge crew used hydraulic jacks to lower the turret onto the flatbed. As we all held our breaths, the transporter began to crawl, very slowly, down the ramp, up the bank, and onto the paved road to the museum. The huge vehicle with its impressive load halted next to a small podium where NOAA, the Navy, and the museum conducted a brief welcoming ceremony.

Then the transporter resumed its slow journey to the conservation area behind the main buildings. There, crews from the museum and Newport News Shipbuilding steered the transporter to a tall steel structure with one side missing—the turret's conservation tank. The turret and Spider were too heavy

for a portable crane, so welders from The Apprentice School at the shipyard had fabricated the cavernous 90,000-gallon tank, and then cleverly removed one side so the turret could be driven inside. Once it was in place, the turret, still cocooned within the Spider, was jacked up so the transporter could be driven away and the missing portion of the tank could be welded back in place.

The Apprentice School welders sealed the tank and Gary Paden, the museum's "go-to guy" for everything mechanical, began filling the tank through an elaborate plumbing system he had just designed and constructed. The turret would now be left alone while we recuperated from the long expedition and organized the next phase of excavation.

BACK IN THE TURRET

On August 27, we were ready to resume excavation inside the turret. Our team consisted of Eric Emery, who had been allowed to return from Hawaii to help complete the removal of human remains; Wayne, Jeff, Tane, and me. Curtiss Peterson (head *Monitor* conservator at the museum) and Gary Paden were in charge of logistics. While Curtiss drained the water from the tank, Tane and I assembled two small mapping frames that would help us record the locations of our finds, including any and all human remains. Also onsite were several heavy riggers from Newport News Shipbuilding, who had volunteered to

On August 10 a truck towed the turret, sitting inside the spider and platform atop a massive multi-axle trailer, from the James River to The Mariners' Museum for a brief arrival ceremony. Courtesy The Mariners' Museum

Daniel J. Basta, Director of NOAA's Office of National Marine Sanctuaries, thanked the major participants for their efforts in preserving parts of *Monitor* for future generations. Courtesy NOAA *Monitor* Collection

help support the guns inside the turret to keep them from shifting during excavation.

After a quick lunch provided by the museum, we entered the turret and worked in two teams until 6:30 p.m., when we stopped to let Curtiss refill the tank. We were back at work by 7:30 the next morning, excavating the human remains, the wool coat and its possible third individual, and several other areas. I spent much of my time just aft of the starboard Dahlgren, where I discovered that the entire area appeared to be filled with coal and concretion.

On August 28, rain fell most of the day, keeping the turret wet, but it made it difficult for us to make notes and drawings. Eric removed the bones from Individual One's right arm, making a poignant discovery: the unfortunate sailor still wore a gold ring on his right hand. We eagerly examined the ring for an inscription that might identify him, but all we found was an inscribed design on the outer surface. The bones were cemented to structural beams and lumps of coal. Individual One's right hand was draped over a lump of coal. We discovered that the object lying beneath the wool coat was a gun tool handle, not a bone, and soon we were fairly certain we would find no additional bodies.

On August 29, Eric and I worked in earnest on the human remains, since he had to fly back to Hawaii the next day. We completed the removal of Individual One, but the upper half of Individual Two

The turret ended its journey in the Museum's conservation area, where it was backed into a waiting steel tank in which it would undergo years of conservation treatment. Courtesy The Mariners' Museum

was embedded in a thick concretion extending down from the breach of the Dahlgren. We discovered a silver spoon that, from its position relative to Individual One, was probably in his pocket. We also removed a comb, stamped "US Navy," that he may have been carrying in his boot. Each such find bonded us more closely with these men, showing us glimpses of them as living people. In fact, I often felt uncomfortable, as if I was invading their privacy.

Because of Eric's tight schedule, the two of us kept working after everyone else went home. Eric

Jeff Johnston (left) and the author, along with other NOAA and museum personnel, spent many hours excavating the contents of the turret as it sat within its conservation tank. Courtesy NOAA *Monitor* Collection

dealt with human remains on his job nearly on a daily basis, and he seemed to be taking this all in stride. For me, however, excavating human bones inside the turret, with only a small electric light to stave off the darkness, was more that a little unsettling. Just after 11:00 p.m., we decided to call it a night, but I learned the next day that Eric had gone back inside after I left, removing all of Individual Two except his head, shoulders, and one arm, which were too deeply embedded to remove. On Friday, August 30, we resumed work while Eric updated his documentation on the remains before leaving for the airport. We excavated until midafternoon, when we needed to refill the turret with water for the weekend.

We resumed the slow excavation on Monday, and as the days became weeks, I became painfully aware that my predicted excavation schedule was embarrassingly optimistic. Not only did I underestimate the number of artifacts we would find, I also badly misjudged the nature of the remaining sediment. Instead of the soft clay I had expected, we discovered that nearly the entire fill consisted of a cement-like mix of iron corrosion product, sand, calcium, shell, sediment, and coal that encased most of the cultural material.

Concretion formation is a fascinating process, influenced by the amount of metal, the chemistry of the surrounding sediment, and also by gravity. The

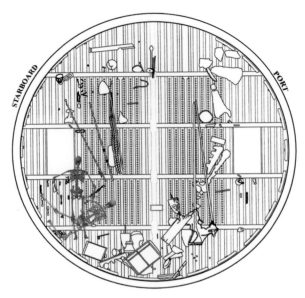

Both of *Monitor*'s crewmen were found as shown, very close to the starboard roof hatch. Courtesy NOAA *Monitor* Collection

fragile, organic material—and the uppermost bones and skull of Individual Two.

We were recording artifact locations using a cumbersome method that required three surveyor tapes to be pulled from reference points on the upper edge of the turret. One day it occurred to Tane and Wayne that it would be simpler to use the turret roof, on which we knelt as we worked, as a reference grid. The roof consisted of iron beams and railroad rails perpendicular to one another, forming a grid that we had already measured and drawn. Everyone agreed with this suggestion and the method proved to be both faster and more accurate.

We continued excavating for another fifteen weeks, recovering more than 400 objects, before securing the turret on December 13. The final weeks were particularly difficult, with our excavation team working inside the cold, wet, constantly dripping turret while museum staff and volunteers sifted through the cold buckets of mud and concretion, retrieving any cultural materials we had missed. Nevertheless, we successfully recovered all of the human remains and a fascinating array of artifacts.

The finds included parts of a wooden chest, a lantern, more than a dozen pieces of silverware, a leather boot and leather shoes, the wool overcoat and buttons, and all of the items required to serve and fire the Dahlgrens. There were powder scoops,

deeper we dug, the thicker the concretion. At the bottom it seemed to pour out across the turret roof and down between the beams and rails. The effect reminded me of stalagmite formation in a limestone cave. The same situation existed beneath the guns, trapping a variety of artifacts—many of which were

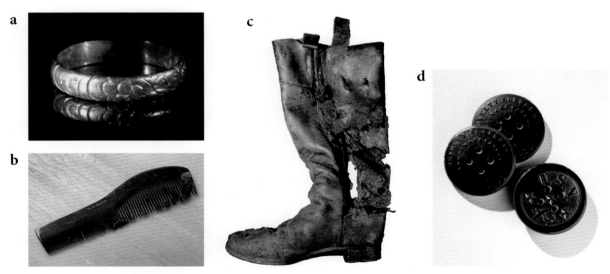

(a) Individual One was wearing a gold ring on his right hand. (b) This hard rubber comb was manufactured for the US Navy by the Goodyear Rubber Company; (c) This boot was recovered from the turret, probably cast off by an officer before abandoning ship; (d) These hard rubber US Navy buttons were made by the Novelty Rubber Company, New York. Courtesy The Mariners' Museum

JPAC: THE ARMED FORCES "CSI"

Since 2002 the US Army Central Identification Laboratory, Hawaii (USACILHI, formerly CILHI), has assisted NOAA and the US Navy with the recovery and identification of human remains from *Monitor*'s turret. On October 1, 2003, the thirty-year-old US Army Central Identification Laboratory, Hawaii, merged with the eleven-year-old Joint Task Force-Full Accounting to form the new Joint POW/MIA Accounting Command (JPAC), located on the island of Oahu in Hawaii. The JPAC is commanded by a flag officer and employs approximately 400 handpicked personnel from all four branches of the military. The JPAC's mission is to achieve the fullest possible accounting of all Americans missing as a result of the nation's past conflicts.

The laboratory portion of JPAC, now referred to as the JPAC Central Identification Laboratory (JPAC CIL), is the largest forensic anthropology laboratory in the world. The CIL's staff consists of more than thirty forensic anthropologists and three forensic odontologists (dentists). The JPAC is an authentic and effective "CSI" unit, except that it deals almost exclusively with "cold cases" dating back to earlier wars. The two *Monitor* crewmen are the oldest US military human remains the agency has processed.

At a recovery site, a JPAC anthropologist directs the excavation much like a detective oversees a crime scene. Each mission is unique, but there are certain steps that all recoveries have in common. First, the anthropologist attempts to define the extent of the site. Then a grid system is established to provide a control reference for careful excavation. Every inch of soil from the site is sifted through a screen to search for potential human remains, personal effects, and related material, such as aircraft parts. Initial analysis occurs at the site, and as soon as possible the material is transported to CIL for further examination.

At CIL, a different forensic anthropologist is assigned the case in the laboratory so that the entire procedure is carried out "blind," meaning that the anthropologist does not know the suspected identity of the individual under analysis, and knows only those details that are required to select the appropriate scientific techniques (e.g., the approximate era of the loss incident). The blind analysis is completed in order to prevent any subconscious bias from influencing the scientist's analysis.

The CIL anthropologists examine all recovered skeletal remains and produce a "biological profile" that includes the sex, race, age at death, and height of the individual. Anthropologists also analyze any trauma caused at or near the time of death and pathological conditions of bone such as arthritis or previously healed fractures. Dental remains are also extremely important, both because they offer the best means of positive identification and because they are durable and may contain surviving mitochondrial DNA (mtDNA).

The JPAC uses mtDNA in more than half of its cases. Successful use of mtDNA for identifications requires a family reference sample and the process of obtaining these can add over a year to the identification process. All mtDNA samples taken at the CIL are analyzed at the Armed Forces DNA Identification Laboratory (AFDIL), Rockville, Maryland, and then compared with reference samples given by suspected family members.

Currently the laboratory is identifying about two servicemen a week—over one hundred a year. There is one American still missing from Operations Desert Shield/Storm, and there are more than 1,750 from the Vietnam War, 120 from the Cold War, more than 8,100 from the Korean War, and more than 78,000 from World War II. The command's motto sums up their mission: "Until they are home."

JPAC's Central Identification Laboratory conducted detailed forensic analyses of *Monitor*'s two crewmen from the turret. Courtesy NOAA *Monitor* Collection

On a steamship, coal heavers shovelled coal into the ship's boilers. The archaeologists were given the same nickname because of the tons of coal that had to be removed from *Monitor*'s turret. Pictured here—with some of the coal they excavated—are Jeff Johnston (left), the author, and Tane Casserley. Courtesy The Mariners' Museum

sponges, rammers, shot tongs, and a bore scraper, all in good condition. We did not find shot or shell, even though one survivor account mentioned shot being in the turret the night of the sinking.[3] So far, no eleven-inch ammunition has been found on the wreck, nor have we discovered any reports of ammunition being thrown overboard from *Monitor*. *Passaic*'s log, on the other hand, notes that most of its shot and shell was jettisoned to lighten the ship.[4] Near the very end of concretion removal from the turret, conservators discovered five unfired rimfire cartridges of approximately .55 caliber, *Monitor*'s only ammunition so far.

REVELATIONS FROM THE TURRET

The turret excavation slowly yielded new clues to events leading up to *Monitor*'s sinking and the subsequent site formation processes—that is, how the ship settled onto the seabed and how it deteriorated over the years. Our interpretation of the wreck site began in 1973, with the realization that *Monitor* lay upside down on its displaced turret. Over the years, scores of historians, archaeologists, naval architects and engineers, and dozens of specialists have contributed to a refinement of that interpretation.

Our recent research has taught us that simulating the sinking sequence of any vessel is difficult, if

Turret excavation required a large team of archaeologists, sifters, conservators, and maintenance personnel. Courtesy The Mariners' Museum

Well-preserved implements used for loading and firing the guns were found near the turret roof, including this powder scoop and a rammer with a wooden head and rope shaft. Courtesy The Mariners' Museum

Mariners' Museum's Colleen Brady conserved this lantern from *Monitor*'s gun turret and painstakingly reassembled its shattered glass globe. Courtesy The Mariners' Museum

not impossible. In *Monitor*'s case, the task is made more difficult by the discrepancies among eyewitness accounts of the event. In order to learn what might be possible, I consulted Otto Jons at CNC Advanced Marine Center, who previously conducted research into *Monitor*'s seakeeping abilities,[5] and the Marine Forensics Committee of the Society of Naval Architects and Marine Engineers. I soon became a member of the committee, which added *Monitor* to its list of active research projects, along with RMS *Titanic* and other famous vessels. We also have an informal *Monitor* forensics committee at The Mariners' Museum that shares research being conducted by conservation staff and volunteers.

Based on input from all sources, and many hours of discussions with colleagues, I have concluded that *Monitor*'s last hours probably progressed somewhat like this: off Cape Hatteras, *Monitor* encountered a storm that built strength during the evening. Huge waves battered the ship, washing out caulking and creating a number of small leaks. As the storm grew in intensity, one of the two towlines parted, causing *Monitor* to yaw broadside to the seas, increasing its distress. The remaining towline was cut, and *Monitor*'s engine had sufficient power to head the ship into the seas.

As the flow of incoming water increased, sloshing through the bilge passages and eventually overcoming the pumps, the heavy weight of machinery (engine, boilers, shaft, propeller) and coal, all located aft of the amidships bulkhead, probably caused water to collect in the stern. We may never know which leak or leaks sank the ship. There is no evidence, his-

torically or archaeologically, of a monitor's upper and lower hulls separating, but water entering the ship through the hawse pipe, coupled with the pounding of the bow, may have given the impression of hull separation, as *Passaic*'s commanding officer concluded. Similarly, the only explanation for the "leak" reported in the fire room is that one or more of the coal scuttles may have worked loose, leaving a hole in the deck through which a large volume of water would have flowed, the deck being awash most of the time. In all likelihood, several leaks contributed to *Monitor*'s loss.

As the situation worsened, and the ship sank lower in the water, a large wave may have struck *Monitor*'s side, causing it to roll over and begin to sink by the stern. This likely would have happened very quickly, causing the turret to dislodge from the deck and plummet to the bottom. The monitor *Tecumseh* rolled over and sank quickly after striking

(a) This spoon is shown exactly where it was uncovered in the deep concretion of the turret roof; (b) A spoon before and after conservation; (c) Researchers are puzzled about why so many items of silverware, some with engraved names or initials, were found deep inside the turret; (d) This wooden drawer may have fallen into the turret from the galley as the ship rolled over. Courtesy The Mariners' Museum

a mine in Mobile Bay in 1864. Another possibility is that *Monitor* sank while still upright, then rolled over before settling to the bottom. Either way, *Monitor*'s hull did not drift far, since it settled atop the turret, which was displaced only about thirty feet.

Adding credence to the former hypothesis is the fact that *Monitor*'s stern is severely damaged, with the aft-most section of the hull essentially crushed, and the rudder missing. These observations strongly suggest that the hull settled stern-first, striking the seafloor and causing the damage visible in the 1974 photomosaic. Since *Monitor* was 172 feet long and the water depth was only 220 to 230 feet, it is not difficult to imagine that if the stern struck first, the bow would still have been near the surface, still being buffeted by the action of waves and swells. That situation would have caused the hull to slam and twist into the ocean floor, displacing the turret and caus-

ing the severe stern damage. During this torturous process, equipment, stores, and furniture would have been torn loose, tossed about, and damaged before coming to rest somewhere aft of the original location.

From this general concept of the sinking sequence, we began to develop a picture of what the trapped crewmen might have experienced as their ship sank to the bottom. It must have been a terrifying way to die. When *Monitor* rolled, water would have rushed into the turret's roof hatches, forcing the crewmen back inside and away from their means of escape. Once the turret dislodged, it would have sunk rapidly, almost straight down, impacting the seabed with considerable force. The huge guns would have dropped, still secured to their carriages, onto the massive diagonal braces, causing restraining tackle and other ropes to shift or part. During the

CONSERVATION OF *MONITOR* ARTIFACTS

In the Batten Conservation Laboratory Complex, a wing of the USS *Monitor* Center, conservators are working to preserve one of the most massive collections of artifacts ever recovered. To date, expeditions to the *Monitor* have produced approximately 1,600 artifacts—an amazing variety of objects and materials, including enormous wrought and cast iron components, copper, bronze, brass, delicate glass bottles, lumps of coal, wood furniture and paneling, a leather book cover, shoes, and a boot, clothing, and even food remains. The iron objects alone represent almost 200 tons of material, most of which require years—if not decades—of conservation treatment. Objects comprised of more than one material, such as the steam engine and condenser, must undergo delicate and time-consuming disassembly before treatment.

After nearly 140 years of immersion in saltwater, each artifact presents a unique challenge to conservators. Iron corrodes rapidly in seawater,

oxidizing into various corrosion compounds that form in unstable layers. Over time, ferrous metals will continue to disintegrate until nothing remains. Objects of iron and other metals become covered with surface encrustations, called *concretion*, a combination of sand, sediment, marine life, and oxides (rust) that bonds to surfaces. Iron and other metals also absorb chlorides (salt) from seawater, which destabilizes the iron and accelerates corrosion. Once-resilient iron components such as the engine, turret, and propeller have been rendered so fragile that they would disintegrate without the years of painstaking treatment they are receiving in the lab. In contrast, glass and ceramic objects can be more easily cleaned and readied for exhibition in just a few weeks. Likewise, brass and bronze objects usually remain relatively intact in seawater and can be conserved in weeks or months. In between these extremes are organic materials, including wood, leather, and fabric, which require deli-

David Krop, chief *Monitor* conservator, is one of the few conservators who actually climbs on artifacts! Here, he is in the process of deconcreting *Monitor*'s steam condenser. Courtesy The Mariners' Museum

cate handling and a conservation plan tailored to each object. All artifacts are kept wet after recovery, since if allowed to dry, chlorides in the objects would crystallize and expand, causing surface damage or even complete structural failure.

Conservators begin by carefully documenting each object to be treated, then entering it into an electronic database to which each step of conservation will be recorded. If disassembly is required, conservators take special care to note and record each component. Although the science of conservation has improved immensely during the past half-century, success sometimes still hinges on the conservator's careful observations and ability to alter treatments as necessary, depending on the response of each

(continued)

The cavernous Batten Conservation Laboratory, part of the USS *Monitor* Center, is where all *Monitor* artifacts are being conserved. Visitors can watch the ongoing process through large windows (far left). Courtesy The Mariners' Museum

object. Ferrous metals, and sometimes copper alloy artifacts, are typically treated with electrolytic reduction before being desalinated, rinsed, dehydrated, and covered with various protective coatings. The most common treatment for organic materials is to soak them in a solution of polyethylene glycol, an inert, waxy substance that replaces the water within the cellular structure of organic objects, thus providing strength and stability. Other treatments are prescribed for different materials and sometimes alternate treatments are chosen for specific objects.

CONSERVING IRON

Conserving iron recovered from the sea involves reduction of the object to arrest corrosion, stabilize the material, and remove the salts. It is important to initially retain the marine encrustations that cover the artifacts because they protect the fragile surfaces from physical damage and atmospheric levels of oxygen that can speed the corrosion process.

After documentation and cataloging, conservators begin deconcretion (removal of corrosion product) and a process called electrolytic reduction, in which an artifact is placed in an alkaline solution of sodium hydroxide in de-ionized or reverse-osmosis water. Metal electrodes are then suspended around the artifacts and a low-voltage, low-ampere current is passed through the object. The negative charge applied to the artifact forces negatively charged chloride (salt) ions from the artifact and into the storage solution. The positively charged electrodes help attract the negatively-charged ions, increasing the rate at which they diffuse into solution. During this process, oxygen and hydrogen bubbles form at the artifact's surface and help loosen and remove concretion from the artifact. The electrical current also consolidates and stabilizes weakened iron and reduces iron corrosion products to more stable forms. The chlorides are trapped in the electrolyte solution, which is changed when it becomes contaminated with chlorides. The process is complete when no more chlorides can be detected in the solution. The required length of time depends on the rate at which salt can be removed from the corroded iron. Large items with thicker corrosion layers, such as the turret, engine, and propeller, require more time than do smaller ones. Conservators estimate that it will require an additional twenty years to conserve all *Monitor* artifacts recovered as of 2010.

les: 1499999
gles: 0

This digital image of *Monitor*'s turret was produced by Epic Scan who scanned the turret inside and out with a laser line scanner, an amazing technology that produces three-dimensional data files with millimeter accuracy. Courtesy NOAA *Monitor* Collection

Heavy riggers from Newport News Shipbuilding expertly rigged *Monitor*'s two Dahlgren guns with padded slings and moved them to custom conservation tanks fabricated at the shipyard.

fall, men trapped inside could have climbed or even been washed out through the deck or roof hatches, but we know that two men did not escape. They may have become entangled or trapped against the deck itself. The rapid rise in water pressure would probably have burst their eardrums and the inrush of water might have brought on vertigo or even shock.

But fate was not done with these unfortunate men. *Monitor*'s hull quickly followed the turret to the bottom, striking stern-first. As trapped air collected in the bow, the rapid rise in pressure may have burst through the thin plating of the lower hull, letting the inverted hull crash down on top of the turret. The force of that impact in turn opened a coal scuttle, bombarding the turret with tons of coal. The trapped men, still alive and probably conscious, were pressed to the bottom of the inverted turret, where they were crushed beneath an avalanche of coal and other debris. That is where we found them, lying di-

rectly against the roof beams beneath tons of coal and silt.

Another possibility is that the coal fell into the turret at a later time, as the hull began to deteriorate. If that was the case, then the two bodies would most likely have floated inside the turret for a time, then settled to the bottom as decomposition progressed. Their bones would have then become disarticulated and scattered in the deepening silt.

We also uncovered mysteries that we may never solve. For instance, why did the turret contain a wooden cabinet, a coffeepot, and a dozen pieces of silverware—some engraved with names or initials? Was the cabinet a turret fixture, used for storing small items such as gunlocks, vent pricks, and tools? Or did the cabinet fall into the turret, along with the silverware and coffeepot, from the galley, which was located just beneath the turret and which could have spilled some of its contents when *Monitor* rolled

WHO WAS IN THE TURRET?

At this writing we have not identified the two men found in the turret. Their boots and clothing suggest they were enlisted men, but officers have not been eliminated from consideration. The JPAC has not released their final forensics report, but they have shared their findings with us. We know that CIL successfully recovered mitochondrial DNA from both sets of remains; they have also provided us with accurate casts of both skulls, from which facial reconstructions will soon give us our first look at the appearance of these unfortunate sailors. Once all the information is in hand the Navy Casualty Office will work with JPAC, NOAA, and The Mariners' Museum to try to identify the two men and reunite them with their families.

Every year JPAC and the Casualty Office provide closure for scores of families of service men and women who have been listed as missing in action, but the odds of identifying our *Monitor* sailors are poor. When the Confederate submarine *Hunley* was raised and its crew removed and examined, excellent forensic details were documented, including personal effects, positions within the hull, examination of human remains, and DNA analysis. Of the eight bodies, three yielded recoverable DNA and two of them were positively identified through matching with the DNA of descendents. The project was well-publicized, yet few prospective descendents came forward and most of the identifications are tentative. Compare those results with our challenge of identifying two bodies out of sixteen possibilities.

We have eliminated a few of the names by exclusion. The two *Monitor* crewmen have been identified as Caucasian, which eliminates three African Americans from the list; there were also eyewitness reports of several men being swept off the deck by waves. At this point, there are quite a few facts, opinions, and guesses, but neither man has been positively identified. In conducting research for his book, *Ironclad*, reporter/author Paul Clancy visited JPAC and in 2006 published his own theories about the two men.[1] We will continue seeking to identify the two *Monitor* sailors until they have been reunited with their families or all possible research options have been exhausted. In either case, we will ensure that these fallen heroes receive proper honors and a secure place to rest.

Casts of the skulls of *Monitor*'s crewmen will be used to create facial reconstructions that may help identify the two men. Courtesy NOAA *Monitor* Collection

Note:

1. Clancy (2006, 223–41).

over? Did *Monitor*'s officers and crewmen always keep their eating utensils with them, or could they have been taking them as mementos of the ship? We may never know for certain. When we find a moment frozen in time, as in the case of the turret, we sometimes get the rare privilege of glimpsing events from long ago, even if the scene has been dimmed by the interceding years.

In other instances, we sometimes find evidence that can be both powerful and ironic. *Monitor* head

As mountainous waves illustrated in *Harpers Weekly* foamed over the *Monitor* and filled her hull with seawater, the ironclad sank by the stern and capsized.

Archaeologists and researchers speculate that *Monitor* sank stern-first then rolled over, dislodging its gun turret before coming to rest atop the turret, upside down, as it was found in 1973. Courtesy NOAA *Monitor* Collection

POSTRECOVERY SITE DOCUMENTATION

In 2003, NOAA again enlisted the aid of David Mindell and Brian Bingham from MIT's Deep Sea Archaeology Research Group (Deep-Arch) for the purpose of acquiring a detailed image of the *Monitor* site as it appeared after recovery of the gun turret. During May 20–21, 2003, with funding from NOAA's Office of Ocean Exploration, the *Monitor* sanctuary and DeepArch conducted an imaging expedition utilizing "SeaBED," an autonomous underwater vehicle (AUV) capable of navigating itself on a preprogrammed path over the wreck. "SeaBED" was a product of the well-respected Wood's Hole Deep Submergence Lab.

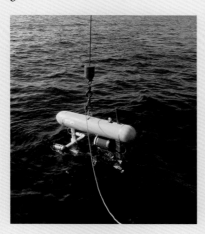

MIT and Wood's Hole attempted to image *Monitor*'s hull using the *SeaBED* autonomous underwater vehicle, but the AUV was overcome by the strong Hatteras currents. Courtesy NOAA *Monitor* Collection

Operating from the R/V *Cape Fear* from UNC-Wilmington, the team deployed a precision navigation system, EXACT, designed by Mindell, which provided SeaBED with the positioning information it needed to conduct a high-precision photomosaic survey of *Monitor*'s hull. Two EXACT transponders were deployed off the southern side of the wreck site, and during drift tests provided reliable readings for distances over 500 feet. Acoustic Doppler Current Profiler (ADCP) readings provided a map of evolving currents between the sea surface and sea floor. Unfortunately, adverse weather conditions and high currents, with which we had become all too familiar, interfered with the successful deployment of SeaBED, and with the limited time available, we were prevented from acquiring the necessary data for a mosaic.

During July 15–20, 2006, NOAA collaborated with the Institute for Exploration, Mystic, Connecticut, to collect high-resolution digital still and video imagery of *Monitor*'s hull in order to generate a high-quality color photomosaic of the entire wreck site. NOAA planned to use this new mosaic as a "baseline" record of exactly how *Monitor* appeared at the time of data collection, giving us an accurate, permanent record of the site that could be compared with subsequent survey data for determination of the rate and severity of continued deterioration.

We conducted the expedition from the 185-foot Research Vessel *Endeavor*, operated by the University of Rhode

In 2006, the towed system *Argus*, operated by a team from the University of Rhode Island, recorded *Monitor*'s hull with multibeam sonar and high-definition video. Courtesy NOAA *Monitor* Collection

Island. We utilized the towed vehicle *Argus* for data collection. *Argus* was equipped with high-intensity lights, a high-definition video camera, and a high-resolution digital still camera. In order to collect imagery for a new photomosaic of the *Monitor* site, we towed Argus over the wreck in a series of closely-spaced parallel passes during which *Argus*' on-board navigation and thrusters kept the vehicle on course at the desired altitude above the bottom. Technical problems and strong currents prevented us from obtaining the quality of data that had been expected, and so far it has not been possible to generate an accurate photomosaic of the entire wreck.

The *Argus* data was used to create a partial photomosaic of *Monitor*'s hull four years after the turret was recovered. Courtesy NOAA *Monitor* Collection

conservator David Krop told me that as he and his team were completing the final excavation inside the turret in 2007 they discovered seven clear glass fragments cemented by concretion to the iron rails of the turret's inverted roof. They were badly iron stained, but when fitted together revealed the head of a Phoenix and the word RESURGAM, which is Latin for "I shall rise again." Krop said, "It was chilling to make this discovery on the last day of excavation because the imagery of a phoenix rising from the ashes is very symbolic of the rebirth of *Monitor* as a result of cumulative research, recovery, conservation, and exhibit."[6]

Epilogue

———————◦⟐◦———————

THE STORY CONTINUES

Their names are for history; and so long as we remain a people, so long will the work of the
Monitor be remembered, and her story told to our children's children. . . . The "little cheesebox
on a raft" has made herself a name which will not soon be forgotten by the American people.

—GRENVILLE WEEKS
Surgeon, USS *Monitor*

A NEW CHAPTER IN *MONITOR*'S STORY

From the Civil War to the present day, the USS *Monitor* has sparked the interest of each new generation until its story has become an amalgam of praise, disparagement, exaggeration, and myth. New books on *Monitor* continue to appear every few years, validating Grenville Weeks' prophecy that the little ironclad would "not soon be forgotten by the American people."[1] Indeed, *Monitor*'s story has continued to grow in volume and breadth, and along the way it has been repeatedly reexamined, reassessed, and augmented by historians, naval architects, and Civil War buffs until it has become difficult to distinguish truth from fiction or to effectively place the story within the context of the society and technology in which *Monitor* existed. By the late twentieth century, historians had mined most (but not all!) of the surviving documentary evidence upon which to base a factual account of the ship's development, naval service, loss, and significance.

But then in 1973, *Monitor*'s discovery off North Carolina opened a new window on the past through which ocean researchers and archaeologists were afforded the rare opportunity to study the ship itself. Investigating *Monitor*'s hull and contents provided a wealth of new data that allowed us to answer some of the most significant questions about its sinking and to write a new chapter in *Monitor*'s story. While preparing our findings and conclusions, we remained aware of the need to weave our new archaeological information into the fabric of the story that had already been so thoroughly—and often skillfully—told.

THE MANY FACETS OF *MONITOR*'S STORY

The *Monitor*'s story began somewhat ignominiously, with the new warship being dubbed "Ericsson's Folly" even before it was completed.[2] Newspapers tended to focus on doubts that the ironclad would float or on controversies about who deserved credit for *Monitor*'s turret design.

Actually, the Northern press had little to say about the "Ericsson battery" until its launching, when the *New York Times* announced, "she was launched successfully" in spite of the opinion of many that she would "break her back or else swamp."[3] That brief announcement, while not exactly derogatory, certainly falls within the category of damning with faint praise. Negative reporting continued through *Monitor*'s sea trials, but then executed an astonishing reversal after the little ironclad's remarkable success at Hampton Roads. Charles MacCord, Ericsson's chief draftsman, later commented somewhat smugly, "The versatility of the modern journalist stood him in good stead on the 10th of March, when the novel fighting machine had proved invulnerable to heavier blows than his pen could deal."[4]

As is common with most famous people and machines, *Monitor* was always dogged by the love-hate attitudes expressed by the press, the public, and even the military. *Monitor*'s tragic loss at sea at year's end provided fuel for renewed debates on the efficacy of low-freeboard monitors. But by that time, two more monitors had been launched and even more were under construction; nothing could reverse the Union's commitment that gambled their coastal blockade—and possibly even the outcome of the war itself—on the monitors. With each new class of monitors came improvements in sea-keeping qualities and firepower, helping sustain the Union Navy's reliance on this type of warship.

Reports on the Battle at Hampton Roads were circulated globally, with varying responses. Contemporary accounts of the battle abound, as do opinions on the outcome and significance. There are published reports and reminisces by participants and eyewitnesses to the building of the two ironclads, their famous battle, the loss of both before a year had passed, and the aftermath and significance. The event generated a myriad of poems, songs, dedications, and memorabilia, and a few pieces of both warships were preserved, especially from *Virginia*'s hull, which was raised and scrapped.

After the war, there were even massive theaters-in-the-round that described the Battle at Hampton Roads through the sights and sounds of "diorama" or "cyclorama" buildings in New York, Omaha, Seattle, and elsewhere.[5] The New York Panorama opened in January 1886 at Madison Avenue and Fifty-Ninth Street, boasting an interpretive painting occupying 20,000 square feet![6] On August 31 of the following year, the Panorama reached 600 performances, rivaling some of New York's longest theater runs; the naval battle panorama was finally replaced by another exhibition in mid-1888.[7]

Writers and poets added their voices to the cacophony, often evaluating *Monitor*'s significance in terms that transcended its fighting abilities, particularly its association with the growing disquiet over possible detrimental long-term effects of the Industrial Revolution on society. Their writings were widely read and discussed, thus expanding the scope and impact of *Monitor*'s story and contributing to the ship's image as an American icon that had, in a single day, altered forever the nature of warfare.

David Mindell, professor of the history of technology, broke free of the conventional mold in 2000 when he published a fascinating book that carefully examined *Monitor*'s actual technological significance and lasting impact, and he discussed these technological aspects within the broader framework of a Western society groping with the good and bad effects of the Industrial Revolution. Making reference to John Keegan's seminal book that examines human aspects of warfare, Mindell likens the nineteenth-century idea that future conflicts would be fought from (or even *by*) machines as the "mechanical face of battle."[8] Mindell presents a range of viewpoints on *Monitor*'s impact and significance, including the reactions of contemporary writers and poets.

Nathaniel Hawthorne visited *Monitor* at Fort Monroe shortly after its battle with CSS *Virginia*, offering his impressions of the ship's significance in the July 1862 issue of *Atlantic Monthly*:

I will allow myself to call [Monitor] devilish; for this was the new war-fiend, destined, along with others of the same breed, to annihilate whole navies and batter down old supremacies. The wooden walls of Old England cease to exist, and a whole history of naval renown reaches its period, now that the Monitor comes smoking into view.[9]

Herman Melville, who may or may not have actually seen *Monitor*, penned a collection of poems under the title *Battle-Pieces and Aspects of the War* that included "The *Temeraire*," a lament on the passing of the sailing warship age, supposedly inspired by the Battle at Hampton Roads:

"*MONITOR MANIA*"—TWO CENTURIES OF ENCHANTMENT

Even though *Monitor* was lost to sight, it was never lost to history. The men in Brooklyn who helped build the first ironclad maintained an institutional pride. The survivors who sailed on *Monitor* formed veterans groups within their local Grand Army of the Republic organizations. The battle was fought over and over again in the popular media of the day (*Harper's Weekly, Leslies Illustrated, Century Magazine, Southern Historical Society Papers*).

Numerous recollections and postwar memoirs told the story and argued about who won.

There were pyrotechnic exhibitions and cycloramas within which mechanical ships recreated the battle for spectators in exciting sight-and-sound performances. A traveling show heralding *Monitor* appeared at the Jamestown Exposition in 1907 and then traveled around the United States and even made its way to Yukon, Alaska. *Monitor* and its battle with

A wartime token, stamped "OUR LITTLE *MONITOR*," one of many objects dedicated to *Monitor* or the Battle of Hampton Roads. Courtesy The Mariners' Museum

THE IMMENSE ARENA OF "THE BATTLE OF THE MONITOR AND MERRIMAC." A GREAT MARINE BATTLE SPECTACLE COSTING $240,000. LOCATED ON THE PAY STREAK, ALASKA-YUKON-PACIFIC EXPOSITION, SEATTLE, WASH., U. S. A.
Copyright 1909
by E. W. McConnell
Riverview Park, Chicago

This postcard advertises "The immense arena of 'The Battle of the Monitor and Merrimac.'" This "great marine battle spectacle" was constructed for the Alaska-Yukon-Pacific Exposition, held in Seattle, Washington in 1909. Courtesy The Mariners' Museum

CSS *Virginia* were commemorated in a remarkable variety of memorabilia and souvenirs including commemorative coins, children's toys, and sheet music. *Monitor*'s name and likeness (loosely speaking) were applied to posters, advertisements, and product names. In the popular culture of the late nineteenth century, *Monitor* was, quite literally, a household word. As time passed, so did the veterans of the battle, but the story of *Monitor* and the clash of armor in Hampton Roads was never forgotten.

> O, Titan Temeraire,
> Your stern-lights fade away;
> Your bulwarks to the years must yield,
> And heart-of-oak decay.
> A pigmy steam-tug tows you,
> Gigantic, to the shore—
> Dismantled of your guns and spars,
> And sweeping wings of war.
> The rivets clinch the iron-clads,
> Men learn a deadlier lore;
> But Fame has nailed your battle-flags—
> Your ghost it sails before:
> O, the navies old and oaken,
> O, the Temeraire no more![10]

In that same collection, "A Utilitarian View of the Monitor's Fight" expresses Melville's belief that sailors fighting from within the protection of their iron box would no longer have an opportunity to demonstrate valor or to reap its honors. He says that war will henceforth consist of "plain mechanic power plied cogently" with

> War now placed—
> Where War belongs—
> Among the trades and artisans.[11]

He continues, stating,

> Yet this was battle, and intense—
> Beyond the strife of fleets heroic;
> Deadlier, closer, calm 'mid storm;
> No passion; all went on by crank,
> Pivot, and screw,
> And calculations of caloric.

He concludes with this prediction of the dehumanization of future wars, which would eliminate opportunities for heroics and, therefore, the recognition of personal accomplishments on the battlefield:

> War yet shall be, but warriors
> Are now but operatives; War's made
> Less grand than Peace,
> And a singe runs through lace and feather.[12]

Melville and Hawthorne felt that future war-fighters would be no more than operatives—a contemporary term for machinery operators.

Hawthorne, like Melville, predicted that mechanized warfare would reduce officers and crews to mere operators of the machines of war:

There will be other battles, but no more such tests of seamanship and manhood as the battles of the past; and, moreover, . . . human strife is to be transferred from the heart and personality of man into cunning contrivances of machinery, which by-and-by will fight out our wars with only the clank and smash of iron.[13]

Certainly, there was no such perception among *Monitor*'s officers and crew after March 9. They were basking in more enthusiastic praise and adoration than any could have imagined. Paymaster Keeler wrote to his wife, Anna, on March 11 that he went ashore to discover that "the *Monitor* is on every one's tongue & the expressions of gratitude & joy embarrassed us they so numerous."[14] On the thirteenth he wrote that as *Monitor* passed close to Newport News, "[t]he whole army came out to see us, thousands & thousands lined the shore."[15] Local dignitaries and citizens by the score visited the little ironclad. Keeler wrote to Anna on the eighteenth that "[w]e

are perfectly over-run with visitors. So many were coming that orders were issued that no one would be allowed on board unless by special invitation."[16] On May 7, President Lincoln and two cabinet secretaries toured the ship. For the time being, the "*Monitor* Boys" were the talk of the town.

Sadly, *Monitor* was quickly relegated to river patrol duties, its continued presence being essential to maintain the Union's control of passage on the James River. During the summer of 1862, *Monitor*'s officers and crew were subjected to extreme heat, boredom, and the frustration of having been denied another opportunity to defeat *Virginia*. Life aboard was dull and almost insufferably hot, and there were few opportunities for visitors or townsfolk to lavish praise on them. When, in late December, *Monitor* received orders to proceed south to engage the enemy, most of the officers and crew were eager to demonstrate their skills and the invincibility of their ship. None could have imagined the terrible tragedy that would soon engulf them.

In his poem, "In the Turret," Herman Melville chillingly, if unintentionally, seems to prophesy *Monitor*'s sinking:

> "Stand up, my heart; be strong; what matter
> If here thou seest thy welded tomb?
> And let huge Og with thunders batter—
> Duty be still my doom,
> Though drowning come in liquid gloom. . . .
>
> First duty, duty next, and duty last;
> Ay, Turret, rivet me here to duty fast!—"
> So nerved, you fought wisely and well;
> And live, twice live in life and story;
> But over your Monitor dirges swell,
> In wind and wave that keep the rites of
> glory.[17]

The discovery of *Monitor*'s remains has allowed the little ironclad to "twice live in life and story," as Melville suggested. Once again the vessel itself, rather than its reputation, became the focus of attention.

NOAA has been at the forefront of *Monitor*'s "second life" almost since the outset, and has headed up efforts to protect it and expand its story. Because of the richness of the story, and the many viewpoints and opinions expressed over a century and a half, NOAA was determined to preserve and disseminate as much of the story as possible while at the same time adding new archaeological and technological details that emerged during our research. During NOAA's quarter-century stewardship of *Monitor*, its officers and crew have not been ignored.

TELLING THE WHOLE STORY

Collecting all the details of *Monitor*'s story was, in many ways, as difficult as recovering its components from the ocean floor. In recent years, more data have come to light, adding new information to the ever-expanding *Monitor* story, and NOAA and The Mariners' Museum in partnership with the National Archives and Records Administration, are capturing this information in the *Monitor* Collection Associated Records. After the *Monitor* National Marine Sanctuary was designated in 1975, NOAA developed a comprehensive management plan that included an education and outreach component. Staff delivered public lectures and published a periodic activities report, *Cheesebox*, to inform colleagues and interested citizens about our activities. We became early users of the World Wide Web to communicate our program and activities to a global audience. We cooperated with public and commercial television producers for documentaries about *Monitor* and our recovery efforts, and we have shared our data with researchers around the world.

Ultimately, though, we needed a permanent facility where we could tell the *Monitor*'s story through professional museum exhibits that would integrate historical information with the actual remains of the ship and its contents. In 1987, NOAA selected The Mariners' Museum to become its principal museum for the *Monitor*, and that same year the museum opened its first *Monitor* exhibit. As more information and artifacts became available, the exhibit grew.

Mariners' also became the repository for NOAA's collection of documents and research material related to *Monitor*. We are continuing to add documents to the *Monitor* Collection Associated Records, which is housed in The Mariners' Museum Research Library, recently relocated to Christopher Newport University, where it is available to the public. NOAA's *Monitor* Collection also includes all the artifacts and other materials recovered from the sanctuary and these, too, are located at the museum. As time passed, NOAA and Mariners' were able to bring new communications tools into play, until information on *Monitor* was available in numerous forms from a wide range of sources.

USS *MONITOR* CENTER

In the mid-1990s, when major recovery plans began to take shape, NOAA, The Mariners' Museum, and the Navy began working together with the common objective of saving parts of *Monitor* from disintegration on the seafloor. From the formation of a three-way partnership and the development of the *Monitor* Long-Range Preservation Plan, NOAA, the Navy, and The Mariners' Museum were committed to a comprehensive range of responsibilities for recovering parts of *Monitor* and then making the information available to the public in an informative and entertaining way. The DOD Legacy Resource Management Program awarded funds for recovery, and NOAA, the Navy, and the museum supplemented those funds with cash and in-kind services. When recovery planning got under way, NOAA and the museum began seeking support to construct a suitable facility to conserve and display the recovered objects.

On March 9, 2007, nearly five years after the turret's recovery and exactly 145 years since the historic day when *Monitor* and *Virginia* fought the world's first battle between ironclad warships, NOAA and The Mariners' Museum officially opened the USS *Monitor* Center. The 162,000 square foot *Monitor* Center is a major exhibition that occupies an entire wing of The Mariners' Museum. It is a comprehensive, multimedia exhibit comprising historical documents and artifacts, a wide range of educational and interpretive material, and interactive displays. The *Monitor* Center gives visitors the opportunity to experience the fear, awe, and excitement surrounding naval aspects of the American Civil War, an extraordinary time in our nation's history.

One component of the *Monitor* Center is the Batten Conservation Laboratory Complex, a cavernous, state-of-the-art conservation facility. From an elevated platform, visitors can peer through large windows to watch conservators at work preserving the engine, turret, and other components, some of which may require nearly twenty years of complex treatment in order to ensure their long-term preservation.

The Center tells *Monitor*'s story by placing the

Outside the USS *Monitor* Center, visitors may step onto the deck of a full-size *Monitor* replica. Courtesy The Mariners' Museum

ship, crew, and battle within the larger context of the mid-nineteenth century. After an introductory section, the exhibit leads visitors through a pathway that uses models and life-size displays to describe the changes in naval technology that were emerging as part of the Industrial Revolution. The next section describes the political situation at that time and discusses the various issues that contributed to the outbreak of rebellion in the southern states. The "Battle Theater" brings the two-day Battle of Hampton Roads to life with dioramas, maps, and sounds that dramatically immerse visitors in the event,

somewhat reminiscent of the 1880s "panorama," but in exciting digital form. Finally, an expansive area displays artifacts from *Monitor* and describes the major recovery expeditions. In this area, visitors can enter the "Recovery Theater," where they will learn how NOAA and the Navy conducted diving operations. Visitors also have the opportunity to make their own decisions about how to recover parts of the *Monitor* and to record their choices via buttons on each chair arm. Just outside this large exhibition area is a full-scale replica of *Monitor*, built and donated by Newport News Shipbuilding, where visitors

The entrance to the USS *Monitor* Center's "Ironclad Revolution" galleries. The corridor to the right leads to the public viewing area for the conservation laboratory. Courtesy The Mariners' Museum

This view shows the two-level gallery with *Monitor*'s propeller, two interpretive turrets, and numerous artifacts and exhibits. Outside the windows to the right is the full-scale replica, and outside on the left is a silhouette of CSS *Virginia* to the same scale as *Monitor*. Courtesy The Mariners' Museum

can walk the deck of the iconic structure and have their photographs taken standing next to the turret.

The museum also created a virtual *Monitor* Center that contains much of the *Monitor*'s history along with other interesting information, including live cameras inside the lab that provide real-time views of the ongoing conservation work, and a conservation blog where new information about the artifact conservation process is posted on a weekly basis.[18]

THE STORY CONTINUES

We recovered more than two hundred tons of material from *Monitor*—one of the largest historic shipwreck recoveries ever conducted—but that staggering tonnage actually represents only about one-fifth of the total weight of *Monitor*'s hull and contents. The area forward of the amidships bulk-

head is virtually undisturbed, and that part of the ship contains the ship's stored supplies and ammunition as well as living spaces for all officers and crew. Therefore, *Monitor* is still a very significant archaeological site with much more information to yield; the site is also a viable and important marine sanctuary where NOAA's efforts at protection and research will continue indefinitely. NOAA and private groups continue to conduct research expeditions, and the new data are added to the growing body of knowledge about *Monitor* and the men who lived and fought on board it.

Since 1977 we have recovered material from the site that sheds new light on the ship's construction details, such as deck plates, the engine, and the turret; on the sinking, such as the lantern that signaled *Monitor*'s distress to *Rhode Island*; and the anchor, still at the end of its chain. We have also learned more about the men who were on board. From the captain's stateroom, we

Since *Monitor*'s turret will be in its conservation tank for many years, the current exhibit includes two full-size interpretive turrets: the near one is a replica showing the turret's construction and guns, while the second is a recreation of the turret as it appeared when it first arrived at the Museum. Courtesy The Mariners' Museum

recovered personal items; from the berth/storage deck we found hair restorative bottles (possibly used to hide a supply of liquor) and a bottle on which someone had scratched "cider." From the machinery spaces came tools, instruments, and spare parts.

But it was the turret that provided the most vivid glimpse of *Monitor*'s men. There we found the remains of those two crewmen: one still wearing a gold ring, and one whose pocket contained personal items. Since recovery, these men have shared space with fallen American warriors from many wars around the world. At the Central Identification Laboratory of the Joint POW/MIA Accounting Command (JPAC) in Hawaii, forensic anthropologists and technicians studied their remains in detail, recovering DNA samples from both men. Efforts by NOAA, The Mariners' Museum, JPAC, and the Navy are now focused on identifying the *Monitor* crewmen and reuniting their remains with their families.

Increased publicity during the past decade about

Monitor's disintegration and the subsequent recovery effort produced numerous queries to NOAA and the museum. Some of those contacts resulted in the acquisition of private papers and documents related to *Monitor* that were previously unknown to scholars. One of the most significant donations was a collection of letters written by *Monitor* fireman George Geer to his wife, Martha.[19]

The NOAA/Mariners' partnership is strong, as is our quest for more details to add to the *Monitor* story. We intend to ensure that the world will never forget the "little cheesebox on a raft."

Publication and Reporting

This book resulted from a partnership between NOAA and Texas A&M University Press, and it represents the next phase in telling *Monitor*'s story to a wide audience. This publication recounts my own

MONITOR'S LASTING SIGNIFICANCE

Rapid advancements in naval technology were under way well before the American Civil War. American ironclad warships in 1862 (both Union and Confederate) were unique and formidable, and they attracted the attention of foreign navies as well as public imagination. They by no means, however, ushered in the age of iron and steam. Historian Brian Lavery notes, "By the time of the Crimean War (1854–6) it was recognized that the purely sailing warship had no place in action."[1] Elsewhere, Lavery concluded, "for the sailing ship of the line, the story ends in 1845, for after that year no more pure sailing ships were built."[2]

Nominating *Monitor* to the National Register of Historic Places was relatively simple, since it qualified on all of the specified criteria. Likewise, *Monitor* was designated a National Historic Landmark, one of the few shipwrecks to achieve that status. *Monitor*'s true significance, however, seems to reside in an intangible, yet significant, attribute: the little ironclad's enduring international recognition as an icon of "Yankee ingenuity." *Monitor*'s continuing legacy stems in part from the nearly universal acknowledgment that it was one of the most successful ship prototypes in history. The concepts of low freeboard, armor on exposed features,

and placement of guns in a rotating turret have remained key elements of modern warship design down to the present day.

In 1988, in a report prepared for NOAA, James P. Delgado assessed the *Monitor*'s significance within the contexts of the development of ironclad warships, the American Civil War, and public perception, among other topics. Delgado argues that *Monitor*'s lasting significance relates primarily to its "mythic" qualities:

*Monitor's impact on the American consciousness was profound, instilling a "*Monitor *mania" that continues to this day.* **Monitor***'s impact is reflected in the popular culture of her era; cartoons, poems, and other forms of social expression of the 1860s are replete with* **Monitor** *references.*[3]

Many examples of historical and recent popular culture support Delgado's argument. Countless writers and poets have heralded *Monitor*'s accomplishments, beginning immediately after the Battle at Hampton Roads. Contemporary luminaries who wrote about *Monitor* include Herman Melville and Nathaniel Hawthorne; popular songs and sheet music extolled *Monitor*'s exploits, and a trademarked *Monitor* image was used in advertisements for "Iron Clad Paint."[4] The trend seems to never end. During the

1990s, as NOAA was developing plans to recover parts of *Monitor*'s hull, a local deejay—a direct descendant of *Monitor*'s first commanding officer—recorded his own *Monitor* song.

The public's loyalty to *Monitor*'s name undoubtedly results in part from a nearly universal tendency to favor the underdog. Before the famous battle, *Monitor* was derided by many in the US Navy, politicians, and the media as "Ericsson's Folly"; the "little cheesebox on a raft" that was no match for the larger and better armed *Virginia*. For many, the battle was a triumph of David over Goliath, preserving the honor of the Union and influencing the progress of the war.

As to *Monitor*'s effect on the Civil War, one historian commented, "To an extent never previously attained, nor ever likely to be equaled, she was precisely the right ship, at precisely the right place, at precisely the right time."[5]

Notes:

1. Gardiner (1992a, 9).
2. Lavery (1983, I.156).
3. Delgado (1988, 1).
4. Ibid., 9; even today, the Benjamin Moore Paint Company advertises its Ironclad® paint line.
5. DeKay (1997, 228).

---

personal recollections and perspective as a key participant in the project, and it will be followed by a detailed archaeological report that will describe in detail our archaeological and technological findings and interpretations. We have accumulated far more data than can be published, even in the technical report, so we have created a dedicated website that will supplement our publications and provide an outlet

for such electronic products as interactive site plans and images, video clips, and other media.

The Sanctuary's Future

I am often asked, "Now that you've recovered all the important parts, is there any reason *Monitor* should still be a National Marine Sanctuary?" My answer is an unhesitating, unqualified, and absolute "Yes!" After all, roughly 80 percent of *Monitor*'s hull and contents still lie on the seabed. Archaeological excavation will unquestionably shed more light on the types and quantities of stores and war materials as well as yield valuable new information on life aboard this unique warship.

As with most major archaeological projects, we expect to uncover new facts for years to come. Further analysis of existing data will continue to generate more knowledge. Already, we have begun to take a new look at *Monitor*'s sea-keeping characteristics, points of hull weakness, and sources of water ingress. With the aid of modern computer analysis tools, we may be able to describe in even greater detail exactly why and how *Monitor* sank. Did the ironclad, criticized in its time and up to the present as a rushed, stopgap design, have a fatal flaw that doomed it? Because of *Monitor*'s fame and significance, we have been able to recruit valuable partners for this research, including the Marine Forensics Committee of the Society of Naval Architects and Marine Engineers, the conservation staff and volunteers at The Mariners' Museum, and other skilled specialists.

New information may also come from historical sources. Publicity from our recovery expeditions and news of plans for the USS *Monitor* Center resulted in the sharing or donation of several significant objects and documents related to *Monitor*. It was a reminder to us that archaeology and history are about people, and that people stories remain paramount in our work and are relevant and exciting to the public. The Mariners' Museum is actively seeking to acquire additional *Monitor* material for the expanding collection of *Monitor* objects and documents. As mentioned, one of the most significant recent acquisitions was a collection of letters from engineer George Geer to his wife, Martha. His letters, since published by the museum, provide a rare opportunity to experience life aboard *Monitor* from the point of view of an ordinary seaman who, in this case, played an important role in trying to save *Monitor* from sinking.[20] Again, history and archaeology are about people, and not just about big events, famous people, and great achievements. People play an important role, and they also pay a price. It was largely through the work of ordinary people that *Monitor* defended the Union ships in Hampton Roads. It was also primarily through the work of otherwise ordinary people that this extraordinary ship was protected, recovered, and put on display; people such as the hundreds of Navy divers, dozens of archeologists, conservators, engineers, and many others who teamed together for extraordinary results. History owes them all, historical and modern, a debt of gratitude.

Just as USS *Monitor* will always have a prominent place in the history of the United States, so too will the *Monitor* National Marine Sanctuary maintain its significance as the little area of seabed that contains the remains of one of the world's most significant warships.

NOTES

CHAPTER ONE   "The *Monitor* Is No More"

1. Confidential order dated December 24, 1862, from Acting Rear Admiral S. P. Lee, commanding the North Atlantic Blockading Squadron to Commander Joseph P. Bankhead, US Navy, Commanding U.S.S. *Monitor*, Hampton Roads, Virginia.
2. Keeler (1862–1863, 232).
3. Letter from Lt. Dana Greene to his father and brother, March 14, 1862.
4. Weeks (1863, 367).
5. Geer letters, January 13, 1863 (Geer 2000).
6. There remain some inconsistencies about the turret transit position and the type of caulking—if any—placed beneath it. Bennett (1898, 297) states that a plaited hemp gasket was used, against Ericsson's instructions, and as the seas washed the hemp out of the seam, it opened wide gaps for water to enter.
7. Bankhead report, 1January1863.
8. No details have been found concerning the method of sealing the hawse pipe, but since the anchor chain had to remain attached, it must have been difficult to effectively seal the opening with the chain running through it. Water pulsing up the anchor well would have created tremendous hydraulic forces, as evidenced by Green's description of the March leak, and most types of packing would have been blown out.
9. Logbook, USS *State of Georgia*, 30Dec1862.
10. Keeler (253).
11. Logbook, USS *State of Georgia*, 30Dec1862.
12. There is no evidence for when Hatteras was first given

the name "Graveyard of the Atlantic," but a mariners' guide published in 1900 (Hoyt 1900, 161), and a government document issued in 1904 (War Department 1904, 1432) applied the term to Hatteras. An article published in *Technical World Magazine* in 1907 stated, "[Cape Hatteras is] the terror of the mariner—the Diamond Shoals, the 'Graveyard of the Atlantic,' being so feared by sailors that comparatively speaking there is no coastwise trade up and down this stretch of coast except by steam vessels. . . . As for barge towing, for freight, it is hardly thought of ten months in the year and the rest of the time essayed with fear and trembling" (Claudy 1907, 402–03).
13. Logbook, USS *Passaic*, 30Dec1862.
14. Determining latitude and longitude were time-consuming exercises in the nineteenth century, requiring accurate fixes on landmarks or celestial bodies at a specific time of day; however, a small line, marked with distances and weighted by a "sounding lead" provided the depth of water and, therefore, a quick estimate of the distance from land. Charts often displayed depth soundings, but depths in areas such as Diamond Shoals were known to change without warning by as much as several fathoms.
15. Logbook, USS *Rhode Island*, 30Dec1862; The Beaufort Scale, developed in England in 1805 by Sir Francis Beaufort, this system is still in use today.
16. Logbook, USS *Rhode Island*, 30Dec1862.
17. Logbook, USS *Passaic*, 30Dec1862.
18. Logbooks, USS *Passaic* and USS *Rhode Island*, 30Dec1862.

19. No details on this procedure have been located, but possibly they rigged block-and-tackle gear from the turret base to the deck below in an attempt to hold the turret in place.

20. This entry points out inconsistencies in *Passaic*'s and *State of Georgia*'s logs: When the two ships stopped at 4:15 p.m. for a burial at sea, *Passaic*'s log stated that the sea was "comparatively smooth," in spite of the fact that the log had been recording Force 4 winds since the previous night, while *State of Georgia*'s log had recorded a 4:00 wind of Force 8! These entries are not only inconsistent with each other, but also with *Rhode Island*, whose log for the same time recorded a steady Force 2. These discrepancies were ignored in favor of other log entries and later reports.

21. Logbook, USS *Passaic*, 30Dec1862.

22. Keeler (254).

23. Ibid.

24. Weeks (1863, 368).

25. Logbook, USS *Rhode Island,* 30Dec1862. Interestingly, throughout this ordeal *Rhode Island* and *Passaic* communicated using a combination of flag and, apparently, light signals, as recorded in both logbooks, while *Monitor* had communicated during the day with a chalkboard!

26. Weeks (1863, 368).

27. Report of Joseph Watters, January 1, 1863.

28. Frances Butts, in *Battles and Leaders*, vol. 1.

29. Bankhead report, 1January1863.

30. Ibid.

31. Report of Captain Percival Drayton. According to Ericsson, who later inspected *Passaic* in drydock, there was not a single sprung rivet, so Drayton was probably seeing water rushing in through the hawse pipe.

32. Logbook, USS *Passaic*, 30Dec1862. Note: Thirty-two-pound solid shot were much too small for either *Passaic*'s XI-inch or XV-inch Dahlgren gun. One must assume that the shot were being carried as ballast, and probably intended for transfer to a Union blockading vessel mounting thirty-two-pdr. guns.

33. Report of Joseph Watters, January 1, 1863. Note: in a letter to his brother, George Geer related that it was he who reported the engine room situation to Bankhead and obtained his permission to start the centrifugal pump (Geer letters; Geer 2000, 235).

34. Report of Captain Percival Drayton.

35. Logbook, USS *Passaic*, 30Dec1862.

36. Ibid.

37. Weeks (1863, 869).

38. Bankhead report, 1January1863.

39. Bankhead, Butts, and Keeler.

40. Keeler letters, January 6, 1863.

41. A *Harper's Weekly* account related that "five or six of the crew of the *Monitor* seized the ropes . . . and started to climb up her side, but only three reached there." None of the other sources corroborate this account.

42. Reports from Bankhead, Trenchard, and other accounts.

43. Neither Bankhead's nor Trenchard's official report mentioned the fouling of *Rhode Island*'s wheel by *Monitor*'s severed hawser; however, the incident is reported later in articles by Weeks and Butts of *Monitor*, and William Rogers and H. R. Smith of *Rhode Island*. It seems reasonable to assume that these later reports are correct, since it is difficult to imagine any other reason for *Rhode Island*'s officers letting the ship drift so far from its own boats and from *Monitor*.

44. Bankhead report, 1January1863.

45. Watters, report of 1 January 1863, appended to Bankhead report of the same date.

46. Ibid.

47. Rodney Browne report, 10 January 1863

48. Bankhead report, 1January1863.

49. Rodney Browne. In the darkness and heavy seas, the cutter became separated from its ship. *Rhode Island* searched for hours, "throwing up rockets and burning blue lights," but the cutter was not located. Fortunately, Browne and his crew were picked up the next day by a schooner and taken to Beaufort, North Carolina.

50. Weeks (1863).

51. Keeler letters, January 6, 1863, 253. *State of Georgia* and *Passaic* saved themselves by turning north and running with the storm. Of the sixty-three men aboard *Monitor* that night, four officers and twelve crewmen lost their lives, many of them washed overboard while attempting to reach *Rhode Island*'s boats. For their heroic efforts in rescuing the crew of *Monitor*, five men from USS *Rhode Island* became the first noncombatants to earn the Congressional Medal of Honor. Of the sixteen men from *Monitor* who lost their lives that night, few details could be discovered concerning their fate. Of *Monitor* itself, its final resting place could only be estimated and no wreckage or human remains were ever reported.

CHAPTER TWO   Discovery

1. According to an Australian source, the UOL Mark IV was the most advanced of a series of "pulse type ahead-searching sonars" developed by the General Electric Company for the US Navy beginning in 1942 and culminating in the AN/UQS-1 sonar (http://users.qld.chariot .net.au/~dialabull/hunter.html, accessed March 5, 2011). Similar information can be found in the *Catalogue of Electronic Equipment*, NavShips 900, 116, 1952 (Update 5,

n.d.), placed on the Internet by the Historic Naval Ships Association (http://www.hnsa.org/doc/ecat/cat-0454.htm, accessed March 5, 2011).

2. Miller (1974, 616–23); this site is almost certainly the YP-389, rediscovered on the 1973 *Eastward* cruise and identified during a NOAA survey in 2009, as described later in the chapter.

3. Mathisson (1955, 5).

4. Blair (1960); Broadwater (1974, 121); Marx (1967); Miller (1974, 635–67).

5. Martin (1968, C-1, C-6); Miller (1974, 670, 694). Magnetometers detect anomalies in the Earth's magnetic field that can indicate the presence of ferrous material (iron, steel).

6. Miller (1974, 671–74).

7. Ibid., 675.

8. Broadwater (1976, 105); Miller (1974, 689; 1978, 96).

9. Miller (1974, 701).

10. Marx (1967, 68).

11. Broadwater (1974, 117–21); Miller (1974, 635–67).

12. Author's personal experience, 1973.

13. The P-3D Orion was equipped with an AN/ASQ-81 metastable helium magnetometer, capable of detecting submerged ferrous objects and fixing their positions within the 0.1 mile accuracy of the LORAN navigation system in use at that time.

14. Miller, Andahazy, and Peterkin (1974, 716, 845–60, 851–59); Andahazy and Miller (1979, 87–94).

15. Miller (1974, 723); Ringle (1973).

16. In-kind equipment and services were provided by numerous organizations, as outlined in the referenced documents.

17. Newton et al. (1974, 1–4, 16); Watts (1975, 301, 325–26). The *Eastward* was supported by two small craft provided by the 824th Transportation Company, US Army Reserve. Major equipment included an EG&G Type 259 (105 kHz) side scan sonar; several fathometers; a Varian proton precession magnetometer; Del Norti, Loran A and C, and Omega positioning systems; and underwater still and video cameras.

18. Newton et al. (1974, 1–2); Watts (1975, 301). Watts and Peterkin each plotted the track of *Monitor* and the other vessels, and both came up with similar survey areas. However, the Watts chart was used during the Eastward cruise and it was not until 1974 that the two researchers compared notes on their research (Watts 2008, pers. comm.).

19. Newton (1975, 49).

20. Ibid.; Watts (1975, 317).

21. ONMS (http://www.noaanews.noaa.gov/stories2009/20090909_battleofatlantic.html, accessed May 28, 2011).

22. Navigation accuracy of plus or minus a quarter mile would have been very good in 1950. Although the upper structure of YP-389 has collapsed since 1973, the overall size, depth, and location make it almost certain that this is the site located in 1950 and 1973.

23. Randt (1973, 11).

24. Newton (1974, Appendix III).

25. Miller (1974, 96–98); Miller, Andahazy, and Peterkin (1974, 853–55). The National Oceanic and Atmospheric Administration (NOAA) plans to investigate these targets in the future.

26. Andahazy, Everstine, and Hood (1976, 19–22); Andahazy and Miller (1979, 93).

27. *Washington Post* (1973). The wire services carried the announcement of the *Monitor*'s discovery, and virtually every major newspaper in the United States, as well as foreign media, reported the story.

28. Ringle (1974b, C1); Miller (1978, 92–93).

29. Newton (1975, 61). In addition to Gordon Watts, presenters included Capt. Ernest Peterkin, probable search area; Midshipman Edward Miller, Project Cheesebox studies and magnetometer search data; William Andahazy, details on the airborne magnetometer survey; John Newton, Duke's *Eastward* survey; and CDR Colin Jones, US Navy, who would be in charge of the *Seaprobe* assessment (Miller 1978, 97).

30. Ringle (1974b, C4).

31. Bascom (1976); Miller (1974, 911–12; 1978, 95); Newton (1975, 61).

32. Craven (2001); Sontag and Drew (1998).

33. Miller (1978, 97). Other participants included JOC Archie Galloway from the Office of the Chief of Naval Operations; Sandra Belock, a North Carolina artist; and Dr. Kent Schneider, archaeologist for the State of North Carolina. The author, a part-time employee with the North Carolina Underwater Archaeology Program at the time, was transferred aboard to assist in the development of the photomosaic. In support on an Army Reserve LCU were Dr. Harold Edgerton, another member of the Duke team, who was operating his side-scan sonar, and several State of North Carolina employees and Army Reserve personnel.

34. Ibid.

35. Watts (1975, 326); Ringle (1974b, G1–G3).

36. Newton, January 1975, 48–61.

CHAPTER THREE   Story of an Ironclad

1. Gardiner (1994, 80–81).

2. Lavery (1983, 155); Lambert (1984, 122). *Victoria* was a three-deck ship of the line, ship-rigged but also fitted with a steam engine.

3. Chappelle (1949, 121); Fowler (1984, 18). The six frigates were *United States*, *Constitution*, *Constellation*,

all launched in 1797, and *President* (1798), *Chesapeake* (1799), and *Congress* (1800) (see Chapelle 1949; Morris 1993).

4. Fowler (1984, 162–84); Morris (1993, 25).

5. Gardiner (1992b, 61).

6. The terms "cannon" and "gun" are often used interchangeably. However, in the early phases of ordnance development a "cannon" was a particular type of gun. Before the eighteenth century there were four main categories, based primarily on the proportion of caliber to length: mortars, Perrier, cannon, and culverin (Lavery 1987, 97). For instance, a sixteenth-century *cannon* was a cast gun whose length was some eighteen to twenty-two times longer than the diameter of its bore, while a *cannon-perier* had a ratio of approximately ten to one (Padfield 1974, 31). There were many other types including bombards, falconets, demi-cannon, culverins, demi-culverins, and so forth, and there were even guns made of wood (Ibid., 25) and leather-clad copper (Lavery 1987, 83)! In any case, the proper term for naval ordnance is "guns." Therefore, this document follows naval convention.

7. Gardiner (1994, 146).

8. Lavery (1987, 86–87).

9. It is beyond the scope of this document to attempt to comprehensively describe the myriad of experiments, testing, implementation, and political decision making involved in the rapid escalation of warship technology, armament, and armor. The interested reader is encouraged to consult the sources referenced in the text and bibliography.

10. This type of projectile was not entirely new; mortars firing powder-filled shells were already in use on land and at sea. However, mortars, which lobbed their shells on high-arcing trajectories, were effective only as siege guns.

11. Baxter (1933, 17); Padfield (1974, 49).

12. An English translation of Paixans' experiments was published by Parlby (1825, 349–58).

13. Baxter (1933, 20–23).

14. English translation by Parlby (1825, 359).

15. Baxter (1933, 69); Gardiner (1992b, 52).

16. Baxter (1933, 33).

17. Ibid., 84–86; Holley (1864). Britain, too, built armored batteries and deployed them to the Black Sea; however, they arrived too late to participate in the shelling of Kinburn (Baxter 1968, 82).

18. *Mechanics Magazine* (1862, VII, 428). *Mechanics Magazine* attributes this quote to Sir John Hay, chairman of the British naval commission, and cites its source as an article in the *Quarterly Review*.

19. Holley (1863, 85–94); Wells (1862, 81–87).

20. Ward (1861, 189).

21. Ibid., 190–95.

22. Ibid., 196–97. Even the mutually assured destruction (MAD) stasis of the Cold War did not reach Ward's "undefined limit," since at the end of that stalemate both sides were developing antimissile missiles that could have neutralized the enemy's offense.

23. Baxter (1968, 10–14); Beach (1986, 148–50); Lavery (1983, I.155). Ericsson was not the sole inventor of the screw propeller but was the first to provide the Royal Navy with a successful demonstration of its effectiveness (Canney 1993, 31).

24. Canney (1993, 14).

25. Baxter (1933, 13–14); Beach (1986, 202–03).

26. For more than a century historians have debated the spelling of this vessel's name: is it "*Merrimac*" or "*Merrimack*"? The Naval Historical Center settled the debate by formally declaring that the name should be spelled with a "k" at the end (Mystery of Merrimac). In 2006, however, the Naval Historical Center declared that a bell belonging to a collector was an authentic watch bell from the USS *Merrimac(k)*. This bell actually bears the name "Merrimac." Interestingly, most nineteenth-century sources spell the name without the "k" as well. However, this document conforms to the declaration of the Naval Historical Center. (See the "Hampton Roads" and "On Assignment" articles in the March 2006 issue of *National Geographic*.)

27. Silverstone (2001, 15–16).

28. Simpson's article, published in 1886, is quoted in Bennett (1900, 29).

29. (Baxter 1968, 152–53). The Stevens brothers eventually were successful in building the ironclad *Naugatuck*, which accompanied *Monitor* and *Galena* up the James River in 1862.

30. *New York Times*, April 24, 1861, 1.

31. Ibid.

32. *New York Times*, April 24 and 26, 1861. Numerous historic accounts describe the abandonment of the Gosport Navy Yard. Northern newspapers played down the loss, the *New York Times* of April 26 smugly stating, "Long before [the Navy Yard facilities] can bring forth new weapons of offence [*sic*], this war will be ended. . . . All that is now spared will then be so much gained!"

33. Miller (1978, 18) states that a sympathetic Union petty officer interrupted the powder train to save the nearby homes of his friends, while Scharf (1887, 133) includes a report from the Virginians stating that the dock was saved by flooding it.

34. Fowler (2001, 47–48).

35. Rawson and Woods (1898, 67–69); ORN (Official Records of the Union and Union and Confederate Navies in the War of the Rebellion), US Navy Department, Series II, vol. 2: 67–69.

36. Still (1985, 11).

37. Ibid.; ONR, 174.

38. Still (1985, 11–15); Baxter (1968, 229). Subsequently, both

men claimed credit for designing the South's first iron-clad, a claim that is still debated today. While it appears that Brooke first suggested submerged ends for his vessel, it was Porter who prepared all conceptual and construction drawings for the CSS *Virginia*. Park (2007) provides details and bibliographic references for both claims.

39. Still (1985, 15).
40. Porter (1892, 342–80); Still (1971, 23).
41. Bennett (1972, 263–72). The Ironclad Board consisted of Commodore Joseph Smith, Commodore Hiram Paulding, and Commander Charles H. Davis.
42. Church (1890, 234).
43. Ibid., 246–47.
44. Related years later in a letter from Bushnell to former Secretary Gideon Wells, as quoted in Church (1890, I.248).
45. A six-inch shot is equivalent to a ball from a thirty-two-pounder cannon, one of the largest naval guns of the eighteenth century, but being replaced by larger guns by the time of the Civil War.
46. Church (1890, I.248). Ericsson's design was well-received by the French emperor, but the Crimean War was coming to a close and the French had no need to build additional warships. Nevertheless, the emperor presented Ericsson with a letter of merit and a gold medal in recognition of his inventive genius.
47. From a letter from Ericsson to John Bourne, quoted in Church (1890, I.240).
48. Ibid.; Miller (1978, 22–24). If the meeting between Bushnell and Delamater had not taken place, Ericsson's ironclad likely would never have been built.
49. Text of a letter from Bushnell to Secretary Gideon Welles after the war, quoted in Church (1890, 249).
50. Related years later in a letter from Bushnell to former Secretary Gideon Wells, as quoted in Church (1890, I.250) and numerous other sources. Davis was making reference to the prohibition against idolatry found in the Bible, Exodus 20:4.
51. Related years later in a letter from Bushnell to former Secretary Gideon Wells, as quoted in Church (1890, I.248–51); Miller (1978, 22–23).
52. Church (1890, I.257). The partners were the prominent New York businessmen Cornelius Bushnell, who presented Ericsson's plan to the Ironclad Board, and iron manufacturers John A. Griswold and John F. Winslow of Troy, New York, who secured the funding.
53. US Navy Department, Letter from the Secretary of the Navy, containing Senate Executive Document 86, 6.
54. Still (1988, 24). Church (1890, 260) estimated the total number of drawings was "at least one hundred." Many of those are reproduced in a NOAA publication complied by Peterkin (1984, out of print).
55. Church (1890, I.258–59).

56. Ibid., I.259; Still (1988, 26).
57. Watts (1975, 64–68, 84–86).
58. Ibid., 88.
59. Church (1890, I.254–55 fn).
60. Watts (1975, 88).
61. *New York Times*, January 31, 1862.
62. "Launch of Ericsson's Battery." Doc. 23. *New York World*, January 31, 1862, in Moore (1862, 57).
63. Miller (1978, 33); "Launch of Ericsson's Battery." Doc. 23. *New York World*, January 31, 1862, in Moore (1862, 57).
64. "Launch of Ericsson's Battery." Doc. 23. *New York World*, January 31, 1862, in Moore (1862, 57); Watts (1975, 96).
65. MacCord (1889, 461).
66. Ibid, 462.
67. Miller (1975, 37–39).
68. The Battle of Hampton Roads has been described in countless publications—commencing immediately after the event and still ongoing. Therefore, this book presents only a brief summary and concentrates instead on recent archaeological investigations. Readers are encouraged to read the very interesting and dramatic details of the battle that are related in several sources listed in the bibliography.
69. Eyewitnesses reported that *Virginia* had a difficult time withdrawing its ram from *Cumberland*'s hull. The incident could have resulted in *Virginia* being pulled under or having its bow torn out as *Cumberland* listed to starboard and sank.
70. Scharf (1887, 165).
71. Church (1890, I.250); Scharf (1887, 167).
72. Hawthorne (1862, 50).
73. After the war's end, the ironclad's remains were salvaged for scrap, with virtually nothing being saved (Broadwater 1984, 113; Scharf 1887, 221–38).
74. Geer letters, June 13, 1862 (Geer 2000).
75. Keeler letters, August 7, 1862 (Keeler 1964).

CHAPTER FOUR   A Sanctuary for America

1. Miller (1978, 89; 1974, 627–31).
2. Miller (1974, 625) speculated that the "group of laymen" referred to in the Navy correspondence was the USS *Monitor* Foundation of Washington, DC, headed by Raynor T. McMullen, a retired postal clerk from Michigan. No information is available on this group or what influence it may have had at the Navy Department.
3. Quoted in Miller, 627–28.
4. USS *Hatteras*, a Union Navy warship sunk off the Texas coast in 1863, was determined to be federal property; see *Hatteras Inc. v. U.S.S. Hatteras*, 1984 A.M.C. 1094 (S.D. Tex. 1981).
5. Milholland (1978, 31). Title III of the Marine, Protec-

tion, Research and Sanctuaries Act of 1972, 16 U.S.C.
s. 1431, *et seq.*

6. Tise (1978, 15).
7. Milholland (1978, 31). The progression of *Monitor* planning meetings and decisions are described in National Trust 1978, a publication of papers from a national conference on the *Monitor* conducted in Raleigh, North Carolina, during April 2–4, 1978.
8. NOAA, *Cheesebox* I: 1, 5.
9. Sheridan (1979).
10. The Regulations became 15 CFR Part 924 (NOAA 1982).
11. Tise (1978, 15–16).
12. The project is described in Bearss (1980).
13. NC ca. 1978.
14. Sheridan (1979).
15. The *Monitor* was not the first shipwreck to be surveyed by human-occupied submersibles. In 1967, Dr. George Bass located a classical Greek wreck off the southern coast of Turkey using side-scan sonar, then examined and photographed the wreck at a depth of nearly 300 feet using the research submersible *Asherah*, designed and built for Bass' research by General Dynamics (Bass 1975, 176–83).
16. Childress (1978); Gwynne (1977).
17. Mankins (1981).
18. National Trust (1978, 16).
19. Ibid., 17.
20. Ibid., 6–8.
21. The media first leaked the story of this incredible achievement in February 1975, and public details were still sketchy at the time of the conference. Several books have since been written, but the Central Intelligence Agency, which directed the recovery under the code name "Project Azorian" (reported erroneously by the press as "Project Jennifer") still blocks the release of all information on the results of the recovery.
22. A search of NOAA files did not produce a copy of the Global proposal, nor even an indication that a copy had been submitted to NOAA or the state of North Carolina.
23. National Trust (1978, 41–42); Sheridan (2004, 105–71).
24. Sheridan (2004, 132).
25. In fact, some of the participants on the *Seaprobe* expedition were actively involved in secret Cold War Navy projects and by 1978 they probably knew a great deal about *Glomar Explorer*'s capabilities and readiness.
26. Cole (1979, 17–25). This brief paper is substantiated by detailed information declassified by the CIA in 2010, which verifies that while the April 1978 *Monitor* conference was taking place, a private consortium of companies was preparing the ship for deepsea mining operations scheduled to begin that fall (see the National Security Archive website at http://www.gwu.edu/~nsarchiv/nukevault/ebb305/index.htm. Retrieved January 10, 2011). These facts also agree with a summary of the ship's history on the NavSource website (http://www.navsource.org/archives/09/49/49193.htm. Retrieved March 7, 2011). Apparently, through a series of mergers, GMDI became Transocean Inc., which purchased the vessel from the US Government in 2010 for $15 million. Renamed *GSF Explorer*, the ship is under hire to an oil consortium to drill off the coast of Indonesia until March 2012 (http://en.wikipedia.org/wiki/Hughes_Glomar_Explorer. Retrieved March 7, 2012).

27. NOAA, *U.S.S. MONITOR National Marine Sanctuary Management Plan*. Washington, DC, 1982.
28. Childress (1979). NOAA does not have a copy of that film.
29. My title was Senior Underwater Archaeologist with the Virginia Historic Landmarks Commission, Virginia's State Historic Preservation Office.
30. Now the Virginia Department of Historic Resources.
31. Watts (1981).
32. Miller (1978).
33. Sadly, just before this book went to press, I received word that Harbor Branch, now part of Florida Atlantic University, has terminated its submersible program, thus depriving scientists of the use of these safe and versatile craft.
34. NOAA *Cheesebox* II:2, April 1984, 1–7.
35. Peterkin, in *Cheesebox* III:1, 3–8.
36. *Cheesebox* VI:1, 6.
37. NPS; *Cheesebox* V:1, 1; *Cheesebox* VI:1, 6–7. The only site designated a National Historic Landmark before *Monitor* was the Truk Lagoon Underwater Fleet (a collection of wrecks, rather than a single ship), which was designated a year earlier. As of 2011, there are only nine NHL shipwrecks (http://www.nps.gov/history/maritime/nhl/wrecknhl.htm).
38. "Corrosion Investigation of the Remains of USS MONITOR," in Arnold et al. (1991, 17–70).
39. Arnold et al. (1988); Arnold et al. (1991).
40. Arnold et al. (1991, 85).
41. Cummings (1987).
42. Peterkin (1983, 1984); Still (1988, 2).
43. NOAA/MHT (1988).

CHAPTER FIVE   Charting a New Course for *Monitor*

1. Price (1984).
2. US Navy, *Diving Manual*; *NOAA Diving Manual*.
3. A NOAA observer accompanied each expedition, in accordance with terms of the permits; however, NOAA regulations prohibited the observer from actually diving.
4. *NOAA Diving Manual*, 2001.
5. Pers. comm., 1992.
6. NOAA (1993). We benefitted from "technical diving"

tri-mix decompression tables, and the feedback on those tables that resulted from hundreds of deep dives, but NOAA's tables were derived independently.

7. NOAA (1995, 4).
8. This mandate was included in section 4 of Public Law 104–283: the National Marine Sanctuaries Preservation Act, 1986.
9. NOAA (1997, 1).
10. Eastport International was the Navy salvage contractor that had participated in the 1985 and 1987 *Monitor* expeditions.
11. NOAA (1998, Apx-5).
12. Ibid., Apx-7, 8.
13. Ibid., Appendix A.

CHAPTER SIX   Implementing the Recovery Plan

1. NOAA/USN (1998). From the very first NOAA-sponsored expedition to *Monitor* in 1977, every site visit was preceded by the development of a detailed operations manual that included all activities, an onsite chain of command, equipment and operating procedures, an emergency plan, and other details deemed important for successful and safe completion of all goals.
2. Funds were received in 1999 from the Department of Defense Legacy Resources Management Program for a Fiscal Year 2000 *Monitor* recovery expedition, but no major funds were available for the 1999 fieldwork.
3. Erickson (1999).

CHAPTER SEVEN   Engineering the Recovery of
Monitor's Machinery

1. The requirement to submit that plan to the House Committee on Resources and the Senate Committee on Commerce, Science and Transportation was enacted as Section 4 of Public Law 104–283, the National Marine Sanctuaries Preservation Act. Section 4 was enacted in October 1996, and the report was submitted June 1998.
2. This historic shipyard was founded in 1886 as Newport News Shipbuilding and Dry Dock Company. In 2011, following several corporate mergers and name changes, the facility became Newport News Shipbuilding, a division of Huntington Ingalls Industries.

CHAPTER EIGHT   *Monitor* Completes Its Final Voyage

1. The tropical depression developed into Tropical Storm Cristobal. We were also getting forecasts from Navy sources.

CHAPTER NINE   In *Monitor*'s Turret

1. The events and comments during the last days of the expedition were skillfully documented by reporters Mark St. John Erickson (2005) and Paul Clancy (2006), and several of the previous quotes appeared in those sources.
2. Jeffrey Johnston, pers. comm. August 9, 2002.
3. Butts (1885).
4. Logbook of USS *Passaic*.
5. Jons (1997).
6. The RESURGAM glass was a somewhat eerie find that we added to other *Monitor* lore, including the fact that the Navy's salvage contractor that developed the turret recovery system is Phoenix International! One could also speculate further about the bottle, since it appears to be a whisky flask made by the Baltimore Glass Works.

BIBLIOGRAPHY

Published Sources

Andahazy, William J., D. G. Everstine, and B. R. Hood. "Magnetometer Search for Shipwrecks from the Battle of Yorktown." *Sea Technology* 17, no. 11 (Nov. 1976): 19–22.

Andahazy, William J., and Edward M. Miller. "In Search of the Monitor: An Application of Magnetic Anomaly Detection." *NAVSEA Journal*, 28, no. 4 (June 1979): 87–94.

Anon. "The Revival of the Monitor." *The Engineer* CXXIV (August 17, 1917): 133–35.

Anon. "Ericsson's Monitor." *The Engineer* CXXIV (August 24, 1917): 161–62.

Appleton, D., and Co. *The American Annual Cyclopaedia and Register of Important Events of the Year 1861*. New York: D. Appleton and Company, 1861.

Arnold, J. Barto, III, G. Michael Fleshman, Dina B. Hill, Curtiss E. Peterson, W. Kenneth Stewart, Stephen R. Gegg, Gordon P. Watts Jr., and Clark Weldon. *The 1987 Expedition to the MONITOR National Marine Sanctuary: Data Analysis and Final Report*. Washington, DC: Sanctuaries and Reserves Division, National Oceanic and Atmospheric Administration, 1991.

Arnold, J. Barto, III, J. F. Jenkins, Edward M. Miller, Ernest W. Peterkin, Curtiss E. Peterson, and W. Ken Stewart. "U.S.S. MONITOR Project: Preliminary Report on 1987 Field Work." In *Underwater Archaeology Proceedings from the Society for Historical Archaeology Conference*, edited by James P. Delgado, 6–9. Reno, NV: Society for Historical Archaeology, 1988.

Atlantic Monthly. "Ironclad Ships and Heavy Ordnance." Vol. XL, 1862.

Ballard, Robert D. *The Discovery of the* Titanic. New York: Warner Books, 1987.

Barthell, Edward E., Jr. *The Mystery of the Merrimack*. Muskegon, MI: Dana Printing Company, 1959.

Bascom, Willard. *Deep Water, Ancient Ships*. Garden City, NY: Doubleday, 1976.

Bass, George F. *Archaeology Beneath the Sea, A Personal Account*. New York: Walker and Company, 1975.

Bathe, Grenville. *Ship of Destiny, A Record of the U.S. Steam Frigate Merrimac 1855–1862 with an Appendix on the Development of the U.S. Naval Cannon from 1812–1865*. Philadelphia: Allen, Lane, and Scott, 1951.

Baxter, James P. *The Introduction of the Ironclad Warship*. Cambridge, MA: Harvard University Press, 1933. (Reprint, Annapolis, MD: Naval Institute Press, 2001.)

Beach, Edward L. *The United States Navy: A 200-Year History*. Boston: Houghton Mifflin, 1986.

Bearss, Edwin C. *Hardluck Ironclad: The Sinking and Salvage of the* Cairo. Baton Rouge: Louisiana State University Press, 1980.

Benedict, George G. "The Builders of the First Monitor." *The Century Magazine* XXXIX (March 1890): 798–99.

Bennett, Frank Marion. *The Steam Navy of the United States: A History of the Growth of the Steam Vessel of War in the U.S. Navy, and of the Naval Engineer Corps*. W. T. Nicholson Press, 1896. Reprint, Westport, CT: Greenwood Press, 1972.

———. *The Monitor and the Navy Under Steam*. Boston: Houghton Mifflin, 1900.

———. "The U.S. Ironclad 'Monitor.'" *Cassier's Magazine* CIII (April 1898): 459–74.

Besse, Sumner B. *C.S. Ironclad Virginia and U.S. Ironclad Monitor with Data and References for Scale Models.* Newport News, VA: The Mariners' Museum, 1937.

Blair, Clay, Jr. *Diving for Pleasure and Treasure.* Cleveland, OH: World Publishing Co., 1960.

Broadwater, John D. "Applying Modern Technology to Save A Historic Warship: The *Monitor* National Marine Sanctuary." Proceedings from the OCEANS 97 MTS/IEEE Conference, 1997.

———. "Ironclad at Hampton Roads: CSS *Virginia*, the Confederacy's Formidable Warship." *Virginia Cavalcade* 33, no. 3 (1984): 100–13.

———. "Managing an Ironclad: Research at the *Monitor* National Marine Sanctuary." In *Excavating Ships of War*, International Maritime Archaeology Series, Volume II, Oxford University, edited by Mensun Bound, 287–93. Oswestry, Shropshire, England: Anthony Nelson Press, 1998.

———. "Rescuing the *Monitor*: Stabilization and Recovery Efforts at the *Monitor* National Marine Sanctuary." *Underwater Archaeology*, edited by D. C. Lakey, 54–61. Tucson, AZ: Society for Historical Archaeology, 1997.

———. "A Search for the USS Monitor." *International Journal of Nautical Archaeology and Underwater Exploration* 4, no. 1 (1974): 117–21.

———. "The Year of the *Monitor*." *Skin Diver* 25, no. 2 (February 1976): 104–08.

Broadwater, John D., and David A. Dinsmore. "1998 NOAA Research Expedition to the *Monitor* National Marine Sanctuary." In *Assessment and Feasibility of Technical Diving Operations for Scientific Exploration*, edited by R.W. Hamilton, D. F. Pence and D. E. Kesling, 17–29. Nahant, MA: American Academy of Underwater Sciences, 2000.

———. "Digging Deeper: Deepwater Archaeology and the *Monitor* National Marine Sanctuary." In *International Handbook on Underwater Archaeology*. Edited by Carol V. Ruppe and Janet F. Barstad, 639–67. New York: Kluwer Academic/Plenum Publishers, 2001.

Broadwater, John D., Dina B. Hill, Jeffrey P. Johnston, and Karen Kozlowski. "Charting a New Course for the *Monitor*: Results from the 1998 Research Expedition to the *Monitor* National Marine Sanctuary." In *Underwater Archaeology*, edited by Lawrence E. Babits, Catherine Fach, and Ryan Harris, 58–63. Tucson, AZ: Society for Historical Archaeology, 1998.

Brodie, Bernard. *Seapower in the Machine Age.* Princeton, NJ: Princeton University Press, 1941.

Brooke, John Mercer. "The Plan and Construction of the Merrimac." In *Battles and Leaders of the Civil War*, 715–16. New York: Century, 1887.

Butts, Francis B. "The Loss of the Monitor, by a Survivor." *The Century Magazine* XXXI (December 1885): 299–302.

———. "The Loss of the 'Monitor.'" In *Battles and Leaders of the Civil War*, vol. 1, 745–47. New York: Century, 1887.

———. "The *Monitor* and the *Merrimac*." In *Personal Narratives of Events in the War of the Rebellion, Being Papers Read before the Rhode Island Soldiers' and Sailors' Historical Society*, 4th ser., no. 6., 1–51. Providence, RI: The Society, 1890.

———. *My First Cruise at Sea and the Loss of the Ironclad Monitor, Personal Narratives of the Battles of the Rebellion, Being Papers Read before the Rhode Island Soldiers' and Sailors' Historical Society*, 1st ser., no. 4, 1–23. Providence, RI: Sidney S. Rider, 1878.

Cain, Emily. *Ghost Ships* Hamilton *and* Scourge: *Historical Treasures from the War of 1812.* Toronto: Musson (Beaufort Books), 1983.

Canney, Donald L. *The Old Steam Navy, Volume Two: The Ironclads, 1842–1885.* Annapolis, MD: Naval Institute Press, 1993.

Chapelle, Howard I. *The History of the American Sailing Navy: The Ships and Their Development.* New York: Norton, 1949

Childress, Floyd. "The Lantern." *NOAA Magazine.* October 1977.

———. "The National Marine Sanctuaries Program As a Cultural Resource Management Tool for the U.S.S. *Monitor*." In *Beneath the Waters of Time: The Proceedings of the Ninth Conference on Underwater Archaeology*, edited by J. Barto Arnold, 187–90. Austin: Texas Antiquities Committee, 1978.

———. "Seeking a New Approach to Ocean Management." In *The Monitor, Its Meaning and Future: Papers from a National Conference, April 2–4, 1978*, 6–8. Washington, DC: The Preservation Press, 1978.

Church, William Conant. *The Life of John Ericsson*, 2 vols. New York: Scribner, 1890.

Clancy, Paul. *Ironclad: The Epic Battle, Calamitous Loss, and Historic Recovery of the USS* Monitor. New York: International Marine/McGraw-Hill, 2006.

Clark, Charles A., and Andrew Dickson White. "Monitor and Merrimac" (Sheet music). New York: H. DeMarsan, 1863.

Claudy, C. H. "To Abolish Cape Hatteras." *Technical World Magazine* 8, no. 1 (September 1907): 402–07.

Cole, Captain C. W. (USN). "The U.S. Navy Ship Whose Time Has Come: Glomar Explorer." *NAVSEA Journal* 28, no. 4 (June 1979): 17–25.

Craven, John P. *The Silent War: The Cold War Battle Beneath the Sea.* New York: Simon & Schuster, 2001.

Cubberly, Norman G. "The Search for the *Monitor*." *Sea Frontiers* (July-August 1974): 212–18.

Cuffey, Roger J., and Shirley S. Fonda. "Bryozoans Encrusting the 1862 *Monitor* Shipwreck off Cape Hatteras." *Cheesebox* I, no. 1 (December 1982): 8–12.

Curtis, Richard. *History of the Famous Battle Between the Iron-Clad* Merrimac, *C.S.N., and the Iron-Clad* Monitor *and the Cumberland and Congress of the U.S. Navy, March*

8th and 9th, as Seen by a Man at the Gun. Norfolk, VA: S. B. Turner & Son, 1907.

Dahlgren, John A. *Shells and Shell Guns.* Philadelphia: King and Baird, 1856.

Daly, Robert W. *How the Merrimac Won: The Strategic Story of the C.S.S. Virginia.* New York: Crowell, 1957.

Davis, William C. *Duel Between the First Ironclads.* Garden City, NY: Doubleday, 1975.

Davison, Louis. *United States Monitors & Confederate Rams.* Published by the author, 1969.

DeKay, James Tertius. Monitor, *the story of the Legendary Civil War Ironclad and the Man Whose Invention Changed the Course of History.* New York: Walker and Company, 1997.

Delgado, James P. *"A Symbol of American Ingenuity": Assessing the Significance of the U.S.S.* Monitor. Washington, DC: National Park Service, 1988.

Eggleston, J. R. "Captain Eggleston's Narrative of the Battle of the *Merrimack." Southern Historical Society Papers,* s. s. III, September 1916.

Erickson, Mark St. John. "Navy AWOL Sea Lion Turns up Near *Monitor* Site." *Daily Press.* June 25, 1999, A1.

———. "Rescuing the *Monitor*: Struggle to Save a Legend." *Daily Press.* (Six-part supplement series published July 11–August 15, 2005.)

Ericsson, John. "The Building of the 'Monitor.'" In *Battles and Leaders of the Civil War,* 4 vols., edited by Robert V. Johnson and Clarence G. Buel, 730–44. New York: The Century Company, 1887–1888.

———. *Contributions to the Centennial Exhibition.* New York: The Nation Press, 1876.

———. "The Monitors." *The Century Magazine* XXXI (December 1885): 280–99.

Farb, Roderick M. "Computer Video Image digitization on the USS Monitor: A Research Tool for Underwater Archaeology." In *Maritime Archaeology: A Reader of substantive and Theoretical Contributions,* edited by Lawrence E. Babits and Hans Van Tilburg. New York: Plenum Press, 1998.

Farr, Arthur. "The Real Genius Behind the *Monitor." Civil War Times Illustrated* XXXVI, no. 3 (June 1997): 34–36.

Fiske, John, and Frank Alpine Hill. *A History of the United States.* Boston: Houghton Mifflin Company, 1894.

Flanders, Alan B. The Merrimac, *The Story of the Conversion of the U.S.S.* Merrimac *into the Confederate Ironclad Warship, C.S.S.* Virginia. Published by the author, 1982.

Fowler, George L. "Ericsson's First Monitor and the Later Turret Ships." *Engineering Magazine* XIV (October 1897): 110–28.

Fowler, William M., Jr. *Under Two Flags: The American Navy in the Civil War.* Boston: Houghton Mifflin, 1984.

Fuller, Howard J. *Clad in Iron: The American Civil War and the Challenge of British Naval Power.* Westport, CT: Praeger Publishers, 2007.

Gardiner, Robert, ed. *Cogs, Caravels and Galleons: The Sailing Ship, 1000–1650.* A volume in the series "Conway's History of the Ship." London: Conway Maritime Press, 1994.

———, ed. *The Line of Battle: The Sailing Warship, 1650–1840.* A volume in the series "Conway's History of the Ship." London: Conway Maritime Press, 1992a.

———. ed. *Steam, Steel & Shellfire: The Steam Warship, 1815–1905.* A volume in the series "Conway's History of the Ship." London: Conway Maritime Press, 1992b.

Geer, George. The Monitor *Chronicles: One Sailor's Account.* Edited by William Marvel. New York: Simon & Schuster, 2000.

Gould, Richard A. "The USS *Monitor* Project Research Design." In *Naval History, the Seventh Symposium of the U.S. Naval Academy,* 83–88. Wilmington, DE: Scholarly Resources, 1988.

Greene, Samuel Dana. "An Eyewitness Account: 'I Fired the First Gun and Thus Commenced the Great Battle.'" *American Heritage* VIII (June 1957): 10–13, 102–05.

———. "In the 'Monitor' Turret." *Century Magazine* XXIX (March 1885): 754–63.

———. "The Fight Between the 'Monitor' and the 'Merrimac.'" *United Service* X (October 1893): 350–56.

Greenhill, Basil, with John Morrison. *The Archaeology of Boats and Ships: An Introduction.* London: Conway Maritime Press, 1995.

Gwynne, Peter, with Evert Clark. "Monitor Mission." *Newsweek,* August 15, 1977, 54.

Harper's New Monthly Magazine, Edited by Henry Mills Alden. Published by Harper & Bros., 1862–1863. [Numerous stories and articles throughout *Harper's,* including the weekly publications and their monthly compilations.]

Harper's Weekly, February 15 and March 22, 1862.

Hawthorne, Nathaniel. "Chiefly about War Matters." (Signed, "By a Peaceable Man.") *Atlantic Monthly* 10, no. 57 (July 1862): 43–61.

Headley, Joel Tyler. *The Great Rebellion: A History of the Civil War in the United States,* 301–15. Hartford, CT: Hurlbut, Williams and Company, 1863.

Hill, Dina B., ed. "Hull Plate Sample Analysis and Preservation." U.S.S. MONITOR Technical Report Series #1. Raleigh: North Carolina Division of Archives and History, 1981.

Hoeling, A. A. *Thunder at Hampton Roads.* New York: Da Capo Press, 1993.

Holley, Alexander. "Iron-Clad Ships and Heavy Ordnance." *Atlantic Monthly* 11, no. LXIII (January 1863): 85–94.

———. *Ordnance and Armor. The Principles, Particulars, Structure, Fabrication, and Results of Standard European and American Guns, . . . , etc.* New York: D. Von Nostrand, 1864.

Hopkins, Garland E. *The First Battle of Modern Naval History.* Richmond, VA: The House of Dietz, 1943.

Howard, Frank. *Sailing Ships of War, 1400–1860.* New York: Mayflower Books, 1979.

Hoyt, John Colgate. *Old Ocean's Ferry, the Log of the Modern Mariner, the Trans-Atlantic Traveler, and Quaint Facts of Neptune's Realm.* New York: Bonnell, Silver & Co., 1900.

Hubinger, Bert. "Can We Ever Raise the *Monitor?*" *Civil War Times Illustrated* XXXVI, no. 3 (June 1997): 38–48.

Hunter, Alvah F. *A Year on a Monitor and the Destruction of Fort Sumter.* Columbia: University of South Carolina Press, 1987.

Jaffe, Jules S., Kad D. Moore, John McLean, and Michael R. Strand. "Underwater Optical Imaging: Status and Prospects." *Oceanography* 14, no. 3 (Special Issue, 2001): 64–75.

Jons, Otto P. "Preservation and Restoration of Historic Vessels in Virtual Environments." *Proceedings of the Third International Conference on the Technical Aspects of the Preservation of Historic Vessels.* San Francisco: National Park Service, 1997.

Johnson, Robert V., and Clarence G. Buel, eds. *Battles and Leaders of the Civil War,* 4 Vols. New York: The Century Company, 1887–1888.

Keegan, John. *The Face of Battle.* New York: Viking Press, 1976.

Keeler, William Frederick. *Aboard the USS* Monitor: *1862, The Letters of Acting Paymaster William Frederick Keeler, U.S. Navy to his Wife Anna.* Edited by Robert W. Daly. Annapolis, MD: United States Naval Institute, 1964.

Konstam, Angus. *Hampton Roads 1862: First Clash of the Ironclads.* Oxford, UK: Osprey Publishing, 1987, 2002.

———. *Union* Monitor, *1861–65.* Oxford, UK: Osprey Publishing, 2002.

Krop, David. "Conserving USS *Monitor.*" *America's Civil War* 18, no. 3 (2005): 74.

———. "Revealing *Monitor*'s Secrets." *America's Civil War* 19, no. 5 (2006): 32–41.

Krop, D., and Hand, S. "Measuring the *Monitor*: 3D Imaging of the Civil War Ironclad's XI-Inch Gun to Support Historical Conservation, Manufacturing Analysis, and Modern Measurement Projects and Techniques." Coordinate Metrology Society Conference post-prints, spring 2010.

Krop, D. S, and Nordgren, E. "Disassembly of USS *Monitor*'s Complex Mechanical Components." Metal 2010: Interim meeting of the ICOM-CC Metals Group. Charleston, SC, 11–15 October 2010.

Lambert, Andrew. *Battleships in Transition: The Creation of the Steam Battlefleet, 1815–1860.* London: Conway Maritime Press, 1984.

———. *Warrior: The World's First Ironclad—Then and Now.* London: Conway Maritime Press, 1987.

Lavery, Brian. *The Arming and Fitting of English Ships of War, 1600–1815.* London: Conway Maritime Press, 1987.

———. *The Ship of the Line,* 2 vols. London: Conway Maritime Press, 1983–1984.

Leslie, Frank. *Frank Leslie's Pictorial History of the American Civil War.* Published by the author, 1863.

Link, Marion Clayton. *Windows in the Sea.* Washington, DC: Smithsonian Institution Press, 1973.

Littleton, William G. *The Cumberland, the Monitor and the Virginia (Popularly called the MERRIMAC) Being an address delivered at the meeting of the Pennsylvania Commandery, Military Order of the Loyal Legion of the United States, held May 10, 1933, at the Union League of Philadelphia.* Privately printed by the author, 1933.

MacCord, Charles W. "Ericsson and His 'Monitor.'" *The North American Review* 149 (1889): 460–71.

Mankins, W. L. "Metallurgical Evaluation of Historical Artifacts from U.S.S. *Monitor* and Blockade Runners Condor and Modern Greece." In *Hull Plate Sample Analysis and Preservation* (U.S.S. MONITOR Technical Report Series #1). Edited by Dina B. Hill. Raleigh: North Carolina Division of Archives and History, 1981.

Martin, Bob. "The Secret Hunt off Hatteras for the *Monitor.*" *The Virginian-Pilot,* August 11, 1968, C-1 and C-6.

Marx, Leo. *The Machine in the Garden: Technology and the Pastoral Ideal in America.* New York: Oxford University Press, 1964.

Marx, Robert F. *Always Another Adventure.* Cleveland, OH: World Publishing Co., 1967.

Mathisson, J. C. "Hydrography, N.C. Coast South of Cape Hatteras." U.S. Coast & Geodetic Survey Report 1955, No. 71, Project No. CS-1377, 14 April-29 October 1955 (courtesy of the NOAA Library).

Mazel, Charles H., et al. "High-Resolution Determination of Coral Reef Bottom Cover from Multispectral Fluorescence Laser Line Scan Imagery." *Limnol. Oceanogr.* 48, no. 1, part 2 (2003): 522–34.

Melville, Herman. *Battle Pieces and Aspects of War.* New York: Harper & Brothers, 1866.

Milholland, John A. "The Legal Framework of the Monitor Marine Sanctuary." In *The Monitor, Its Meaning and Future: Papers from a National Conference, April 2–4, 1978,* 19–22. Washington, DC: The Preservation Press, 1978.

McKinney, Chester M. "The Early History of High Frequency, Short Range, High Resolution, Active Sonar." *Echoes,* the newsletter of the Acoustical Society of America 12, no. 2 (Spring 2002): 4–7.

Miller, Edward M., ed. "Bound for Hampton Roads." *Civil War Times Illustrated* XX, no. 4 (July 1981): 22–31.

———. "The USS *Monitor* as a National Marine Sanctuary." In *Naval History, the Seventh Symposium of the U.S. Naval Academy,* 72–74. Wilmington, DE: Scholarly Resources, Inc., 1988.

———. *U.S.S. MONITOR: The Ship That Launched a Modern Navy.* Annapolis, MD: Leeward Press, 1978.

Miller, Edward M., W. J. Andahazy, and E. W. Peterkin. "The Search for the *Monitor*: A Journey into History." In *Proceedings of the Tenth Annual Conference of the Marine*

Technology Society, September 23–25, 1974, 845–60. Washington, DC: Marine Technology Society, 1974.

Miller, Francis T. *The Photographic History of the Civil War, the Navies*. New York: Castle Books, 1957.

Mindell, David A. *War, Technology, and Experience Aboard the USS* Monitor. Baltimore, MD: Johns Hopkins University Press, 2000.

McClure, Alexander Kelly, ed. *The Annals of the War Written by Leading Participants North and South*. Philadelphia: The Times Publishing Company, 1879.

McNeil, Ben Dixon. *The Hatterasman*. Winston-Salem, NC: John F. Blair, 1958.

Monitor National Marine Sanctuary. *Cheesebox* VII, no. 1 (September 1995): 4.

———. *A Look at the Monitor National Marine Sanctuary: Past, Present, and Future*. Newport News, VA: The Mariners' Museum, 1994.

———. *Charting a New Course for the Monitor: A Comprehensive, Long-Range Preservation Plan with Options for Management, Stabilization, Preservation, Recovery, Conservation and Exhibition of Materials and Artifacts from the* Monitor *National Marine Sanctuary*. Newport News, VA: The Sanctuary [Washington, DC] US Dept. of Commerce, National Oceanic and Atmospheric Administration, National Ocean Service, Office of Ocean and Coastal Resources Management, Sanctuaries and Reserves Division, 1998.

———. The 1987 Expedition to the MONITOR National Marine Sanctuary: Data Analysis and Final Report.

———. *U.S.S.* Monitor *National Marine Sanctuary Management Plan*. Washington, DC: NOAA, 1983.

Moore, Frank, ed. *The Rebellion Record: A Diary of American Events with Documents, Narratives, Illustrative Incidents, Poetry, Etc.*, 4 vols. New York: G. P. Putnam, 1862.

Morris, James M. *History of the U.S. Navy*. Stamford, CT: Longmeadow Press, 1993.

Morris, Kenneth. "A Conservation Viewpoint of the *Monitor* Project." In *Underwater Archaeology: The Challenge Before Us, the Proceedings of the Twelfth Conference on Underwater Archaeology*, edited by Gordon P. Watts Jr., 246–49. San Marino, CA: Fathom Eight, 1981.

National Oceanic and Atmospheric Administration (NOAA), *Monitor* National Marine Sanctuary. *Cheesebox, Monitor* National Marine Sanctuary activities report, 1982–2003. Program in Maritime History and Underwater Archaeology, Dept. of History, East Carolina University, Greenville, NC (early volumes) and NOAA's *Monitor* National Marine Sanctuary.

National Oceanic and Atmospheric Administration, NOAA Dive Office. *NOAA Diving Manual* (4th ed.). Flagstaff, AZ: Best Publishing Company, 2001.

National Trust for Historic Preservation. *The* Monitor, *Its Meaning and Future: Papers from a National Conference, April 2–4, 1978, Raleigh, NC*. Washington, DC: The Preservation Press.

Nelson, James L. *Reign of Iron: The Story of the First Battling Ironclads, the* Monitor *and the* Merrimack. New York: William Morrow, 2004.

Newton, John G. "How We Found the Monitor." *National Geographic* 147, no. 1 (January 1975): 48–61.

Newton, John G., O. H. Pilkey, and J. O. Blanton. *An Oceanographic Atlas of the Carolina Continental Margin*. Raleigh: North Carolina Department of Conservation and Development, 1971.

New York Herald. "The Monitor Disaster." January 6, 1863.

Nordgren, E., Krop, D., Secord, E., Sangouard, E., Saul, M., Paden, P. and Hanley, L. "USS Monitor Conservation: Preserving a Marvel of 19th Century Technology." Incredibly Industry 2009, conference post-prints.

Osborne, Philip R., "The American Monitors." *United States Naval Institute Proceedings* 63, no. 2 (February 1937): 235–38.

Padfield, Peter. *Guns at Sea*. New York: St. Martin's Press, 1974.

Park, Carl. *Ironclad Down*. Annapolis, MD: Naval Institute Press, 2007.

Parlby, Samuel. "Translation from the *Bulletin Des Sciences Militares* for May 1825 of a work entitled, 'Experiments carried on by the French Navy with a new Piece of Ordnance; the Changes which must result therefrom; and a fresh Examination of some Questions relative to the Navy, to the Artillery, and to the Attack and Defence of Places,' by M. Paixans, Lieutenant Colonel of Artillery. Paris, 1825.'" *The British Indian Repository* IV, no. VIII (July 1825): 349–58.

———. "Containing Remarks Drawn Forth by A Treatise on Hollow Projectiles, by Montgery, Is Offered to Our Readers, with A View to Exhibit the Notions Entertained by the French on This and Other Military Subjects with Which It Is Connected." *The British Indian Repository* IV, no. VIII (July 1825): 359–70.

Patterson, H. K. W. *War Memories of Fort Monroe and Vicinity, Containing an Account of the Memorable Battle Between the "Merrimac" and "Monitor," the Incarceration of Jefferson Davis, and Other Topics*. Fort Monroe, VA: Pool & Deuschle, 1885.

Peterkin, Ernest W. "Building a Behemoth." *Civil War Times Illustrated* XX, no. 4 (July 1981): 12–19.

———. "To Raise Her." *Civil War Times Illustrated* XX, no. 4 (July 1981): 42–43, 46–49.

———. *Drawings of the* U.S.S. Monitor: *A Catalog and Technical Analysis*. Raleigh: North Carolina Division of Archives and History, 1984.

Peterson, Curtiss E. "Conserving the *Monitor*." In *The Underwater Archaeology Proceedings from the Society for Historical Archaeology Conference, 1987*, 139–40. Pleasant Hills, CA: Society for Historical Archaeology.

———. "The Role of Conservation in the Recovery of the USS Monitor." In *Search of Our Maritime Past: Proceed-*

ings of the Fifteenth Conference on Underwater Archaeology, Williamsburg, Virginia, January 5–8, 1984, edited by J. W. Bream, 195–96. Greenville, NC: East Carolina University, 1984.

Poilpot, Theophile. *A Comprehensive Sketch of the* Merrimac *and* Monitor *Naval Battle.* New York: The New York Panorama Company, 1886. (Accurate reproduction by Kessinger Publishing, LaVergne, Tennessee, 2010.)

Porter, David D. *Naval History of the Civil War.* New York: Castle Books, 1984.

Porter, John L. "The Plan and Construction of the Merrimac." In *Battles and Leaders of the Civil War*, 715–17. New York: Century, 1887.

Porter, John W. H. *A Record of Events in Norfolk County, Virginia from April 19th, 1861, to May 10, 1862.* Portsmouth, VA: W. A. Fiske, 1892.

Randt, John. "Investigators Believe Wreck is the *Monitor.*" *Wilmington Star News.* October 24, 1973, 11.

Ringle, Ken. "Monitor Is Shown In Mosaic Photo." *Washington Post.* October 12, 1974, G1–G3. 1974a.

———. "Monitor Seekers Map Spring Search." *Washington Post.* March 12, 1974b, C1, C4.

———. "Pursuing the Mystery of the *Monitor.*" *Washington Post*, September 23, 1973.

Sangouard, E., and S. Grieve. "Evaluating Treatments for Waterlogged Lignum Vitae Objects from the USS *Monitor.*" WOAM 2010, Greenville, NC, 24–29 May 2010.

Scharf, John Thomas. *History of the Confederate States Navy from its Organization to the Surrender of Its Last Vessel.* New York: Rogers and Sherwood, 1887.

Scientific American. "Ericsson's Revolving Turreted War Ship." September 6, 1890, vol. LXII.

Scientific American. "The Steam Battery 'Monitor.'" March 22, 1862, vol. VI, 1.

Searle, W. F., Jr. "Salving the Monitor." *Marine Technology Society Journal* 13, no. 4, (August-September 1979): 31–37.

Sheridan, Robert E. *Iron from the Deep: The Discovery and Recovery of the USS* Monitor. Annapolis, MD: Naval Institute Press, 2004.

———. "Site Charting and Environmental Studies of the *Monitor* Wreck." *Journal of Field Archaeology* 6, no. 3 (1979): 252–64.

Shreeves, Karl. "CVID: An Emerging Power Tool of Underwater Research?" *The Undersea Journal*, Second Quarter, 1992, Professional Association of Diving Instructors (PADI) (1992): 86–87.

Silverstone, Paul H. *Civil War Navies, 1855–1883.* Annapolis, MD: Naval Institute Press, 2001.

Sontag, Sherry, and Christopher Drew, with Annette L. Drew. *Blind Man's Bluff: The Untold Story of American Submarine Espionage.* New York: PublicAffairs (Perseus Books), 1998.

Sprout, Harold Hance, and Margaret Sprout. *The Rise of American Naval Power, 1776–1918.* Annapolis, MD: Naval Institute Press, 1990.

Stewart, Ken. "Computer Modeling and Imaging Underwater." *Computers in Science* 1, no. 3 (November/December 1987): 23–32.

Still, William N. "Confederate Naval Strategy: The Ironclad." *The Journal of Southern History* XXVII, no. 3 (August 1961): 330–43.

———. "The Historical Importance of the USS *Monitor.*" In *Naval History, the Seventh Symposium of the U.S. Naval Academy*, 75–80. Wilmington, DE: Scholarly Resources, 1988.

———. *Iron Afloat: The Story of the Confederate Armorclads.* Nashville, TN: Vanderbilt University Press, 1971.

———. *Ironclad Captains: The Commanding Officers of the USS Monitor.* Washington, DC: National Oceanic and Atmospheric Administration, 1988.

———. *Monitor Builders: A Historical Study of the Principal Firms and Individuals Involved in the Construction of USS* Monitor. Washington, DC: National Park Service, 1988.

———. "To Begin in the Middle." *Civil War Times Illustrated* XX, no. 4 (July 1981): 10–11.

———. "A Spotted Career: The Most Cowardly Exhibition." *Civil War Times Illustrated* XX, no. 4 (July 1981): 32–37.

Stimers, Alban C. "An Engineer Aboard the *Monitor.*" *Civil War Times Illustrated* IX, no. 1 (April 1970): 28–35.

Stringer, John. "Sanctuary at 36 Fathoms." *NOAA* 14, no. 1 (Winter 1984).

Tennent, James Emerson. *The Story of the Guns.* London: Longman, Green, Longman, Roberts and Green, 1864.

Terrell, Bruce. *Fathoming Our Past: Historical Contexts of the National Marine Sanctuaries.* Newport News, VA: The Mariners' Museum, 2005.

Thulesius, Olav. *The Man Who Made the* Monitor: *A Biography of John Ericsson, Naval Engineer.* Jefferson, NC: McFarland & Co., 2007.

Tise, Larry E. "Jacques Cousteau, the U.S.S. *Monitor*, and the Philosophy and Practice of Public History Institutions." *The Public Historian* 5, no. 1 (Winter, 1983): 31–45.

———. "The *Monitor*; An American Artifact." In *The Monitor, Its Meaning and Future*, 63–65. Washington, DC: The Preservation Press, 1978.

———. "The Monitor: Its Meaning." In *The Monitor, Its Meaning and Future: Papers from a National Conference, April 2–4, 1978*, 13–17. Washington, DC: The Preservation Press, 1978.

———. "Off Carolina Searching for the *Monitor.*" *Civil War Times Illustrated* XX, no. 4 (July 1981): 38–41, 44–45.

US Congress. Title III of the Marine, Protection, Research and Sanctuaries Act of 1972, 16 U.S.C. s. 1431, *et seq.* ("The National Marine Sanctuaries Act"), 1972.

US Government Printing Office (GPO). *Report of Navy Department Documents Relating to the Harbor and River Monitors Manhattan, Mahopac, and Tecumseh.* Washington, DC: GPO, 1912.

———. *Report of the Secretary of the Navy in Relation to Armored Vessels*. Washington, DC: Government Printing Office, 1864.

———. *Hearing on the U.S.S.* Monitor *National Marine Sanctuary. Hearing before the Subcommittee on Fisheries Conservation, Wildlife and Oceans of the Committee on Resources, House of Representatives, One Hundred Fifth Congress, First Session, Serial No. 105–68 (November 6, 1997)*. Washington, DC: Government Printing Office, 1998.

US Navy Department. *Official Records of the Union and Confederate Navies in the War of the Rebellion*, 32 vols. Washington, DC: Government Printing Office, 1898.

US Navy Department, Naval Sea Systems Command. *U. S. Navy Diving Manual* (Revision 6, April 2008). (Available as a free download from http://www.supsalv.org/00c3_publications.asp., www.MilitaryBookshop.co.uk), 2010.

US War Department. *Annual Reports of the War Department for the Fiscal Year Ended June 30, 1904, Volume VI: Report of the Chief of Engineers, Part 2*. Washington, DC: GPO, 1904.

Van Hoek, Susan, with Marion Clayton Link. *From Sky to Sea: A Story of Edwin A. Link*. Flagstaff, AZ: Best Publishing Company, 2003.

Ward, James H. *Elementary Instruction in Naval Ordnance and Gunnery* (New edition, revised and enlarged). New York: D. Van Nostrand, 1861.

Washington Post. "*Monitor* Found?" September 1, 1973.

Watts, Gordon P., Jr. "A Decade of Research: Investigation of the USS *Monitor*." In *The Underwater Archaeology Proceedings from the Society for Historical Archaeology Conference*, edited by Alan B. Albright, 128–39. Pleasant Hills, CA: Society for Historical Archaeology, 1987.

———. "Deep-water Archaeological Investigation and Site Testing in the *Monitor* National Marine Sanctuary." *Journal of Field Archeology* 12, no. 3 (Fall 1985): 315–32.

———. *Investigating the Remains of the U.S.S. MONITOR: A Final Report on 1979 Site Testing in the MONITOR National Marine Sanctuary*. Raleigh: North Carolina Department of Cultural Resources, 1981.

———. "The Location and Identification of the Ironclad USS Monitor." *International Journal of Nautical Archaeology and Underwater Exploration* 4, no. 2 (1975): 301–39.

———. "*Monitor* '83." *Cheesebox* 2, no. 2 (April 1984): 1–7.

———. "Systematic Planning and Sophisticated Technology: An Approach to Management of the Nation's First Marine Sanctuary." In *Underwater Archaeology: The Proceedings of the Eleventh Conference on Underwater Archaeology*, edited by Calvin R. Cummings, 45–52. San Marino, CA: Fathom Eight, 1982.

Watts, Gordon P., Jr., and James A. Pleasants Jr. *U.S.S. Monitor: A Bibliography*. Raleigh: NC Division of Archives and History, 1981.

Webber, Richard H., ed. *Monitors of the U.S. Navy 1861–1937*. Washington, DC: Naval History Division, US Navy, 1969.

Weeks, Greenville Mellen. "The Last Cruise of the *Monitor*." *Atlantic Monthly* XI (March 1863): 366–72.

Welles, Gideon. "The First Ironclad Monitor." *The Annals of the War* XXI (1879): 17–31.

Wells, David A., ed. *Annual of Scientific Discovery . . . for 1862*. Boston: Gould and Lincoln, 1862.

White, E. V. *The First Iron-Clad Naval Engagement in the World, History of Facts of the Great Naval Battle Between the* Merrimac-Virginia, *C.S.N. and the Ericsson* Monitor, *U.S.N. Hampton Roads, March 8 and 9, 1862*. Privately printed by the author, 1906.

White, Ruth. *Yankee from Sweden: The Dream and the Reality in the Days of John Ericsson*. New York: Holt, 1960.

Williams, Robert. *The United States from the Discovery of America to the Close of the Year 1862*. Philadelphia: Sower, Barnes & Co., 1863.

Wilmington Morning Star. "Monitor Find is Confirmed." March 8, 1974, 1.

Archival Sources

Anonymous. *Minutes of Meeting Held at the Smithsonian Concerning the U.S.S. MONITOR*. Raleigh: North Carolina Division of Archives and History, 1978.

Beachem, C. D., D. A. Meyn, and R. A. Bayles. *Mechanical Properties of Wrought Iron from Hull Plate of USS MONITOR*. Washington, DC: Naval Research Laboratory, 1979.

Berent, Irwin M. *The Crewmen of the USS Monitor*. Raleigh: North Carolina Division of Archives and History, 1982.

Broadwater, John D. "Applications of Technology in the *Monitor* National Marine Sanctuary." In *The Coastal Ocean—Prospects for the 21st Century, Proceedings from the OCEANS 96 MTS/IEEE Conference*, 1269–73, 1996.

Casserley, Tane R. "NOAA's 2002 Excavation of the USS *Monitor*'s Gun Turret." NOAA's *Monitor* National Marine Sanctuary, 2004, *Monitor* Collection.

———. "NOAA's 2002 Expedition to the *Monitor* National Marine Sanctuary." NOAA's *Monitor* National Marine Sanctuary, 2004, *Monitor* Collection.

Childress, LCDR Floyd. "Cruise Summary of Filming Project by Cousteau Society, Inc., *Monitor* Marine Sanctuary, 9 June-14 June, 1979." NOAA Office of Coastal Zone Management, Washington, DC, 1979.

Childress, LCDR Floyd, Gordon P. Watts Jr., Roger W. Cook, and Chester C. Slama. "Stereo Photography and Artifact Retrieval, July 16-August 2, 1977, *Monitor* National Marine Sanctuary." NOAA Office of Ocean Management, Washington, DC, ca. 1978.

Cummins, Calvin. *USS Monitor National Marine Sanctuary Research Management Plan*.

D'Angelo (Schoenewaldt Associates). *Preliminary Recovery Feasibility Study, USS* Monitor. Raleigh: North Carolina Division of Archives and History, ca. 1978.

Eastport International Inc. *Draft Report on the 1985* Monitor *Expedition, Which Appended a Bottom Currents Study and a Geophysical Data Acquisition Report from Ocean Surveys, Inc.* Submitted to NOAA's Marine and Estuarine Management Division, ca. 1985. (No final report was produced.)

Edgerton, H. E. Unpublished letter to Dr. Melvin Payne, National Geographic Society, entitled, "Research at the MONITOR Site off Cape Hatteras, N.C., Report on the August 12–28, 1974 Effort." Dated September 5, 1974, *Monitor* Collection.

———. Unpublished report to the National Geographic Society Research Committee, entitled, "Cape Hatteras Expedition, August 17–31, 1973." Dated September 6, 1973, *Monitor* Collection.

Farb, Roderick M. "Farb *Monitor* Expedition 1990 Final Report." Unpublished report submitted to NOAA, dated September 30, 1991.

Gentile, Gary. Letter to NOAA dated August 5, 1990, with subject, "1990 *Monitor* Photographic Expedition Sponsored by Gary Gentile."

Greene, Lt. Samuel Dana. Letter dated March 14, 1862, to his father and brother. British National Archives, ADM 1/5809, PRO D350.

Lusardi, Wayne. "Archaeological Investigations of the USS *Monitor*'s Gun Turret: Interim Field Notes and Artifact Catalog." Newport News, VA: The Mariners' Museum, 1 November 2002.

Miller, Edward M., ed. *Project Cheesebox: A Journey into History*, 3 vols. Annapolis, MD: Research Manuscript, United States Naval Academy, 1974.

Mindell, David A., and Brian Bingham. "Cruise Report: USS *Monitor*–NOAA *Monitor* National Marine Sanctuary, August 2–4, 2001." Unpublished cruise report on a survey of *Monitor*'s turret using a sub-bottom profiler, submitted to NOAA's *Monitor* National Marine Sanctuary, August 6, 2001.

Muga, Bruce E. *Engineering Investigation, USS* Monitor. Raleigh: North Carolina Division of Archives and History, 1982.

National Archives and Records Administration (NARA). Record Group 24, Records of the Bureau of Naval Personnel, official logbooks of US naval vessels.

National Oceanic and Atmospheric Administration (NOAA). *Final Report on the 1990 Assessment and Placement of Permanent Reference Markers at the Monitor National Marine Sanctuary.* US Department of Commerce, 1994.

———. *The MONITOR National Marine Sanctuary Draft Revised Management Plan.* Newport News, VA: NOAA, 1992.

———. *Operations Manual, MONITOR Marine Sanctuary, A Photogrammetric Survey July 1977.* Washington, DC: NOAA, 1977.

———. *Operations Manual, Monitor Marine Sanctuary, An Archaeological and Engineering Assessment August 1979.* Washington, DC: NOAA, 1979.

———. *Operations Plan Monitor Expedition 87–1.* Washington, DC: NOAA, 1987.

———. NOAA prepared detailed operations manuals for all *Monitor* expeditions conducted during the following years: 1993, 1995, 1998, 1999, 2000, 2001, and 2002. All manuals can be found in the *Monitor* Collection Associated Records.

———. *U.S.S. MONITOR National Marine Sanctuary Management Plan.* Washington, DC: NOAA, 1982.

———. *U.S.S.* Monitor *National Marine Sanctuary Management Plan.* Washington, DC: NOAA, 1983.

———. *U.S.S.* Monitor *National Marine Sanctuary Research Management Plan.* Washington, DC: NOAA, 1987 (prepared in cooperation with the National Park Service).

NOAA Office of Coastal Zone Management. 1977. *Operations Manual:* Monitor *Marine Sanctuary, A Photogrammetric Survey.* In cooperation with Harbor Branch Foundation Inc., July 1977.

NOAA Office of Coastal Zone Management and North Carolina Department of Cultural Resources. "U.S.S. *Monitor* National Marine Sanctuary Management Plan." January 1982 (revised February 1983).

NOAA, Office of National Marine Sanctuaries. Monitor *Site Recorder Database*, 2008.

NOAA, Sanctuaries and Reserves Division. "Strategic Plan for the 21st Century," April, 1997.

NOAA, Sanctuary Programs Division. "The Monitor National Marine Sanctuary in Perspective," Sanctuary Programs Division, Office of Ocean and Coastal Resource Management, NOAA. Management Report Series, July 1984 (no author given).

———. "The Monitor National Marine Sanctuary Management Plan," 1992 draft.

National USS Monitor National Marine Sanctuary Research Management Plan .

National Undersea Research Center at the University of North Carolina at Wilmington. "Dive Procedures Manual: Procedures for Specialized Diving Operations [at the *Monitor* National Marine Sanctuary] Using Open Circuit, Self-contained Underwater Breathing Apparatus with Required, in-Water Decompression Procedures for Conducting Undersea Science Exploration." Prepared for the *Monitor* National Marine Sanctuary, Office of National Marine sanctuaries, National Ocean Service, National Oceanic and Atmospheric Administration, 2003.

Newton, John G., H. E. Edgerton, R. E. Sheridan, and G. P. Watts Jr. "Final Expedition Report–Cruise E-12-73." Unpublished report submitted to Duke University Marine Laboratory, Beaufort, NC, ca. February 1974.

North Carolina Department of Cultural Resources, Division of Archives and History (NCDAH). "Minutes of Meeting

Held at the Smithsonian Concerning the *Monitor*, October 23, 1978."

———. "The *Monitor* Marine Sanctuary Research and Development Concept." Submitted to NOAA by the North Carolina Department of Cultural Resources under terms of a Memorandum of Agreement, undated, ca. 1978. Raleigh, NC.

Oceaneering International Inc. "Preliminary Proposal for the Emergency Recovery, Stabilization, and Preservation of the *Monitor*." Submitted to the Office of the Director of Ocean Engineering, Supervisor of Salvage and Diving, Naval Sea Systems Command, SEA OOC, Department of the Navy, 25 April 1997.

Peterkin, Ernest W. "Contents of the *Monitor*: A Catalog at the Time of Sinking." U.S.S. *Monitor* Historical Report Series, vol. 1, no. 2. Manuscript prepared for the NC Division of Archives and History and NOAA's Sanctuary Programs Division, 1983. *Monitor* Collection.

Price, William S., Jr. Letter to Gary Gentile dated December 4, 1984. In *Monitor* Collection Associated Records, Series 2, MS390, NOAA Subject File.

Sheridan, Robert E., H. E. Edgerton, and J. G. Newton. "Preliminary Report: Environmental Studies of U.S.S. MONITOR Wreck Site." Unpublished report, *Monitor* Research and Recovery Foundation, ca. 1977.

Southwest Research Institute. *Feasibility Study for Transmission of a Live Television Picture*. Raleigh: North Carolina Division of Archives and History, 1982.

Still, William N. *Archival Sources*. Raleigh: North Carolina Division of Archives and History, n.d.

Tucker, Rockwell G. [*Monitor*] *Environmental Data*. Raleigh: North Carolina Division of Archives and History, 1981.

US Commerce Department. "Designation Document, *Monitor* National Marine Sanctuary, January 30, 1975." Document on file in the NOAA *Monitor* Collection, The Mariners' Museum Library.

US Department of Commerce, NOAA, and the State of Maryland. Cooperative Agreement dated November 1, 1988.

US Navy Department. "Letter of the Secretary of the Navy, Communicating . . . Information in Relation to the Construction of the Ironclad Monitor," 40th congress, 2nd Session, Senate Executive Document 86, Washington, DC, 1868.

Watts, Gordon P., Jr. "Investigation of the Commerce Raider CSS *Alabama*, 2001." Report produced by the Institute for International Maritime Research Inc., Washington, DC, North Carolina, 2001. Document on file in the NOAA *Monitor* Collection, The Mariners' Museum Library.

———. "*Monitor* of a New Iron Age: The Construction of the U.S.S. *Monitor*." Unpublished Master's Thesis, Department of History, East Carolina University. Document on file in the NOAA *Monitor* Collection, The Mariners' Museum Library.

Watts, Gordon P., and James A. Pleasants Jr. *The* Monitor: *A Bibliography*. Raleigh: North Carolina Division of Archives and History, 1978. Document on file in the NOAA *Monitor* Collection, The Mariners' Museum Library.

INDEX

Acoustic Doppler Current Profiler
    (ADCP), 205
Age of Exploration, 29
Alcoa Marine, 23
Anaconda Plan, 37
Andahazy, William J., 15, 22, 23
Anderson, Eric, 133
The Apprentice School, 191
Arapahoe Chief, 155, 157
Argus, 205
Armed Forces DNA Identification Labo-
    ratory (AFDIL), 196
Arnold, J. Barto, III, 94, 95
Askew, Tim, 73, 86
Atlantic Monthly, 208
Atlantic Wreck Divers, 100
Autonomous underwater vehicles
    (AUVs), 68, 69, 70, 205

Bailey, Tom, 151, 153, 170
Baker, D. James, 109
Bankhead, John P., 5, 8–13
Bascom, Willard, 24
Basta, Daniel J., xi, 178, 193
Bateman, Herbert H., Congressman,
    139
Batten Conservation Laboratory Com-
    plex, 200, 211
Battle of the Atlantic, 17, 19
Battle at Hampton Roads, ix–x, 208–209,
    215
    125th anniversary, 91, 93
    destruction of both ironclads, 61

progression
    Day 1, 49–51
    Day 2, 51–53, 59–61
    spectators to the battle, 51
Battle-Pieces and Aspects of the War, 208
Battle of Trafalgar, 29–30
Battle of Yorktown, 79
Bearss, Edwin C., 92
Beierl, Philip, 133, 135, 140, 146, 147
Benn, Nathan, 23
Bingham, Brian, 163, 205
Bingham, Wade, 179
Blair, Clay, 15
Bomford, George, 30
Brady, Colleen, 198
Broadwater, John, 121, 125
Brooke, John M., 37–38, 39
Browne, D. Rodney, 12
Buchanan, Chester, 23, 25
Buchanan, Franklin, 49–50, 52
Bushnell, Cornelius, 40, 41
Butts, Francis, 10
Byrd, Gary, 148
Byron, Ilene, 97, 135

Cabled Observation and Rescue Device
    (CORD), 69, 70, 71
Caddigan, Craig, 87
Caloric engines, 42
Cambrian Foundation, 101, 119, 127, 131
Caravels, development of, 29
Carlstedt, Richard, 149
Carracks, development of, 29

Casemate, 39
Casserley, Tane, 148, 153, 170, 197
Cavey, Rick, 180, 181, 183, 189
Central Identification Laboratory (CIL).
    See Joint POW/MIA Accounting
    Command (JPAC)
Century Magazine, 209
Challenger, use of *J-S-L* in locating wreck-
    age, 68
Charting a New Course for the Monitor, 111
Cheesebox, 90, 211
Childress, Floyd, 71, 74, 81
Christine J., 147
Christopher Newport University, 211
Chu, Jeff, 135
Church, William C., 40, 44
Clancy, Paul, 203
Clelia, 68–69, 134, 135, 143
CNC Advanced Marine Center, 198
CNN, 131
Cold War, 196
Coles, Brian, 134
Coles, Cowper, 33
Columbiad, 30–31
Computer-aided drawing (CAD), 151, 159
Concretion formation, 194–195
Continental Iron Works, 44, 47, 48
Convention on the Protection of Under-
    water Cultural Heritage, 76
Cook, Roger, 1, 71, 81, 83
Corrpro Companies Inc., 93, 137, 138
Council of American Maritime Muse-
    ums, 91

Cousteau Society, 76
Creamer, Kyle, 147–148
Crimean War, 31–32
C. S. Bushnell and Co., 60
CSS *Alabama,* 139
CSS *Virginia,* ix–x, 27, 191, 208, 209, 213
  battle with
    USS *Congress,* 50
    USS *Cumberland,* 50
    USS *Monitor,* 4, 5
  built from *Merrimack*'s remains, 39
  design specifications, vs. *Monitor*'s, 53
  initial launch, 49–50
  scale model of, 49
  sinking of, 60
Cubberly, Norman, 25
Cupola, rotating, 43
Cussler, Clive, 181
Cycloramas, 208, 209

Davis, Charles, 43
Deck decompression chamber (DDC),
  123, 127
Deep Drone, 69, 70, 93, 94, 95
Deep Sea Archaeology Research Group
  (DeepArch), 163, 205
Deep Submergence Elevator Support Ship
  (DSESS), 118, 119
Deep Submergence Rescue Vehicles
  (DSRVs), 119
Deepwater Horizon, 70
Delamater, Cornelius, 41
Delamater & Co., 44
Delamater Iron Works, 41
Delgado, James P., 92, 215
Delta Force, 185, 189
Demologus, 33
de Montgéry, Jacques Merigon, 31
Dennis, Donnie, 129
Department of Defense. See Legacy Re-
  source Management Program
Diamond Shoals, 9
Differential Global Positioning System
  (DGPS), 157
Dinsmore, David, 119, 138
Diver Debriefing Form, 123
Diver propulsion vehicle (DPV),
  147–148
Diver Underwater Color Television Sys-
  tem (DUCTS), 121, 129
Diving:
  lockout training, 79, 80, 81–82
  safety, 82–83
  saturation, 153
  technical, 100, 101, 127
Dolan, Hugh, 100
Drayton, Percival, 10, 11
Drewry's Bluff, 59

Dry Dock No. 1, 39, 40
Duke Center for Hyperbaric Medicine
  and Environmental Physiology, 79, 80
Duke University Marine Laboratory, 16,
  17, 18, 73

East Carolina University (ECU), 85, 88,
  163
  Maritime Studies Program, 141
  NOAA transfers responsibilities to,
  89–90
Eastport International Inc., 91, 93, 110
Edgerton, Harold E., 17, 18, 23, 62, 70
Edison Chouest Offshore Company,
  118–119
Electrolytic reduction, 201
Emery, Eric, 170, 179–180, 191
Emmanuel, 176
Engine lifting frame (ELF), 142, 151, 158,
  159, 162
Engine Recovery System (ERS), 141, 142,
  143, 145, 149, 151, 158, 162, 167
England, 28, 31
Environmental Protection Agency, 91
Epic Scan, 201
Erickson, Mark, 189
Ericsson, John, ix, 5, 187
  background, 42
  blamed for gun explosion, 35
  design considerations, 45
  propeller design, 33
  shares design with Bushnell and Ironclad Board, 41, 43–44
  signs contract to build *Monitor,* 44
  soured relationship with Navy, 40
  Swedish perceptions of, 131

Fahey, Larry, 188
Farb, Roderick M., 101, 104
Federal Archaeological Program, 110
Federal Register, pre-designation protec-
  tions in, 66
Fenwick, James, 11
Floating batteries, 31–32, 34, 43
Fly-Away Mixed-Gas Diving System
  (FMGS), 118, 122, 142
Foster, Nancy M., 85, 90, 93
Fox Television, 131
Fox, Gustavus V., 46
France:
  development of shell guns, 31
  early iron-armored warships in, 28
  involvement in Crimean War, 31
Fulton, Robert, 33

Galleons, development of, 29
Geer, George Spencer, 8, 57, 60, 214, 216
Gentile, Gary, 100, 101

Global Marine Development Inc.
  (GMDI), 74–76
La Gloire, 32, 34
General Services Administration (GSA),
  62
Gosport Navy Yard, 36, 39
Grand Army of the Republic, 209
Gremlin, 135, 136
Guillotine saw, 125
Gulf Stream, 1–2, 6, 9, 63–64, 66, 137,
  149, 153
Guns:
  cast iron guns, 30, 31
  CP, 138
  Dahlgren, 57, 59, 148, 187, 195
  howitzers, 60
  Parrott rifles, 60
  shell ammunition, 29–31
  technological advancement of, 29–30
  turret (see USS *Monitor,* turret)
Gyrocompass, 23

Hall, Wesley K., 86
Hampton Roads. See Battle of Hampton
  Roads
Harbor Branch Oceanographic Institu-
  tion (Harbor Branch Foundation), 1,
  70, 71–72, 103, 134, 143
Harper's Weekly, 209
Harris, John, 18, 23
Hawthorne, Nathaniel, 58–59, 208, 210,
  215
Haydel, Oren, 176, 181
Heineman, Scott, 170, 188, 190
Henry VIII, 98
Hess, Peter, 100
Hill, Dina, 102, 110
H. L. Hunley, ix, 98, 139, 203
HMS *Victory,* 29, 30
HMS *Warrior,* 33, 34
Holmes, Oliver Wendell, ix–x
Houma, Louisiana, 154–155, 168
Hulls:
  use of iron for, 30–33
  See also USS *Monitor,* hull
Huntington Alloys Inc., 73
Hurricane Felix, 107
Hurricane Humberto, 108
Hurricane Iris, 108
Hydroblaster, 160

Industrial Revolution, 30–33, 40, 64, 208,
  212
Institute for Exploration, 205
Ironclad, 203
Ironclad Board, 40
"Iron Clad Paint," 215
Iron-Clad Steam-Vessels-of-War, 40

Ironclad warships:
    Confederate production of, 34, 36–39
    Union production of, 39–41, 43–44,
        47–48
    Wards' classification of, 32–33
Isherwood, Benjamin F., 44

James River, 58
Jamestown Exposition, 209
Janek, Steve, 181
Johnson, 71
Johnson-Sea-Link (*J-S-L*), 1, 3, 68, 71, 72,
    73
    1979 archaeological excavation and as-
        sessment expedition, 81
    lockout dive training, 80, 88–89
    MARSS expedition, 104
    visual data collected from, 88
Johnston, Jeff, 110, 118, 121, 125, 133, 140–
    141, 151, 163, 197
Johnston, John Paul, 107
Joint POW/MIA Accounting Command
    (JPAC), 196, 203, 214
Jones, Catesby, 51, 52
Jones, Colin M., 23
Jones, Walter B., Sr., Congressman, 63
Jons, Otto, 198

Kearny, William N., 9
Keegan, John, 208
Keeler, William F., x, 10, 11, 13, 54, 58, 60,
    210
Keeney, Timothy, 190
Kellie Chouest, 118–119, 120–121, 122, 125,
    127, 129, 130, 141
Kelly, Fred, 19
Kelly, Jim, 151, 167, 170, 182
Kesling, Doug, 138
Key West Divers, 108
Kirby-Morgan KMB-10 band masks, 69
Kirby-Morgan Superlite 17, 122
Kirchner, Art, 100
Kobukson, 34
Korea, builds first armored ship, 34
Korean War, 196
Krop, David, 200, 206
Kure Beach, 21

Labrador Current, 9
Laser line-scanning system (LLS), 134
Lavery, Brian, 215
Lawrence, Richard, 79, 80
Lay-by days, 112
The Learning Channel, 131
Legacy Resource Management Program
    (Department of Defense), 139, 140,
    150, 211
Leslie's Illustrated, 58, 209

Letcher, John, 36
Liberatore, Don, 1
Life magazine, 15
Lillestolen, Ted, 71, 81
Lincoln, Abraham:
    contacted by Ericsson, 40
    expands naval blockade after fall of
        Gosport, 37
    orders *Monitor* to avoid another battle
        with *Virginia*, 53, 61
    visit to *Monitor*, 54
Link, Edwin, 80
Little, Chris, 142
Little Creek Naval Amphibious Base, 119,
    133, 142, 147
Lockout dive training. *See* Diving, lock-
    out training
Lockwood Brothers, 161, 162
Lusardi, Wayne, 176, 178, 190

MacCord, C. W., 44, 48, 208
Magnetic survey. *See* Project Magnet
Magnetometer, 15
Mallory, Stephen R., 37, 38
Malone, Vernon, 179
Mariano, Jim, 181, 189
Marine Archaeological Research Services
    Inc., 15, 67
Marine Forensics Committee of the So-
    ciety of Naval Architects and Marine
    Engineers, 198, 216
Marine Protection, Research, and Sanctu-
    aries Act of 1972, 63
Mariners' Museum, The, x, xi, 57, 91, 131,
    166
Mariners' Museum Research Library, 211
The Mark One Eyeball, 83
Mars Rover, 70
Marx, Robert, 14–15
Mary Rose, 30, 98
Massachusetts Institute of Technology,
    17, 18, 140, 163, 205. *See also* Deep Sea
    Archaeology Research Group (Deep-
    Arch)
McLean, Craig, 108
Melville, Herman, ix, 208, 209, 210, 215
Merrick and Sons of Philadelphia, 60
Miami, 54
Miller, Edward M., 15, 18, 23, 25, 86, 90, 191
Mindell, David, 163, 205, 208
MiniROVERs, 70, 157, 174
Mitchell, Mike, 82
mitochondrial DNA (mtDNA), 196, 203
Mobile Diving and Salvage Unit TWO.
    See US Navy, MDSU TWO
Monitor. *See* USS *Monitor*
Monitor Archaeological Documentation
    Subcommittee, 91

Monitor Archaeological Research, Re-
    covery, and Stabilization Expedition
    (MARSS), 1995 expedition, 106–108
Monitor Archaeological Research and
    Structural Survey (MARSS), 1993 ex-
    pedition, 103–106
Monitor Mix, 104, 127
Monitor Research and Recovery Founda-
    tion (MRRF), 67
Moon pool, 25
Morehead City State Port, 133
Mullen, Craig, 23, 110
Murray, Christopher, 117–119, 121, 129,
    139–140, 151–152, 168–169, 178
MV *Hughes Glomar Explorer*, 74
Mythology, American, ix–x

Napoleon III, Ericsson's design to, 41
NASA, 68, 70
National Geographic Channel, 131
National Geographic Explorer, 105
National Geographic magazine, 23, 27, 70
National Geographic Society, 17, 23, 105
National Historic Landmark (NHL),
    91–92
National Marine Sanctuaries Act, 63, 100
National Oceanic and Atmospheric Ad-
    ministration (NOAA), xi, xii, 19, 63
    assessment surveys, 90–96
    Diving Manual, 100
    Diving Program, 103, 104, 106, 119, 127,
        130
    Diving Safety Board, 127
    Experimental Diving Unit, 103
    long-range preservation plan, 109–115
    management issues, 98–108
    Marine and Estuarine Management Di-
        vision (MEMD), 97
    Maritime Heritage Program (NOAA),
        65
National Hurricane Center, 180
National Marine Sanctuary Program, x,
    xi, xii, 63, 71, 109–110, 130, 166
National Undersea Research Center, 127
Office of Coastal Zone Management,
    63, 70
Office of National Marine Sanctuaries
    (ONMS), x, xi, 65
    Channel Islands National Marine
        Sanctuary, 178
    Florida Keys National Marine Sanctu-
        ary, 119
    Monitor National Marine Sanctuary,
        6, 63, 65, 66, 90
    recreational divers seeking site access,
        negotiations with, 100–102
    Sanctuary Programs Division (SPD), 85
    Sanctuaries Programs Office, 71

National Oceanic and Atmospheric Administration (NOAA) (*continued*)
Sanctuaries and Reserves Division (SRD), 97, 103, 117
site assessment and documentation survey, 93
Tri-Mix, 106
National Park Service (NPS), 91–92
National Register of Historic Places, 63
National Science Foundation, 17
National Trust for Historic Preservation, 90, 91
National Undersea Research Program, 131, 163
Naval Sea Systems Command (NAVSEA), Supervisor of Salvage and Diving, 158
NAVSEA Journal, 75
Navy. *See* US Navy
Nelson, Keith, 181
Newell, Cliff, 104, 106
Newport News Shipbuilding, 131, 140, 162, 166, 191, 212
Newton, John G., 17, 18, 22, 23
New York Panorama, 208
New York Times, 48, 208
Nicholson, Dorothy, 23
Nitrogen narcosis, 100
Nitrox, 103–104
NOAA Ship *Ferrel,* 131, 135
NOAA Ship *Ronald H. Brown,* 189
North Carolina Division of Archives and History (NCDAH), 17, 23, 63
Monitor Technical Advisory Committee, 63
North Carolina Tidewater Services Inc., 15
North Carolina Underwater Archeology Branch, 70
Northrop Grumman Oceanic Systems, 135
NOVA documentary, 128, 131
Novelty Ironworks, 44

Oceaneering International Inc. (OII), 110–111, 140–141, 142
Oculina varicosa, 148
Offshore oil fields, 120
Operation Desert Shield/Storm, 196
Ott, Michael, 138

Paddlewheels, drawbacks of, 33
Paden, Gary, 166, 191
Paixhans, Henri-Joseph, 30
Penn steam engine, 34
Peterkin, Ernest W., 15, 17, 18, 23, 25, 86
Peterson, Curtiss, 137, 162, 166, 176, 190, 191, 193
Phoenix International Inc., 151, 153–155, 157, 166, 168

Pierce, Mitch, 178
Porter, John L., 38, 39
Portsmouth Historic Dockyard, 29
Project Cheesebox, 15, 23, 86, 90. See also *Cheesebox*
Project Magnet, 15, 22–23
Propeller, screw, 33, 35, 42
Public Broadcasting Network, 131

Rayfield, John, 139
Raytheon Electronic Systems, 134
Rebel Monster, 41
Rechnitzer, Andreas, 23
Remotely operated vehicles (ROVs), 24, 69–70, 71
RESURGAM, 206
Riendeau, Ken, 189
RMS *Titanic,* 198
Roesch, Richard, 4, 73
Rosencrantz, Donald, 71, 135
Rowland, Thomas F., 44, 48, 55
Russia, early use of shell guns, 31
R/V *Alcoa Seaprobe,* 23–27, 62, 134
R/V *Calypso,* 76
R/V *Cape Fear,* 119, 131, 138, 141, 163, 183
R/V *Cape Henlopen,* 67
R/V *Eastward,* 16–22, 73
R/V *Edwin Link,* MARSS expedition, 104–105
R/V *Elusive,* 107, 109
R/V *Endeavor,* 205
R/V *Johnson,* 72, 81
R/V *Peter W. Anderson,* 91
R/V *Seward Johnson,* 176

Santísima Trinidad, 29–30
Schneider, Randy, 105
Scholley, Barbara, 151, 157, 170, 183, 189
Schwemmer, Robert, 178, 188
Science Applications International Corporation (SAIC), 135
SeaBED, 205
Sea Diver, 71
Search Area A, 15. *See also* Marx, Robert
Searle, William F., Jr., 15
SeaROVER, 143
Shell guns. *See* Guns, shell
Sheridan, Robert E., 17, 18, 67, 69, 74, 81
Simpson, Edward, 35
Smithsonian Institution, 63, 67
Sonar, development of, 17
Southern Historical Society Papers, 209
Spain, warships, 29–30
Spider and Platform, 168, 169, 173, 176, 178
Steam engines:
caloric vs., 42
transition to, 33, 35
Stevens, Edwin A., 35

Stevens, Robert L., 35
Stirni, 15
Stocking, John, 11
Stockton, Robert, 42
Stodder, Louis, 11
Strand, Michael, 134
Surface decompression (SUR-D) tables, 122
Surplus property, 62
Swedish Television, 131

Taliaferro, William B., 36
"The *Temeraire,*" 208–209
Teredo navalis, 105, 176
Terrell, Bruce, 102, 105
Texas A&M University Press, 214–215
Tillman, Glen, 25
Time capsules, shipwrecks as, 76
Tise, Larry E., 74
Torpedo Junction, 17
Trade-off study, 111
Trenchard, Stephen D., 9, 11
Trible, Paul S., Jr., 93
Tri-mix, 104, 106
Tropical Storm Allison, 155
Tropical Storm Arlene, 133
Tropical Storm Cristobal, 183, 185–186
Tudors, warships, 30
"In the Turret," 210
Turtle Ships, 34
Tysall, Terrence, 101, 119, 138, 147–148

U-Boats, 17
Ulu Burun, 98
Underwater Archeological Associates Inc., 15
Underwater Object Locator (UOL), 14, 16, 19
United Nations Educational, Scientific, and Cultural Organization (UNESCO), 76
University of Delaware, 17, 18, 67–68
University National Oceanographic Laboratory System (UNOLS), 102
University of North Carolina at Wilmington (UNC-W), 107, 119, 127, 131, 163
University of Rhode Island, 205
US Army:
Central Identification Laboratory in Hawaii (CILHI), 170, 196
Reserve, 23
US Coast Guard, 62
US Naval Academy, 15, 18, 90
US Navy:
abandonment vs. surplus, 62
Casualty Office, 203
Coastal Systems Station, 134

Experimental Diving Unit, 155
formally abandons *Monitor* project, 62
Intelligence Support Center, 27
MDSU TWO, 117, 118, 121, 123, 125, 133, 140, 142–143, 166
Oceanographic Office, 15
Research and Development, 15
ROVs, 69
searches for USS *Monitor,* 14, 15
Ship Research and Development Center, 22
site assessment and documentation survey, 93
Supervisor of Salvage, Diving, and Ocean Engineering (SUPSALV), 93, 111, 151, 166
Undersea Operations, 110
US Navy Diving Manual, 100
USNS *Apache,* 93
USS *Cairo,* 67
USS *Chinook,* 189
USS *Commanche,* 149
USS *Congress,* 50–51
USS *Constitution,* 30
USS *Cumberland,* 50–51
USS *Edenton,* 107–108
USS *Fulton,* 33
USS *Galena,* 41, 60
USS *Grapple,* 153
USS *Grasp,* 133, 135, 136, 154
USS *Merrimack,* 33, 35, 36, 37, 41. See also CSS *Virginia*
USS *Michigan,* 31
USS *Minnesota,* battle with CSS *Virginia,* 50
USS *Mississippi,* 33
USS *Monitor*:
  anchor recovery expedition, 85–89
  armor belt, removal of, 113, 114
  assessment
    site, 79–90
    surveys, 90–96
  Comprehensive Plan:
    data collection expedition 1999, 131–138
    funding, 117
    propeller recovery expedition 1998, 118–131
  data collection from, 67–73

description of site at time of designation, 63–64, 66
design
  considerations, 45
  controversy over credits, 47–49
  vs. *Virginia* specifications, 53
drive train, removal of, 113, 114
Fort Monroe, returns to, 189–191
hull
  shoring beneath and removal of, 113, 114
  stabilization, 140–150
launch, 47–49
leakage at sea, 8–9, 10–12
ownership issues, 63
preservation, 61–67
  plans beyond, 73–79
  threats to, 96–97
recreational divers seek access, 100–102
red-lens signal lantern, 73
research expeditions, list of, 77–79
steam engine recovery
  2000, 140–150
  2001, 150–165
turret
  exploration of interior, 186–189, 191–197
  findings, 197–206
  recovery planning, 166–182
  removal of, 113, 114
  secured, 183–186
U-Boat in WWII, possible confusion with, 17
USS *Monitor* Center, 211
USS *Monitor* Foundation, 15
USS *Monitor National Marine Sanctuary Research Management Plan,* 96–97
USS *Monitor* Project, Project Planning Committee, 90–91
USS *New Ironsides,* 60
USS *Ortolan,* 104, 105
USS *Passaic,* 5, 7, 9, 10–11, 18, 197, 198
USS *Princeton,* 35, 42
USS *Rhode Island,* 5, 7, 9, 10, 11–12, 18, 213
USS *Roanoke,* 50
USS *St. Lawrence,* 50
USS *State of Georgia,* 9, 11, 18
USS *Tecumseh,* 198
USS *United States,* 30

"A Utilitarian View of the Monitor's Fight," 209

Valsalva maneuver, 2
Vasa, 98, 99
Vietnam War, 196
Viking ships, 98
Virginia Historic Landmarks Commission, 79, 80
Virginia Sea Grant, 79
Vlcek, Jan, 135
Voith-Schneider cycloidal propellers, 24

War of 1812, 30
Ward, James, 32
Warner, John, Senator, 139
Washington Post, 23
Watters, Joseph, 10, 11, 12
Watts, Gordon P., Jr., 2, 17, 18, 20, 21, 23, 67
  1979 archaeological excavation and assessment expedition, 81
  advice for expedition, 70–71
  determines accelerated rate of corrosion, 95
  development of research plan, 79, 80
  establishes Program in Maritime History and Underwater Research, 90
  Monitor announcement, 22
  site assessment and anchor recovery, 86
  work with ECU, 85
Weeks, Grenville, 8, 10, 11, 207
Wells, Morgan, 103, 104, 106
Western Electric Company, Hydrographic Division, 18
William Laird and Sons, 31
Williamson, William P., 38, 39
Wommack, Roland, 16
Wooden warships, 29–30
Woods Hole Deep Submergence Lab, 205
Woods Hole Oceanographic Institution, 94–95
Worden, John L., 46, 51
World War II, 17, 196
Wotan, 154, 155, 157, 168, 179, 183, 185

York River, 58
Young, Chuck, 162